Enhancing global governance

Foundations of Peace

Note to the reader

The United Nations University Press series on the Foundations of Peace addresses themes that relate to the evolving agenda of peace and security within and between communities. Traditional or conventional conceptions of security, primarily military and interstate, have been supplemented, or perhaps even surpassed, by a definition of security which rests upon much broader tenets, including human rights, cultural and communal rights, environmental and resource security, and economic security. To resolve the dialectic between state security and human security it is necessary to envision a wide agenda of international peace and security that embraces these tenets and the potential tensions that exist between them and the interstate context. International actors, such as the United Nations and non-governmental organizations, are also increasingly playing a central role in building the foundations of sustainable peace. This series promotes theoretical as well as policy-relevant discussion on these crucial issues.

Titles currently available:

Enhancing global governance:
Towards a new diplomacy?

Edited by Andrew F. Cooper, John English, and
Ramesh Thakur

**United Nations
University Press**

TOKYO · NEW YORK · PARIS

United Nations University Press
The United Nations University, 53-70, Jingumae 5-chome,
Shibuya-ku, Tokyo, 150-8925, Japan
Tel: +81-3-3499-2811   Fax: +81-3-3406-7345
E-mail: press@hq.unu.edu (sales and marketing) sales@hq.unu.edu
http://www.unu.edu

United Nations University Office in North America
2 United Nations Plaza, Room DC2-2062, New York , NY 10017, USA
Tel: +1-212-963-6387   Fax: +1-212-371-9454
E-mail: unuona@ony.unu.edu

United Nations University Press is the publishing division of the United Nations University.

Cover design by Andrew Corbett

Printed in the United States of America

UNUP-1074
ISBN 92-808-1074-X

Library of Congress Cataloging-in-Publication Data

Enhancing global governance : towards a new diplomacy? / edited by Andrew F. Cooper, John English, and Ramesh Thakur.
    p.   cm.
Includes bibliographical references and index.
ISBN 92-808-1074-X
1. International organization. I. Cooper, Andrew Fenton, 1950– II. English, John, 1945– III. Thakur, Ramesh Chandra, 1948–
JZ4850 .E54 2002
341.2—dc21   2002005674

Contents

Preface

This edited collection is derived from papers presented at two conferences, one in Canada in September 1999 and another in Japan in July 2000. The conferences focused on the theme of the United Nations and "new diplomacy". Participants at these conferences analysed both the structural and the situational conditions opening up (and imposing constraints) on a diplomacy that is changing in form, scope, and intensity. The operating assumption guiding the research project was that alternative sources of innovation were developing through bottom-up modes of leadership from both so-called "like-minded" states and the enhanced role of civil society in contemporary diplomacy. The questions of how and where these alternative leadership forms were expressed through the UN system underpinned the papers and the discussion.

To gain a better insight into this dynamic the Canadian conference examined two specific cases, namely the development of the Ottawa Treaty to ban anti-personnel land-mines and the campaign to establish an international criminal court. In the case of the land-mines initiative, the triggering effect of organizational frustration was brought to the fore. Deemed to be an inadequate means of resolution, several states and a variety of NGOs mounted what can be called an "end run" around the Conference on Disarmament. In some ways, therefore, the land-mines case represented a challenge to the established power/institutional structure. In other ways, though, the case demonstrates the capacity of the UN system to allow improvisation and innovation. Similar lessons can be drawn from the case of the International Criminal Court. As in the land-mines episode, the creation of the ICC faced formidable opposition not only from members of the P5 in the UN Security Council but also from leading jurists associated with the existing International War Crimes Tribunal. Yet, akin to the model developed on land-mines, support for the ICC was mobilized by a diverse coalition of like-minded countries and NGOs.

Both of these cases were thought by the participants at the conference to emphasize the diffuse and uneven nature of the emerging international system. While some expressed concern that the effect of these initiatives would be to overextend the UN system, others expressed enthusiasm about the implications these "end runs" would create in terms of fragmenting authority.

The Tokyo conference helped sustain a variety of themes that emerged from the Canadian discussions. Moreover, a number of other important points were developed more fully. For one thing, the question of the generic or exceptional quality of the land-mines and the ICC campaigns was examined. Although the land-mines and ICC cases possessed many unique features, both practitioners and academics felt that there may be lessons to be learned from the land-mines treaty/ICC for other humanitarian issues such as child soldiers and small-arms trafficking. For another thing, the question of individual as well as collective leadership within the United Nations was brought into the equation. In both the land-mines and the criminal court campaigns, the majority of the P5 on the Security Council were opposed until well into the campaign, yet the Secretary-General gave strong support to the movement, especially in the case of the land-mines campaign. Finally, the question of whether the process of change introduced by the land-mines/ICC processes is reformist or transformational was raised more comprehensively.

These wider questions are reflected in the two major concerns of the Tokyo conference: the impact of the "new diplomacy" on the Security Council and the effectiveness, legitimacy, and possibility of "codes of conduct" that would affect both states and global business. The keynote speaker at Tokyo was the then Canadian Foreign Minister Lloyd Axworthy. Canada was finishing up a term on the Security Council and had tried to place "human security" questions at the forefront of the Security Council's agenda. In his remarks at the Tokyo conference, Minister Axworthy assessed the effectiveness of that attempt and addressed some of the promise and prospects for the Security Council itself in dealing with these issues. As Canada was coming to the end of its term on the Security Council, it made a great effort to "hand the baton" to other like-minded countries. This activity has targeted not only traditionally like-minded countries such as Norway and Australia but non-traditional like-minded countries such as South Africa and Jordan.

The other concern at the Tokyo conference highlighted the development of codes of conduct. As Richard Falk reminds us, the focus of UN activity over the decade will most likely shift from the peace and security area to other areas of global activity where the call for action will accelerate and where the United Nations remains a "vital actor". For all of its importance, much of this form of activity will be behind the scenes, as the United Nations tries "to engineer a myriad of useful activities beyond the gaze of the media". Specific papers studied the attempt to develop voluntary codes of conduct dealing with apparel and other industries in Western countries, and considered the tension between and within international institutions as they face these questions. Are these ad hoc functional arrangements simply tools of opportunism, serving particularistic interests, notably labour and protectionists in the developed world? Furthermore, the question must be asked: do they undermine existing international institutions with clear mandates on labour standards? Or, rather more constructively, are these initiatives imaginative and innovative responses to the added complexity and the loss of primacy of the sovereign state? Within the context of this debate, the attempts to develop codes in other areas are illuminating. Some of these cases will look at areas where work has been done to promote codes of conduct, most notably in the areas of small-arms trafficking, child soldiers, and the protection of civilians. Other cases are even more forward-looking, as in the case of the campaign against "conflict" diamonds, where the push for action has only recently being galvanized.

Although confident that this research programme provides a useful lens into the nuances of contemporary diplomatic practices, the participants appreciate that its design must be extended to capture fully all of this complexity. To begin this process another conference was held in Amman, Jordan, in April 2001 to consider the implications of these studies of the United Nations and new diplomacy for the development of international law. To be sure, this linkage was made implicitly throughout the Canadian and Tokyo proceedings. Participants at the Canadian proceedings, for example, emphasized the importance of placing the landmines treaty within humanitarian law. The aim of the Jordan conference was to make this connection more central and explicit. One question that remains significant here is the widening interpretations of sovereignty to allow a balance between a state's internal legitimacy and the expansion of international "community" standards. A second question revolves around the process for extending established international norms, such as the one that proscribed the use, stockpiling, production, and transfer of anti-personnel mines, and the relationship of such norms to the development of international law. A third question revolves around the interplay between the United Nations, governments, and NGOs in the development of new agendas and regimes. A fourth intertwined question focuses on the growing cooperative/conflictual relationship between public and private authorities as the sources for international law. A fifth question will look at the relative salience between quiet and public diplomacy in the creation of international norms.

Stretching this framework still further, the participants are now engaged in a study of the nexus between ideas and institutional development in the context of the UN system. It is a commonplace assumption that the space for ideas *vis-à-vis* global governance has opened up in the post-Cold War years. But little attention has been paid to the question of where and how these ideas have been generated and come to influence international public policy. Equally, the United Nations must be taken seriously in terms of its agency as a conduit for ideas.

The catalyst for this project was a luncheon meeting in Tokyo on the land-mines treaty, and the editors are grateful to so many people who helped with ideas, support, and financial assistance. Above all they wish to acknowledge the United Nations University for its generous support of this research programme. The Rector of the United Nations University, Professor Hans van Ginkel, was an active participant in the conference and a champion of the broader project. Yoshi Sawada, and other staff at the UNU, did a splendid job of organization in Tokyo. The editors would also like to thank the Centre on Foreign Policy Development in Ottawa, and the Canadian Department of Foreign Affairs and International Trade (DFAIT). Steven Lee, together with Marketa Geislerova, played a central role in the planning, facilitation, and operation of the conferences. The Canadian Embassy in Tokyo was extremely helpful, and the editors would like to thank the then Ambassador Len Edwards for his hospitality in Tokyo. He also hosted the initial luncheon where the idea for this project developed. The editors wish him well in his new role as Deputy Minister of International Trade, a position for which he is superbly trained.

A number of other prominent individuals actively participated in the proceedings of the two conferences, including Dr Guenter Altenberg, Louis Delvoie, Bill Graham MP, Professor John Groom, Ambassador Paul Heinbecker, Kirsten Hoffman, and Dr H. G. Sulimma. The editors appreciate the willingness of *Canadian Foreign Policy* to grant permission to reprint in slightly modified form the chapter by Deirdre van der Merwe and Mark Malan (Vol. 8., No. 1 (July 2000), 67–81) and to Oxford University Press for allowing publication of the chapter by Maxwell Cameron, which appeared in *To Walk Without Fear: The Global Move-*

ment to Ban Landmines (OUP, 1999). The editors also wish to highlight the support provided to a number of contributors by the Social Sciences and Humanities Research Council of Canada.

At the University of Waterloo, the editors benefited from the enthusiasm of Professor Robert Kerton, Dean of Arts, and Professor Bruce Mitchell, Associate Vice-President (Academic). Lena Yost was the conference organizer, and without her talent and dedication this project could not have been realized. Irene Majer and Nancy Birss offered invaluable assistance, and Professor Geoffrey Hayes provided sound advice and helped whenever necessary. Two students, Andrew Thompson and Ryan Touhey, helped throughout. Andrew Thompson deserves special thanks. He is an excellent young scholar who did splendid work in technically managing this manuscript.

The final thanks are to the people associated with the United Nations University Press. Cherry Ekins, in copy-editing the manuscript, considerably tightened the presentation of the book. Janet Boileau, publications officer, and Gareth Johnston, editorial assistant at the UNUP, provided a model of efficiency.

1

Like-minded nations, NGOs, and the changing pattern of diplomacy within the UN system: An introductory perspective

Andrew F. Cooper

A good deal of contestation has emerged about the nature of international leadership in the post-Cold War period. This debate is especially prevalent with respect to the multilateral architecture generally and the activities of the United Nations more specifically. As the global system underwent a major transformation in the late 1980s and early 1990s, a widely shared view developed of the United Nations moving to the forefront of an expanded form of global governance. As played out over the subsequent decade, though, progress towards this goal has become far more convoluted. Instead of a sense of comprehensive achievement, generated by the passing of the East/West ideological/military divide, the process of transition has been far more complex, uneven, and awkward. The challenges in the way of creating and maintaining new forms of consensus-building, multi-centred governance networks and the negotiation of rules based on transparency and accountability remain formidable. Yet signs of transformation are visible in terms of the pattern of collective decision-making. The brake on the evolution of international organization remains the structural constraints imposed by the hierarchical state system, and the embedded role of agenda-setting among the established powers.[1] The motor for this dynamic of change, by way of contrast, has become the agency of innovative and non-hegemonic diplomacy. Given enhanced freedom from the disciplines of the Cold War era, room has opened up for a variety of actors in an array of areas. While far from unrestricted, the hallmark of this diplomacy has become its form (with a heavy emphasis on coalition-building), scope (its extension from the economic and the social into the security domain), and its intensity.

The frustrations of top-down leadership

This mixture of obstacles and momentum is provoked and underscored by a number of theoretical and policy-related questions concerning the source and application of leadership in the post-Cold War period. Most practitioners and academic/journalistic observers took it as a given that leadership would continue for the most part to emanate in a top-down fashion from the core permanent members of the UN Security Council, the so-called P5 states, as a "trusteeship of the powerful".[2] This type of arrangement would allow efficiency and order, if not necessarily equity and justice. As Robert Jervis suggested in 1993: "Concerts have provided a significant measure of security in the past and the conditions for establishing related arrangements are propitious."[3]

By moving its role to centre stage in the burst of enthusiasm for the creation of the "new world order", the performance of the United Nations seemed to match these expectations. As the Security Council became engaged in a widened cluster of focused problem-solving activities, a tilt took place in the overall image of the United Nations, from a "talking shop" to a constructive agent making a difference.[4] As the UN's agenda expanded, however, so did the gap between its capabilities and its commitments. These delivery problems were most pronounced in the peacekeeping/humanitarian intervention arena, as witnessed in Somalia, Rwanda, and the former Yugoslavia. Each of these operations suffered from weak and confused mandates and logistical deficiencies.[5]

From a more comprehensive institutional perspective, this backlash became intertwined with a widening and deepening backlash against the hierarchical organizational structure of the United Nations itself. On a problem-solving basis the target of this criticism was the closed nature of the decision-making process; a process increasingly used not to drive initiatives forward but to block activity through backroom deals and the use of the "hidden veto".[6] On a more critical trajectory, the main focus has been on the question of whether or not the Security Council has become increasingly unrepresentative and illegitimate.

Indeed, it is this combination which constitutes the crucial ingredients of the chapters by Andy Knight and David Malone. Knight's contribution closely examines the critical conundrum of the Security Council. After a comprehensive review of the process of systemic change, featuring both the release of creativity in the immediate post-Cold War period and the subsequent sense of overstretch, Knight homes in on the issue of legitimacy and representation. As he argues: "For an apex body to be representative of the broader membership it must portray the values of the larger group; present the ideas or views of that group; be typical of that group's geographical make-up, population base, and political views; [and] act as a delegate of that group." The Security Council falls short on all of these criteria. Moreover, despite a proliferation of proposals to make the United Nations more transparent and equitable, there has been little in the way of tangible progress towards a reform agenda. Knight therefore ends with list of principles of his own which would not only be normatively attractive but provide a sound instrumental basis for a re-structuring project for the Security Council.

Malone's starting point is the blockage imparted to the UN system by the informal process within the evolving design of the Security Council. Reinforcing the argument made by Knight, Malone points to the un-anticipated consequences of the post-Cold War settlement in terms of the marginalization of many member states because of the privileging of private consultations between the UN Secretariat and the P5. In contra-diction to this image of exclusion, however, Malone also points to a num-ber of countervailing trends central to the thematic structure of this book. Malone highlights in some detail the ability of NGOs to exploit new spaces in the international architecture to win access and input on selective areas of decision-making. Although careful to underscore the unevenness of this process, Malone captures the tensions between clo-sure and immobilization and openness and innovation found within the UN system. Part and parcel of this notion of duality is Malone's depic-tion of middle states or like-minded states within the UN system. Having lost a good part of their traditional role as go-betweens or helpful fixers, this cluster of countries is portrayed as having the will and capacity for issue-specific forms of leadership.

This prevailing sense of ambivalence about the terms of settlement in the post-Cold War system has been accentuated by growing confu-sion and concern about the style of US leadership. Through any lens of waning hegemony (or, to use Ruggie's term, "hegemonic defection"),[7] scenarios opened up concerning the possibility of a collaborative ar-rangement forming at the top of the international system. From this per-spective, the future held the prospect of some condominium with a strong element of joint responsibility and burden-sharing. Other lenses, nonetheless, provided very different images of American behaviour. One dominant alternative image has been that that of "renewal" and/or "tri-umphalism" on the part of the USA.[8] A US-driven "new world order", or at the very least a US-centred "assertive multilateralism", contains some putative potential to be viewed as a benign force in the international arena.[9] But this interpretation remains far from universally shared, with opinion in other countries varying "from agreement, to scepticism, to down-right disbelief".[10] Still another image is that of a heightened shift towards parochial introspection and insularity, with a marked withdrawal of the USA from its commitment to the United Nations and its own internationalist tradition. Signs of these latter two scenarios extend from the declaratory to the operational, as epitomized by the drawn-out saga concerning the USA's insistence on the right of taking military actions outside the United Nations, and its approach to UN dues.

Whatever scenario is favoured, the bottom line is that the US international personality and profile remain highly exceptional. As James Reed argues, the USA makes no pretence to be "like-minded" in either its coalition or issue-based behaviour. Unlike the cluster of middle countries that constitutes the bulk of the "like-minded" constellation, the USA not only possesses a global reach but massive hard power resources. Given its unique identity and multiple set of interests, consequently, the USA's opposition to the best-known initiatives associated with the "new diplomacy" (land-mines and the International Criminal Court) may come as no surprise. As Reed demonstrates in his chapter, though, the USA's estrangement from the United Nations and multilateral global governance goes much deeper than situational conditions. According to Reed, the key behind the USA's estrangement can be found in the structure of American society.

Having demonstrated the gap between the USA and the like-minded countries, Reed extends his argument to catch another important component of this puzzle. If "un-like-minded" as a state or country, the USA nonetheless contains a mass of "like-minded" citizens who have forged transnational linkages on an issue-by-issue basis. Ted Turner, Bill Gates, and other members of the American business élite remain highly international in their outlook. The Vietnam Veterans of America and Jody Williams have been at the core of the International Campaign to Ban Land-mines. US-centred groups such as Human Rights Watch and the Lawyers Committee for Human Rights moved to the forefront of the campaign for the ICC.

Diplomatic initiatives from below

In rehearsing the manner by which international leadership is shape-shifting, this chapter looks at alternative sources of initiative and innovation. Animating this discussion is the argument that there is a need to look at how sources of leadership "from below" have adapted to change and modified their tactics to (re)work the UN system better. One long-standing source of alternative leadership, as suggested above, is located among the group of countries termed the traditional first followers of the UN system in the ranks of secondary states.[11] This sense of commitment among this cluster of middle or like-minded states came out in diverse areas such as peacekeeping, and within the economic and social agendas. It also came out in the willingness of this cohort of states to put their money where their mouth is in terms of the payment of UN fees, contributions to specific UN operations, etc. While lacking the power capabilities of the inner circle of states at the apex of the global hierarchy, some compensatory element has been provided through diplomatic skill and focused use of resources. In the case of the United Nations, this active engagement by the like-minded revolved around a multiplicity of activities (as exemplified by the Canadian approach), such as "getting together sponsors for compromise resolutions, lobbying to avoid dangerous conflicts, collaboration with the efforts of the Secretary-General, and in a thousand ways seeking to reduce tension".[12]

An awareness of the functional abilities displayed by this set of secondary countries should not minimize the constraints under which they had to operate. Self-selected like-minded countries such as Canada, Australia, and the Nordic countries were unrepresentative of the wider society of nations. Not only were they developed countries, with membership in the Western European and Other group (WEO) within the United Nations, but they were countries which straddled regions. Such distinguishing characteristics disconnected these countries from other putative coalition partners among the less developed countries (such as India, Indonesia, Nigeria, and Mexico) through the 1970s and 1980s. Even in disagreement, these like-minded countries could in foreign policy terms be considered the USA's loyal opposition in the international system.[13] Structurally, the space available for these countries to make a difference remained severely bounded by the context of the Cold War and the system of tight bipolarity. What influence these countries had in international affairs contained the distinctive flavour of both leadership and followership.

A key argument in this volume is that the character of this source of innovation and initiative is in the process of being transformed. With the release of many of the disciplines of the Cold War, like-mindedness has become more agile. The role of the gadfly long built into the like-minded concept has become far more accentuated, with the best known of these coalitions of the willing directed towards nudging and tweaking the P5 and especially the USA on selected issues in a determined and time-sensitive manner. The range of candidates for like-minded status has also expanded. From a narrow and well-established cohort of countries, the scope for possible coalition partners has become far more inclusive. The element of continuity that has remained, and indeed has been reinforced, through this changing dynamic highlights the limitations of its issue-specific nature. Instead of providing leadership everywhere and on everything, an element of selection has come into play in a more explicit fashion. In other words, a form of country/activity differentiation is made by which individual countries make a choice as to which functional areas they will specialize in. This niche orientation offers secondary countries both an instrument and a rationalization for targeting their behaviour in a segmented fashion. As Gareth Evans, the former Australian Foreign Minister, has observed, niche diplomacy involves "concentrating resources in specific areas best able to generate returns worth having, rather than trying to cover the field".[14]

This country-specific source of leadership has been supplemented, in turn, by the expanding diplomatic role of civil society generally and NGOs more specifically. One prominent former UK diplomat, in a book entitled *Positive Diplomacy*, has argued that: "Good governance depends increasingly on non-governmental factors."[15] A similar message has been delivered by the UN Secretary-General Kofi Annan. Embracing non-governmental organizations as "essential partners of the United Nations", he defined their role in a multifaceted way, salient "not only in mobilizing public opinion, but also in the process of deliberation and policy formation and – even more important – in the execution of policies, in work on the ground".[16]

Conceptualizing a new model of interactive leadership

Having laid out the potential for innovation, it becomes contingent to examine how these alternative sources of leadership have been expressed through the UN system. The working assumption here is that the relative (though far from absolute) shift from a concentrated top-down to a multifaceted bottom-up mode of leadership merits more detailed research. Indeed, this type of diplomatic practice has become so prevalent, fluid and fast-moving that it has raced ahead of intellectual formulations. A period of catching up is therefore required. At a conceptual level, the shift must be examined as a critical response to the status quo.[17] Certainly, the shift represents an attempt to look beyond the status quo. Unlike more radical challenges to the international system, however, this alternative source of leadership has not been incorporated into a process of disengagement from the established rules and institutions. Although this expression of leadership exposes many limitations in that system, it does not constitute a bid to work from without. The focus remains very much one of trying to deal with frustrations and blockages in the UN system through new problem-solving techniques.

At an operational level, the style established by this alternative source of leadership comes to the fore in a number of ways. One dimension that needs to be examined is the intensity of this ascendant approach. There is a profound feeling of impatience at forms of diplomacy conducted at a slow speed – or no speed at all – behind closed doors. Rather than quiet diplomacy, the alternative leadership impulse is conducted via public diplomacy. Appeals are made directly and clearly over the heads of other negotiators/governments to opinion leaders and the mass public. Instead of the formality of traditional statecraft, considerable onus is placed on informal mechanisms via information technology. Ideas from the traditional leaders are no longer absorbed fully, if at all. Mission-oriented diplomacy, to use Gil Winham's words, is offered on an ad hoc basis, "when and where you needed it".[18]

Another dimension that requires attention is the form of this diplomatic approach. The core component that needs to be discussed here is the nature of the interaction between the secondary/like-minded countries and the NGO community. In some select cases, there does seem to be some evidence of the implementation of a concerted joint-venture strategy or strategic alliance. But in a variety of other cases, there is a considerable element of flexibility built into the approach, with a great deal of short-term assessment about the value-added benefits of striking a constructive arrangement on an issue-by-issue basis. In overall terms this pattern of interaction remains fuzzy, fragmentary, and awkward, but nevertheless vital and important. Like-minded countries and NGOs rub up against and off each other in an uneven fashion. Contacts and coalitions are built in an improvisational manner, but few in the way of co-terminous roles are established. A premium is placed on bargaining and open-ended arrangements.

Another aspect of these alternative sources of leadership that needs discussion pertains to their multiple roles. One form of activity which stands out is that of a catalyst, by which the activity of NGOs stimulates corresponding or complementary activities by like-minded countries. At the core of this pattern is a triggering effect, in which the out-in-front behaviour on the part of like-minded countries and/or NGOs helps frame the agenda for action by the United Nations. This triggering component of the state-NGO relationship may be detected in a wide variety of cases and situations. For example, the reciprocal nature of this push-pull dynamic comes out strongly in the diplomatic efforts of NGOs with respect to other international conferences. As recognized by Baroness Chalker, the UK's former Conservative Minister for Overseas Development, much of the catalyst for action at the Beijing conference on women and development was stimulated by the NGOs' entrepreneurial ability to push this agenda forward:

at [Beijing], women's concerns moved up the policy-making agenda. Their relevance to a wide range of economic, political, and social problems was acknowledged. Much of the inspiration for change has come from thousands of women's groups all over the world. The impact of [Beijing] will depend largely on their success in working with men and with governments to turn words into action.[19]

A second type of activity which stands out is that of an agent, a pattern by which NGOs take on some type of go-between or subcontracting facilitative role which supports the work of the United Nations. At a functional level, what appears novel is the amount of activity which may be described as micro-mediation. The prime illustration of this trend may be found in the area of negotiated access of relief deliveries in war zones either through non-protected and/or cross-border operations. As one insightful critic mentions, micro-mediation serves as the backbone of these types of operations: "to secure the consent of warring parties has become the principal means of establishing internationally mandated relief operations that cover all sides in an ongoing conflict".[20]

A third form of activity which stands out is that of a joint manager, a pattern by which the activities of secondary countries and/or NGOs lend themselves to some type of enhanced institution-building. Integral to this dynamic is some further type of partnership or multi-party cooperative venture through which know-how is shared and some mode of formal or informal division of labour established. Arguably the best illustrations of this pattern of joint managership are located within the arena of Western responses to complex humanitarian emergencies. At the more formalized end of the institution-building scale, there exist firmly established partnerships in which government and NGOs work together. The exemplar of this integrative model is the Norwegian Emergency Preparedness System (NOREPS).[21]

A final dimension that merits discussion is the scope of this alternative source of leadership. What appears highly salient about the domain of these non-traditional sources is that they take account of the changing agenda of the international order. On the one hand, much of the focus of these alternative sources of leadership is on the ascendant issue areas in the economic and social domains. To be sure, one of the key elements of this volume will be to tease out case studies where this dynamic has already occurred. One possible set of case studies comes out in the area of the interaction between trade, environmental, and labour "standards" issues, in which both secondary countries and NGOs have an increasingly high profile. Another potential cluster of case studies exists in the area of human rights. Children's rights come to mind as one good illustrative case study. The skill and determination of both secondary countries and NGOs in idea formulation and dissemination come out in their agenda-framing activities with respect to the development of a wide variety of protective regimes in this area.

On the other hand, a considerable amount of focus needs to be directed to the evolving debate about security. Driven by the sea change in circumstances created by the end of the Cold War, the "essentially contested" nature of the concept of security has surfaced in a provocative and comprehensive fashion.[22] During the post-1945 era, there existed a consensual understanding about what the essence of security implied. In terms of both thinking and policy practice, the concept was applied to state security, and the security of states was predicated on the existence of some physical threat to territorial sovereignty. With the enormous changes in international politics precipitated by the collapse of the Soviet Union in 1991 and the end of the bipolar rivalry between the USA and the Soviet Union, this uniformity of opinion ended. With many of the secondary countries and NGOs in the lead of the rethinking, the concept of security has been extended to a much wider range of issues. Under this wider lens, security threats are more pervasive than traditional rivalries and confrontations between states. Removing the privileged status of the nation-state, alliance structures, and concerns of external aggression from other states, the definition of security is refined and expanded to cover the holisitic concerns of private citizens.[23] The essence of security, or safety, from this standpoint rests on negative as well as positive criteria, namely the lack of insecurity on the part of individuals and groups.

Prototype or anomalous case studies?

Two case studies from the security domain provide suitable introductory entry points into the larger debate, in that these case studies highlight the breadth and diversity of the emergent alternative sources of leadership in the international architecture generally and the UN system more specifically. By providing a number of highly detailed contributions on these cases, we can better tease out the conceptual complexity and operational realities concerning the nature of the "new diplomacy" dynamic.

The first case study is the campaign for a global ban on anti-personnel land-mines. As laid out by Maxwell Cameron, the land-mines case was unique in a number of ways. Above all, it revealed how a combination of like-minded small and middle-sized states, as well as mine-affected states located mainly in the South, could work in partnership with transnational social movements and NGOs (in the International Campaign to Ban Land-mines) in particular. This combination of forces created a larger normative environment which non-signatories and the non-compliant could not ignore.

Looking at the case in further detail, it appears to fit the model laid out above. To begin with, the alternative sources of leadership acted as catalysts. The preparatory work of a constellation of NGOs was crucial in getting the campaign off the ground. Beginning in the early 1990s, the International Committee of the Red Cross (ICRC) was mobilized into action against the humanitarian "scourge" of land-mines by its field workers. Going beyond the organization's traditional low-key/technical mode of operation, the Red Cross took the lead in gathering a broad-based NGO coalition calling for a "total ban on the production, export, and use of anti-personnel mines".[24] Eventually united under the auspices of the International Campaign to Ban Land-mines, this NGO coalition included the Vietnam Veterans of America, the German group Medico International, and the French group of Handicap International, together with Human Rights Watch and Physicians for Human Rights.

In terms of intensity, the campaign featured a good deal of speed and energy. Rather than waiting for results to happen via a lowest-common-denominator diplomatic solution by governments, the NGOs constantly forced the pace of the negotiations through savvy use of publicity and the demand for real deadlines. When negotiations stalled through the ongoing arms control talks, the NGOs pressed for action through alternative channels. As Cameron points out, the pace of this process was unprecedented. No other multilateral disarmament treaty has ever come into being more rapidly.

Throughout this campaign a sense of strategic or at least tactical alliance stands out. Jody Williams lauded the actions of Canada and other like-minded countries for challenging the status quo. The main conclusion showcased by Cameron is that non-hegemonic states and transnational social movements can achieve diplomatic ends by working in partnership. The process in effect established the "basis for new mechanisms of horizontal accountability by bringing together like-minded states, in partnership with NGOs, outside of traditional arms control fora".

William Maley and Iver Neumann do much both to embellish and to nuance Cameron's conclusion. At the country-specific level, Maley's chapter deals with the Australian experience with the Ottawa process. As in a number of other countries, the issue of land-mines engaged the attention of diverse elements of Australian civil society and resulted in a broad campaign for total abolition. Mobilized under the umbrella organization, Australian Network of the International Campaign to Ban Land-mines, this network maintained a well-informed campaign, the expertise of which eventually trumped the claims of their bureaucratic opponents. Brought to the fore in particular through the hearings and work of the Joint Standing Committee on Treaties, Maley points out that there can be few better illustrations of deliberative democracy at work. At a more generalized level of analysis, Maley draws a number of wider conclusions from the land-mines process and its success in Australia.

Neumann is particularly interested in the relationship between the Norwegian Foreign Ministry and NGOs in the context of the land-mines initiative. As in many other countries, the Norwegian Foreign Ministry was caught between a NGO-led campaign and resistance in the military and defence establishment. On the one hand, sensitivity to the issue in the NGO community was triggered by the loss of some members of the Norwegian Afghan Committee (NAC) in a land-mines accident. On the other hand, the land-mines issue remained an idea that clashed with traditional Norwegian security policy, rooted in the experience of sharing a common border with Russia.

Yet Neumann points out as well that an analysis emphasizing a transnational NGO network pressuring a state to act is overly simplistic. States themselves have their own motivations for providing agency in terms of initiative and leadership. Not all states, of course, are able to adopt new diplomacy. One requirement is a richness of knowledge and skills. A second requirement is a good working relationship among different segments/components of society and the state (for example, a good working relationship between intellectuals and NGOs and the Ministry of Defence/Foreign Affairs). Third, financial capacity must exist. A final prerequisite for new diplomacy is the existence of good lines of contact between Northern states and the South.

A second case study of interest is the push for a permanent international criminal court. Again, the catalytic function of middle powers and NGOs stands out. From 1995 to 1998, a like-minded group of approximately 60 countries pushed for progress on this agenda. A core group of countries supplemented this declaratory support by skilful legal work in developing a draft treaty. At the heart of this core group remained the self-identified cohort of traditional middle powers such as the Nordics, Australia, New Zealand, and Canada. Nonetheless, there was an additional group of non-traditional states within the leadership group. Of these states South Africa stands out. South Africa played a key role in the so-called group of "Lifeline Nations" advocating an independent court and independent prosecutor as opposed to an ICC under the control of the Security Council. Individual South Africans (notably Chief Justice Richard Goldstone) also played key roles. In all of this activity, furthermore, the like-minded states were supported by a wide variety of NGOs, ranging from the World Federalists to Amnesty International, Human Rights Watch, and the Lawyers Committee for Human Rights. The focal point of all this entrepreneurial and technical work was the June-July 1998 UN-sponsored Rome conference.[25]

Alistair Edgar's chapter highlights in a number of ways the salience of the ICC for new diplomacy. Not only can the ICC campaign be identified with the growing visibility of partnerships between like-minded countries and NGOs, but the substance of the initiative itself is indicative of the process of transformation in the development of the international normative system. One of the hallmarks of the ICC is the independence of the prosecutor from the UN Security Council. Another is the potential for the erosion of state sovereignty through the court's jurisdiction. Still another is the implications of the UN Assembly vote allowing the court to have a role in individual countries.

If recognizing the new, Edgar cautions against any claim that the ICC is revolutionary. Indeed, he argues that in many ways the ICC is a blend of the new and the old. Edgar highlights the various ways by which the ICC comes up against the traditional world of power. While the court has jurisdiction, it is not clear whether or not the ICC can actually enforce its decisions.

Philip Nel argues that the establishment of the ICC brings another major dilemma into focus. Are the tendencies associated with the creation of the ICC part of a counter-hegemonic or a post-hegemonic movement? While a counter-hegemonic movement may lead to the creation of another form of dominance, a post-hegemonic movement may actually transform the character of the international system. From Nel's point of view, the establishment of the ICC should be seen as part of the latter process. While he acknowledges that the ICC is still contested by many developing countries, which feel that unchecked development of humanitarian intervention will contribute to arbitrary intervention, Nel concludes that the opportunities of the ICC as part of a new diplomacy outweigh these concerns. In terms of process, the ICC helps undermine the élitism associated with the P5 and the veto. At the ICC NGOs can claim representation. In normative terms, the ICC represents an excellent innovation to humanitarian law.

Narratives of these case studies are interesting in themselves. The more ambitious purpose of the research programme described in this volume, however, is to use these case studies to bring out some answers to bigger questions concerning global governance and the UN system. Arguably the most fundamental of these questions is whether these cases are prototypes of further activity of this sort, or anomalous episodes.

Certainly the pattern of activity found in the new diplomacy *vis-à-vis* land-mines and the ICC does not exhaust the range of possible ways in which this dynamic is played out. To be fully comprehensive, the typology would have to be extended still further in terms of both actors and the range of issues to be covered. In form, one important dimension of new diplomacy that should not be neglected is so-called "triangular" diplomacy, including not only states and NGOs but states, NGOs, and the business community.[26] In scope, this type of interaction moves beyond the security domain to encompass various aspects of commercial diplomacy.

Virginia Haufler's chapter provides comprehensive coverage of the impact on global governance of corporate codes of conduct and "co-regulation" between governments, the corporate community, and NGOs. Haufler shows the impressive scope of this process through a survey of both national and international regulatory and self-regularity practices. She argues that the adoption of corporate codes of conduct is uneven and depends on the differing effects of globalization. Among the incentives for companies to adopt codes of conduct are attitudes of shareholders, the danger of state-imposed codes, and reputation. In pushing for new forms of governance in the global workplace, NGOs have become a vital component in this dynamic. Nonetheless, as NGOs become embedded in their operations, Haufler suggests that these organizations face similar tests with respect to reputation and credibility.

Haufler argues that several core challenges remain in the process of trying to develop codes of conduct. What is included and what is left out? Who participates in the code's development? What is the best way to monitor such codes? In conclusion she notes that while business accepts some measure of government involvement, there exists fundamental distrust between business and NGOs, leaving little room for facilitation.

John English's chapter on the Canadian experience of trying to negotiate a code of conduct for Canadian companies elaborates on the question of opportunities and challenges. In common with other countries, the Canadian government has faced growing pressure by NGOs for a code of conduct in the apparel and related sectors. Yet despite its success in triggering the creation of a Task Force on Sweatshops, the mainstay organization in this campaign (the Ethical Trading Action Group or ETAG) has remained frustrated by the outcome of this process. The result was not a code but only loose guidelines companies could adopt for their use at the recommendation of the Retail Council (the representative organization of the business side). It lacked reference to ILO standards, did not address monitoring, and the freedom of association component was weak.

Instead of blaming the breakdown of this sort of initiative on the government's unresponsiveness to bottom-up approaches, the NGO assessment of what went wrong with the process is markedly state-centric. The ETAG complained that the Canadian government did not come through with needed funding, and was not willing to pressure business associations and companies in support of ILO core labour rights. The ETAG also pointed out to the obstacles posed by the international environment, because of both the limits imposed by Chinese sovereignty and the shadow of American legislation.

The chapter by Brian Hocking and Dominic Kelly is informed directly by the central theme running through this collection: the sources and impact of diplomatic innovation from multiple actors. More specifically, their chapter locates the changing role of the business community in the diplomatic milieu through a focused study on the activities of the International Chamber of Commerce via its relationship with the United Nations. In common with a number of the other contributors, Hocking and Kelly make some caveats to the extent of the actual "newness" in new diplomacy. Still, they emphasize that under conditions of globalization, the International Chamber of Commerce has become part of a multi-dimensional or polylateral diplomacy. Driving this new diplomacy on the part of the International Chamber of Commerce is not only a greater appreciation of the mutual benefits to be derived from this interactive process, but also the fact that multilateral strategies and norms are taken more seriously in the international system.

By their linkage of this component of new diplomacy to Kofi Annan's Global Compact initiative, Hocking and Kelly cut in as well to the additional question about the role of the UN Secretary-General. Whereas this volume has concentrated on the frustrations with the United Nations as a trigger for new forms of activity from outside the P5, there may be some other cases where the actions of key agents within the UN system may prove to be catalysts for accelerated action. Hocking and Kelly locate both the motivations and the institutional impetus for this type of advance in the case of the International Chamber of Commerce and the United Nations.

The final set of contributions to the volume returns to the question of where new diplomacy can become ripe in the security domain. One sign of an operational advance in this direction has been the Human Security Network initiated by Canada and Norway. Broader in scope than the Canada-Norway bilateral Lysoen Declaration, this initiative included 11 countries and nine NGOs at its first meeting in May 1999 at Bergen. On top of this broadly based initiative, as Deidre van der Merwe, Mark Malan, and Kim Richard Nossal testify, some considerable potential for cross-cutting partnerships on an issue-specific basis is available.

The van der Merwe and Malan chapter outlines exisiting initiatives aimed at the protection of children in armed conflict, and argues that they be complemented by a voluntary code of conduct. They concentrate their attention on three areas where codes of conduct could have a positive impact on the plight of children in armed conflict: in specific forms of humanitarian action, in small arms, and in the incorporation of and emphasis on the rights of children in armed conflict in military codes of conduct.

While van der Merwe and Malan acknowledge there exists abundant controversy about the feasibility and effectiveness of voluntary codes, they argue that these mechanisms increase ethical sensitivity and judgement. Codes are reflections of the morally permissive standards of conduct which members of a group make binding upon themselves. The principle that children's interests should be held in higher regard than military interests is viewed as being particularly valuable.

Nossal's chapter targets more specifically the role of innovative leadership in the case of UN sanctions and "conflict diamonds" in Angola. Nossal is fully aware of the defects of sanctions when used in an indiscriminate and blunt fashion. What his chapter demonstrates, however, is the salience of these instruments when mobilized in a smarter, sharper, and stronger fashion on an issue-specific basis. Replicating the triangular shape detected on codes of conduct, Nossal traces the links in an emergent partnership between NGOs (most notably Global Witness), a variety of like-minded states (including Britain), and, after some considerable initial reluctance, the global diamond industry generally and De Beers more specifically.

As a case study of new diplomacy in action, the issue of conflict diamonds underscores the relevance of the model depicted above. Catalysts, in terms of individual change agents, were on tap. An accentuated intensity was provided by the tactic of "naming and shaming". And some sophisticated division of labour was developed, as witnessed most clearly by the creation of the World Diamond Council in September 2000.

Normative and practical considerations

Two last points need to be raised about new diplomacy and innovative leadership. The first is that a larger set of normative questions should not be lost amidst the focus on case studies as illustrative devices. From this perspective, Ramesh Thakur's concluding chapter is illuminating. Building on the concept of global governance, he makes the linkage between a new and more diffuse form of diplomacy and the change from an agenda based on national security to the ascendancy of human security. The implications of the new diplomacy transcending traditional state-centred interests and activities via an extended agenda of human rights, humanitarian intervention, and the concept of international law are highlighted. As Thakur delineates: "The goal of global governance is not the creation of world government, but of an additional layer of international decision-making, multisectoral, democratically accountable, and inclusive of civil society actors in the shared management of the troubled and fragile world order."

Despite all its limitations, the United Nations remains at the legislative and normative centre of the international system. Its authority is rooted in the sense of international solidarity transcending national perspectives and sectarian affectations. Because of its authenticized procedures and capacity for standard-setting, norm generation, and regime creation, there is no alternative to the United Nations. In Thakur's words, the United Nations remains indispensable because it has "the moral legitimacy, political credibility, and administrative impartiality" to make a difference.

On the practical side, questions must be asked about what techniques have and/or should be used by these sources of alternative leadership. What comes out through this volume is an image that these alternative set of leaders and innovators are increasingly prepared to use any and all tactics to get results. If momentum is stymied in one direction, the push for change is rerouted in other directions. As one observer has put it, in quite a positive vein, this multifaceted process has produced an indirect style in which some results are won not through the front door of the UN system but at the edges and around the back of the system. In other words, "some progress has been made since the end of the Cold War, through the backdoor rather than the major reform".[27]

The positive virtues of this process of adaptation are obvious. The possibility of opening up the UN system is enhanced not only in procedural terms but in terms of getting results. The result will be a big step towards efficiency and democratization. This sense of instrumentality is picked up as well in the less enthusiastic analysis of other commentators. Two Canadian academics, for instance, have suggested in a recent article that episodes such as the land-mines campaign have a subtlety and sophistication built into them: "it can perhaps be described as an end-run around the practical and political roadblocks that are a frequent feature of international discourse".[28] The difference is that Hampson and Oliver cast this change in a more negative or subversive light, threatening, not reinforcing, the operational capacity of the United Nations.

All of this added complexity in the international system demands greater nuance of analysis. As James Rosenau has recognized,[29] a considerable element of "fragmented authority" has been introduced into the international system. What have been neglected are the implications of these changes with respect to the application of diplomacy. Whatever view is taken concerning the extent and impact of "turbulence" within the specific context of the United Nations, it seems clear that the emergent pattern of diffuse interaction and multiple forms of leadership matters. Rather than discarding or avoiding the UN system, this activity aims to rework this system to make it more operational and transparent. The need, then, is to look more closely at these non-traditional sources of leadership and innovation so as to be able to understand and deploy this multifaceted dynamic better.

Notes

1. Richard Higgott, "Issues, Institutions and Middle-power Diplomacy: Action and Agendas in the Post-Cold War Era", in Andrew F. Cooper, ed., *Niche Diplomacy: Middle Powers after the Cold War* (London: Macmillan, 1997), p. 25.
2. Stanley Meisler, *United Nations: The First Fifty Years* (New York: Atlantic Monthly Press, 1995).
3. Robert Jervis, "International Primacy: Is the Game Worth the Candle?", *International Security* 17, no. 4 (Spring 1993), p. 65.
4. Erskine Childers and Brian Urquhart, *Renewing the United Nations System* (Uppsala, Sweden: Dag Hammarskjöld Foundation, 1994).
5. See, for example, Carnegie Commission on Preventing Deadly Conflict, *Preventing Deadly Conflict; Final Report* (New York: Carnegie Corporation of New York, 1997).
6. See for example Margaret P. Karns and Karen A. Mingst, "Multilateral Institutions and International Security", in Michael Klare and D. C. Thomas, *World Security, Trends and Challenges at Century's End* (New York: St Martin's Press, 1998).
7. John G. Ruggie, "Multilateralism: Anatomy of an Institution", *International Organization* 46, no. 3 (Summer 1992), p. 593.
8. Samuel Huntington, "The U.S. – Decline or Renewal?", *Foreign Affairs* 67, no. 1 (Winter 1988–1989), pp. 75–96.
9. Richard N. Haass, *The Reluctant Sheriff: The United States After the Cold War* (New York: Council on Foreign Relations, 1997).
10. Higgott, note 1 above, p. 34.
11. Andrew F. Cooper, Richard A. Higgott, and Kim Richard Nossal, *Relocating Middle Powers: Australia and Canada in a Changing World Order* (Vancouver: University of British Colombia Press, 1993).
12. John W. Holmes, *Canada: A Middle-Aged Power* (Toronto: McClelland and Stewart, 1976), p. 36.
13. Arthur Andrew, *The Rise and Fall of a Middle Power: Canadian Diplomacy from King to Mulroney* (Toronto: James Lorimer, 1993), p. 166. See also Andrew F. Cooper, "Coalitions of the Willing: The Seach for Like-Minded Partners in Canadian Diplomacy", in Leslie A. Pal, ed., *How Ottawa Spends 1999–2000 Shape Shifting: Canadian Governance Toward the 21st Century* (Don Mills, Ont: Oxford University Press, 1999), pp. 221–250.
14. Gareth Evans and Bruce Grant, *Australia's Foreign Relations in the World of the 1990s* (Melbourne: University of Melbourne Press, 1991), p. 323.
15. Sir Peter Marshall, *Positive Diplomacy* (London: Macmillan, 1997), p. 49. See also Richard Langhorne, "Diplomacy Beyond the Primacy of the State", paper presented to annual conference of the International Studies Association, Minneapolis, 20 March 1998; and Strobe Talbott, "Globalization and Diplomacy: A Practioner's Perspective", *Foreign Policy* 108 (Autumn 1997), pp. 69–83.
16. Quoted in "Opening Address to the Fiftieth Annual Department of Public Information/ Non-govenmental Organization (DPI/NGO) Conference", United Nations Press Release, SG/SM/6320,PI/1027, 10 September 1997.
17. Robert W. Cox, "Multilateralism and World Order", *Review of International Studies* 18, no. 2 (April 1992), pp. 161–180; Michael Schechter, *Future Multilateralism: The Political and Social Framework* (Basingstoke: Macmillan/Tokyo: United Nations University Press, 1998).
18. Gilbert Winham, "The Impact of System Change on International Diplomacy", paper delivered to Canadian Political Science Association, Ottawa, 1993.

19. Quoted in Marshall, note 15 above, p. 82. For a further analysis of the process of integration of these issues into the UN human rights mechanisms see Elizabeth Riddell-Dixon, "Mainstreaming Women's Rights: Problems and Prospects Within the Centre for Human Rights", *Global Governance* 5, no. 2 (April–June 1999), pp. 149–171.
20. Mark Duffield, "NGO Relief in War Zones: Towards an Analysis of the New Aid Paradigm", *Third World Quarterly* 18, no. 3 (1997), p. 534. For a more general treatment of the emergent role of NGOs in "negotiating outcomes" see P. J. Simmons, "Learning to Live with NGOs", *Foreign Policy* 112 (Autumn 1998), pp. 82–96.
21. For an expansion of this typology see Andrew F. Cooper and Brian Hocking, "Governments, Non-governmental Organisations and the Re-calibration of Diplomacy", *Global Society* 14, no. 3 (2000), pp. 361–376.
22. Barry Buzan, *People, States and Fear: An Agenda for International Security Studies in the Post-Cold War Era* (Hemel Hempstead: Harvester, 1991).
23. See, for example, Charles Tilley, "Prisoners of the State", *International Social Science Journal* 44, no. 3 (1992), pp. 329–343.
24. Quoted in John R. English, "The Landmine Initiative: A Canadian Initiative?", in Andrew F. Cooper and Geoffrey Hayes, eds, *Worthwhile Initiatives? Canadian Mission-Oriented Diplomacy* (Toronto: Irwin Publishing, 2000). On some of the wider implications of this process see Ramesh Thakur and William Maley, "The Ottawa Convention on Landmines: A Landmark Humanitarian Treaty in Arms Control?", *Global Governance* 5, no. 3 (1999), pp. 273–302.
25. For an overview of the ICC process see Fanny Benedetti and John L. Washburn, "Drafting the International Criminal Court Treaty: Two Years to Rome and an Afterword on the Rome Diplomatic Conference", *Global Governance* 5, no. 1 (January–March 1999), pp. 1–39.
26. Susan Strange, "States, Firms and Diplomacy", *International Affairs* 68, no. 1 (January 1992), pp. 1–16.
27. Edward Newman, *The UN Secretary-General From the Cold War To the New Era* (Basingstoke: Macmillan, 1998).
28. Fen Osler Hampson and Dean F. Oliver, "Pulpit Diplomacy: A Critical Assessment of the Axworthy Doctrine", *International Journal* 50, no. 3 (Summer 1998), p. 397.
29. James N. Rosenau, *Turbulence in World Politics: A Theory of Change and Continuity* (Princeton, NJ: Princeton University Press, 1990).

2

The future of the UN Security Council: Questions of legitimacy and representation in multilateral governance

W. Andy Knight

Introduction

The Security Council is the apex body of the United Nations. It is the pre-eminent authoritative body within the UN system. It has the primary responsibility of maintaining international peace and security, and was given specific and detailed powers through the UN Charter to carry this out.[1] As part of that responsibility the Council is charged with establishing a system to regulate armaments; identifying threats to global peace and security; calling on disputing parties to end their conflicts through peaceful means (negotiation, inquiry, mediation, conciliation, arbitration, judicial settlement, resort to regional agencies and arrangements, etc.); and referring legal disputes to the International Court of Justice. In addition, it is the only body within the UN system whose decisions are binding on all UN members.[2] Thus it should come as no surprise that as the issue of UN reform reaches a crescendo the spotlight has been focused on the Security Council.

Like the rest of the UN system, the Security Council is being critically scrutinized by observers of multilateral governance who recognize that analyses of the nexus between evolving global order and changes to the concrete manifestations of multilateralism[3] can reveal much about the extent of the relevance and legitimacy of multilateral institutions. These observers first ask "What are the ways in which international society and global order are changing?" and then, "Do we have the correct institutional structures and arrangements to deal with the new demands that emerge from such changes?" This chapter uses this critical framework to examine first the systemic changes that have impacted on the UN Security Council, then to understand the reasons why the Council has been charged by some with becoming illegitimate and unrepresentative, and finally to describe the reform process that has been initiated to address the perceived inadequacies of the Council.

Brief history of systemic changes that affected the UN Security Council

Clearly there have been changes in international society and global order since the United Nations was founded in 1945 that have had an impact on international governance institutions, particularly on the UN system. One of the major post-Second World War changes that had a major impact on the UN system was the Cold War – a clash of political, ideological, and strategic interests of the rival superpowers, the USA and the Soviet Union. The climate of mistrust that characterized this period dashed any hopes for the continuation of the great-power cooperation witnessed during the Second World War. The stalemate over the Military Staff Committee exemplified the problems associated with this ideological rivalry. The end result was that the Security Council could not function in the way the UN founders expected it to function, and "the grand scheme that the Charter envisaged for the collective enforcement of peace and security was never operationalized".[4] Excessive use of the veto by both superpowers and the use of the so-called hidden veto resulted in sustained circumvention of possible Council actions. The USA and its allies did find a way out of the Council's impasse for a brief period in 1950 with the adoption of the Uniting for Peace resolution by the General Assembly. This measure allowed the United Nations to become militarily involved in the Korean conflict (1950–1951) and later the Suez crisis (1956). The Assembly in those cases acted as a substitute for the paralysed Council.

However, by the 1960s the USA could no longer depend on the Assembly to assist it in circumventing the Council. A period of decolonization resulted in the admission of several countries, mostly from Africa and the Caribbean, into the UN system. This "new aggressive majority" of mostly poor, underdeveloped countries began to push its own agenda within the Assembly. That agenda was concerned with issues affecting the people of those impoverished former colonial countries – issues such as economic development, anti-racism, and anti-imperialism. The USA (and its allies) became more isolated in the General Assembly, and consequently there was a tendency to reverse its earlier pro-Assembly policy and revert back to the Council on issues dealing with international peace and security. During this decolonization period, UN membership grew from 51 to 118. The membership in the General Assembly had thus grown disproportionately to the size of the Council, which consisted of five permanent and six non-permanent members. Pressure was placed on the Security Council to expand its membership, and by 1965 the General Assembly agreed to amend the UN Charter to allow for an increase in the non-permanent seats on the Council from six to 10.[5]

The expansion of the Council's membership facilitated the emergence of a new coalition within that body, namely the Non-Aligned Group. The strength of that group ranged from six to eight votes depending on the issue, and that solidarity "became a factor to be reckoned with in the political process of the Council".[6] This presence helps explain Security Council actions against the pariah regimes of Rhodesia (1966) and South Africa (1977). But it also goes towards explaining the increase in the paralysis of that body.[7] This, combined with a rapid deterioration in the international political climate during the mid- to late 1970s, caused the Council once again to succumb to a period of futility and stagnation. For about a decade the Council was unable to act decisively in any international conflict situation. Indeed, the superpowers worked outside of the Council to address conflicts affecting international peace and security. Murthy observes that "the Council's prestige was at its lowest from 1979 to 1987, i.e. till the end of the Cold War".[8] The Council was unable to take action on conflicts in Afghanistan, Cambodia, Angola, Nicaragua, and the Gulf, among other places.

The end of the 1980s brought a thaw in the Cold War conditions. The sharp ideological distinctions between East and West began to fade, and as a result a new era in the history of the Council was heralded. The fall of the Berlin Wall and the reunification of East and West Germany were symptomatic of this new post-Cold War period. It was this change of climate that allowed the Security Council in 1990 to act decisively in forcing Iraq to withdraw from Kuwait and to give up its annexation plans. Although the permanent members were not entirely harmonious (China having abstained on Resolution 678), the success of Operation Desert Storm promised a "new global order" in which the Security Council would assert its Charter powers to achieve international peace and security. This period of assertive multilateralism, marked by the first-ever Security Council summit (January 1992), brought the Council to the centre of international activity in Angola, Bosnia-Herzegovina, Haiti, Liberia, Rwanda, and other conflict theatres.

At the same time we have been witness to the merging of the first and second worlds, the rise of new economic powers within the international hierarchy (such as Japan and Germany), the expansion of the nuclear power club (India and Pakistan), an increase in secession activity leading to the creation of new states (note the break-up of the Soviet Union and Yugoslavia), the growing role of regional organizations in regional conflicts, the intensification of globalization, and a shift from interstate to largely intrastate conflicts. The Security Council has been kept busy with internal conflicts, ethic and tribal clashes, terrorism, humanitarian emergencies, human rights abuses, etc. during the immediate post-Cold War era.[9]

The increase in the Council's activity during the immediate post-Cold War period transformed that body literally overnight. There was a sense of a "new-found solidarity" among the permanent members of the Council[10] which translated into a new-found efficiency measured in terms of an increase in the number of formal meetings, informal consultations, agenda items, resolutions adopted, observer missions, and peacekeeping operations. All this was made possible because of "a striking reduction in the use of the veto and a significant improvement in the decision-making capacity" of the Council.[11] Indeed, the Council stretched certain aspects of the Charter to develop peacekeeping-plus operations, peace-building and peace maintenance operations. An entirely new tool, preventive deployment, emerged to deal with regional conflicts.[12] Some critics have suggested that the Council, instead of designing "a concept commensurate with the challenges encountered", decided to embrace the easy path of "tinkering with the peacekeeping concept in the hope that it would work in all conflict situations equally effectively – an exercise with none too happy consequences for the continued credibility of the concept".[13]

To sustain this flurry of activity in the peace and security area, the Council adopted the practice of contracting out and used troop contributions by its permanent members – a break with past tradition which has proven to be more of a liability than an asset.[14] In addition, as Murthy observes, Council members interpreted "the Charter so liberally" that they "tended to trample upon the powers and privileges of other UN organs".[15] However, one could suggest that without such liberal interpretation it would have been difficult to address adequately the "new" security problems facing the UN organization. The flexibility built into the Charter allowed the Council to create the Sanctions Committee to deal with recalcitrant states and disarm a potential nuclear power (such as Iraq), to set up ad hoc international tribunals for investigating and prosecuting crimes against humanity committed ostensibly in civil conflicts by individuals (as in Rwanda and the former Yugoslavia), to address state terrorism in unique ways (note the Libyan case), and to initiate a process (a conference of plenipotentiaries) which resulted in the creation of a permanent international criminal court.[16]

However, it is ironic that just as the UNSC seems to be operating in the way in which the UN founders had intended, many UN member states "began to have second thoughts about the legitimacy of that body's use of its collective authority".[17] This second guessing occurred during and after the "successful" Gulf War,[18] and when the UNSC acted with respect to Libya.[19] Also, the failed Somalia operation in 1995 so tarnished the new-found reputation of the Council that the permanent members became much more tentative about committing troops and resources in civil conflict situations, particularly in Africa.[20] This tentativeness can be blamed for the failure of the United Nations to prevent the genocidal activity in Rwanda and limit the gross human rights violations by the Revolutionary United Front (RUF) in Sierra Leone. But more importantly, what these cases of internal conflicts revealed was that the Security Council did not have the rapid reaction capability to respond in a timely fashion to incipient conflicts.

The capacity and resources of the United Nations were so stretched by the later 1990s[21] that we witnessed a downturn in Council activity just when the notion of assertive multilateralism seem to be taking hold. The Council was sidelined during the NATO-Yugoslavia conflict. It has been barred from dealing with the conflict in Chechnya because of a Russian threat to use the veto. It was stymied on the issue of extending UNPREDEP's mandate in Macedonia because of a Chinese veto.[22] It has been unsuccessful in resolving the impasse over Iraqi weapons inspection. As if this was not enough, the Council has had to deal with charges that it is losing its collective legitimacy[23] and has become unrepresentative of the UN membership.

Legitimacy and representation

To assess the charges being levied against the UN Security Council, it is important to understand what is meant by legitimacy and representation in the context of multilateral institutions.

The issue of legitimacy in multilateral organs has been examined by international legal scholars[24] as well as political scientists for some time.[25] While the term "legitimacy" may be considered a nebulous one – used rather loosely in the international organization and international law literature[26] – one can decipher from a cursory survey of those literatures a number of specific ways in which this term is employed. For an institution to be considered legitimate it must be recognized as a lawful authority; one that conforms to a particular standard and operates in such a manner that its actions and decisions are seen as legally or morally justified and proper.[27] Thus allegations of illegitimacy are made when an institution or process is perceived to be unjust or unfair, or when the decisions of such institutions are no longer capable of being justified, especially when measured against expected standards of what is considered proper or lawful. Absence of legitimacy will ultimately lead to mistrust in the institution in question.

Perceptions of illegitimacy are ultimately subjective but could affect the effectiveness of an institution in one of two ways. They could undercut the perceived legitimacy of the rules that emanate from the institution, and might influence the willingness of the members of the institution to obey and support the decisions made by that institution in the future.[28] Hurd puts it well when he says: "The power of social institutions in a society is largely a function of the legitimacy of the institution." An institution that is perceived as legitimate will therefore be treated with respect and "will be endowed with a corporate existence above and beyond the units that make it up, and will find compliance with its rules more easily secured, than in the absence of legitimacy".[29] Caron contends in the case of the United Nations: "The likelihood of continued collective action depends in part on the perceived legitimacy of the decision maker, the Council itself."[30] Clearly, the perception of legitimacy or illegitimacy of the Council held by the majority of members of the General Assembly will have a significant impact on the authority of this apex body. The Council's authority[31] is derived from the UN Charter as well as from the delegated power of the community of nations it represents. That authority is called into question by the general UN membership if it perceives that the Council has acted in ways that are unjust, unfair, improper, or not in keeping with the promise and spirit of the UN Charter.[32] Since the effectiveness of the Council is predicated on that body's ability to get states to comply with the decisions it makes, it is exceedingly important for the Council to be perceived as legitimate by the rest of the UN membership.

A major charge of illegitimacy of the Council stems from the perception that the Council is dominated by a few states and is not truly representative of the rest of the UN body. This perception is widespread among states from the developing world. For an apex body to be representative of the broader membership in an organization it must portray the values of the larger group; present the ideas or views of that group; be typical of that group's geographical make-up, population base, and political views; and act as a delegate of that group. The Security Council, therefore, can be considered unrepresentative in a wide array of senses.

The Council's composition

The Italian delegation at the United Nations recently pointed out that 77 countries have never been members of the Council and 47 have served only a single term.[33] The reason for this has to do with the fact that the membership of the United Nations has grown disproportionately to the size of the Council. Although, as mentioned earlier, there was one expansion in the Council's membership in 1965, further growth in UN membership (today there are 185 UN member states) would seem to require a further expansion in the size of the Council. Implicit in the charge of "unrepresentation" is the idea that since much of the increase in the general membership of the United Nations has come from the admission of states from the developing world, there should be a corresponding increase in the Security Council membership of developing states.

It is noted that the dissolution of the Soviet Union, Yugoslavia, and Czechoslovakia resulted respectively in the creation of 15, five, and two new state entities – all new members of the UN organizations. Additionally, the United Nations has recently admitted a number of micro states into the family of nations, bringing the total UN membership to 185. The momentum being gained by a number of secessionist movements around the world makes it likely that new states will be added to the UN General Assembly in the not too distant future. It is conceivable, for instance, that the Russian Republic could further disintegrate. Ultra-national political parties exist in Scotland and Wales which are calling for separation from the United Kingdom. And, in Canada, the Parti Québécois came exceedingly close to forcing the federal government to negotiate terms of separation from Canada. These changes and potential changes require that some thought be given to the issue of broadening representation within the Security Council.

Geopolitical representation

From a geopolitical perspective, four out of the five permanent members on the Council are European or linked through history to Europe. China is the only permanent member not from the industrialized world. None of the permanent members is from the southern hemisphere. Therefore, one can appreciate the calls of several third world states for the inclusion of a number of countries representing the developing world – "the South" – in the permanent category of the Council. Developing countries see expansion of the Council as an opportunity to increase their power and influence within the United Nations and in global governance. Such a move could also have the effect of diminishing somewhat the power and influence of those states that are currently dominant within the Council, particularly the USA.[34] It will be difficult to deny for too much longer the agitation of developing states for greater representation on the Council, whether it be within the permanent category or the non-permanent category of seats.

Regional representation

From a regional perspective, the current permanent members of the Council represent North America, Western and Eastern Europe, and Asia. Neither Central America and the Caribbean, South America, nor Africa has a claim to representation among the permanent five. As we shall see below, there are calls for this situation to be corrected. Regional representation is considered one of the value planks of the UN Security Council's legitimacy and authority.[35] This explains why in 1965, when reform to the composition of the Council was entertained, a custom was established to distribute non-permanent seats in such a way as to give five seats to states in Africa and Asia, one seat to Eastern European states, two seats to Latin American states, and two seats to the states in the category of Western Europe and Other (WEO). These 10 seats are rotated on a staggered two-year basis. Today, the argument particularly among African states is that this is not enough. Something must be done in the non-permanent category to reflect better representation of the African continent on the Council.

Representation by population

From the perspective of representation by population, "[i]t seems absurd to think that in 50 years – when China, India, Pakistan, Nigeria, and Indonesia are projected to account for more than four billion people – the Security Council will still look the same".[36] While 46 per cent of the states on the Council today are European in origin or associated with Europe, the areas they represent contain only 20 per cent of the world's population.[37] If population is used as a criterion to ensure representation, then clearly the North is over-represented and the South is under-represented on the Council. Another related point that is sometimes made is that, particularly since the end of the Cold War, the Council's agenda has grown in ways that affect the large population groups of the globe. This expanded agenda, the argument goes, requires more members on that body to handle the corresponding increase in tasks. And it would make sense that the enlargement of members of the Council should come from those areas most affected by the decision-making fall-out of the Council.

Capacity representation: The functionalist principle

One of the major criteria for Council membership at the UN founding conference was the capacity to contribute to the maintenance of international peace and security – based on the functionalist principle. However, as Russett, O'Neill, and Sutterlin effectively argue, "the council is no longer representative of those countries with the greatest capacity to contribute to the maintenance of international peace and security as the founders had intended".[38] Based on economic strength alone, Germany and Japan "together are now able to offer a contribution to the maintenance of international security comparable to that of the United States, and greater than any of the others".[39] Schwartzberg has developed what he calls an "entitlement quotient" (EQ) that could be used to determine whether or not a state can qualify for Security Council membership based on the functionalist principle. He assigns an EQ to each member of the General Assembly that is determined by the average of three percentages: its population as a percentage of the total population of all member states, its UN assessed contribution as a percentage of the total for all member states, and its unitary percentage of the total UN membership.[40] Based on his EQ formula, the permanent membership of the Security Council would look very different from the existing arrangement. The USA and China would remain, but other countries like India and Japan would nudge out the UK and France.

There is flexibility built into Schwartzberg's model that would allow for adjustments to the composition of the Council as material capabilities of states undergo changes. As he is careful to point out:

there is no guarantee that today's economic giants will maintain their preeminence. Japan, for example, though rich in human and capital resources, is endowed with a meager natural resource base and faces increasing competition from other emerging "tigers" of the Pacific rim. Will it loom as prominently on the global stage a generation hence as it does at present?[41]

While the EQ formula needs some refinement, there is merit in establishing a means of determining the material capacity of states – since the Charter states that the main criteria for election of non-permanent members to the Council is the ability of potential members to contribute to the maintenance of international peace and security and to the other purposes of the organization.

The veto

Another related matter that affects both the legitimacy and the representativeness of the Council is the fact that the veto is held by five states, some of which may no longer be considered to be worthy of having this kind of exclusive power. The idea of giving the veto to an exclusive group of states stems from the practice of great-power management of the international system that can be traced back to the Concert of Europe. This idea was preserved in the League Council of the League of Nations and later adopted in the UN Security Council. "The right of the veto in the Security Council was given to those powers who would share principal responsibility for the maintenance of peace."[42]

When the United Nations was formed, a clear distinction was made between permanent members of the Council (consisting primarily of the victors of the Second World War)[43] and non-permanent members. The intent behind this differentiation was to maintain a form of great-power executive control over the entire UN operation. The permanent five powers were given the right to veto substantive resolutions emanating from the Council,[44] giving these powers a tremendous amount of clout with respect to key issues such as addressing security problems. The decision to allocate this power of veto to the permanent five was, in large part, based on the dominant political realist thinking of the immediate post-war period that the effectiveness of the United Nations would be severely constrained if great-power unanimity was not forthcoming. In addition, it became clear during the UN founding discussions, as noted by Cordell Hull, that the USA may not have remained a member of the United Nations had it been denied the veto.[45] Bearing in mind that great-power absence in the League of Nations contributed to one of the critical defects in that organization, the framers of the Charter learned a valuable lesson and incorporated the veto principle into the UN's constitutional structure in the hopes that the new organization might avoid the same fate as its immediate predecessor.

There was another reason why the veto principle was adopted. Again drawing lessons from the experience of the League's failed attempt to squash Italy's aggression against Ethiopia in 1935, it was generally felt that if the United Nations wanted to be successful in a similar situation it would require the solid backing of the states which controlled most of the global material and political power. In this regard, the veto became a "safety valve" to prevent the UN system from over-committing itself, politically, economically, and/or militarily. But it also was hoped that this device would ensure that whenever the coercive power of the United Nations was utilized, those powers with substantial material capabilities would back the effort. As Murthy put it: "The Council was designed to act not against *a* permanent member, but at the behest of *the* permanent members in the furtherance of its mandate."[46]

Several states expressed reservations at the UN founding conference in San Francisco about giving veto power to this exclusive group of states. The concerns then were quite similar to those being expressed today. The debate concerning the veto is dominated by four positions: eliminate the veto altogether; limit the scope of the veto's use; allow the existing permanent five countries to retain the veto, but not extend it to potential new permanent members; and extend the veto power to new permanent members.[47]

As was evident particularly during the Cold War period, the veto severely limits the possibility of discourse within the Council, and it reinforces the perception of the dominance of the P5. This situation also has created élitism within the UN organization that runs contrary to the Charter principle of sovereign equality of states. Yet it was intended to reflect the realities of *realpolitik*, and will most likely remain with us for sometime to come.

It is very unlikely that the permanent members of the Security Council would agree to relinquish the veto altogether. Indeed, as Patrick McCarthy puts it, this idea is "a non-starter since all permanent members have indicated that they are not willing to relinquish their right of veto".[48] For the permanent members, the veto is necessary for ensuring that when military or other coercive action is being undertaken by the United Nations, the states which possess the most substantial capabilities are in agreement with such action. Of course, the permanent members of the Council are aware as well that the veto ensures that concerted action taken by the United Nations will never be taken against any one of them. Even when the permanent members agree to limit the use of the veto, some of them utilize what has been called the "hidden veto", the threat of using the veto, to deter other states from bringing certain issues to the Council. This tool has been particularly effective since the end of the Cold War. With the culmination of the ideological divisions that characterized the Cold War and the advent of a new cooperative spirit in the Council, there was a "gentleman's agreement" among the permanent five to refrain from using the veto. However, from time to time, when a permanent member feels that a potential Council action might run against that state's interest (however defined), threatening to use the veto can accomplish the same thing as using the veto.

Before considering the elimination of the veto, one has to reflect on what substitute voting procedure will be likely to replace it. It is clear that any attempt to democratize the voting procedures of the Council will have to be balanced against the realities of the concentration of power among a limited number of states. Those realities would ensure that some alternative method of maintaining an element of great-power control over the outcomes of substantive issues will replace the veto tool.

In any event, the Charter's amending formula (in Article 108) poses a formidable obstacle to proposals calling for the elimination of the veto. Procedurally, this means that "the permanent members have a veto over any effort to take away their right of veto".[49] Given the present mood of the US Congress regarding the United Nations, it is highly unlikely that there would be domestic ratification of any UN resolution that would take away the right of veto from the USA. It is also highly unlikely that the UK, France, Russia, and China could be induced into supporting a move to relinquish the veto. Until such a time when all permanent five members of the Council agree to phase out the veto, there seems little point in contemplating that option.

Initiating the reform process

Responding to widespread demands for changes to the Council, the General Assembly in December 1992 placed on its agenda the item "Question of equitable representation on and increase in the membership of the Security Council". All UN member states were invited to contribute proposals and written comments on this matter.[50]

The question implicit in the comments submitted by so many member states is whether the council can meet the unprecedented current and future challenges while structured essentially as it was fifty years ago and following procedures that, aside from increased reliance on informal consultations, have remained remarkably unchanged.[51]

The proposals for change in the Security Council have been wide-ranging. There have been calls for increased transparency; closer cooperation between the Security Council and the General Assembly; wider consultations between the Security Council and concerned parties, including regional organizations and groups within civil society; limiting the right of the veto currently enjoyed by the five permanent members of the Council; extending the veto to a few more states; eliminating the veto altogether; making the Security Council more representative by adding states from under-represented regions to both the permanent and non-permanent seats; lessening the monopoly of power held by the permanent five; and curtailing the practice of informal consultations among the permanent five.[52]

Some of the main concrete proposals being entertained are described and assessed below.

- Create between eight and 10 new non-permanent seats (based on countries' ability to assume greater responsibility for UN finances, peacekeeping operations, etc.) that would be shared by 20–30 countries through frequent rotation.[53] The problem with this proposal is that an increase of that magnitude could negatively impact on the effectiveness of the Council and its ability to take decisive action.
- A two-plus-three permanent seat formula which would assign two permanent seats to industrialized states (with Germany and Japan added

as candidates) and three permanent seats to one country each from Africa, Asia, and Latin America and the Caribbean. This, however, begs the question of whether or not existing P5 states would legislate themselves out of a permanent seat on the Council. It also raises the possibility of extending the veto to countries in the developing world – something that the current P5 members are unwilling to entertain.

- The so-called "two permanent plus three permanent but rotating" formula.[54] This would grant two industrialized countries permanent seats, in addition to the current P5, but also allow for three regional rotating permanent seats assigned to states in Africa, Asia, and Latin America and the Caribbean. This proposal has been dubbed by some "a quick fix". It has been criticized by others who argue that a permanent seat cannot be "rotating"; it is either permanent or non-permanent. The fact that the two permanent additional seats from the industrial world would have a veto while the permanent rotational seats would not has become a major concern for states in the developing world. The latter states argue that the permanent rotational seats would thus become little more than regular non-permanent seats. This formula also would divide the Council into four categories of membership – simply increasing the inequality among members.

- Increase in the Council membership from its current 15 members to a total of 26.[55] This proposal would see the addition of both new permanent and non-permanent seats. The new permanent seats would be assigned to countries from "less advantaged" continents in order to redress what is perceived as a major gap in the current ranks of the permanent members between industrialized and developing countries.[56] The Non-Aligned Movement (NAM) has also placed on the table a proposal that calls for the expansion in the number of non-permanent seats only, should there be a failure to reach agreement on expanding the membership in the permanent category. The call for expansion in the non-permanent seats is predicated on the need to redress the imbalance between the current size of the UN Security Council and the expansion that has occurred in the overall membership of the UN General Assembly. The purpose is to have the Council become more representative of the general membership of the UN organization. However, the same concerns about maintaining Council effectiveness mentioned earlier would apply to this proposal.

- Increase the size of the Council from 15 to 20 seats – creating five new non-permanent seats in the process, to be divided as follows: one for Africa, one for Asia, one for Latin America and the Caribbean, one to alternate every two years between the WEO and the East European group, and one to alternate every two years between Germany and Japan.[57] While this increase seems more reasonable, the idea of alter-

nating seats between the WEO and East European group and between
Germany and Japan does not sit well with these countries and seems
very awkward indeed.

- Add two permanent seats (with veto) to be assigned on a rotational
basis to countries in Africa only, as well as five non-permanent seats.[58]
African states have insisted on the importance of ensuring that the
veto be given to the new permanent members so that these members
would be on equal footing with the current P5 members. This proposal
from the OAU does not sit well with the USA and its allies. Also, Pakistan is clearly opposed (as are other developing states) to this idea.
As the UN delegation from Pakistan recently put it:

We are against any enlargement of the permanent membership of the Security
Council since this concept is against the principle of sovereign equality of
states. We would not support an expansion which would merely serve to accommodate the interests of only a few countries, and conversely, alienate the
small and medium sized countries, who constitute an overwhelming majority in
the General Assembly. We will continue to oppose the creation of new centres
of privilege and aggravation of imbalances within the UN system as these are
anachronistic, anti-democratic and contrary to the principle of sovereign equality of states enshrined in the UN Charter.

It continues: "Any decision on Security Council reform that is not
backed by the consensus of all the UN Member States will erode the
credibility and undermine the legitimacy of the Council as well as the
United Nations."[59]

- The Arab countries have proposed the increase in permanent seats
(with veto power) by one – which should be assigned to Arab countries on a rotational basis, as well as the addition of at least two non-
permanent seats to be assigned to that group of states.[60] This proposal
suffers from the same problem as that proposed by the OAU.

Essentially the discussion of the last eight years in the open-ended working group established by the General Assembly to consider "the Question of Equitable Representation on and Increase in the Membership of
the Security Council and Other Matters Related to the Council" has resulted in virtual "log-jam".[61]

Conclusion

Has the Council become an anachronism? Is it now a dysfunctional and
unrepresentative body? Paul Knox writes:

The Security Council – the ossified nuclear unit of the UN's extended family – does not accurately reflect the distribution of population, wealth, contributions to the UN, or ability to project military force in today's world. As long as this remains true, not only will it lack credibility in many of the most acute security crises, but key members and coalitions will have structural incentives to paralyze or undermine it.[62]

Can the Council adapt to shifts in the relative power of UN members?

It seems to the author that the mandate of the Council is not being challenged. All UN member states seem to agree that the Council still should be the primary body responsible for maintaining international peace and security. What is being questioned is "whether the authority of the council can endure if its structure remains unchanged and, conversely, whether in an enlarged form it would retain the effectiveness on which its authority also depends".[63] So expansion of the Council and its ability to function effectively form the basis of the questions concerning its legitimacy. As Russett, O'Neill, and Sutterlin put it: "Ultimately, legitimacy and effectiveness depend substantially on each other."[64]

The aim of expansion of the Council should be to achieve the objectives outlined below.

• Improve the rate of participation. Not very many states will be afforded the opportunity of being on the Council.
• Improve geographical representation. Since 1945 there has been a redistribution of the weight and responsibilities of geographical areas as far as international peace and security is concerned specifically and global governance in general. Some regions are emerging in importance economically (such as Asia). In some parts of Africa there are signs of renaissance and resumption of economic growth. Democracy seems to have taken root in a big way in Latin America. The European Union has developed into a major economic powerhouse. Some states have acquired nuclear power capability (Israel, India, Pakistan). Others seem to be on the verge of doing so. These new balances of relations between and within continents cannot be ignored when discussing the possible recomposition of the UNSC.
• Improve the democratic character of the Council. This means reducing élitist claims and positions of privilege over time, and raises questions about the need for the veto power within the Council. It also raises the notion of reducing rather than expanding the use of the veto, or perhaps limiting it to issues that involve Chapter VII actions. Democratizing the Council also means that this body should represent a clear majority of the world's population as well as the resources that can be made available to the organization to pursue the maintenance of international peace and security.

- Improve efficiency. At a time when expansion of the Council is being proposed, one must also be aware that a large increase in membership could make this body unmanageable and perhaps affect its ability to function efficiently and effectively.
- Improve transparency. The procedures of consultation and decision-making should be as transparent as possible to all the members of the organization. This result can be obtained through greater involvement of non-permanent members of the Council and by involving states that are not members of the Council, particularly on questions that pertain to them.

These five principles ought to form the basis of any restructuring of the UN Security Council. Flexibility ought to be the key in any proposed reforms to the composition and function of the Council. Only if it can be flexible enough to adjust to these shifts can it be considered a relevant institution of multilateral governance.[65] At the same time, a recognition of the potential constraints to any planned change will keep reform proposals "realistic".

The ultimate goal of the reform of the Security Council should be to make that body less élitist, more democratic, and thus more representative of the rest of the UN membership. There should not be an attempt simply to reward a few countries with the privileges that the P5 currently enjoy. Rather, the objective should be to identify a number of solutions that would result in a more participatory and representative Council while at the same time holding on to the elements that allow the Council to be efficient and effective in carrying out its Charter mandate.[66] Bearing this in mind, the establishment of new permanent seats with veto power is not the answer. Such permanent members, particularly if they are from the European region or are part of the industrialized world, may simply carry on the élitist and domineering practices of the exiting permanent five. Such actions would certainly not strengthen the legitimacy of the institution. In any event, such a solution would not be permanent since there will always be calls by other states for inclusion into the rank of veto-wielding permanent members.

Recognizing the likelihood that the existing permanent five will not agree to an expansion in the ranks of permanent membership, it would probably be wiser at this stage to opt for the more modest reform strategy of expanding the non-permanent category of seats within a specified limit that would still allow for an efficiently run Council. This solution would offer the best hope for a more representative Council, provided that the elective seats are available to every regional grouping, and it would allow all member states of the United Nations a potential chance to serve for a specified term on the Council at some point. The NAM has offered this as a fall-back position in the case that no agreement can be reached on the other categories of seats. Support for this position seems to be strong among the 113 NAM states.[67] And countries like Italy have supported it as well.

In the meantime, Council members as representatives of the UN body should give preference to consultation rather than dictation. They should try to win the confidence and support of the majority within the UNGA. They should avoid exclusivity and secrecy, and should uphold standards of fairness and justice in their decision-making and actions. Decisions made should be acceptable to the majority of the UNGA and the international community. All actions taken by the UNSC should be justifiable legally in the context of the UN Charter. This is necessary for the legitimacy of that body to be retained. As the former UN Secretary-General Perez de Cuellar once noted: "The greater the Power, the higher is the responsibility to act and to be seen to act with justice."[68]

Notes

1. See UN Charter, Articles 24–26 and Chapters VI, VII, VIII and XII.
2. See UN Charter, Article 25, and David D. Caron, "The Legitimacy of the Collective Authority of the Security Council", *American Journal of International Law* 87 (1993), p. 552.
3. See Robert Cox, "Towards a Post-Hegemonic Conceptualization of World Order: Reflections on the Relevancy of Ibn Khaldun", in James Rosenau and Ernst-Otto Czempiel, eds, *Governance without Government: Order and Change in World Politics* (Cambridge: Cambridge University Press, 1992), p. 137.
4. C. S. R. Murthy, "Change and Continuity in the Functioning of the Security Council since the End of the Cold War", *International Studies* 32, no. 4 (1995), pp. 424–425.
5. UNGA Resolution 1991A (XVIII).
6. Murthy, note 4 above, p. 427.
7. See Richard Jackson, "The Role of the Nonaligned in the UN Security Council: A Western Perspective", *The Nonaligned World* (New Delhi) 1, no. 4 (1983), pp. 464–482; Davidson Nicol, "The Major Powers in the United Nations and the Nonaligned Group: The US as a Special Case", in M. S. Rajan, V. S. Mani and C. S. Murphy (eds), *The Nonaligned and the United Nations* (New Delhi: Oceana Publications/South Asia Books, 1987), pp. 158–177.
8. Murthy, note 4 above, pp. 427–428.
9. B. G. Ramcharan, "The Security Council: Maturing of International Protection of Human Rights", *The Review*, International Commission of Jurists, no. 48 (1992), p. 24.
10. Karen Mingst, *Essentials of International Relations* (New York: W. W. Norton, 1999), p. 249.
11. Patrick A. McCarthy, "Personality, Tension, and Instability in the UN Security Council", *Global Governance* 3 (1997), p. 149.
12. UNPREDEP in Macedonia.
13. Murthy, note 4 above, p. 434.
14. Note the Rapid Reaction Force in Bosnia-Herzegovina that consisted of British and French troops and the Quick Reaction Force, the United Task Force (UNITAF), in Somalia that was made up of US troops.
15. Murthy, note 4 above, p. 431.

16. W. Andy Knight, "Soft Power and Moral Suasion in Establishing the International Criminal Court: Canadian Contributions", in Rosalind Irwin, ed., *Ethics and Security in Canadian Foreign Policy* (Vancouver: University of British Columbia Press, 2001).
17. Caron, note 2 above, p. 553.
18. See Erskine Childers, "Gulf Crisis Lessons for the UN", *Bulletin of Peace Proposals* 129 (1992); Peter J. Fromuth, "The Making of a Security Community: The United Nations after the Cold War", *Journal of International Affairs* 341 (1993), p. 363.
19. Badi M. Ali, "White House Plays the Libya Card", *New York Times*, 5 May 1992, p. A18.
20. See W. Andy Knight and Kassu Gebremariam, "UN Intervention and Peacebuilding in Somalia: Constraints and Possibilities", in W. Andy Knight, ed., *Adapting the United Nations to a Post Modern World: Lessons Learned* (London: Palgrave/Macmillan/St Martin's Press, 2001), pp. 77–94; Mohamed Sahnoun, *Somalia: The Missed Opportunities* (Washington, DC: United States Institute of Peace Press, 1994).
21. See John G. Ruggie, "Wandering in the Void: Changing the UN's New Strategic Role", *Foreign Affairs* 72, no. 5 (November–December 1993), pp. 26–31.
22. Despite Chinese denials, it seems that this was done in retaliation against Macedonia's decision to establish diplomatic ties with Taiwan.
23. On the issue of collective legitimacy see Inis L. Claude, Jr, "Collective Legitimation as a Political Function of the United Nations", *International Organization* 20 (1966), pp. 367–379.
24. See for example Thomas M. Franck, *The Power of Legitimacy Among Nations* (New York: Oxford University Press, 1990); Jose E. Alvarez, "The Quest for Legitimacy: An Examination of *The Power of Legitimacy Among Nations* by Thomas Franck", *New York University Journal of International Law and Politics* 199 (1991).
25. Claude, note 23 above.
26. Caron, note 2 above, p. 556.
27. Karen Mingst defines legitimacy as "the moral and legal right to rule, which is based on law, custom, heredity, or the consent of the governed". See glossary in Mingst, note 10 above, p. 269.
28. Caron, note 2 above, p. 558, note 24.
29. Ian Hurd, "Legitimacy, Power, and the Symbolic Life of the Security Council", paper presented to the 1999 ISA Conference (updated May 2000), p. 3.
30. Caron, note 2 above, p. 554.
31. Authority is the power or right to enforce obedience irrespective of the goodwill of those who are subjugated to the authority.
32. Caron, note 2 above, p. 559.
33. See "The Italian Proposal for the Reform of the Security Council of the United Nations", at http://www.esteri.it/archivi/documenti/rifcosen.htm.
34. Some have argued that expansion of the Security Council will inevitably undermine US power and influence, hamper US support for Israel, aid the spread of weapons of mass destruction, complicate and possibly prevent the formation of UN military coalitions to protect US security, undermine the ability of the Council to act decisively and effectively, add to the amount of money the USA pays for the costs of peacekeeping, and basically harm US interest overall. See Brett D. Schaefer, "The United States Should Oppose Expansion of the U.N. Security Council", Heritage Foundation Roe Backgrounder No. 1140, 22 September 1997, http://www.heritage.org/library/categories/forpol/bg1140.html.
35. Joseph E. Schwartzberg, "Editorial: Toward a More Representative and Effective Security Council", *Political Geography* 13, no. 6 (November 1994), pp. 483–491.

36. See Paul Knox, "Canada at the UN: A Human Security Council?", in Maureen Appel Molot and Fen Osler Hampson, eds, *Canada Among Nations 2000: Vanishing Borders* (Don Mills, Ont: Oxford University Press, 2000), pp. 317.
37. Bruce Russett, Barry O'Neill, and James Sutterlin, "Breaking the Security Council Logjam", *Global Governance* 2, no. 1 (January–April 1996), p. 67.
38. *Ibid.*, p. 68.
39. *Ibid.*
40. Schwartzberg, note 35 above, p. 486.
41. *Ibid.*, p. 484.
42. Russett, O'Neill, and Sutterlin, note 37 above, p. 66.
43. Those powers were China, France, the USSR, the UK, and the USA.
44. While each member of the Council has one vote, decisions on crucial matters are made by an affirmative vote of nine members including the concurring votes of the permanent five.
45. As recorded in Inis Claude, *Swords into Plowshares: The Problem and Progress of International Organization*, 4th edn (New York: Random House, 1971), p. 143.
46. Murthy, note 4 above, p. 424.
47. McCarthy, note 11 above, p. 159.
48. *Ibid.*
49. Caron, note 2 above, p. 570.
50. These proposals and comments can be seen in the Report of the Secretary-General to the Forty-Eight Session of the General Assembly, A/48/264.
51. Russett, O'Neill, and Sutterlin, note 37 above.
52. See for instance Schwartzberg, note 35 above, p. 484.
53. See the Italian proposal.
54. A proposal presented by Norway.
55. A proposal of the non-aligned countries.
56. See http:/www.esteri.it/eng/foreignpol/multilater/council.htm.
57. A proposal from Mexico.
58. This is an African proposal which was re-emphasized at the June 1997 Harare summit of the OAU.
59. Pakistan delegation, see http://www.un.int/pakistan/19971204.htm.
60. This proposal was put forward by the Arab group at the open-ended working group on the reform of the Security Council in May 1997.
61. Russett, O'Neill, and Sutterlin, note 37 above, pp. 65–66.
62. Knox, note 36 above.
63. Russett, O'Neill, and Sutterlin, note 37 above, p. 66.
64. *Ibid.*
65. McCarthy, note 11 above, pp. 147–169.
66. See Italy's position on reform of the Security Council at http://www.italyun.org/sc.html.
67. See the Pakistan Mission to the United Nations – "Statement by the Foreign Secretary of Pakistan on Agenda Item 59: 'The Question of Equitable Representation on and Increase in the Membership of the Security Council and Related Matters' in the Plenary of the General Assembly on 4 December 1997" – http://www.un.int/pakistan/ 19971204.htm.
68. In the *Report of the Secretary-General on the Work of the Organization* (New York: United Nations, 1990), p. 41.

3

The new diplomacy at the United Nations: How substantive?

David Malone

Introduction

In the post-Cold War era, new channels for diplomacy have opened up while others have become more opaque. The international institutional framework has been under severe pressure, presenting rare opportunities for some actors, notably non-governmental organizations, while placing others, often including governments, on the defensive. For example, negotiations for the international convention banning the use of anti-personnel land-mines took place largely outside the framework of the UN's disarmament fora – a fact that has been seized upon by some to argue that international negotiations need no longer be dominated by states. However, the negotiations towards a statute for the International Criminal Court suggest that while a shift may be taking place in some cases, an intergovernmental umbrella will continue to occupy a privileged position.

The involvement of non-state actors in pushing the development of international norms is hardly novel. One of the most remarkable developments in the nineteenth century was the emergence of codified rules regulating the conduct of armed conflict. This was initially driven not by states but by individuals, most notably Jean-Henri Dunant, whose travels led him to encounter a particularly brutal battle in the Austro-Italian war of 1859. His subsequent calls to establish "relief societies for the purpose of having care given to the wounded in wartime" and "international principles" to serve as the basis and support for these societies led to the establishment of the International Committee of the Red Cross and the development of international humanitarian law.

Nevertheless, there does appear to have been a certain renovation in the architecture of the international system over the past decade, with NGOs playing a more formal part in the process of norm creation. This chapter examines some distinct phenomena at the United Nations relating to security issues that may suggest an evolution in international negotiating patterns. It looks specifically at NGO involvement in global agenda-setting. As an example of a state open to NGO influence over its work in the Security Council, Canada will be examined.

Security Council decision-making at the end of the Cold War

With the thaw of the Cold War in the mid-1980s, the increased ability of the five permanent members of the UN Security Council (P5) to cooperate with each other seriously diminished the margin for manoeuvre of other Council members. Some of them had in earlier times developed skills and occupied political space as "helpful fixers" or, in the case of some developing nations, had learned how to play the permanent members off against each other, greatly amplifying the voice and enhancing the apparent influence of the Non-Aligned Movement within the Council. Now, non-permanent members were grumbling that they were systematically marginalized, a complaint lent more weight by a tendency of the UN Secretariat to consult privately with some or all of the P5 before advancing recommendations to the Council as a whole. This tacit, largely invisible, collusion between the P5 and the Secretariat was aggravated, from the perspective of other members, by the growing resort to "informal consultations" for decision-making purposes. These mechanisms increasingly replaced the open Council meetings that had served as the principal forum for Council decision-making in earlier decades. The "informals", of which no record is kept by the UN Secretariat, frustrated not only non-members of the Security Council, but also NGOs, journalists, academics, and others with an interest in the UN's key decisions in the security sphere. The altogether deliberate absence of transparency may have proved counterproductive, since the Council's track record during the 1990s suggests that sober second thoughts and public questioning of its impulses might have led to more responsible decision-making.

However, public opinion increasingly did influence Council deliberations. Under intense pressure from member states not serving on the Council, it quite reluctantly allowed some light to shine on its autocratic and opaque proceedings in the early 1990s. This pressure came particularly from the "troop-contributing nations" which provided personnel and materiel to the United Nations for peacekeeping operations, and which were intensely irritated by the Security Council's working methods.

The Security Council and NGOs

The role and interaction of NGOs with respect to the Security Council both grew significantly and evolved in nature during the 1990s. NGOs have for many years been accredited by the UN Economic and Social Council (ECOSOC) to monitor and contribute to UN activities in a broad range of fields.[1] The accrediting body itself suggests how NGOs were traditionally viewed. They were seen as focused on economic and social issues such as the environment, human rights, health, labour, education, population, and humanitarian issues.

In the 1990s, conflicts, particularly of an internal nature, were increasingly seen as featuring economic and social causes as well as effects. Partly for this reason, NGOs clamoured for access to the Security Council, for which the Charter and the Council's long-established working methods made no provision. The role of NGOs as major UN partners in humanitarian operations, the success of many NGO programmes in the field, the mandate for the Secretariat's Department of Humanitarian Affairs to offer coordination services to NGOs as well as official agencies, the media-genic nature of some NGO activity, and a rapidly spreading trend late in the decade in favour of interaction with "civil society" (a term never satisfactorily defined) all conspired to encourage the Council to display greater openness to NGO views and more generous recognition of NGO achievements. Within the Council, a number of governments, including Sweden, Portugal, the Netherlands, Germany, and Canada, advocated greater access for NGOs, while the Secretary-General lavishly praised them.[2] This was achieved in two ways: in a breakthrough of sorts, the Council met informally with a small group of NGOs in 1998. More meaningfully, although less visibly, Council members increasingly met with NGOs on their own and in groups, not only to brief them on recent developments and upcoming debates in the "informals", but also to seek their input for Council decision-making.[3] While the sincerity of some Council members in engaging in these exchanges might be questioned, the achievement of genuine access, and the growing recognition of NGOs as significant and mostly constructive contributors to international peace and security, marked a new departure for the Council in its relations with the "outside" world.

Security issues at the United Nations in the 1990s

This section looks at security-related issues and decisions before the UN Security Council in the 1990s. As becomes apparent, NGOs have influenced, or attempted to influence, most of the important proceedings.

National sovereignty

Arguably the most important, although one of the least noticed, consequence of Security Council decisions in the 1990s – and one of great interest to NGOs and other non-governmental actors – has been the shift at the international level of the understanding of national sovereignty. By 1999, it was widely, although not universally, accepted that tyrants could no longer seek refuge behind the walls of sovereignty to shield themselves from international concern, and even action, over massive human rights violations and humanitarian catastrophes. The Council has intervened repeatedly to address the humanitarian consequences of mostly civil wars, often authorizing coercive measures and designing increasingly complex and intrusive mandates for international action within UN member states. Sometimes this has been done without their consent. These actions have not so much overridden Article 2(7) of the Charter (which exempts Chapter VII decisions from its non-intervention provisions), but rather sharply redefined in practice the conception of what can constitute a threat to international peace and security. The degree of intrusiveness the Council was prepared to mandate throughout the 1990s was striking, even though its own members were not always helpful in implementing decisions involving risks to their nationals, for example in the arrests of those indicted by the international criminal tribunals.

Sanctions

Resort to the provisions of Chapter VII of the UN Charter by the Security Council greatly increased during the 1990s.[4] These measures fell broadly under three headings: authorization of the use of force by UN peacekeeping or enforcement missions; naval blockades; and sanctions. The most common were mandatory economic (and, increasingly, diplomatic) sanctions. While arms embargoes remained in vogue, imposition of comprehensive trade and other economic sanctions, seen as more gentle than the resort to force, faded noticeably once the humanitarian costs of sanctions regimes against Haiti and Iraq became widely known late in the decade. The ability of government regimes in countries struck by sanctions to enrich themselves greatly by controlling black markets in prohibited products also became clear. By then more targeted sanctions, such as the ban on air flights to and from Libya (aimed at inducing Libyan cooperation with Council efforts to address several terrorist aircraft bombings), and diplomatic sanctions (such as the reduction in the level of diplomatic representation mandated by the Council against Sudan following an assassination attempt in Addis Ababa against Egyptian President Hosni Mubarak) were more in favour. Some advantages, but also the difficulty of designing and implementing effective financial sanctions, were brought to light by a useful research and dialogue initiative, the Interlaken process, sponsored by the Swiss government in 1998–1999.[5] The German government launched a similar project on arms embargoes and other forms of targeted sanctions in 1999.[6]

NGOs played a major role in these developments, both by participating in the multilateral fora that advanced these processes and by encouraging national governments to confront issues that they might otherwise have ignored – notably in highlighting the humanitarian cost of sanctions.

Land-mines

The proceedings leading to the Land-mines Convention,[7] also called the Ottawa Convention, fits squarely into the pattern of NGO influence. What has been labelled the "Ottawa process" was conceived, and to a large extent led, by international NGOs, in partnership with a few like-minded governments, notably Canada (Lloyd Axworthy, Canada's Foreign Minister, saw this process as part of a transformation of Canada's foreign policy towards emphasizing "human security"). Early on in the process, the NGOs organized themselves through the International Campaign to Ban Land-mines (ICBL). After a series of preliminary meetings, the ICBL was formally launched in 1992. At the outset it included a handful of international NGOs, but over the next few years the campaign grew to over 1,200 NGOs in 60 different countries.[8] These NGOs varied from those focusing on human rights and humanitarian law to those working on development issues. Despite different approaches, what they had in common was their dedication to end the use of anti-personnel mines which kill and maim dozens of people every day, most of them civilians.[9]

The Ottawa process stands out because of the close relationship it produced between NGOs and states sympathetic to their cause. Because of the strong NGO involvement, this process has been seen as more democratic than other treaty formulations. However, there are individuals who have questioned whether NGOs can really be seen as legitimate representatives of citizens – they are not elected and most of them do not have a membership base (a notable exception is Amnesty International). The Ottawa process did not take place under the auspices of the United Nations but between the NGOs and a select number of governments. This has been called "fast-track" treaty-making and seen as a model for the future, but it raises important questions about legitimacy and the role of international institutions – such as the United Nations – which were set up as fora for international cooperation.[10]

Recognizing the groundbreaking nature of the Ottawa process, Jody Williams, coordinator of the ICBL, won the Nobel Peace Prize in 1997, a worthy tribute to the new power and effectiveness of grassroots organizations and campaigns when endowed with a sophisticated political strategy.[11]

Humanitarian issues

In the 1990s, the UN Security Council developed an acute concern over the humanitarian plight of civilian victims of conflicts, particularly refugees. This concern was driven largely by the media, NGOs, and public opinion. The intense, if highly selective, media scrutiny (the so-called "CNN effect") of horrendous conditions endured by civilian victims of war and targeted advocacy by NGOs impelled populations worldwide to press their governments to alleviate extreme suffering arising from a variety of conflicts. Several factors conspired to focus attention on the United Nations to act on behalf of the international community: the limited impact of most bilateral assistance in these dramatic circumstances; the existence of several UN specialized agencies with the skills and "critical mass" required; and the possibility for the United Nations to deploy peace missions of various types and sizes with mandates focused on humanitarian objectives or at least including them. The most important consideration for many governments was that in delegating to the United Nations the responsibility to act, mostly in situations where few vital national interests were at stake, the costs and risks of response nationally were usefully curtailed. At the peak of media and public fervour for humanitarian initiatives, in the early 1990s, a lively debate unfolded over not only the international right to intervene in the internal affairs of countries to save civilian lives but also a purported duty to do so.[12] By the bleaker end of the decade, with millions suffering untold horrors unassisted, mainly in Africa, this debate rang hollow in the absence of any actual desire to intervene on the part of those governments with the capacities to do so.

In addition to the debate over the legitimacy of using force in response to humanitarian crises, there have been a number of developments in the area of the international community's non-forcible responses. In September 1999, for example, the Carnegie Corporation of New York, led by Vartan Gregorian, together with the International Peace Academy launched work on how to move beyond the normative framework developed since the first Hague Peace Conference in 1899 on the regulation of war to the actual protection of civilians today in actual theatres of war. NGOs – most notably, though not exclusively, the International Committee of the Red Cross – continue to play a major role in this area also.[13]

Children and war

In the 1990s, the United Nations increased its focus on the role of children in armed conflict. Children are not only the targets of violence but also participate actively – as soldiers, guerrilla fighters, spies, saboteurs, sexual slaves, porters, and suicide commandos. In 1993, on the recommendation of the Security Council, the Secretary-General appointed an independent expert panel led by Graça Machel to study the impact of armed conflict on children. The resultant report, undertaken with the support of the UN Centre for Human Rights, UNICEF, and UNHCR, was released in 1996.[14] Rooted in the Convention on the Rights of the Child,[15] the report was the first comprehensive and systematic human rights examination of the way war affects children. The Machel report led to the appointment of Olara Otunnu as the Secretary-General's special representative for children and armed conflict in 1997.[16] Otunnu, who enjoys high rank (Under-Secretary-General) and tremendous credibility within the UN system and beyond, works as an advocate for war-affected children, aiming to place their rights and welfare on the international agenda and to advance them through further agreements and programmes.

These institutional changes provided a framework for high-level NGO involvement on the issue. This was reflected in the participation of many NGOs which have been active in working for children's rights at the Canadian government's International Conference on War-Affected Children in September 2000.[17]

Human rights

Human rights issues were long cloistered within intergovernmental machinery and UN Secretariat bureaucracy designed in part to keep the topic at a safe distance from those responsible for international peace and security at the United Nations. Eventually, human rights burst on to the Security Council's agenda with the realization that civil strife was not amenable to negotiated solutions as long as human rights continued to be massively violated. For this reason, the protection, promotion, and monitoring of human rights (often by staff trained within the NGO movement) formed an important and uncontroversial part of the mandates of several UN peacekeeping operations, notably in El Salvador and Guatemala. Where this was not the case, as in Rwanda and Haiti, the UN General Assembly, as part of the broader UN strategy, often deployed parallel human rights missions. This tendency to address human rights objectives in Security Council debates and decisions coincided with the appointment of a UN High Commissioner for Human Rights as of 1994.[18] However, the High Commissioner and the Security Council have yet to develop a meaningful working relationship. Somewhat making up for this, Kofi Annan has proved a powerful advocate within the Council and beyond for the protection of human rights (and for the prosecution of egregious human rights offenders), for example criticizing with vigour Russian methods in subduing Chechnya and Serb exactions in Kosovo. Reporting by human rights organizations such as Human Rights Watch and Amnesty International has significantly influenced Security Council delegations in the selection of the crises it has chosen to address and also in the means of addressing them.

Democratization

The Council also appeared to be increasingly engaged in the promotion of democracy by mandating the organization and monitoring of elections, a trend as unlikely during the Cold War as would have been the driving force of humanitarian considerations and the Council's role on human rights in the 1990s. Nevertheless, the Council favoured electoral processes not so much as an end in themselves, but rather as a means of effecting a "new deal" in countries emerging from civil war in which power could, in some cases, be shared with former combatants in rough proportion to electoral results. Such elections proved an unreliable indicator of the extent to which genuinely democratic cultures would take root. The stilted, power-driven, and unstable coalition arrangements resulting from Cambodia's UN-monitored elections of 1993 and 1998 contrast with the more natural, relaxed electoral rhythms apparently achieved in El Salvador, where an alternation of power between rival parties seems more likely in the long run.

Various NGOs have become active in this area. In the Secretary-General's recent report on "Support by the United Nations system of the efforts of governments to promote and consolidate new or restored democracies", he makes extensive reference to the work of the International Institute for Democracy and Electoral Assistance (IDEA), in particular to a report identifying key challenges to United Nations involvement in democratization assistance.[19]

International criminal law and judicial review

The Security Council in the 1990s may be remembered in part for its contribution to radical innovation in international criminal law, notably through its creation of ad hoc international criminal tribunals – for the former Yugoslavia in 1993 and Rwanda in 1994 – to bring to justice those responsible for war crimes, crimes against humanity, and genocide. Building on calls from NGOs for action against impunity, the foremost champion of these tribunals was the USA (possibly because of frustration over its own inability at the time to influence the course of events on the ground in the former Yugoslavia due to sharp policy differences with European allies, and guilt over its refusal to confront genocide in Rwanda). The creation of the tribunals greatly intensified pressures for a permanent international criminal court (ICC) with universal jurisdiction, but when a statute for this court[20] was adopted in Rome in 1998, the USA, with six other countries of varying respectability, voted against the text out of concern over its potential implications for US citizens, particularly US troops serving abroad. NGO coalitions played a major role in generating support for the ICC both domestically, in countries such as Canada, and internationally.[21] Negotiations continued throughout 1999 and 2000 on operational modalities for the court and efforts were quietly made to frame understandings of the statute allowing the USA, some day, to sign on. NGOs continued to follow these discussions closely and to shape them through targeted lobbying campaigns. A number of NGO staffers and members (many of them students) surfaced within national delegations to the ICC negotiating process (often in the service of developing countries), mirroring a trend that had earlier developed in the economic and social field.[22]

The Security Council's expanding role in the early 1990s and both the number and sweeping scope of its resolutions gave rise to growing calls for judicial review of its decisions by the World Court. Libya contested the Council's decisions targeting it, clearly embarrassing the court, which prudently awaited the 1999 diplomatic solution to the impasse pitting the Council against Tripoli throughout most of the decade before addressing the merits of the case (over which it did accept jurisdiction, much to the annoyance of some of the P5). Pressure for judicial review, as well as for access to advisory opinions from the court on peace and security issues by the Secretary-General (a proposal advanced by Boutros Boutros-Ghali in *An Agenda for Peace* in 1992), was resisted by the P5, but a sense of inevitability developed over growing involvement of the court in the Council's institutional life.

Small arms

A challenge that remained largely unaddressed at the decade's end was that of the threat posed by the pervasive presence and continued spread of small arms throughout the world, particularly in theatres of conflict. Most recent conflicts have been fought primarily with small arms and light weapons. The extensive accumulation of and trade in these weapons contribute to the continuing destabilization of conflict-prone areas. Under strong pressure from a number of developing countries which have suffered from the prevalence of small arms within their own countries, and prodded by several industrialized countries, including Canada, and international NGOs, the United Nations established a negotiating framework towards an international agreement in this area. An international conference on the trade of small arms was held in New York in July 2001.[23]

Many NGOs active on this issue have organised themselves into the International Action Network on Small Arms (IANSA).[24] The IANSA founding document was published in May 1999 after two international conferences with participants from over 100 NGOs, and focuses on measures to control both the supply of, and demand for, small arms.[25] Together with the NGO Committee on Disarmament, IANSA coordinated NGO participation in the New York conference as well as its preparatory committee. Even though it is too early to determine the extent of NGO influence and effectiveness in this area, developments so far show yet another example of the increasing NGO involvement in UN activities in the security sphere.

Canada and the UN Security Council

One government that helped considerably to advance a new diplomatic agenda, and simultaneously the role of NGOs, was Canada. As of early 1996, Canadian Foreign Minister Lloyd Axworthy sought, with considerable success, to harness civil society as well as government actors to an evolving human security agenda focused on the rights of individuals rather than those of states. Axworthy contributed significantly to the development of this agenda at the international level, often working in partnership with other "middle powers", notably Norway, through such ministerial ginger formations as the Lysoen Group (named after the Norwegian venue of a meeting between Axworthy and his Norwegian counterpart). He was also able to introduce and promote a number of "new" issues into G8 discussions, frequently relying on the UK for support (once a Labour government replaced the Conservative regime in that country in 1997). It is too early to assess the lasting impact of his approach and the extent to which his substantive objectives were achieved, but there can be little doubt that he did affect the way business is done internationally. This was clear at the final international meeting he hosted as Foreign Minister, the International Conference on War-Affected Children in Winnipeg in September 2000, which brought together ministers, NGOs, and youth and other activists addressing a component of the human security agenda in an informal, cross-cutting fashion. Very consciously, he contributed to international decisions (largely improvised and inconsistent though they were) that, for good or ill, eroded the foundations of absolute conceptions of state sovereignty, and fundamentally altered the way in which many of us see the relationship between state and citizen the world over.

In part in deference to lobbying by public interest groups, Security Council members in the late 1990s sought to address cross-cutting, thematic security issues during Council debates. Canada chose the plight of civilians in war as the theme of its Security Council presidency in February 1999. Axworthy's advocacy on this front paid off: UN Secretary-General Kofi Annan and many others have been increasingly echoing his calls for action in this area, not least by instituting effective accountability for those violating humanitarian norms pertaining to civilians.

During its second presidency in April 2000 and more broadly, Canada focused attention within the Security Council on the need for more effective, less counterproductive sanctions regimes. Long before Canada was elected to the Council, Axworthy launched in-depth work within the Department of Foreign Affairs and International Trade, drawing extensively on Canadian and foreign experts, on how Canada might bring some order, clarity, and humanitarian focus to the Council's disparate sanctions regimes. From the outset of Canada's term in the Council, 1999–2000, he pursued energetically his interest in more effective sanctions that would spare civilian populations from their brunt.[26] Canadian advocacy led to a critical public debate on sanctions on 17 April 2000, followed by the creation of a Security Council working group to develop guidelines for future sanctions regimes.[27] The Canadian Ambassador to the United Nations, Robert Fowler, meanwhile proved a creative and energetic chair of the Council's Sanctions Committee for Angola, pressing for more rigorous application of its mandate to suffocate UNITA's ability to fund its war effort through the sale of diamonds. His advocacy, elaborated upon in Kim Nossal's chapter, has been rewarded *inter alia* by the decision of the De Beers corporation to close down its operations in Angola.[28] A commission of experts on sanctions in Angola, championed by Fowler and chaired by Swedish Ambassador Anders Mollander, provided detailed and embarrassing information on the role of a number of state actors, in Africa and elsewhere, in profiting from the illicit trade in Angolan diamonds.[29] This work drew heavily on scholarly and NGO sources in order to achieve policy results.

Axworthy also initiated new forms of diplomacy within Canada. A voracious reader himself, he sought to encourage policy-relevant research within the academic community and quite frequently acted upon ideas he gleaned from the academic literature. He appointed an independent advisory team, largely drawn from the academic world and led by Janice Stein of the University of Toronto, to provide him with independent views on Canadian foreign policy (and actually listened to it!). He worked through the Center for Foreign Policy Development (CFPD), an arm's-length unit within the Canadian Foreign Ministry, to consult Canadians on specific issues.[30] In sum, he was always on the lookout for new ideas and new allies, sometimes in unlikely places, often with excellent results.[31]

Conclusion

The United Nations, in the year 2001, remains an organization of member states. Its intergovernmental nature is frequently emphasized by a large number of members, notably those from the developing world. That being said, the United Nations is increasingly influenced by the "open-sourcing" approach to information and policy development that has been characterizing international relations in the cyber era. Both the Secretariat (enthusiastically) and member states (somewhat less enthusiastically) have been recognizing that information well beyond their control is shaping the international pressures for UN action in a variety of fields. NGOs, information networks of a bewildering diversity, academics, and individual experts have been accessing UN actors through the news media, the internet, and e-mail;[32] at the same time a wide variety of interactive fora (including those provided by the International Peace Academy in New York) have been strikingly successful in attracting a wide cross-section of interveners to exchange views rather than restate positions or otherwise adopt sterile debating postures.[33]

Unfortunately, NGOs often overstate their claims to drive the international agenda. They do this, perfectly understandably, in order to impress funders in the highly competitive market for financial support. Their influence has, in fact, varied from issue to issue: very strong on the

Land-mines Convention, the International Criminal Court, population issues, and many environmental questions, but much less so on complex issues generating divided opinions within global civil society, for example on the debate over humanitarian intervention.[34] The NGOs that have proved most successful are those that have mastered the technique of interaction with governments and have taken the trouble to grasp the intricacies of intergovernmental negotiating processes (and of methods of access to the mainstream media). NGOs, particularly in the USA, have also been learning how to relate to and interact with the international private sector, rather than merely protesting against it. Further progress in this area will be important in years ahead, given the central role of the private sector in a globalizing world.[35]

Some concern has been expressed about the proliferation of NGOs, many of them with overlapping goals and mandates. Such fears may be exaggerated. In fact, a global market-place for NGOs has arisen. Those (big and small) with good ideas, sound working methods, and well-channelled energy attract favourable notice and funding. Those essentially engaged in self-promotion with few ideas and little programming of value tend to sink and disappear without a trace. It is the diversity, fractiousness, and competitiveness of the NGO world that generate added value.[36]

Naturally, large and highly professional NGOs such as Amnesty International, Human Rights Watch, International Planned Parenthood, the World Resources Institute, and the Worldwide Fund for Nature tend to attract a large share of the media's attention and, perhaps consequently, of available funding. However, size is no guarantee of quality (Greenpeace seems very much on the wane these days, its strident tone and tactics out of tune with more results-oriented activists and those who fund them).[37] Small NGOs can also produce outstanding work and gain recognition, as demonstrated by Global Witness (on the misuse of natural resources in war-torn societies) and Saferworld (on questions such as the pervasive threat posed by small arms).

The great weakness of the international NGO community is its dominance by organizations of the industrialized world. This asymmetry led to a hijacking of the NGO agenda on trade issues, notably at the Seattle WTO meeting, by NGOs of the North, with perspectives from the South drowned out or altogether absent. The protectionist whiff of the NGO platform at Seattle, so damaging to the interests of developing countries, was deeply disturbing, and the NGO community needs to engage in serious reflection on the extent to which it has been and can be manipulated by forces, such as the labour movement in industrialized countries, with their own agendas.

A paradox for the NGO world (one highlighted in an excellent Finnish study of the NGO community) is that while its component organizations derive much of their legitimacy from their grassroots origins, for NGOs to achieved impact globally some of them at least must operate at the international level, far removed from grassroots constituencies.[38] This reality, along with the frequently incestuous relationship between leading NGOs and governments (which often largely fund them), leaves NGO credibility ambiguous in many circles. This need not undermine the quality of contributions to international debates and programmes by NGOs, but needs to be borne in mind by them.

The new diplomacy, with governments remaining the critical actors but with many other participants shaping the context for negotiations and serving in advisory capacities, has proved better equipped to tackle challenges of institutional reform and identify and promote important emerging issues than the hidebound world of established multilateral diplomacy. The latter is exemplified by the stultified UN General Assembly and such vacuous jamborees as the World Bank and International Monetary Fund annual meetings. It is partly because of the mix of international actors it has sought to attract that the World Economic Forum at Davos has proved the largest "draw" of the post-Cold War era.

Canada has played an important role in helping to encourage the new diplomacy. Its contribution in this regard, very much in line with a long history of international institutional innovation fostered by successive Canadian governments, should be a source of pride to all Canadian practitioners and students of foreign policy.

Notes

1. Under the UN Charter, the Economic and Social Council may consult with NGOs concerned with matters within the Council's competence. See UN Charter, Article 71. This relationship is defined in ECOSOC Resolution 1996/31.
2. See, for example, *Supplement to An Agenda for Peace*, UN Document A/50/60-S/1995/1, para. 81.
3. These consultations, bringing together individual Security Council ambassadors with a group of NGOs, have been organized by the Global Policy Forum, itself a policy-oriented NGO, since 1995. These off-the-record exchanges have generally proved extremely frank and useful. Since 1997, the working group has met increasingly regularly with delegations sitting on the Council, including monthly meetings with delegations in the Council presidency.
4. See David Cortright and George Lopez, *The Sanctions Decade: Assessing UN Strategies in the 1990s* (Boulder, CO: Lynne Rienner, 2000).
5. See references available at http://www.smartsanctions.ch.
6. See *Smart Sanctions, the Next Step: Arms Embargoes and Travel Sanctions*, Executive

Summary of First Expert Seminar, Bonn, 21–23 November 1999, available at http://
www.germany-info.org/UN/un_press_04_18b_00.htm.
7. Convention on the Prohibition of the Use, Stockpiling, Production, and Transfer of
Anti-Personnel Mines and Their Destruction, 18 September 1997, entered into force 1
March 1999.
8. Jody Williams and Stephen Goose, "The International Campaign to Ban Landmines",
in Maxwell A. Cameron, Robert Lawson, and Brian W. Tomlin, eds, *To Walk Without
Fear: The Global Movement to Ban Landmines* (Toronto: Oxford University Press,
1998).
9. International Committee of the Red Cross, *Landmines Overview*, 1999, available at
http://www.icrc.org.
10. For a discussion on this topic, see Kenneth Anderson, "The Ottawa Convention Banning Landmines, the Role of International Non-Governmental Organizations and the
Idea of International Civil Society", *European Journal of International Law* 2, no. 1
(2000).
11. Another NGO, Médecins Sans Frontières, won the Nobel Peace Prize in 1999.
12. This debate was fuelled to a large extent by Médecins Sans Frontières' founder Bernard
Kouchner, by then Secretary of State for Humanitarian Affairs within the French government (and later Minister of Health). Perhaps ironically, by the decade's end he was
the UN Secretary-General's special representative in Kosovo, coping with the consequences on the ground of just such a humanitarian intervention (by NATO). To his
credit, he discharged these responsibilities with great panache, displaying strong leadership (although, also, weak administrative skills).
13. See Simon Chesterman, ed., *Civilians in War* (Boulder, CO: Lynne Rienner, 2001);
Karma Nabulsi, *Traditions of War: Occupation, Resistance, and the Law* (Oxford: Oxford University Press, 2000).
14. UN Document A/51/306: *The Impact of Armed Conflict on Children – Report of the
Expert of the Secretary-General, Ms Graça Machel.*
15. Convention on the Rights of the Child, 20 November 1989.
16. See General Assembly Resolution A/RES/51/77, *The Rights of the Child*, 20 February
1997.
17. Information on this conference, including agendas and documents, can be found on the
conference website: http://www.waraffectedchildren.gc.ca/.
18. José Ayala-Lasso of Ecuador assumed the post of the first UN High Commissioner for
Human Rights on 5 April 1994. Mary Robinson of Eire succeeded him on 15 March
1997 and proved a much firmer advocate of universal respect for international human
rights standards.
19. See Report of the Secretary-General, *Support by the United Nations System of the Efforts of Governments to Promote and Consolidate New or Restored Democracies*, UN
Document A/55/489, 2000.
20. Rome Statute of the International Criminal Court, UN Document A/CONF.183/9.
21. The World Federalist Movement, perhaps more than any other single NGO, played a
leading role in organizing effective NGO interaction with key delegations prior to and
during major ICC negotiations and was also active in certain capitals. See the Coalition
for an International Criminal Court website (http://www.igc.org/icc/) or the UN website
(http://www.un.org/law/icc/general/public.htm) for an overview.
22. For example, Canada and many other countries included NGO representatives as full
members of their official delegations to several of the major UN conferences of the
1990s. While a mutually useful arrangement, this new trend also exposed some of the
NGOs to accusations of "selling out" to governments while other constituencies, notably parliamentarians, wondered how NGOs could claim to be as representative (or

more so) as elected officials. Such discomfort was least evident when NGOs brought much-needed expertise (rather than simply advocacy) to the negotiating table.

23. UN Conference on the Illicit Trafficking in Small Arms and Light Weapons in All its Aspects, 9–20 July 2001. For information, see the conference website: http://www.un.org/Depts/dda/CAB/smallarms/.

24. For more information, see the IANSA website: http://www.iansa.org/index.htm.

25. This includes reducing the weapons trade as well as peace-building measures such as security sector reform and reintegration programmes.

26. For this purpose, Canada commissioned, through the International Peace Academy, a comprehensive volume on the 12 sanctions regimes mandated by the Security Council during the 1990s. This volume, Cortright and Lopez, note 4 above, will be followed by another in 2002 focusing on the progress (if any) achieved by the Council in crafting better sanctions decisions in the new millennium and on key cross-cutting themes in the sanctions debate.

27. UN Press Release SC/6845, 17 April 2000.

28. "De Beers Negotiates Diamond Rights with Angola", *Financial Times*, 17 October 2000.

29. *Report of the Panel of Experts on Violations of Security Council Sanctions Against UNITA*, UN Document S/2000/203, 10 March 2000.

30. While this latter effort was sometimes naively implemented – with those consulted not always having relevant specific views or knowledge to contribute to occasionally rather mechanical exercises – the message to public servants was clear: public views and perceptions mattered. Occasionally, these consultations produced interesting insights, although the centre experienced mixed results at best in transmitting them to those actually responsible for foreign policy development within the ministry under Axworthy. The CFPD experiment needs retooling to ensure that efforts to glean academic and public views actually feed into the formulation of policy. Having achieved significant reach within Canadian society, the CFPD now needs to focus more on quality control, effective evaluation, and improved dissemination.

31. The author served under Mr Axworthy as Director-General of Global Issues and International Organizations in the Canadian Foreign Ministry, 1997–1998, and experienced personally the often galvanizing impact of his *modus operandi* on the ministry.

32. It is important here to recognize the distinction between international policy networks, focusing on policy development grounded in research, and transnational advocacy networks that lobby in favour of predetermined goals. Both discharge valuable functions on the international scene. However, it is dangerous to conflate their roles in assessing actors in the "new diplomacy". On the former, see Wolfgang H. Reinicke and Francis Deng with Jan Martin Witte, Thorsten Benner, Beth Whitaker, and John Gershman, *Critical Choices: The United Nations, Networks and the Future of Global Governance* (Ottawa: IDRC, 2000), and on the latter Cynthia Hewitt de Alcantara, ed., *Social Futures: Global Visions* (London: Blackwell, 1996) and Margaret E. Keck and Kathryn Sikkink, *Activists Beyond Borders* (Ithaca: Cornell University Press, 1998). More broadly, the following are of interest in this field: James Rosenau, *Along the Domestic-Foreign Frontier: Exploring Governance in a Turbulent World* (Cambridge: Cambridge University Press, 1997); Jackie Smith, Charles Chatfield, and Ron Pagnucco, eds, *Transnational Social Movements and Global Politics: Solidarity Beyond the State* (Syracuse: Syracuse University Press, 1997).

33. An example of this was a symposium on humanitarian action launched by Dutch Foreign Minister A. van Aartsen and UN Secretary-General Kofi Annan at the International Peace Academy (IPA) on 20 November 2000 under Chatham House rules of non-attribution, with over 150 UN Ambassadors, NGO representatives, academics,

journalists, and others thrashing out often controversial views, notably on humanitarian intervention. (Report forthcoming on IPA website: www.ipacademy.org.) Such discussions bring home the fact that no single international actor or group of actors, including states and NGOs, can offer easy answers to tough policy dilemmas.

34. The massive Hague Appeal for Peace meeting in the Netherlands in May 1999, for example, was split down the middle on the extent to which NATO intervention in Kosovo should be supported, with human-rights-oriented NGOs squaring off against many others. See http://www.haguepeace.org.

35. Resistance by a number of NGOs and NGO coalitions to initiatives aimed at enhancing the involvement of private sector actors in UN programmes and within the United Nations itself arises in part from suspicion of corporate motives (for example, in relation to the UN Secretary-General's new Global Compact initiative), but does not show NGOs in a particularly attractive light. Why insist on access for themselves, but not for private sector actors who provide the vast bulk of global employment and are involved in the creation of much welfare as well as misery internationally?

36. Efforts by some NGOs to secure "access" to intergovernmental processes without much to bring to the table are unlikely to succeed on their own terms (although they do, occasionally, attract media attention). Suggestions that only NGOs provide added value to such processes and that somehow governments are illegitimate can only prove counterproductive over time. However, considerable progress continues to be made in exploring productive relationships between intergovernmental, governmental, business, academic, and civil society actors in most fields of international endeavour.

37. It is striking that the NGOs which seem to have proved most influential in the failed international talks on climate change at the Hague in November 2000 were those that worked hard to bridge the positions of the EU and the USA on the one hand and countries of the North and the South on the other. Their expertise and commitment seem to have been a major factor in bringing negotiators close to success in the early hours of 25 November 2000, before the negotiations collapsed. On the other hand, the commitment of even large NGOs to bedrock principles is well understood by governments (and admired by many of them, from both North and South): at the Cairo Conference on Population and Development in 1994, major NGOs in the field of population and development were able to play an important, constructive role, greatly influencing negotiations, without compromising on their mandates.

38. See Antti Pentikainen, *Creating Global Governance: The Role of Non-Governmental Organizations in the United Nations* (Helsinki: Finnish UN Association, 2000).

4

Why is the USA not a like-minded country? Some structural notes and historical considerations

James Reed

To an American historian of liberal internationalist persuasion, the suggestion of a "new diplomacy" inevitably brings to mind the first "new diplomacy" envisioned by the USA during and after the First World War of 1914–1919 – and of its original genius, President Woodrow Wilson. From the promulgation of Wilson's 14 Points, to the President's triumphant arrival in Paris for the peace conference, to his strenuous campaign across the USA for ratification of the Treaty of Versailles, the "new diplomacy" meant something truly new and utterly monumental in international affairs. Open covenants openly arrived at the freedom of the seas, the self-determination of peoples, a community of power rather than a balance of power, and, above all, a League of Nations "where the moral forces of the world are mobilized": these watchwords echo still in the world's imagination.

Over 80 years later, after the wreckage of the League, the mixed record of the UN system, and decades of severe strains between the USA and the international community, it is not always easy to remember that the twentieth century's principal institutions for global governance were largely American in origin and inspiration.

This is of course true not only of the League but of the United Nations, which was conceived at Dumbarton Oaks in Washington, proclaimed at the Fairmont Hotel in San Francisco in 1945, and eventually took up residence on the Upper East Side of Manhattan. Yet relations between the USA and the United Nations are so tenuous today that the

New York location may actually contribute to the international organization's problems, by exposing it to the chauvinist gaze of certain American media and the vindictive mischief of Senator Jesse Helms and his staff, who are only a few hours away in Washington by train or shuttle from the Security Council chamber. Almost by definition diplomats love the high life, but from the standpoint of institutional effectiveness there is something to be said for the recurring suggestion that in the twenty-first century the UN Secretariat might more sensibly be based in Geneva or the Hague.[1]

How and why did this remarkable estrangement come about? To answer this question in depth and with precision would require a book-length work, beginning at least before the First World War, with considerable attention to the period since 1970, and a detailed examination of the post-Cold War years when a new but perhaps not yet definitive dynamic began to assert itself. Such a study would give particular attention to the changing structures of élite public opinion in the USA – to the subtle, necessarily impressionistic, and finally rather elusive play of ideas, values, and assumptions within the class of Americans specially concerned with international affairs. Finally, such a study would emphasize the interplay between policy and opinion, and would relate the shifts in state policy over time to fundamental changes in the structure and attitudes of the concerned public. A work on this scale would occupy a diligent researcher for several years. There may no more urgently needed work – one with policy-relevant implications – in the entire field of American foreign relations.

What this chapter will attempt to do, quite simply, is to raise some of the key questions concerning the growing hostility of the USA toward the international community at the end of the twentieth century, and to suggest some reasons why this extraordinary development has come about. The study began as an attempt to sketch the deep background to the period 1995–2000, when a group of middle-size states which are traditional stalwarts of the UN system – including Canada, the Nordic countries, the Netherlands, Australia, New Zealand, and other "like-minded countries" – made common cause with leading NGOs in unique and ultimately successful campaigns culminating in the Ottawa Treaty banning land-mines (1997) and the Rome Treaty establishing the International Criminal Court (1998). This "new diplomacy", melding the time-honoured practices of the diplomatic trade and the moral force of international civil society, was adamantly opposed by the USA.[2]

Why did this happen? What broad forces have contributed to the progressive alienation of the USA from the international community and its evolving humanitarian, pacific, and legal norms? Is the estrangement permanent? What does the immediate future hold, now that a new presidential administration has assumed power in Washington? And what are the implications for the world community as it searches for standards and mechanisms of global governance? In an attempt to suggest answers to these questions, some of the structural features of the American polity and historical record will be discussed. Inevitably a historian goes back and back forever.

An exceptional country: State, civil society, and public opinion in America

A recent study of Americans' ambivalent attitudes toward the United Nations lays much of the blame – the writer is a former president of the United Nations Association of the USA – on America's persistent belief in its own "exceptionalism". No doubt this is true if by exceptional one means wholly unlike, and morally superior to, every other nation. Puritan conceptions of "a city set upon a hill" and the new American nation's revolutionary proclamation of a *"novus ordo seclorum"* – literally "a new cycle of the ages", which still announces itself on the Great Seal of the USA – make plain that America's self-conception has from the beginning involved a sense of world historical uniqueness and ineluctable destiny.[3]

Such a self-image is, inevitably, not easily reconcilable with the equality of nations and the protocols of world community, and the massive self-deception to which it leads is finally self-defeating, both at home and abroad. For this reason the critique of "American exceptionalism" is a cottage industry in American academia, to the point where the mere mention of American exceptionalism or uniqueness is typically greeted with a scepticism bordering on derision.

This is mostly well and good, but taken to an extreme it can blind American and foreign analysts alike to certain unique and, yes, exceptional features of the American polity which are key to explaining America's peculiar role in the world, past and present, and the prospects for global governance. Any "new diplomacy", now or in the future, must deal centrally and creatively with these structural characteristics of the American scene. Both comparative government and the classic authors point to the same conclusions.

First, we are dealing here with a relative anomaly among modern countries, in that the USA has what is finally a rather weak state and, indisputably, an exceptionally strong, vibrant, and astonishingly creative civil society. Visiting the USA in the 1830s, Alexis de Tocqueville was struck by these fundamental features of democracy in America which contrasted so sharply with the centralized state and anaemic civil society of both old regime and post-revolutionary France.

Today, viewed from abroad, where the USA is almost universally described as a "superpower" or even as a "hyperpower", Tocqueville's America of a lightly governed society with an engaged citizenry building their community through a myriad of "voluntary associations" may seem impossibly remote, even irrelevant. But viewed from within, Tocqueville's America seems alive and well at the end of the twentieth century, as those "voluntary associations" have matured and proliferated into a vast array of foundations, philanthropies, universities, advocacy groups, non-governmental organizations, research institutes, and civic associations – a far-flung, decentralized, and financially independent civil society which is typically referred to as the "third sector" or the "non-profit sector". It is the object of advanced study and expanding research in leading universities, where Tocqueville is repeatedly and almost ritually cited for his prescient probe into the heart of the American polity. Even the recent lament by a leading political scientist that too many Americans are "bowling alone" – insufficiently active in voluntary associations – illustrates the degree to which Tocqueville still sets the standard.[4]

Importantly, many of the institutions of American civil society have long had significant operations overseas or have taken a special interest in international affairs. The Rockefeller Foundation's medical work in China early in the twentieth century, the complex of American educational institutions in the Middle East, periodic campaigns for famine relief, and, today, the overseas work of foundations established by Ted Turner and Bill Gates – these are but a few of the more visible examples of a long tradition of American civil society's engagement in international affairs. The comparison may seem strained, but one has to ask if these institutions of American civil society, taken as a whole, do not exceed in prestige and influence – and as a force for good in the world – the aggregated foreign policy apparatus of the American bureaucratic state. In any event, the overseas interests and ambitions of America's "third sector" are clearly exceptional.[5]

The second unique characteristic of the American polity which must be included in any discussion of the prospects for a "new diplomacy" or "enhanced global governance" is the long-recognized (if in some quarters long-resented) supremacy of public opinion in American foreign relations. As noted above, there is a substantial body of literature on this subject which is familiar to American historians and political scientists. Since knowledge is power, this literature deserves to be scrutinized by practitioners as well as students of diplomacy, particularly representatives of foreign governments and international organizations, who may well find the deep structure of American public opinion – its delicate mechanisms, informal patterns of influence, and subterranean channels to power – to be as novel and exceptional, not to say intricate, as US civil society.[6]

Where the French-born historian Tocqueville was the original authority on American civil society, it was the British historian James Bryce, long-time Ambassador to Washington, who identified public opinion as the key to American government, and laid bare its essential morphology. In his classic work *The American Commonwealth* (1888), Lord Bryce wrote:

Towering over Presidents and State governors, over Congress and State legislatures, over conventions and the vast machinery of party, public opinion stands out, in the United States, as the great source of power, the master of servants who tremble before it.

In the American community, Bryce concluded in an analysis which holds up today, "public opinion can with truth be said not only to reign but to govern".[7]

What Lord Bryce described as a uniquely American system of "government by public opinion" has been amplified by the invention of "scientific" opinion-polling in the 1940s, the political uses of television since the 1950s, and the instantaneous reach of the internet in the 1990s. Collectively these innovations have encouraged the American state to seek out assiduously, even obsessively, the general will on all public issues, foreign as well as domestic.

On foreign policy issues, however – which are typically of interest to only a small minority of citizens – American scholars emphasize the continuing and often radical difference between "élite" and "mass" opinion. A public opinion poll, especially if it weighs the saliency of an issue as well as the raw numbers, can enable the policy-maker to judge the boundaries of public tolerance, but generally it does not translate into foreign policy unless the issue involved is of overwhelming public importance. Typically the official has considerable margin for manoeuvre, regardless of polls. Thus, on matters involving the United Nations, for example, an American official will receive no real guidance from the often-cited polls showing that the public overwhelmingly thinks the United Nations is a good thing. On any particular issue involving global governance, the policy-maker instinctively realizes that the vast majority neither know nor care.[8]

The group that matters is the relatively small "foreign policy public" and the even smaller élite of "foreign policy opinion leaders" to whom this highly educated, well-informed, professional, and influential body of citizens look for guidance. The policy-maker who would defy the consensus of opinion within the foreign policy public and among its opinion élites is running a considerable risk. In America, the foreign affairs bureaucracy is so politically vulnerable – and the American political class so transient – that foreign policy ideas generally trickle up, as it were, into the state apparatus from the vigorous and always opinionated institutions and organs of America's independent foreign policy community. Hence the extraordinary collective influence of the think-tanks and academic research institutes, the Council on Foreign Relations and the World Affairs Councils, and the journals *Foreign Policy* and *Foreign Affairs*.

This "community" is by no means monolithic in structure or of one mind philosophically. There is a rough-and-ready division, for example, between the nationalist and often military-oriented institutions based in Washington and the more liberal and internationalist groups and opinion leaders "outside the Beltway". The foreign policy community is typically "entrepreneurial" in the best American tradition – it is open to new groups, organizations, and voices at any time. One could argue, of course, that this unique system of "government by public opinion" is also American in the worst sense, in that it encourages too much individualism and too little responsibility. The point is simply that any foreign friends advocating a "new diplomacy" or wishing to start a dialogue on global governance or the future of the UN system must penetrate the non-governmental "foreign policy community" – or the game is over before it even begins. Yet, oddly, there are foreign governments and experienced diplomats of pronounced liberal internationalist inclination who, even today, behave as if they can treat with the American bureaucratic state without paying appropriate attention to American civil society and the American foreign policy community.[9]

The historical dimension: The USA and global governance, 1776–1992

To appreciate the official American resistance to the new global activism of the 1990s, by the United Nations and like-minded countries, culminating in the "new diplomacy" initiatives regarding land-mines and the International Criminal Court, it is essential to survey briefly the broad sweep of American engagement in world affairs over the past two centuries. In fact the briefer that survey the better, because it is precisely in the quick, bird's-eye view – a vertical view rather than a horizontal one – that one can see with clarity the peculiar lay of the land.

From the American Revolution to 1917 – for nearly 150 years – the USA was basically preoccupied with creating a new society on the North American continent. Its activities, energies, and attitudes – the country's sense of itself – were overwhelmingly continental. Of course there were wars aplenty – with Canada (1812–1815), Mexico (1846–1848), a terrible civil war (1861–1865), and virtually constant warfare against the Indian nations until the 1890s – but these were seen as "internal" matters related to the new nation's manifest destiny to create a *"novus ordo seclorum"* – liberally, a new world order – on the American continent.

To secure this continental empire, the country proclaimed a hemispheric sphere of influence via the Monroe Doctrine in 1823, but otherwise the American government largely avoided involvement in international politics until the Spanish-American war of 1898, a brief overseas adventure which was precipitated by a split in the country's foreign policy élite, led to a bitterly divisive debate over imperialism, and was not repeated. There were military skirmishes here and there (China, Japan, the Barbary Coast), but these were of modest scale and almost always in defence of America's trading interests or to protect American citizens. Even Theodore Roosevelt, who wielded a "big stick" rhetorically and involved himself in Central American affairs and the diplomacy of North-East Asia, held aloof from the great-power politics of Europe and the rivalries of their overseas empires. On the eve of the First World War, the American people – even its governing classes – had had little experience of world affairs apart from the trading activities and overseas missionary, educational, and philanthropic work at which Americans had long excelled.

If nineteenth-century Americans chose not to think about what we now call global governance – or found its principal vehicle, imperialism, to be morally repugnant (particularly when practised by cynical Europeans) – the world wars of the twentieth century finally forced the issue. The point that should be remembered, however, is that the American people – including a substantial body of its foreign policy élites – had to be dragged, three years late, into the First World War by a basically pacifist President Wilson, and then led into the Second World War (this time two years late) by a President Roosevelt who had charted an isolationist course in the 1930s because of the strength of isolationist public opinion. The wars were emergency situations, requiring emergency responses; and when the wars were over, the instinctive American reaction – nurtured by deep historical memory – was to return to their usual preoccupations on the North American continent. Global governance, if needed at all, was somebody else's problem.

This was clearly the case after the First World War, with the American repudiation of the Treaty of Versailles and refusal to join the League of Nations. The reaction after the Second World War was more ambivalent and complex, and took longer to play itself out.[10]

Americans, it is true, took the lead in creating the United Nations, and a system of global governance was by the mid-1940s generally seen to be in America's enlightened self-interest after the myriad disasters of the 1930s. But in the flush of military victory the USA approached the new United Nations with certain assumptions which were shortly to prove illusory. One founding assumption was FDR's notion that the Security Council would be comprised of "four policemen" working in tandem to maintain law and order on their global beat. There was the further assumption – shared by congressional Republicans who now gave their tentative support to internationalism of a kind – that the UN organization would become a principal vehicle to enforce the *Pax Americana*. But these assumptions were shattered by the advent of the Cold War, which led President Truman and the "wise men" of that day to "scare hell out of the American people" and create NATO as the principal international organization to resist Soviet expansion and secure the "free world". This was undoubtedly necessary, but the inevitable corollary was to marginalize the UN system, particularly after the Korean War, when the USA lost its dominance in the Security Council, and after decolonization, when it lost control of the General Assembly. In the context of Cold War confrontation, the American instinct for unilateralism expressed itself early and often. It is also true that the USA, like all the major powers, tended to conduct its diplomacy through the United Nations only when the international organization served to advance the American nation's power and interests.[11]

That said, the United Nations still played an important (if subordinate) role in American conceptions of international order and global governance for approximately 30 years, from the mid-1940s to the mid-1970s. From the 1956 Suez crisis onward, the USA appreciated the value of the peacekeeping function and supported peacekeeping operations; and the USA solicited the approval of the international community on many occasions, including the Cuban missile crisis of 1962, when the greatest of US ambassadors, Adlai Stevenson, gave his command performance at the Security Council. The United Nations was still controversial at the grassroots and in the hinterlands, but liberal internationalists of various stripes dominated the foreign policy élites; and the great foundations (Ford, Rockefeller) and other institutions of American civil society pursued a liberal internationalist agenda through massive overseas programmes, often working in tandem with UN specialized agencies in fields such as health, literacy, poverty, and economic development. This was hardly a golden age – and there were deep disagreements in the liberal internationalist community over issues like Viet Nam, Cuba, and Palestine – but from today's standpoint it seems astonishing to recall that the USA could not bring itself to cast a veto at the United Nations until 1970.[12]

The critical period in the estrangement of the USA from the UN system came in the years 1975–1989. While detailed research is needed on this pivotal subject, it seems clear that the estrangement was partly the fault of the United Nations but largely the result of factors internal to the USA. In any event the attack came first from the left, and then – with blistering fury – from the right. The devastating effect on the foreign policy public's esteem for the United Nations was created especially by the inflammatory rhetoric of two US Ambassadors, Daniel Patrick Moynihan and Jeane Kirkpatrick, who from rather different ideological perspectives found it politically useful to make the United Nations their whipping boy. Moynihan's attack was not unprovoked – the 1975 General Assembly resolution describing Zionism as a form of racism was patently outrageous and merited the sharpest rebuke. But instead of stopping there, Moynihan went on the attack on a variety of UN issues, often sacrificing cosmopolitan nuance to his local ambition to represent New York in the US Senate.[13]

Moynihan was followed in the Reagan years by Ambassador Kirkpatrick, a neo-conservative intellectual who spat contempt at the UN system, eloquently reflecting the Reagan administration's consistent anti-internationalism. Foreshadowing developments in the 1990s, the Republicans resisted arms control initiatives, however modest in scope, and in 1984 refused to accept the jurisdiction of the World Court in the matter of American intervention in the Nicaraguan civil war. During the Reagan years the USA became more estranged from the international community than was even the case during the 1920s, when it remained outside the League of Nations but nonetheless pursued a vigorous diplomacy focusing on disarmament.[14]

Under Reagan, so complete was the collapse of support for the institutions of global governance in the USA that a 1985 article in *Foreign Policy* announced "the twilight of internationalism".[15] Inevitably, a shift of this magnitude involves more than state policy, which tends to be epiphenomenal under the American system. Behind the anti-UN diplomacy of the Reagan years lay such factors as the shattering of the liberal-international consensus in the foreign policy public during the Viet Nam era. This turning inward was paralleled by civil society institutions progressively cutting back their overseas programmes in order to focus on domestic problems. During the Reagan years, the foreign policy public was exposed to a vigorous onslaught by the neo-conservative opinion élite, with their aggressively nationalist and fundamentally military preoccupations.

To a Wilsonian or FDR liberal, the 1980s may have witnessed "the twilight of internationalism", but to Reagan and the neo-conservatives it was "morning in America" – an exquisitely beautiful sunrise over God's Own Country that held all the promise in the world. Reagan's concept of American exceptionalism was vintage nineteenth century, and the triumphalism attendant on the end of the Cold War served to reinforce this pre-modern strain in American thinking.

The USA and global governance since the Cold War

More than 10 years after the Cold War, it is still not clear what the shape of the new international system will be, or how the world will be governed in the twenty-first century. There have been several initiatives looking to give new direction in this period of extraordinary flux: from 1990 to 1992 by the USA during the administration of George Bush senior, from 1992 to 1996 by the United Nations under Secretary-General Boutros Boutros-Ghali, and subsequently by the "new diplomacy" pioneered by Canadian Foreign Minister Lloyd Axworthy and other "like-minded" middle powers long supportive of the UN system. But each of these, after some momentary success, foundered in its turn. And what lies just ahead, under the newly elected administration of George Bush junior, cannot be contemplated without a degree of apprehension. In each initiative the fundamental difficulties were really all aspects or instances of the same underlying problem; namely, how to reconcile America's status as sole remaining superpower – and its pretensions to global hegemony – with the standards and norms of a self-governing community of nations.

The case of George Bush senior is perhaps the most peculiar and the least well remembered. As a former ambassador to the United Nations (1971–1973), Bush understood the ways that the United Nations can be used to advance American interests, assemble coalitions, and secure legitimacy for American-led military action. With some nostalgia perhaps for the liberal internationalists of the mid-1940s, Bush sincerely thought there could be a "new world order", with the USA once again triumphantly leading the United Nations. But the US victory in the UN-authorized Gulf War of 1991 was the product of historically unique opportunities that would not be presented again.

Moreover, the Gulf War period exposed underlying contradictions in American foreign policy. Saddam Hussein was a bad actor, to be sure, but even General Colin Powell doubted whether American public opinion would countenance the sacrifice of American lives for gasoline at $1.50 a gallon. As the Senate debate preceding the war revealed, the foreign policy élites were deeply divided on the need to defend the sovereignty of Kuwait; and when the war had ended, President Bush promptly plummeted in the opinion polls, opening the way to a Clinton presidency. In the years since the Gulf War, the Pentagon's fear of public opinion became so extreme that it is practically military doctrine that US wars must now be fought without loss of American lives. This is an odd doctrine for a putative global hegemon, but it was equally peculiar for Bush to think that post-Cold War America could maintain the confidence of the United Nations as the linchpin of world order when the USA approved of so little of the organization's ambitious global agenda.[16]

If Bush's agenda for global governance was blinkered by American Cold War triumphalism, Secretary-General Boutros-Ghali's ambitious *Agenda for Peace* collided head-on with American nationalism and the global ambitions of the Pentagon, and soon ran afoul of the new Clinton administration, which lacked the courage of its convictions. Boutros Boutros-Ghali may well go down in history as the best Secretary-General since Dag Hammarskjöld. He saw clearly the unique opportunity to revitalize the UN system now that superpower rivalry and ideological confrontation had largely ended with the Cold War.

But Boutros-Ghali ran up against a stubborn truth: while there may be differing approaches to foreign relations within the Washington establishment, and ambient confusion about what to do with all its "hyperpower", there is rough consensus within the Beltway that the world will be ordered, if it is ordered at all, on American terms rather than UN terms. Boutros-Ghali's elaborate plans for a United Nations with its own army for peacekeeping, and its own endowment for a measure of financial independence, implied a freedom of action for the international organization that was perceived as threatening to American hegemony. The expansion of UN peacekeeping operations in the early 1990s – so central to Boutros-Ghali's vision of a new world order – troubled the Pentagon, particularly after the abortive Somalia mission in 1992, and angered congressional Republicans, especially after the massive victory of conservative Republicans in the congressional elections of 1994. Yet the Clinton administration, though internationalist by comparison, fully shared the antipathy toward the UN Secretary-General and his agenda. It is notable that UN Ambassador Madeleine Albright was elevated to Secretary of State on the strength of having terminated Boutros-Ghali's career at the United Nations. In 1996 the Republicans derided Boutros-Ghali in their election campaign rhetoric, but it was the Clinton-Gore Democrats who did him in.[17]

This body-blow to global governance, and the consequent humanitarian catastrophes of the mid-1990s – notably the American blockage of international assistance to halt the genocide in Rwanda – created the need for novel diplomatic approaches to what Canadian Foreign Minister Lloyd Axworthy called "the human security agenda". Axworthy, a Princeton PhD in political science, understood well the distinction between the American state and its vigorous civil society institutions, with their unique ability to mobilize public opinion. Axworthy's innovation was to harness the energy of leading NGOs – which proliferated in the 1990s to meet urgent humanitarian needs – and the diplomatic skills of "like-minded countries" among the middle powers. His diplomacy led global movements culminating in the Ottawa Treaty to ban land-mines (1997) and the Rome Treaty (1998) to create the International Criminal Court for prosecution of war criminals and perpetrators of genocide.

Both of these campaigns deserve further monographic study, but it seems clear that their rapid initial successes depended on having a clearly focused "single issue" of broad humanitarian appeal to international civil society. Importantly, these campaigns took place at arm's length from the American state, though they depended heavily on American NGOs, the International Campaign to Ban Land-mines and Human Rights Watch, respectively. They also represented "end runs" around the bureaucratic rigidities of the UN system, even though the United Nations quickly embraced them. Predictably, these initiatives of the "new diplomacy" were opposed by the USA. US opposition was less vociferous in the case of land-mines, which the Pentagon appeared to oppose on grounds of global principle rather than interest. But congressional Republicans vowed that they would kill the International Criminal Court, even if they have to punish allied countries in the process.[18]

These were classically "worthy Canadian initiatives". The land-mines effort, in particular, has already been implemented to a considerable degree and probably can be sustained in the longer term by Canada and the other "like-minded countries". The prospects for the International Criminal Court, however, appear to be doomed under the administration of George W. Bush, whose military-minded associates are determined that no American, however wanton his deeds, will ever be brought to the bar of international justice.[19]

Do these initiatives herald a "new diplomacy"? Yes, in the sense that they are clearly in the Wilsonian tradition of mobilizing the moral forces of the world, and their successes could be repeated if there is adequate political will in the world community. But the limitations of this approach need to be recognized. The problem with "niche diplomacy" is that its proponents must keep finding new niches and raising new coalitions for every "single issue" they choose to address. Inevitably, the Viet Nam veterans and the human rights lawyers will drift off to other preoccupations. But there is a problem here of continuity in state policy as well. Niche diplomacy is easily abandoned once the "single issue" has been addressed, even if inconclusively. This may even prove to be the case with Canada, where the departure of Foreign Minister Axworthy in late 2000 apparently spells the end of his global, if niche-specific, human security agenda and its replacement by an agenda fostering broad-gauged integration into the North American community. The "new diplomacy" deserves to be continued, if not by Canada then by other traditional stalwarts of the UN system; but one must recognize that it cannot be a comprehensive answer to the problem of global governance.

Looking ahead, from the perspective of the UN system it is not easy to contemplate the administration of George W. Bush without experiencing a premonition of trouble. A columnist for the *New York Times* has observed that "your average TWA pilot knows more about the world than George W. Bush",[20] but the root problem is an apparent deep-seated antipathy to international organizations and mechanisms of global governance on the part of the new Republican administration. To judge by their campaign positions, a Bush administration will have so hard-boiled a conception of the national interest as to rule out support for many UN peacekeeping operations. A Bush administration seems likely to indulge its congressional allies in their efforts to keep the United Nations broke by continued refusal to pay UN dues, and to keep it weak by hampering peacekeeping activities. If the Bush people have their way, the USA will build its national missile defence system in short order, may well abrogate the ABM treaty, and there will be no ratification of the comprehensive nuclear test ban treaty. No doubt there will be many surprises in store, few of them conducive to human security and global governance.

In this historical overview of two centuries and more, this chapter has tried to argue that while the American state's engagement with global governance has been fitful and episodic – and largely confined to the 1945–1975 period – its civil society institutions and the influential body of citizens interested in world affairs have long played a role in creating a better world. The USA is not, finally, a "like-minded country", nor is it likely to be any time soon; but it contains many like-minded institutions and like-minded people. Under the doleful circumstances of the George W. Bush administration, the need for a "new diplomacy" appears to be more acute than ever.

Notes

1. See the verbatim text of speech by US Senator Jesse Helms to the UN Security Council, 20 January 2000, available in the archives of www.nytimes.com.
2. For background see the collected essays in *Canadian Foreign Policy* 7 (Fall 1999), published by the Norman Patterson School of International Affairs, Carleton University.

3. Edward C. Luck, *Mixed Messages: American Politics and International Organization 1919–1999* (Washington, DC: Brookings, 1999), chapter 2 and passim.
4. See the new translation of Alexis de Tocqueville, *Democracy in America* (Chicago: University of Chicago Press, 2000), by Harvey Mansfield and Delba Winthrop.
5. Walter W. Powell, ed., *The Nonprofit Sector: A Research Handbook* (New Haven: Yale University Press, 1987). See also John K. Fairbank, ed., *The Missionary Enterprise in China and America* (Cambridge, MA: Harvard University Press, 1974).
6. The literature is summarized in Ernest R. May, *American Imperialism* (New York: Athenaeum, 1968). See especially James R. Rosenau, *Public Opinion and Foreign Policy* (New York: Random House, 1961), and subsequent works by this author.
7. James Bryce, *The American Commonwealth*, II (New York: Macmillan, 1910), pp. 267, 284.
8. The point is given expansive emphasis in James M. Lindsay, "The New Apathy", *Foreign Affairs* 79 (September/October 2000), pp. 2–8; but see also William H. Luers, "Choosing Engagement", *ibid.*, pp. 9–14.
9. For deep background see May, note 6 above, passim; and for recent iterations, Jessica T. Mathews, "Power Shifts", *Foreign Affairs* 76 (January/February 1997), pp. 50–66; Anne-Marie Slaughter, "The Real New World Order", *Foreign Affairs* 76 (September/October 1997), pp. 183–197.
10. See Selig Adler, *The Isolationist Impulse: Its Twentieth Century Reaction* (New York: Free Press, 1996).
11. Townsend Hoopes and Douglas Brinkley, *FDR and the Creation of the UN* (New Haven: Yale University Press, 1997). See also Gary B. Ostrower, *The United Nations and the United States* (New York: Twayne Publishers, 1998), chapters 1–3.
12. Ostrower, *ibid.*, chapters 4–5.
13. *Ibid.*, pp. 125–137, 139, 159, 230, 235.
14. *Ibid.*, chapter 9.
15. Thomas L. Hughes, "The Twilight of Internationalism", *Foreign Policy* 61 (Winter 1985–1986), pp. 25–48.
16. Ostrower, note 11 above, chapter 10.
17. *Ibid.*, chapter 11.
18. Richard Prince, "Reversing the Gun Sights: Transnational Civil Society Targets Land Mines", *International Organization* 52 (Summer 1998), pp. 613–644; "U.S. Accord Being Sought on UN Dues and on Court", *New York Times*, 7 December 2000, p. A6.
19. Thomas Friedman, "The World According to Bush", *New York Times*, 4 August 2000, p. A27.
20. *Ibid.*

5

Global civil society and the Ottawa process: Lessons from the movement to ban anti-personnel mines

Maxwell A. Cameron

Introduction[1]

Debate on the emergence of a global civil society has oscillated between guarded optimism and explicit scepticism. R. B. J. Walker cautions that analysis of social movements in world politics invites trouble: "the elusive transience of the one is no match for the monolithic presence of the other, fables of David and Goliath notwithstanding".[2] The movement to ban anti-personnel (AP) mines is a tale of David triumphing over Goliath, but if previous social movements led observers to conclude that "global civil society is more potential than actual",[3] and that the promise of global democratization is more fable than fact, the success of the mine ban movement suggests that global civil society may be an emerging reality in the global system. That, at least, was the view of a coalition of non-governmental organizations, united under the umbrella of the International Campaign to Ban Land-mines (ICBL), which participated as delegates in the international conference to ban land-mines held in Ottawa in early December 1997. At the signing ceremony the partnership between NGOs and like-minded states was even proclaimed "a new superpower" by NGO leaders.[4] Hyperbole aside, does the ban on land-mines portend a shift or transformation in the post-Cold War global system? This chapter undertakes a preliminary assessment of the lessons of the mine ban movement from the perspective of the prospects for global civil society.

Global civil society and social movements

The idea of global civil society is often contrasted with the image of an anarchic interstate system in which self-help is the dominant organizing principle.[5] According to Ronnie D. Lipschutz, for example, global civil society refers to the "self-conscious constructions of networks of knowledge and action, by decentred local actors, that cross the reified boundaries of space as though they were not there".[6] In a similar vein, Martin Shaw defines civil society as "the network of institutions through which groups in society in general represent themselves – both to each other and to the state". It is globalized "to the extent that society increasingly represents itself globally, across nation-state boundaries, through the formation of global institutions". These institutions may include formal organizations, international linkages of informal networks and movements, and globalist organizations with a "specifically global orientation, global membership, and activity of global scope".[7] For Lipschutz, the existence of such networks holds the promise of modifying "the conflictual nature of a socially constructed anarchy". The "fading away of anarchy"[8] occurs as systems of rules begin to govern global economic transactions and then extend into such areas as human rights, humanitarian law, or the environment. The idea of anarchy giving way to global civil society is an attractive one, but it is at best fuzzy and vague and at worst extravagant rhetoric.

Such criticisms could not be directed at Martin Shaw, whose useful analysis of global civil society begins with a crucial distinction between civil society and social movements. In his view, civil society is defined in relation to the state. As the site of multiple political struggles, the boundaries between the state and civil society are constantly being shifted and renegotiated according to the balance among social groups, civil institutions, and state power. Social movements, defined as collective actors constituted by individuals with common interests and a shared identity who use mass mobilization or its threat as their source of power, operate within the political spaces provided by civil society. A major ambiguity of social movements, which bedevils analysts and frustrates political strategists, is the ambivalent relation many such movements have with the major institutions of the state, including representative assemblies and parties. If the location of social movements outside formal party and parliamentary structures can be a weakness "when it comes to seeking particular concessions from the state",[9] then that weakness is much amplified in the sphere of interstate politics. Truly global social movements face the formidable task of coordinating their actions through transnational linkages spanning a large number of countries, and this challenge is compounded by the reluctance of state élites to tolerate the intrusions of such movements into the sphere of international power politics.

Shaw is pessimistic about the potential of social movements within globalized civil society. He devotes considerable attention to both peace movements and humanitarian organizations, two currents that came together in the mine ban movement. Of the former he suggests that they failed to prevent the deployment of new weapons in the 1980s, in spite of their substantial impact on public opinion. This can be explained by the mutual solidarity of NATO governments,[10] as well as the inability of peace activists to mount parallel movements in the Warsaw countries. Of the latter he argues that efforts by humanitarian organizations to offer ameliorative assistance to war-torn countries in the 1990s have failed to generate participatory mobilizations. The reasons for this failure lie in the lack of simple moral-political questions around which the public might coalesce in a shared conviction that their own governments need to take responsibility for change. Shaw concludes that "there appears to be a crisis of popular responses in Western societies to even the most appalling situations in the new post-Cold War crises. Peace movements of the old kind are no longer viable, and there is no alternative social movement development around these new global/international issues."[11]

Shaw's pessimism may require revision in the light of the movement to ban AP mines. Yet an appreciation of the achievements of this movement should not blind us to the difficulties that may be encountered in attempting to replicate its success. A realistic assessment should begin by immediately dispensing with wishful thinking about the "fading away of anarchy" or the transformation of the structure of the interstate system. After all, AP mines have never been a weapon of strategic importance in the arsenal of states, and have little impact on the distribution of capabilities among states: they rarely confer a long-term advantage on any military force; they have never caused a country to win or lose a war, although they are still widely deployed by many states with border conflicts; they are more commonly used in civil conflicts than interstate conflicts; and, moreover, the major producers of AP mines have not signed the ban treaty.[12] The purpose of banning AP mines was not to change the interstate system but to alleviate the appalling humanitarian effects of a particularly cheap and abhorrent weapon.

By reframing the terms of the debate on AP mines from an arms control to a humanitarian issue, the ban advocates shifted the focus from military security to human security. The public was encouraged to think of AP mines not in terms of disarmament but as an obstacle to development, a hindrance to humanitarian relief, a form of pollution, and, above all, a source of widespread human suffering. Theorists of international relations have for some time insisted that the pay-off structure and rewards for cooperation are especially weak in the security area, where the potentially grave losses associated with cooperation are great and the risks associated with inadequate surveillance and monitoring are high. By reframing the problem, AP mines were removed from an exclusive focus on security and shifted into an arena more amenable to cooperative solutions.[13] This line of reasoning is quite obvious. More intriguing is the possibility that transnational social movements were the decisive agents responsible for reframing the debate on AP mines.

The ban on AP mines points, as Richard Price observes, to denser patterns of political engagement across borders which "do not amount by themselves to a qualitatively novel challenge to state authority – understood in a Hobbesian sense of who wields the sword", and yet may "constitute a transnational civil society, the thin and uneven public sphere that can coalesce at the global level where individuals interact for common purposes and shape collective life".[14] One possible implication of global civil society is the emergence of new networks of decision-making and public deliberation, partnerships between states and non-state actors, and mechanisms of accountability.[15] Transnational political activities may result in new flows of information that bring publicity to previously neglected problems, thereby requiring public decision-makers to account for their actions before new actors, in new fora, and on new issues. In short, global civil society implies emergent patterns of what might be called "global horizontal accountability".

Horizontal accountability is a term coined by Guillermo O'Donnell to describe a type of political responsibility that "depends on the existence of state agencies that are legally empowered – and factually willing and able – to take actions ranging from routine oversight to criminal sanctions or impeachment in relation to the possibility of unlawful actions or omissions by other agents or agencies of the state".[16] Vertical accountability, where a subordinate public agency is held accountable to a higher agency ("the people" in a democracy), is ruled out at the international level by the structure of interstate politics. Anarchy, and its self-help corollary, imply that each state is responsible for its own preservation, and none is accountable to a higher authority. Insofar as a system is anarchic, all states are formally equal, though in practice they are unequal in capabilities. Horizontal accountability is weaker in the international system than in democratic or republican polities, yet the Ottawa Treaty is one of a number of developments – including the creation of the International Criminal Court and the growing acceptance of the universal obligation to punish human rights abusers (dramatically illustrated by the detention of the former Chilean dictator Augusto Pinochet) – that suggest the potential fruitfulness of this concept for understanding the impact of global civil society.

The ban convention

The Ottawa Treaty, formally known as the Convention on the Prohibition of the Use, Stockpiling, Production, and Transfer of Anti-Personnel Mines and on Their Destruction,[17] is a legally binding and comprehensive ban based on the principle that the means of warfare are not unlimited and weapons that cause excessive injury and suffering, especially those that are indiscriminate in their effects on civilians and military personnel, are prohibited. It contains both negative and positive obligations. On the negative side, there are disarmament measures which, as the title of the treaty implies, require that states not use, stockpile, produce, sell, or otherwise transfer AP mines. These measures are supported by transparency provisions to ensure accurate reporting and data collection to enable the international community to understand the scope and magnitude of the problem. The treaty also contains positive humanitarian obligations to redress the existing problem by clearing mined areas and providing assistance to victims. Its architects envisaged a global effort to eradicate AP mines modelled on other humanitarian efforts like campaigns against preventable disease.

The Ottawa Treaty establishes a clear norm: AP mines cannot be used as weapons under any circumstances, in times of either war or peace. They are defined unambiguously as mines "designed to be exploded by the presence, proximity or contact of a person and that will incapacitate, injure, or kill one or more persons" (Article 2.1). The treaty does not cover anti-vehicle mines, but it does explicitly apply to anti-handling devices attached to anti-vehicle mines.

The onus of compliance is, naturally, on sovereign states. However, the same partnership between states, NGOs, and regional and intergovernmental organizations that was developed in the advocacy phase of the ban movement provides the transnational network that undergirds the treaty in the implementation phase. The treaty provides a set of deadlines and annual review conferences, and outlines measures of progress and tasks to be performed in which NGOs, above all the ICBL, will play a crucial role. NGOs are responsible for a substantial part of all mine clearance and most victim assistance, and they will provide crucial reports on progress in these areas. To this end, the ICBL has established 75 grassroots monitors covering 105 countries.[18] Mine-afflicted countries are encouraged to work with UN agencies, NGOs, and other states to assess the scope of their problems, to provide baseline data for assessing compliance, and to undertake the legislative, administrative, and regulatory measures necessary to implement the convention.

The compliance mechanism, one of the most contentious issues in the development of the treaty, involves a hybrid of fact-finding, modelled on human rights enforcement, and more intrusive verification mechanisms, modelled on disarmament law. The treaty establishes a rather cumbersome process involving requests for information regarding allegations of non-compliance, responses and further clarification, fact-finding missions, and review and reports on findings. Sanctions for non-compliance have not been spelled out, but may include suspension of benefits arising from the convention. Although this is clearly a weak compliance mechanism, it provides an institutionalized vehicle for NGOs and states to monitor and oversee the effective implementation of the convention by other signatories – in short, a mechanism, albeit weak, of global horizontal accountability. The weakness of the compliance mechanism does not necessarily mean the ban will be ineffective. Since mines are easy to produce, conceal, and use covertly, a coercive and intrusive compliance regime would not necessarily be more effective than an unequivocal norm backed by the moral suasion that comes from global public engagement in the issue. AP mines will never completely disappear, but their humanitarian burden may be substantially lightened as states expose themselves to intense scrutiny and criticism under the convention whenever they fail to comply with its provisions.

The Ottawa Treaty is a short, clear, unambiguous document with remarkably few loopholes, exemptions, or reservations. The heavy price tag for such a treaty was the refusal of some nations, most notably the USA, to sign. The leaders of the core group decided that it was preferable to seek a comprehensive and unequivocal ban on AP mines and then seek to universalize it, rather than make the concessions necessary to win the immediate support of the USA, China, Russia, India, and other holdouts. The reason for this decision was that since the goal was to solve a humanitarian problem, it was more important to win the support of mine-afflicted nations than producer nations. Once mine-afflicted nations have signed the treaty, as most of them have, the demand for AP mines is expected to diminish. Moreover, the existence of a widely embraced treaty has already had an impact on a number of non-signatories. AP mine producers are caught in a larger norm system that they cannot ignore. Fewer than 10 mine-producing countries continue to export AP mines. The USA, which largely supports the goal of eliminating AP mines over time and has dedicated significant resources to demining efforts, has ceased to export mines, has engaged in transparency measures, and is beginning to destroy its stockpiles. Mine action has become a central aspect of peacekeeping initiatives, and was a major element in the efforts by the Organization of American States to provide assistance to victims of hurricane Mitch in Central America. In the year after the treaty was signed, 10 donor countries initiated 98 mine action programmes in 25 countries.[19]

A weaker norm that more countries could have signed would have undermined the supportive coalition that had driven the Ottawa process. The ICBL leadership fought hard for a strong treaty and, in spite of the fact that the US leaders of the coalition were particularly disappointed by the refusal of the USA to sign, most of the NGO leadership would have been more upset by a ban riddled with loopholes and exceptions. Such a ban, lacking the enthusiastic support of the ICBL and its allies, would have lost momentum at the implementation stage. It was deemed better to get a strong treaty and then universalize its membership quickly, since the willingness of signatory states actually to comply with the provisions of the treaty will be stronger if the treaty is widely accepted. So far, judging by the extremely rapid pace of ratification, the prospects for sustaining momentum into the implementation phase look good. On 16 September 1998 the fortieth state ratified the treaty, making 1 March 1999 the date of its entry into force. No multilateral disarmament treaty has ever entered into force more rapidly. As of January 1999, 133 countries had signed the treaty and 60 had ratified it. To show how this remarkable treaty came about, the next sections examine the ICBL and draw lessons from the Ottawa process.

The ICBL and the mobilization of shame

The ICBL is a paradigmatic example of what Shaw calls a "globalist organization".[20] It is an umbrella composed of over 1,000 non-governmental organizations from over 60 countries around the world, all unified by a single purpose: to ban AP mines. The original founders included Handicap International of France, Human Rights Watch (another globalist organization), Medico International of Germany, Physicians for Human Rights/USA and the Vietnam Veterans of America Foundation (which hired Jody Williams, a coordinator of the ICBL[21] and Nobel Peace Prize winner for 1997, and invested substantial resources into the ban movement). Today the ICBL includes an extraordinarily heterogeneous assortment of groups and organizations, including humanitarian assistance organizations, refugee and medical relief workers, human rights and development NGOs, arms control and peace advocates, church groups, unions, and professional associations. Like many social movements, the ICBL remains a loosely organized and unstructured network of groups and individuals – with only a handful of key full-time and paid activists – that draws upon the resources, both financial and human, of a broad spectrum of member organizations interconnected by fax machines, the internet, and periodic conferences. The decentred and flexible organization of the ICBL, which reflects what Shaw calls the "messy aggregation of global and national state power which comprises the contemporary interstate system",[22] allows member organizations to pursue the strategy most efficacious in their own national setting at the same time as they share information and coordinate "messaging" with the media and opinion leaders around the world.

The ICBL has performed exactly the function expected of a globalist organization: to "make a reality of global civil society by bringing the most exposed victims among the world's population into contact with more resourceful groups in the West".[23] Jody Williams argues that the awareness of the AP mines problem followed UN-brokered peace agreements:

When peace-keeping missions entered these countries – Afghanistan, Angola, Cambodia, Mozambique, to name just a few – what they found were millions of land mines. As the work of United Nations, governmental, and non-governmental agencies began to feel the impact of these weapons, there followed a dramatic increase in attention to land mines as well as coordinated efforts to mitigate their impact.[24]

A powerful instrument in the hands of the ICBL was a list it maintained and regularly updated documenting the policies on land-mines taken by states around the world. This list, produced under the heading "The Good, the Bad, and the Ugly", was started around the time of the campaign to lobby the ongoing negotiations under the aegis of the conference on the Convention on Certain Conventional Weapons (or CCW). This "frequently roused the ire of governments" but "it also pressured them to bring their public statements in line with the realities of their negotiating position – or vice versa".[25] Some governments began to lobby the ICBL to get on to the "good" list.

Raising public awareness of the issue of AP mines was one of the most important tasks performed by the ICBL, and it was a task that no single state, or even group of states, could have undertaken with comparable results. Yet the ICBL went far beyond such a role, breaking new ground in terms of the participation of a social movement in the actual negotiation of an international convention. This new role of civil society has been made possible by what is now widely referred to as the Ottawa process, a term that denotes three related components: a partnership between states and NGOs in the conduct of international diplomacy; the practice of bringing together small and medium-sized like-minded states into a coalition; and a willingness to operate outside of the normal channels and fora on a diplomatic "fast track" to ban mines. The ICBL was able to lead a worldwide ban movement to the successful negotiation of an international convention because it worked creatively and tenaciously in a partnership with like-minded states. Had the ambivalence on the part of governments and NGOs about working together in partnership not been overcome, the mine ban would almost certainly not have been negotiated or signed. The Ottawa process suggests that, at least in the post-Cold War international environment, non-hegemonic states and transnational social movements can achieve impressive diplomatic ends by working in partnership.

Was the Ottawa process unique, or did it set a precedent for partnerships between governments and NGOs that might be attempted on a larger scale or in other issue areas in the future? The next section takes up these questions. It will be demonstrated that the Ottawa process established the basis for new mechanisms of horizontal accountability by bringing together like-minded states, in partnership with NGOs, outside of traditional arms control fora.

Lessons from the Ottawa process[26]

Partnership pays

The unprecedented level of cooperation between governments and NGOs was essential to the success of the ban. The partnership was intense, in that it involved daily contact among government and NGO leaders, and an unprecedented degree of equality was achieved between state and non-state actors. In fact, the Canadian government initially proposed that states and NGOs would be equal participants in the October 1996 Ottawa conference, and both official and NGO delegates would partake in all discussions. Bitter rejection of this formula by some officials, who accused Canada of selling out to the NGOs, led to a compromise in which there would be two tracks of meetings, one for the official delegates and closed to NGOs (unless they attended, as they were invited to do, as members of government delegations), and another open to NGO "observers" as well as government officials. Roughly 15 countries brought NGO leaders on their official delegations, and 20 NGO delegates attended on behalf of the ICBL. To give a sense of how important NGO participation was, and how uncomfortable it made some delegates feel, consider the fact that when a French delegate outlined France's position in terms that, stated crudely, implied France was prepared to ban land-mines until it needed them, Jody Williams was given the floor to respond, which she did with the following statement: "Your policy is contradictory. You are saying that you want to ban land-mines, except when you want to use them. I suppose this is better than a stick in the eye, but it is not what we are looking for here." A better example of mobilizing shame would be hard to find.[27]

NGO participation in international negotiations, although not totally unprecedented, is uncommon in the security field. NGO involvement in the treaty-drafting process was also unusual. The ICBL composed its own draft treaty which it submitted as a model, attended all preparatory meetings, and commented on every draft written by the Austrian delegation throughout the Ottawa process. The ICBL intervened in key moments of the decision-making process and watched over the negotiations to ensure that no loopholes or reservations were carved into the treaty. They insisted, for example, on an unambiguous definition of AP mines and, at the end of the process, were able to say that they had commented on every single provision of the treaty. A careful comparison of the original goals of the NGOs and the text of the final convention shows that, in terms of substance, the NGOs got all or more than they had demanded.[28]

The leaders of the ICBL were self-conscious of the fact that, as one South African put it, "civil society is globalizing, leading to cross-border civil society". But just as there are governments nervous about working with NGOs, many NGOs are also nervous about working with governments. Some national leaders of the ICBL felt that they could trust certain policy-makers, but remained sceptical about entering into partnership with governments. This was particularly true of the larger powers, such as France, Japan,[29] and the UK; partnership was more feasible in small and medium-sized democracies like Canada, Austria, and Belgium. The ICBL was sufficiently flexible to enable each national campaign to adopt what it felt would be the most effective strategy. However, the dominant view in the ICBL, as summed up by one of its principal leaders, reflected the sense that partnership, at least with certain governments, was indispensable to the success of the movement:

Partnership does not mean that you agree on everything or are in the government's pockets. You have the same goals and bring comparative advantages to the achievement of these goals. Not all national campaigns work in partnerships with government. We have overall agreement, but we also have differences. We should not be afraid of word "partnership" ... we're not always adversaries. The government is *me*; I have a voice, they should listen.

In focus groups with government representatives, held during the signing of the convention in Ottawa, an effort was made to probe more deeply the nature of the partnership with NGOs. Some government officials involved in the ban movement were surprised that the NGO leaders "turned out to be reasonable people who understood international diplomacy". At the same time, government leaders were as interested as the NGOs in carefully defining the boundaries of the partnership. As a senior Canadian official put it:

The role of governments and NGOs is different. NGOs don't want to be public servants. There will always be some mistrust and competition for ideas and leadership; yet we have seen a real change in many issues, leading to cooperation between government and NGOs.

Coalitions of the like-minded can lead

Small and medium-sized states, in partnership with NGOs, led the Ottawa process. What is remarkable is not merely the fact that the ban was achieved without the cooperation of the big powers, but that it was achieved in the face of stiff opposition from certain big powers. All five permanent members of the UN Security Council opposed the AP ban, or supported the ban but were initially critical of the Ottawa process.[30] An obvious lesson, one that evokes painful winces among members of the Washington establishment, is that the USA does not always have to be the leader in the new post-Cold War global politics.

The ICBL leadership was intellectually responsible for a strategic decision that was critical to initiating the Ottawa process. They proposed the idea of bringing together like-minded pro-ban states (based on the ICBL's list of "good states") into what came to be known as the "core group", and thereby proceeding outside of the UN CCW process. In late 1995, at the start of the CCW negotiations, there were only a dozen states with a clear pro-ban policy. In Geneva in January 1996, 14 countries were invited to informal talks to discuss alternatives: some of the eight that showed up were later to be members of the core group.

An Austrian official from the core group said: "We had this coalition of small and medium-sized countries. There was no 'big brother'. Canada was in the lead, but it was a democratic process. We were never bullied; on the contrary, it was a particular joy the way we cooperated." That same official pointed out that one of the advantages of small- and middle-power leadership was that "some who did not want us to succeed did not take us seriously". Most government officials had to acknowledge that the Ottawa process could never have been conducted during the Cold War.

Leaders of the core group who orchestrated the Ottawa process went to pains to ensure that their coalition would not appear to be a "Northern" initiative because they feared that a North–South split would fatally undermine the ban movement. Thus a number of key developing country states were invited to play critical roles. South Africa's Jacob Selebi and his delegation presided over the Oslo endgame, and his strong leadership helped prevent the convention from unravelling in the face of intense US demands for a carve-out for South Korea. Mexico was also an extremely helpful member of the core group. However, the most vital players were Canada, Austria, Norway, Sweden, and Belgium – all small, established democracies, and all countries comfortable with the active participation of civil society in foreign policy. The convention may be interpreted as evidence in support of the proposition that democracies are more peaceful, not only because they do not fight other democracies,[31] but also because their decision-makers may be predisposed to foster the rule of law and mechanisms of horizontal accountability at the international level. People in less democratic, mine-afflicted countries may benefit from the potential use of the treaty as an instrument to strengthen civil society. The success of the treaty at the implementation stage depends on the ability of NGOs involved in mine clearance and victim assistance to do their work. They will raise their voice on thorny issues like whose land is cleared first and who gets victim assistance.

Obsolete diplomatic fora can (and should?) be subverted

The Ottawa process worked outside of traditional diplomatic processes. As one NGO leader put it, "Canada decided to play the negotiation game by subverting traditional diplomatic schemes". The desire to move rapidly meant that it was impossible to work through the CCW. Its consensus rules were too cumbersome and slow. The pro-ban states were unwilling to move at the pace of the most reluctant states. A new form of ad hoc diplomacy was required. The core group, working with the ICBL and the International Committee of the Red Cross, opted to bypass the CCW and create their own process. A key ingredient of the new "ad hoc" approach was that it would not be held hostage to the tyranny of consensus. One Canadian official said "the Ottawa process was open to all, but hostage to none".[32]

A virtue of the non-consensus-based approach was that it was precisely this feature of the negotiation process that produced a treaty largely free of exemptions. There were few votes on exemptions because diplomats knew they were dealing with a collection of states and non-state actors determined to achieve a total ban; at least at the outset, the half-hearted were not at the table. As one diplomat put it: "We worked outside regular bodies and organizations, so we were not subject to little games played in these bodies." Since the clarity of the goal – a total ban on AP mines – was essential to maintaining core group unity, when faced with the trade-off between increasing the number of supporters of a ban treaty and avoiding exceptions, the core group opted for a clean convention that would establish an unequivocal norm.

Another virtue of the Ottawa process was its breathtaking pace. For some time now observers of global politics have noted public impatience with the glacial quality of normal diplomatic processes.[33] Arms control negotiations can take decades to complete and longer to ratify and implement; they were a poor model for the kind of problems confronting the global commons in the 1990s. As is became clear that the CCW would not deliver adequate results, the Canadian fast-track initiative seemed like a welcome, if initially startling, gamble.

The problem that emerged after the CCW was how to remain open to the participation of any country without becoming mired in disputes with countries that did not share the core group's objectives. The solution, as articulated by a Canadian government official, was self-selection: "Who to invite? Everyone. They decided if they were ready enough to join with these rebels in the ban group." Once the open invitations to participate were sent out, a special effort was made to win representation from all regions of the world. The pay-off came in Oslo: in the crucial final stages of the negotiation, no cleavage emerged between Western and non-aligned blocs of nations. Selebi stewarded the talks to a successful conclusion in the face of a last-ditch effort by the USA – with, much to the surprise of many, Canadian support – to seek a delay in an effort to find a compromise. Had the US negotiators been authorized to break up their package of demands, it is quite possible that major rifts would have appeared among the core group states and their NGO partners. The Ottawa process could have had a very different denouement.

The diplomatic process leading to the ban on land-mines raises difficult questions about the role of the UN system as a forum for negotiations and about the relationship between NGOs and the United Nations. Should diplomatic initiatives take place at the margins of the United Nations in other areas? Should the United Nations itself be "democratized" by expanding the role of NGOs? The Ottawa convention was negotiated outside the United Nations, but was embraced by Secretary-General Kofi Annan and is currently housed in the United Nations. Annan also called for a People's Assembly to be held in the year 2000. Advocates of democratizing the United Nations suggest that the effectiveness of UN policies requires democratic deliberation at the international level. Two trends must be confronted by the United Nations if it is to remain relevant. First, the growth of interdependence means that national regulations and policies cannot internalize many economic and environmental externalities (volatile capital flows, or pollution, for example). If we accept that decisions must be transferred to a higher, supranational jurisdiction, should we not expect as much public input into such decision-making as occurs at the national level? Second, the major threats to human security are overwhelmingly intranational, and the most serious violators of individual rights and freedoms are non-democratic states. Thus, it makes sense for the United Nations to champion democratization as part of the process and as a goal of UN decision-making.

How should such a transformation of the United Nations be effected? Not surprisingly, many NGOs advocate greater NGO participation in UN decision-making. The Campaign for a More Democratic United Nations, the World Federation of United Nations Associations, and former Secretary-General Javier Perez de Cuellar favour a greater role for NGOs. The arguments advanced are not always self-serving. NGOs point to the enormous gap between the knowledge that UN bureaucrats bring to discussions of issues like land-mines and the expertise NGOs acquire as a result of working on the ground with victims of these weapons. NGOs can serve as crucial transmission belts for information from affected populations to decision-makers.[34] The same is true in other areas, such as human rights, the rights of women, and environmental and labour standards. The United Nations has begun to respond to these calls. The UN Economic and Social Council (ECOSOC) has changed its rules on the consultative status of NGOs, but NGO leaders call for a greater role in the General Assembly and Security Council as well. Others have advocated a Second Assembly, composed of national parliamentarians or accredited NGOs.[35]

Critics recoil in horror at the idea of NGOs, unelected, largely government-funded, self-appointed spokespersons for "civil society", using the UN system to, as one editorialist put it, "effect changes that would be difficult or impossible democratically".[36] These fears are often exaggerated and misplaced. The value of NGOs is that they can bring publicity to certain issues, raise public awareness about what is being done, bridge the knowledge gap between international negotiators and real-world conditions, and push for accountability by public officials. Part of the backlash against NGOs lies in the failure to make the distinction noted at the outset of this chapter between civil society and social movements. If we think of NGOs as "representing" global civil society, then we tend to exaggerate the impact their participation in diplomacy will have on the interstate system. Advocates overstate their case when they see this impact as affecting the anarchic structure of the interstate system, while critics similarly exaggerate when they fear that states will be hijacked by NGOs.

If we think of coalitions of NGOs as transnational social movements, we get a clearer picture of their potential and limitations. Transnational social movements are contentious movements that operate at both the national and international levels. They are, almost by definition, impossible to institutionalize. The best way to democratize the United Nations would be for states to promote the changes that such social movements advocate by incorporating NGOs on official delegations, giving them access to negotiation fora as participants, and accrediting them not as individual NGOs but as international coalitions.

Idiosyncrasies of the ban movement

The Ottawa process will not be replicated in other issue areas in exactly the same way because of the uniqueness of the issue, the fortuitous circumstances surrounding the ban movement, and the willingness of key leaders to go way out on a diplomatic limb. To what extent do these unique features of the Ottawa process limit its utility as a model for the future?

The issue was unique

The mine ban issue posed what Shaw calls "a simple moral-political question, in which the issues of responsibility were direct".[37] "It is a moral, black-white issue," said a European official, "one that is easy to transport to the media." The central argument made by ban advocates was that the limited military utility of land-mines was far outweighed by the destructive humanitarian consequences of their use. These humanitarian consequences could be dramatized in simple but compelling images and symbols. The argument that mines had limited military utility also highlighted the fact that the use or abolition of mines would have little impact on the global military balance, while significantly improving human security.

The uniqueness of the AP mine issue comes into sharper focus when compared with other similar problems, such as small arms. The main argument against AP mines was their indiscriminate character. AP mines are designed to be detonated by actions that may be as innocent as a farmer ploughing a field or a child collecting an attractive object. They are often used to inflict horrifically painful wounds on soldiers and civilians alike in a deliberate effort to raise the human cost of war for an adversary. Even though many states have regulations governing the use of mines, such regulations are often abandoned in the field conditions of actual warfare. It is difficult to make similar arguments against the use of small arms, which are certainly used as weapons of mass terror, but are not inherently indiscriminate. Unexploded ordinance is a problem in many war-torn areas, but such explosives are not deliberate government policy. Fuel-air explosives and cluster bombs may be used as weapons of mass destruction, and they are frequently deployed with indiscriminate effects, but they are not obviously part of a large-scale humanitarian crisis.

Another unique feature of the AP mines issue was that it could be treated in relative isolation from other issues that might have complicated the need for a ban in the public mind. Issues such as child labour are linked to deeper problems of underdevelopment and poverty and cannot be banned without altering basic social conditions; similarly, environmental issues raise complex trade-offs between growth and conservation, and between the consumption of one generation and the next, between population growth and environmental scarcity. The AP mines issue was relatively free of such complexity in the minds of the public. Banning a whole class of weapons complicates entrenched military doctrine, but there were few linkages to other issues around which opposition to the ban might mobilize.

Luck played a role

The mine ban movement benefited from a series of fortuitous events that could not be expected to occur again in quite the same way. Support for the ban by such high-profile public figures as Archbishop Desmond Tutu, and Princess Diana prior to her death, helped the campaign. Britain and France would not have come to the bargaining table had it not been for the outcome of their 1997 general elections. Many policy-makers among the core group states felt that chance played a role. Said a Norwegian government official: "We benefited from circumstantial luck – not *sheer* luck, but we had the advantage of incidentally beneficial factors. This will not easily reappear in a similar mix." A Canadian official elaborated, emphasizing how the conclusion of the CCW created an open playing field for new diplomatic initiatives. He said: "Serendipity, good luck played a huge role. We began at a time when the agenda was largely there. In October, within days of concluding the test ban treaty, there was nothing on the horizon. We were undistracted: the agenda parted like the Red Sea."

A big gamble paid off

The leaders of the ban movement, on the part of both governments and the NGO community, included a group of singularly effective people.

One part of that group – the NGO leadership – was recognized by the Nobel committee. However, the leaders among the core states were also unusual in their willingness to take diplomatic risks. In particular, Canadian Foreign Minister Lloyd Axworthy's announcement in the strategy conference in October 1996 that he would host a conference at the end of 1997 to sign a convention banning AP mines was a big gamble. By setting a public deadline, Axworthy could have exposed himself – and the Canadian government – to considerable embarrassment. At the time, Canada could not even count on the support of the core group. Indeed, only a handful of his own staffers and two members of the ICBL knew he was going to make the announcement before he entered the final plenary session – senior bureaucrats did not know, nor even the Prime Minister. The extent to which Axworthy and the Canadian foreign service went out on a diplomatic limb at this crucial junction cannot be overestimated.[38]

Government-NGO partnerships, publicity, and horizontal accountability

In spite of the idiosyncrasies aiding the movement to ban AP mines – the nature of the issue, luck, and risk-taking leadership – there were precedent-setting features of the process that may become more frequent features of the post-Cold War diplomatic landscape, including government-NGO partnerships, a larger role for smaller and middle powers, and new possibilities for subverting and replacing traditional diplomatic fora and procedures. The crucial lessons are that states and social movements can work in partnership to enhance their capacities mutually, to bring publicity to neglected issues, and to create new mechanisms of global horizontal accountability.

The idea of partnership with states is anathema to many NGOs, which are deeply suspicious of state institutions and traditional mechanisms of representation, and many policy-makers are equally sceptical of NGO politics. Yet the Ottawa process confirms a view articulated by M. J. Peterson: "States and transnational societal actor networks not only need each other, they can alter each other's capacities."[39] The partnership between the core states and the NGO coalition enhanced the capacities of both. Without the ICBL, the core states would not have been able to mobilize the skills and resources of foreign social actors; without the core group, the ICBL would never have been able to engage in the diplomatic lobbying necessary to negotiate a convention.

Yet the clash between NGOs and governments is inevitably rooted in differing concepts of the political. Martin Shaw notes that social movements invite us to broaden conventional views of politics (as in the femi-

nist slogan that the "personal is political"), but he cautions against ig-
noring the reality of state power.[40] NGOs brought a broader conception
of politics to the Ottawa process. Whether it was creating mock mine-
fields that the diplomats had to walk through to the negotiation centre in
Oslo, creating shoe mountains near the negotiation centres, or bringing
the pain of victims into public view by introducing mine victims to the
international media, the NGOs were able to recast the problem in human
terms, create evocative symbols and messages that were conveniently
adapted to media and communications technology, and build the climate
of public opinion that made policy change both possible and politically
attractive to governments. At the same time, the ICBL had the political
maturity to work with sympathetic governments in ways that acknowledged diplomatic politics on the one hand, and domestic constraints on
the other. For example, the NGOs worked closely with allies in legislatures in established democracies. Parliamentarians – whether in the
European Parliament, the US Congress, or the Italian Senate – tended to
be quite receptive to the ICBL's message. In countries with weak civil
societies, different strategies were used. Often, the existence of a worldwide movement against AP mines emboldened both domestic political
authorities and local grassroots organizations. NGOs in Africa reported a
major shift in the willingness of the public to endorse the mine ban cause
as global momentum built behind the ban; international pressures provided political cover for local activists. Moreover, the compliance provisions of the convention build on the human rights model, and require efforts to enhance civil society capacities to ensure enforcement.

The ICBL helped make the AP mines issue public, not just by transmitting images and information about the problem, but by working with
states to ensure that arguments about AP mines were exposed to criticism from civil society so that all actors were compelled to provide public
reasons for their actions. Based on deliberative polls held in Ottawa
during the signing of the convention, there existed a clear consensus
among government and NGO delegates that the ICBL's most important
function was in building public support for the ban, influencing the media, and thereby bringing about change in government policies. Members
of the ICBL believed that the surprising success of the movement rested
in the extraordinary outpouring of support from the public.

It would be a mistake to argue that the ICBL "represented" global
civil society. Representation, at least in democratic theory, means an assembly is authorized to speak on behalf of a larger community. The
ICBL was no such assembly and had no such authority. Parties and legislatures can be thought of as crucial aspects of representative government; social movements may be an increasingly important constituent of
civil society, but do not replace the representative functions of parties
and parliaments. The point is an obvious one, but it needs to be empha-

sized because there are many advocates of the Ottawa process who will argue that the greater openness of the negotiation process made it more democratic because it was more "representative" of civil society – a claim that invariably provokes a hackneyed but pertinent question: who voted for the NGOs?

The distinctive feature of the Ottawa process was not greater representativeness but greater publicity. By including NGOs in the negotiation process, as delegates in meetings and as equals with states in certain negotiation fora, the Ottawa process guaranteed that the reasons provided by diplomats for the policies of their governments were made in public and exposed to criticism by groups from civil society and other governments. Military bureaucrats, unaccustomed to providing public justification for their weapon systems, found themselves unable to explain the need for mines, and their arguments failed in the court of global public opinion. This is the essence of global horizontal accountability.

The leaders of the ICBL could take the microphone at international conferences and directly challenge the policies of governments. Similarly, government officials in countries like Canada, Norway, Austria, and Sweden – all of which had NGOs on official negotiation teams – were compelled to make their policies under the public scrutiny of a highly attentive and electronically "wired" civil society. And, although this reduced the bargaining "wiggle room" for policy-makers, it stiffened their position internationally, as became evident in the final round of the negotiations in Oslo.

The role of global civil society will be to ensure that existing democratic institutions and practices at both domestic and international levels are supported and given vitality, that they are transformed through innovative praxis and experimentation, and that they become more powerful, accountable, and enduring by being anchored in world opinion. There are good reasons for scepticism about the "fading of anarchy" and some of the other more heroic tasks often assigned to global civil society. Nevertheless, the fact that an entire category of weaponry, widely used by armies around the world, has been banned from the arsenals of most of the world's states following negotiations of astounding rapidity suggests that world politics has begun to change since the Cold War in ways that we are only beginning to intimate. The Ottawa process provides reason to believe that global civil society is a basic ingredient of this change.

Notes

1. This chapter began as part of a research project under the umbrella of the Center for Negotiation and Dispute Resolution at Carleton University, funded by the Government of Canada, Department of Foreign Affairs and International Trade. It benefited from a

series of round tables and deliberative polls conducted during the Mine Action Forum in Ottawa that accompanied the signing of the convention on 2–4 December 1997, as well as an Ottawa Process Forum on 5 December 1997 attended by over 200 representatives from states and NGOs around the world. The author is grateful to Bob Lawson, senior policy adviser in the Mine Action Team in Canada's Department of Foreign Affairs, for sharing his detailed knowledge of the Ottawa process, to David Long, and to Brian Tomlin for comments on an earlier draft.

2. R. B. J. Walker, "Social Movements/World Politics", *Millennium: Journal of International Studies* 23, no. 3 (1994), p. 669.

3. Martin Shaw, "Civil Society and Global Politics: Beyond a Social Movements Approach", *Millennium: Journal of International Studies* 23, no. 3 (1994), p. 655.

4. This contention was reiterated in Jody Williams and Stephen Goose, "The International Campaign to Ban Landmines", in Maxwell A. Cameron, Robert Lawson, and Brian W. Tomlin, eds, *To Walk Without Fear: The Global Movement to Ban Landmines* (Toronto: Oxford University Press, 1998), p. 47.

5. Kenneth N. Waltz, *Theory of International Politics* (Reading, MA: Addison-Wesley, 1979).

6. Ronnie D. Lipschutz, "Reconstructing World Politics: The Emergence of Global Civil Society", *Millennium: Journal of International Studies* 21, no. 3 (1992), p. 390.

7. Shaw, note 3 above, p. 650.

8. See Lipschutz, note 6 above.

9. Shaw, note 2 above, pp. 655–656.

10. *Ibid.*, p. 663.

11. *Ibid.*, p. 664.

12. Robert G. Gard, Jr "The Military Utility of Anti-Personnel Mines", pp. 140–144, Alex Vines, "The Crisis of Anti-Personnel Mines", pp. 127–130, and Stuart Maslen, "The Role of the International Committee of the Red Cross", pp. 87–89, in Cameron, Lawson, and Tomlin, note 4 above.

13. Alluding to a substantial literature on cooperation, much of which has its roots in Kenneth A. Oye, ed., *Cooperation Under Anarchy* (Princeton, NJ: Princeton University Press, 1986).

14. Richard Price, "Reversing the Gun Sights: Transnational Civil Society Targets Land Mines", *International Organization* 52, no. 3 (Summer 1998), p. 627.

15. David Held, *Democracy and the Global Order* (Stanford: Stanford University Press, 1995), pp. 267–286, and "How to Rule the World", *New Statesman*, 29 August 1997, p. 8.

16. Guillermo O'Donnell, "Horizontal Accountability in New Democracies", *Journal of Democracy* 9, no. 3 (1998), p. 117.

17. The convention is reproduced in the Appendix to Cameron, Lawson, and Tomlin, note 4 above, pp. 464–478. For a detailed analysis of the treaty by three of the legal experts who helped draft it, see Thomas Hajnoczi, Thomas Desch, and Deborah Chatsis, "The Ban Treaty", in *ibid.*, pp. 292–313.

18. Letter from International Campaign to Ban Land-mines, *Landmine Monitor*, 31 December 1998.

19. Government of Canada, *One Year Later: Is the Ottawa Convention Making a Difference?* (Ottawa: Department of Foreign Affairs and International Trade, 1998), pp. 2–3.

20. Shaw, note 3 above, p. 650.

21. Her current title is International Ambassador for the ICBL.

22. Shaw, note 3 above, p. 650.

23. *Ibid.*, p. 655.

24. Jody Williams, "Land Mines: Dealing with the Environmental Impact", *Environment and Security* 1, no. 2 (1997), pp. 107–108. In a seminar with Jody Williams and Stephen

Goose at Carleton University, Ottawa, 3 November 1997, Williams stated that the Gulf War had a profound impact on her decision to shift attention from Central American solidarity to work on the humanitarian consequences of war. Perhaps Shaw's claim that the Gulf War "produced only brief intimations of anti-war movements of the kind seen in previous Western wars" (see Shaw, note 3 above, p. 664) should be placed in the context of Albert O. Hirschman's principle of the conservation and mutation of social energy: failures of collective action can lead to later success if the actors involved draw upon the lessons of previous mistakes. See Albert O. Hirschman, "The Principle of Conservation and Mutation of Social Energy", in Sheldon Annis and Peter Hakim, eds, *Direct to the Poor: Grassroots Development in Latin America* (Boulder, CO and London: Lynne Rienner, 1988), pp. 7–14.

25. Williams and Goose, note 4 above, p. 31.
26. Unless otherwise indicated, the views cited in this section are based on comments made by delegates in the Mines Action Forum held in Ottawa, 2–4 December 1997, either in the organized panels or focus groups conducted by Ekos Research Associates, or in the Ottawa Process Forum sponsored by the Government of Canada, Department of Foreign Affairs and International Trade, held on 5 December 1997. The results were published in a report, entitled *"A Global Ban on Landmines"*, *Survey of Participants: Technical Report* (Ottawa: Ekos Research Associates, 1997), which is available upon request. In the case of direct quotes, the anonymity of the delegates has been preserved because they spoke on a not-for-attribution basis.
27. Brian W. Tomlin, "On a Fast Track to a Ban: The Canadian Policy Process", in Cameron, Lawson, and Tomlin, note 4 above, p. 201.
28. Maxwell A. Cameron, "Democratization of Foreign Policy: The Ottawa Process as a Model", in Cameron, Lawson, and Tomlin, note 4 above, pp. 430–441.
29. The Japanese government shifted in response to international rather than domestic pressures. The defence establishment opposed the ban, but the Foreign Minister favoured it on the grounds that Japan should not spend overseas development assistance on mine clearance in places like Cambodia but not support the ban. The Prime Minister sided with his Foreign Minister.
30. Robert Lawson, "Toward a New Multilateralism: Canada and the Landmine Ban", *Between the Headlines* 54, no. 4 (1997), p. 21.
31. For an introduction to this voluminous literature, see Bruce Russett, *Grasping the Democratic Peace* (Princeton, NJ: Princeton University Press, 1993).
32. Interview, Ottawa, 6 January 1998.
33. Jessica Tuchman Mathews, "Redefining Security", in Robert J. Art and Robert Jervis, eds, *International Politics: Enduring Concepts and Contemporary Issues* (New York: Harper Collins, 1992), p. 556.
34. Interview with land-mine ban activist, Vancouver, 17 September 1999.
35. For a brief discussion of these proposals, see Volker Rittberger and Tanja Brühl, "Global Governance: Civil Society and the UN", *Work in Progress: A Review of the Research Activities of the United Nations University* 15, no. 3 (Summer 1999), pp. 7–8.
36. Lorne Gunter, "Whose World is It, Anyway?", *National Post*, 28 August 1999, p. B7.
37. Shaw, note 3 above, p. 664.
38. The role of "powerful people" – policy entrepreneurs as well as articulate and active citizens – is stressed in the literature on global civil society. See James N. Rosenau, *Turbulence in World Politics: A Theory of Change and Continuity* (Princeton, NJ: Princeton University Press, 1990), p. 333–387.
39. M. J. Peterson, "Transnational Activity, International Society and World Politics", *Millennium: Journal of International Relations* 21, no. 3 (1992), p. 387.
40. Shaw, note 3 above.

6

The UN, NGOs, and the land-mines initiative: An Australian perspective

William Maley

In December 1997, Australia was one of the states which signed the Convention on the Prohibition of the Use, Stockpiling, Production, and Transfer of Anti-Personnel Mines and Their Destruction. Australia's signature was accompanied by a ringing denunciation of anti-personnel mines by the Australian Foreign Minister, Alexander Downer, who travelled to Ottawa to sign on Australia's behalf. Yet just a few weeks before the signing ceremony, Australia's attitude to the treaty appeared distinctly ambivalent. In contrast to states which had hastened to board the "Ottawa express", Australia reacted to the Ottawa process with a high degree of caution, avowedly for fear that it would undermine the possibility of a more inclusive (if less extensive) set of prohibitions on anti-personnel mines negotiated within the Conference on Disarmament established by the UN General Assembly in 1978.

Yet ultimately, Australia *did* sign the Ottawa Treaty. The aim in this chapter is to investigate why this was the case, with a view to shedding light somewhat more widely, if indirectly, on the nature of mobilization and agenda-setting in contemporary world politics. The chapter is divided into five sections. The first offers an overview of pertinent elements of the Australian political process. The second looks at the management of foreign policy in Australia. The third examines the emergence of pressures within Australia for a ban on anti-personnel mines, and looks at some of the venues in which the case was argued. The fourth traces the evolution of government policy towards anti-personnel mines, and identifies key moments at which the direction of debate shifted. The fifth offers some conclusions, of which the central is that Australia's signature was the product of a creative coalition of forces whose efforts flourished in part because of the specific nature of the issue in point.

The context of the Australian political system

Foreign policy decisions in Australia are taken in a context defined in part by the character of Australia's constitutional system.[1] Australia has a federal system of government with a bicameral Commonwealth Parliament consisting of a House of Representatives comprising 148 members elected from single-member constituencies, and a Senate comprising 76 senators, 72 chosen in equal numbers from each of the six original states, with a further four from the two mainland territories. The Australian Constitution, originally enacted by the British Parliament as part of the Commonwealth of Australia Constitution Act 1900, functions as fundamental law and in general divides legislative responsibilities between the Commonwealth (or central) government and the governments of the various states, which enjoy law-making powers in the areas not specifically granted to the Commonwealth. As the story unfolds, the Australian states were not significant actors, and will not be discussed further. What is pertinent from the point of view of this analysis is rather the fact that the Constitution specifically grants the Commonwealth Parliament law-making power in respect to two areas of great relevance to interstate relations. First, s. 51(vi) of the Constitution grants law-making power with respect to "The naval and military defense of the Commonwealth and of the several States, and the control of the forces to execute and maintain the laws of the Commonwealth". Second, s. 51(xxix) grants law-making power with respect to "External affairs".

The Constitution provides not for a complete separation of powers, but for a system of responsible government. Ministers are drawn from that party or coalition which can command the support of a majority in the House of Representatives,[2] and s. 64 of the Constitution provides that "no Minister of State shall hold office for a longer period than three months unless he is or becomes a senator or a member of the House of Representatives". As in the UK, the most senior ministers make up the Cabinet, and the ministry as a whole is headed by the Prime Minister, on whose advice the Governor-General of Australia – representing the Queen of Australia – acts as long as the government retains the confidence of the Parliament.

The Australian system is robustly pluralistic, with high levels of competition between political parties.[3] "Politics in Australia," one observer goes so far as to say, "are party politics."[4] The Australian party system at the Commonwealth level, the broad outlines of which have been securely in place for over half a century, pits a coalition of the Liberal and National Parties against the Australian Labor Party, with a range of smaller parties also offering candidates for election. The coalition formed the government from 1949 to 1972, 1975 to 1983, and since 1996; Labor ruled from 1972 to 1975 and from 1983 to 1996. The system is entrenched by relatively high levels of socialized party identification and by compulsory voting. However, in the Senate, a system of proportional representation permits minor party candidates to secure election, and groups as diverse as the post-materialist Australian Democrats (who currently hold the balance of power) and the extremist One Nation party have succeeded in winning Senate seats.[5] The difficulty faced by major parties in securing a Senate majority offers considerable scope to minor parties to bargain for the adoption of elements of their own platforms by the government of the day. The ideological differences between the major parties should not be exaggerated: their need to appeal to "middle Australia" as well as to their core support bases discourages hot-headed politics. Nonetheless, for electoral purposes they often attempt "product differentiation", and this can assist interest groups in pursuing their objectives, although it also means that it is unrealistic to expect parties to show a high degree of consistency.[6]

In addition to political parties, Australian political life is enlivened by a rich array of altruistic and non-altruistic interest and pressure groups. In the sphere of humanitarian action, many take the form of non-governmental organizations which conceive public advocacy to be a legitimate part of their activities. For example, aid agencies such as AUSTCARE, World Vision Australia, CARE Australia, Community Aid Abroad, the Australian Red Cross Society, and Save the Children regularly circulate material to their donors which highlights the nature of the problems which the agencies' activities are designed to address. This dissemination of material can assist the mobilization of opinion around particular issues. Their efforts are augmented by those of bodies more directly concerned with advocacy, such as the Medical Association for the Prevention of War and the Refugee Council of Australia, and by the "umbrella organization" of aid agencies, the Australian Council for Overseas Aid (ACFOA). However, it is important to note that many interest groups view their areas of concern in expansive terms. Thus, the Returned and Services League (RSL) is concerned not simply with the welfare of veterans, but also with issues of contemporary defence policy, while Registered Engineers for Disaster Relief (RedR) can turn their attention to any matters which potentially affect the safety and security of their staff in the field.

A point which is critical to note is that organizations of this nature tend to enjoy a high level of respect from the community at large, in sharp contrast to political parties. While it would be an exaggeration to say that this forces parties to "court" such bodies – the NGOs' ability to mobilize votes directly is too weak for that – it does have the effect of winning them a degree of access to ministers, MPs and senators which individual members of the public could not so readily secure.

Finally, bureaucratic actors play an important role in the Australian policy process. It is somewhat unusual for ministers, other than in specialized portfolios such as that of the Attorney-General, to have professional expertise directly relevant to their work. They are professional politicians.[7] Most ministers are therefore heavily dependent upon the departments which they head for specialized briefing and advice, and this of course gives power to bureaucrats. This in turn increases the importance of bargaining and conflict within and between bureaucracies as advice to ministers is being shaped. Australian bureaucracies are as marked as any other by turf wars ("where you stand depends on where you sit") and by variations in procedures according to whether decisions to be taken are of a routine, stressed, or crisis variety. However, on many issues of policy there are no obviously "correct" answers, but merely a range of policy options with varying costs and benefits for different people. Some may be more morally defensible than others, but even here there is scope for honest divergence between those whose ethic is utilitarian and those who are concerned to do right irrespective of the consequences.

The complexity of the foreign policy dimension

Australian foreign policy is less a rational statement of coherent objectives, priorities, and means for their realization than the outcome of a complex process of interaction between different actors and agencies. This raggedness tends to be somewhat masked in accounts of the process from the pens of senior bureaucrats and ministers,[8] but it is a reality with which everyone associated with the process rapidly becomes familiar. This dynamic is even more markedly the case when one is talking about issues which straddle a number of portfolios. To turn to the case in point: is the banning of anti-personnel mines an issue of *foreign* policy (given the concern of a number of states to see such a ban brought into effect) to be handled by the Department of Foreign Affairs and Trade; or of *defence* policy (given that the tactical use of anti-personnel mines figured in the standard operating procedures of the Australian Defence Force) to be handled by the Department of Defence; or of *foreign aid* policy (given that scarce overseas aid dollars can be absorbed by the need to clear anti-personnel mines before other aid projects can be attempted) to be handled by the Australian Agency for International Development (AusAID)? The answer is that it is all three, and normally in such circumstances final decisions cannot be taken by any single portfolio minister but must be brought to Cabinet, chaired by the Prime Minister.

Furthermore, decisions relating to such subjects are not as a rule contextualized simply in narrow terms of Australian preference, but also in terms of Australia's security relations with alliance partners, most importantly the USA. This alliance relationship is an unusually powerful shaper of policy: as Hugh Smith has observed, "The Departments of Defence and Foreign Affairs and Trade, in particular, tend to be 'closed shops' as a consequence of their exclusive access to information, possession of expertise and need for confidentiality in dealing with foreign governments."[9]

One area in which there has been something of a breach in the wall of silence in recent years relates to the ratification of treaties. As a matter of common law, the signing and ratification of a treaty was a prerogative right of the Crown, which under s. 61 of the Australian Constitution formed part of the "executive power of the Commonwealth", to be exercised by the Governor-General. However, the mere ratification of a treaty, while creating obligations under *international* law, does not as a rule give rise to obligations which are enforceable as a matter of *domestic* law.[10] For this, further legislation may be required, and this opens the way for Parliament to become involved in the treaty process. As noted earlier, s. 51(xxix) of the Constitution permits the Commonwealth Parliament to legislate with respect to "External affairs". Until the early 1980s, judicial interpretation of the Constitution by the High Court of Australia held that for a treaty to be implemented domestically, it had to deal with a subject matter which was *itself* a matter of "external affairs". However, in 1983 a majority of the High Court abandoned this requirement, and ruled instead that it was sufficient that a treaty be ratified in good faith for its subject matter then to be implemented.[11] In a subsequent case, it was held that treaty obligations could be taken into account in interpreting domestic law.[12]

These developments created great apprehension on the part of the Australian states that the treaty process would be used as a "back-door" route either to alter the effects of Australian law or to expand the powers of the Commonwealth at the states' expense, and prompted the Liberal and National Parties to commit themselves to the establishment of a process by which treaties could be reviewed *before* they were ratified and thus became binding upon Australia under international law. The result was the establishment on 30 May 1996 of the Joint Standing Committee on Treaties. It is now general practice that treaties be tabled in Parliament, together with a "national interest analysis", at least 15 days before any action is taken to give them binding effect. The committee routinely invites public submissions and holds hearings on such treaties, and, as we shall shortly see, such hearings have become an important avenue by which groups can bypass established bureaucracies in voicing their concerns to legislators, or challenge the positions adopted by bureaucratic witnesses.

Amidst all these bureaucratic and domestic political considerations, Australia's relationship with the United Nations is not in itself a major factor shaping individual foreign policy decisions. On the one hand, Australia was a founding member of the world body, and Dr H. V. Evatt – Australian Minister for External Affairs from 1941 to 1949 and President of the UN General Assembly in 1948 – was a vigorous participant in the early life of the organization, as was Paul Hasluck, who subsequently held the same ministerial portfolio.[13] A great deal of Australia's diplomatic activity is focused on multilateral interactions with other permanent missions to the United Nations in New York, and UN offices in Geneva and Vienna. But on the other hand, no particular authority is attached to UN representations or requests for commitments emanating from the UN Secretariat.

Senator Gareth Evans, Australian Foreign Minister from 1988 to 1996, articulated an interest for Australia to be viewed as a "good international citizen", and sought to give effect to this with a volume of good advice to the world on issues of global order.[14] However, this did not prevent him from pursuing a distinctively Australian position on issues of perceived strategic importance – for example in accommodating Indonesia's annexation of East Timor, which Evans described as "irreversible in effect so far as the international community is concerned"[15] – despite the existence of Security Council resolutions of contrary import, such as Resolutions 384 and 389. The disjunction between Australian rhetoric and behaviour may have been one of the factors which contributed to Australia's humiliating failure to win a non-permanent seat on the Security Council in 1996. The value of the United Nations to Australia is rather as a venue through which perceived Australian interests – whether bilateral or multilateral – can be advanced. This applies also to UN fora such as the Conference on Disarmament, in which Australia has been an active player.[16]

Pressures from civil society

Having made these preliminary points, the chapter will now turn to the question of how the issue of anti-personnel land-mines came to engage the attention of elements of civil society in Australia in such a way as to result in a broad campaign for their total abolition. The process was a complex one with a great deal of "grassroots" activity that is impossible to summarize. In the following remarks, the aim is simply to highlight a number of landmark developments which illustrate different forms of constructive political activity that contributed to the campaign.

Australia has long had a diverse range of pressure groups concerned with peace and disarmament, but in the late 1970s and early 1980s land-mines were not at the forefront of their concern. Deriving their agendas largely from European groups that were then extremely active,[17] they focused their attention on nuclear weapons.[18] This was extremely unfortunate, as it diverted the attention of many people of goodwill from the emerging problem of anti-personnel mines at a time when it could have been strangled in its cradle. However, the rationale for the existence of many of these groups was undermined by the collapse of the Soviet system, and most of the remainder were discredited by their tepid response to the Iraqi invasion of Kuwait.[19] Yet this paradoxically had the effect that the groups around which the campaign to ban land-mines crystallized in the 1990s were vastly more reputable than those which had dominated peace and disarmament debates in the previous decade.

The exact date of birth of a "campaign" in Australia against anti-personnel mines is difficult to identify, for different agencies initially campaigned on their own, and only with the passage of time did they begin to act concertedly. Nonetheless, it is clear that the lead in highlighting the problem of anti-personnel mines was taken by NGOs. Aid agencies in the early 1990s were in no doubt that anti-personnel mines threatened the security not only of aid workers in previously war-torn societies, but more importantly of the civilian populations whom they aimed to assist. An important early development was a visit to Australia in November 1993 by Jody Williams, at the time coordinator of the Land-mines Campaign of the VVAF (Vietnam Veterans of America Foundation), who spoke at a conference at Parliament House organized by the Human Rights Council of Australia and Community Aid Abroad entitled "Land-mines, A Human Rights Crisis". In December 1994, at Parliament House, Senator Stephen Loosley, Chair of the Joint Standing Committee on Foreign Affairs, Defence, and Trade launched a book on anti-personnel land-mines, and Abdul Rahman Sahak, a multiple amputee and President of the Afghan Disabled Society, presented the senator with an AUSTCARE petition calling for a land-mines ban.[20] Concerted NGO activities on a large scale began in 1995, with the focus of attention being a "national day of awareness" on 28 August. In connection with this event, Rae McGrath, founder of the Mines Advisory Group, took part in a panel discussion hosted by the Peace Research Centre at the Australian National University.[21] This "day of awareness" involved a range of activities to highlight public awareness of the issue, through the circulation of petitions (signed by 243,000 Australians) and the organizing of street theatre. Others agencies engaged in more direct forms of lobbying: ACFOA coordinated a "lobbying blitz" on 19 September 1995 in which teams of volunteers furnished with detailed background material on anti-personnel mines met with ministers and other MPs and senators to press the case for a total ban.

From 1993, Sister Patricia Pak Poy served as coordinator of the Australian Network of the International Campaign to Ban Land-mines. The choice was an inspired one. Sister Pak Poy, a Sister of Mercy who had studied the effects of land-mines on Cambodian refugees while working on secondment to the Mercy Refugee Service in Thailand, proved capable of dealing constructively not only with the (often quite radical) NGO workers at the grassroots of the campaign, but also with the (often quite conservative) officials and army officers addressing the issue from varying bureaucratic perspectives. She rapidly developed an enviable degree of technical expertise with respect not only to the various types of anti-personnel mines, but to the various types of legal instrument that might be used to regulate them. It is a tribute to her skills that she was eventually to be included as an NGO representative in official delegations to the First Review Conference of the States Parties of the Inhumane Weapons Convention (in Geneva in 1995), the continuation of that conference (in Vienna and Geneva in 1996), and finally the 1997 Oslo diplomatic conference that finalized the text of the Ottawa Treaty. Sister Pak Poy was also deft in lobbying in the region: she secured wide regional attendance at a major colloquium in Sydney in July 1997, and at a conference in November 1997 in Fiji she brought together an influential network of activists from Pacific island states who then successfully lobbied their home governments to sign the Ottawa Treaty.

This highlights a broader factor which worked in favour of the campaign, namely its ability to develop and mobilize expertise of a type which could trump the claims to expertise of bureaucratic opponents of a total ban. Many of the issues involved in the campaign were quite straightforward – the horrific nature of the injuries to which anti-personnel mine blasts give rise, the dubious legitimacy in moral and legal terms of weapons which are ultimately victim-activated, and the long-term menace posed by anti-personnel mines in war-torn societies – and to the extent that more complex issues of military tactics and legal drafting arose in the course of debate, there was as much expertise at the disposal of the critics as of the defenders. An important development was the emergence of a range of scholarly works on anti-personnel mines,[22] with a study on the military utility of land-mines commissioned by the International Committee of the Red Cross proving especially useful for lobbyists.[23] Also of value, albeit somewhat later, was the final declaration of participants at the Asian Regional Seminar for Military and Political Experts organized in Manila in July 1997 by the International Committee of the Red Cross in cooperation with the Philippine Department of Foreign Affairs and the Philippine Red Cross Society. The signatories to the declaration, including senior serving and retired generals from a number of different countries, as well as academics in the area of strategic studies, argued in detail that in "most conflicts, the appalling humanitarian consequences of the use of anti-personnel mines have far outweighed their military utility".[24]

The impact of such expertise was strikingly apparent during the inquiry of the Joint Standing Committee on Treaties into Amended Protocol II to the Inhumane Weapons Convention. There could be few better illustrations of "deliberative democracy" at work.[25] Because there was bipartisan support for the ratification of the protocol, the hearings instead became a forum in which further steps to be taken could be canvassed by the witnesses and those MPs and senators who were exposed to their views. Apart from witnesses provided by government departments, submissions and testimony came from ACFOA, the International Committee of the Red Cross, the Australian Red Cross Society, AUSTCARE, Caritas Australia, the Medical Association for the Prevention of War, the Australian Network of the International Campaign to Ban Land-mines, and the Returned and Services League; this writer testified as a private individual.

The release of the committee's report vindicated the lobbyists' efforts: it recommended that "Australia destroy its stockpile of anti-personnel landmines, except for a small number to be retained for training purposes to ensure that the Australian Defence Force retains its skills" and that "Australia prepare for consideration at the December 1997 meeting in Canada a proposal for the creation of an agreed international timetable for the destruction of anti-personnel land-mines of all nations".[26] This was a notable result in that the committee had heard as witnesses not simply NGO representatives, but also energetic defenders of the military utility of anti-personnel mines such as Colonel Geoff Pearce, Director of Engineers (Army). The defenders' arguments had been weighed in the balance and found wanting, and the verdict was contained in an official report to the Commonwealth Parliament.

The response of the Labor and Liberal-National governments

These, then, were the kinds of pressure to which the state was exposed from various elements of civil society. What paths did the state take on its road to Ottawa? In addressing this question, it is useful to draw a distinction between the approach of the Labor government up to March 1996, and the approach thereafter of the Liberal-National Party coalition.

For the Labor Party, anti-personnel land-mines were never a high priority, although a number of its policies addressed the issue in one way or another. In 1989, the Hawke government agreed to contribute Australian military personnel to the UN Mine Clearance Training Team (UNMCTT) for Afghanistan, but in 1993 the Keating government decided to withdraw the contingent. The decision, taken by Defence Minister Robert Ray, was somewhat casually endorsed by the office of Foreign Minister Senator Evans, but by the time the implications fully dawned on Senator Evans he was tied to a position of acceptance from which he could not extract himself. The author has elsewhere examined this decision in considerable detail, and will not repeat that analysis here.[27] However, the decision did attract some wider critical attention. In a hearing of the Defence Sub-Committee of the Joint Standing Committee on Foreign Affairs, Defence, and Trade, witnesses from the Defence Department were sharply interrogated by committee members over the reasons for the decision, and did not acquit themselves with particular distinction. Furthermore, disgruntled voices from within the Australian Defence Force who regarded the testimony of the official witnesses as at best misleading were able to share their concern with committee members through a later hearing, and their concerns were reflected in the committee's final report, which concluded that "Australia's 'good international citizen' image has been somewhat tarnished by its withdrawal of support of UNMCTT".[28] This episode was important because it exposed to members of the Commonwealth Parliament that the façade of a clear official policy masked a swirling diversity of perspectives within the Defence Department and other spheres of government.

Further divisions surfaced in time broadly between those (in both the Defence and Foreign Affairs Departments) who saw the issue of anti-personnel mines as a military issue to be addressed by arms control, and those (in both the Defence and Foreign Affairs Departments) who saw the issue as a humanitarian issue to be addressed through norms of international humanitarian law.[29] For the former, the 1995–1996 negotiations which resulted in the drafting of Amended Protocol II to the Inhumane Weapons Convention were a step forward, while for the latter they offered a weak and inadequate response to a problem of desperate urgency. Yet while these schools of thought were undoubtedly gripped by differing senses of urgency, they also had different approaches to the management of the problem. The "arms controllers" in general favoured either "taming" anti-personnel mines (through restrictions on the use of lower-tech "dumb" mines) on the assumption that states such as Australia would be responsible users, or laboriously building consensus for a ban that the Conference on Disarmament could then ratify. Some of them at least retained an image of war as conflict between institutionalized standing armies. The "norm-builders" for the most part were scornful of the possibility of taming a weapon which remained victim-activated, regarded the Conference on Disarmament as altogether too slow and unreliable to offer an adequate solution to the landmines problem, and were alert to the wider humanitarian consequences of the transformation of war.[30]

The change of government in March 1996 brought an immediate breath of fresh air. On 15 April 1996 the Foreign Affairs Minister Alexander Downer and the Defence Minister Ian McLachlan jointly announced "support for a global ban on the production, stockpiling, use, and transfer of anti-personnel land-mines and a unilateral suspension on their operational use by the Australian Defence Force".[31] With the benefit of hindsight, the statement was a development of enormous importance: from this point onwards, the debate became one about means rather than ends. However, the scope for debate about means remained wide, and this debate was to dominate Australian discussion until almost the eve of the Ottawa diplomatic conference. The sheer speed with which the Ottawa process took off left Australian officials flustered and flabbergasted,[32] and not a few resented the fact that Canadian Foreign Minister Lloyd Axworthy's October 1996 call to states to return in a year's time to sign a ban treaty took them completely by surprise. Particularly distressing was the fact that the USA in May 1996 had identified the Conference on Disarmament as its preferred forum for action: this confronted the Australian government with the risk of offending a friendly government (the USA or the Canadians) no matter what step it took – never a position comfortable for the professional diplomat. The official Australian response was to sit on the fence for as long as possible, arguing the case for using the Conference on Disarmament but not actually rejecting the Ottawa process.

This position was apparent at the July 1997 colloquium at Sydney University.[33] The government's equivocal stance was presented by John Griffin, a polished, witty, and thoroughly professional spokesman. However, it was undermined in off-the-record interventions by others connected to government, and while some activists present wanted to publicize these divisions, it was put to them persuasively (not least by Professor Ramesh Thakur, who chaired the conference) that this could only have the effect of disabling those within bureaucracy who were in effect pressing the case for the Ottawa process. In another respect the activists again proved themselves politically sophisticated. The opposition spokesman on foreign affairs, Laurie Brereton, offered a *mea culpa* for his party's inadequate response to the issue when in government, and when the spokesperson for the Australian Democrats, Senator Vicki Bourne, proposed moving in the Senate a resolution supporting the Ottawa process, the suggestion was greeted with some enthusiasm, since such a motion would have had an excellent chance of passing. However, once it was pointed out that this tactic could lead to otherwise-sympathetic government senators having to *oppose* the motion since the government remained officially uncommitted, the idea was quietly dropped. As a result, when the government ultimately agreed to sign the Ottawa Treaty, it did not need to fear loss of face by doing so.

After the Sydney meeting, the government signed the Brussels declaration, and subsequently took part in the Oslo diplomatic conference that drafted the Ottawa Treaty. But it was only on 17 November 1997 that the Foreign and Defence Ministers finally announced that the government had decided to sign the Ottawa Treaty. The statement issued by the ministers described it as "a difficult decision for the government", and argued that the next step would be "to get negotiations under way as soon as possible in the Conference on Disarmament on an agreement to ban transfers and exports of land-mines as a way of complementing the Ottawa Treaty".[34] The story behind the final decision to sign is an interesting one. Even after the Oslo conference concluded, Australia's position was uncertain, with "norm-builders" and "arms controllers" still at odds within the bureaucracy, although with the latter increasingly on the defensive. In October, however, the Australian Prime Minister, John Howard, travelled to Edinburgh for the Commonwealth Heads of Government Meeting (CHOGM). Prime Minister Howard took with him a proposal for an international trade and investment access facility, and also had strong views on the form which any declaration on gas emissions and climate change should take. He raised them in a meeting with Canadian Prime Minister Jean Chrétien, whose support for Australia's position he sought. Prime Minister Chrétien in turn sought Australia's support for the Ottawa Treaty. Through this, the deadlock in Canberra was broken. Once an Australian Prime Minister makes a commitment to a foreign head of government, it normally takes more than bureaucratic politics to turn back the tide.

Conclusions

What conclusions are we to draw from this case study? There are five that seem to be of importance. The first four relate to the circumstances that militated in favour of successful lobbying, while the fifth is concerned more with the salience of the issue as a whole.

First, the issue of anti-personnel land-mines was one which lent itself extremely well to the organizing of a campaign of concerted action. The questions involved were relatively simple and straightforward. Furthermore, they were ones over which diverse agencies could cooperate. In large part they were insulated from the struggle for resources which often turns potential partners into competitors, and Australia was not touched by the tensions which saw the International Campaign to Ban Land-mines come under attack from disgruntled former deminers who failed to see that the campaign actually improved the climate in which funds for demining could be solicited.[35]

Second, the Australian example points to the importance of *maturity* in campaigning. The agencies involved in the campaign approached their lobbying with a high degree of professionalism and expertise. In general they did not seek to embarrass political and bureaucratic actors, but to build a case which would be impregnable in the face of counterattack. Such counterattack as did come (for example when a senior military defender of anti-personnel mines spoke in abusive terms of the International Committee of the Red Cross at a seminar organized by the Institution of Engineers, Australia) proved counterproductive.

Third, the Australian case points to the importance of insulating an issue of this type from domestic party politics. At a number of points the agitational efforts of campaigners would have been undermined had an injection of partisanship forced basically sympathetic members and senators to line up behind the less-than-satisfactory positions to which various governments of the day were committed. That this was avoided meant that there were no serious issues of "loss of face" to overcome in moving towards the ultimate position of support for a total ban.

Fourth, the case points to the virtues of building extensive coalitions. Australian decisions were positively shaped not simply by those working for a ban from outside government, but also by those working for a ban from inside government. The mixed messages even from different Defence Department circles were clearly audible to those with acute political hearing. But beyond that, the international governmental connections upon which campaigners could draw were a real source of bargaining authority. The role of the Canadian government in legitimating the arguments put by Australian campaigners was extremely important (and amongst the defenders of anti-personnel mines, bitterly resented). However, in quieter ways governments such as South Africa also played a significant role in increasing pressure on Australia. Since these governments were officially Australia's "friends", and protected from direct criticism by considerations of protocol, their activities provided a kind of protection for the Australian activists who were promoting the same position. And as noted earlier, ultimately the intervention of the Canadian Prime Minister was to play a decisive role. The emulation effect of which

Richard Price has written[36] undoubtedly came into play as far as Australia was concerned.

Yet we need to draw a fifth, and in some ways more sobering, conclusion. Ultimately lobbying proved successful because the need to retain anti-personnel mines was simply not seen by civilian political leadership as a fundamental aim of policy. Military opinion on the value of such mines was at best ambivalent, and with tactics increasingly emphasizing the need for mobility and flexibility, the mine as a conventional weapon was decreasingly relevant. There was no "core national interest" to be served in retaining mines, and they had few ardent defenders. The US alliance was not at threat from an Australian signature on the Ottawa Treaty, and there were no domestic costs whatsoever to be incurred by the decision: it was unlikely that a single Australian would shift his or her vote in protest that the Conference on Disarmament was overtaken by the "Ottawa express". All in all, the decision to relinquish anti-personnel mines was *not* in the final analysis a difficult one to take, despite the ministers' statement. It would be a grave error to believe that other issues of concern to NGOs will be configured in such a fortunate fashion.

Notes

1. For more detail on the Australian constitutional system, see David W. Lovell, Ian McAllister, William Maley, and Chandran Kukathas, *The Australian Political System* (Melbourne: Addison Wesley Longman, 1998).
2. On the character of responsible government in the Australian system, see Chandran Kukathas, David W. Lovell, and William Maley, *The Theory of Politics: An Australian Perspective* (Melbourne: Longman Cheshire, 1990), pp. 147–169.
3. See generally Ian McAllister, *Political Behaviour: Citizens, Parties and Elites in Australia* (Melbourne: Longman Cheshire, 1992); Brian Graetz and Ian McAllister, *Dimensions of Australian Society* (Melbourne: Macmillan, 1994); and Ian Marsh, *Beyond the Two Party System: Political Representation, Economic Competitiveness and Australian Politics* (Cambridge: Cambridge University Press, 1995).
4. Dean Jaensch, *The Australian Party System* (Sydney: Allen & Unwin, 1983), p. 10.
5. On the Australian Democrats, see John Warhurst, ed., *Keeping the Bastards Honest: The Australian Democrats' First Twenty Years* (Sydney: Allen & Unwin, 1997); on One Nation, see Chandran Kukathas and William Maley, *The Last Refuge: Hard and Soft Hansonism in Contemporary Australian Politics* (Sydney: Issue Analysis no. 4, Centre for Independent Studies, 16 September 1998).
6. See William Maley, "Ethical Actors in Australian Foreign Policy: Political Parties, Pressure Groups and Social Movements", in Paul Keal, ed., *Ethics and Foreign Policy* (Sydney: Allen & Unwin, 1992), pp. 81–97.
7. Patrick Weller and Michelle Grattan, *Can Ministers Cope? Australian Federal Ministers at Work* (Melbourne: Hutchinson, 1981), p. 34.
8. See, as examples, Alan Watt, *The Evolution of Australian Foreign Policy 1938–1965* (Cambridge: Cambridge University Press, 1968); and Gareth Evans and Bruce Grant,

Australia's Foreign Relations in the World of the 1990s (Melbourne: Melbourne University Press, 1995).

9. Hugh Smith, "Politics of Foreign Policy", in F. A. Mediansky, ed., *Australian Foreign Policy into the New Millennium* (Sydney: Macmillan, 1997), pp. 13–32 at p. 23.

10. *Attorney-General for Canada v Attorney-General for Ontario* [1937] AC 326 at 347.

11. *The Commonwealth v Tasmania* (1983) 46 ALR 625.

12. *Minister for Immigration and Ethnic Affairs v Ah Tin Teoh* (1995) 128 ALR 353.

13. See H. V. Evatt, *The United Nations* (Melbourne: Oxford University Press, 1948); Paul Hasluck, *Workshop of Security* (Melbourne, F. W. Cheshire, 1948). On Australian relations with the United Nations more generally, see Norman Harper and David Sissons, *Australia and the United Nations* (New York: Manhattan Publishing, 1959); Alex C. Castles, *Australia and the United Nations* (Melbourne: Longman Australia, 1974).

14. Gareth Evans, *Cooperating for Peace: The Global Agenda for the 1990s and Beyond* (Sydney: Allen & Unwin, 1993).

15. See Heike Krieger, ed., *East Timor and the International Community: Basic Documents* (Cambridge: Cambridge University Press, 1997), p. 337.

16. See Ramesh Thakur, "Arms Control", in Mediansky, note 9 above, pp. 130–161.

17. See Philip A. G. Sabin, *The Third World War Scare in Britain: A Critical Analysis* (London: Macmillan, 1986); Clive Rose, *Campaigns Against Western Defence: NATO's Adversaries and Critics* (London: Macmillan, 1986).

18. For a striking indication of these groups' priorities, see Michael Denborough, ed., *Australia and Nuclear War* (Canberra: Croom Helm, 1983). For a critique, see William Maley, "Armageddon in the Antipodes", *Quadrant* 28, no. 10 (October 1984), pp. 81–83.

19. See William Maley, "The Gulf and the Australian Peace Movement", *Quadrant* 35, no. 10 (October 1991), pp. 41–44.

20. See *War of the Mines*, Canberra: Research and Information Series no. 3, Australian Council for Overseas Aid, May 1995.

21. Somewhat more comically, Mr McGrath was advised to "f ... off" by a minister in the Keating Labor government whose views on anti-personnel mines he had forcefully challenged during a meeting from which he and an accompanying World Vision journalist were escorted by this writer. This was a very interesting illustration of the hypersensitivity of the then government to criticism of its position on anti-personnel mines, something which will be returned to later in this chapter.

22. See *Landmines: A Deadly Legacy* (New York: Human Rights Watch, 1993); Rae McGrath, *Landmines: Legacy of Conflict* (Oxford: Oxfam Publications, 1994); Paul Davies, *War of the Mines: Cambodia, Landmines and the Impoverishment of a Nation* (London: Pluto Press, 1994); Kevin M. Cahill, *Clearing the Fields: Solutions to the Global Land Mines Crisis* (New York: Basic Books, 1995); Shawn Roberts and Jody Williams, *After the Guns Fall Silent: The Enduring Legacy of Landmines* (Washington, DC: Vietnam Veterans of America Foundation, 1995).

23. *Anti-personnel Landmines: Friend or Foe? A Study of the Military Use and Effectiveness of Anti-personnel Mines* (Geneva: ICRC, 1996).

24. Final Declaration of Participants, Regional Seminar for Asian Military and Strategic Studies Experts on Anti-personnel Landmines: What Future for Asia?, Manila, 23 July 1997.

25. See John Uhr, *Deliberative Democracy in Australia: The Changing Place of Parliament* (Cambridge: Cambridge University Press, 1998).

26. Joint Standing Committee on Treaties, *Restrictions on the Use of Blinding Laser Weapons and Landmines* (Canberra: Australian Government Publishing Service, February 1997), para. 3.137.

27. See William Maley, "Australia and Mine Clearing in Afghanistan", in William Maley, ed., *Dealing with Mines: Strategies for Peacekeepers, Aid Agencies and the International Community* (Canberra: Australian Defence Studies Centre, 1994), pp. 63–75.
28. Joint Standing Committee on Foreign Affairs, Defence, and Trade, *Australia's Participation in Peacekeeping* (Canberra: Australian Government Publishing Service, December 1994), para. 4.35.
29. On this distinction see Ramesh Thakur and William Maley, "The Ottawa Convention on Landmines: A Landmark Humanitarian Treaty in Arms Control?", *Global Governance* 5, no. 3 (July–September 1999), pp. 273–302.
30. See Martin van Creveld, *The Transformation of War* (New York: Free Press, 1991).
31. "Support for Global Ban on Anti-Personnel Landmines", *Insight* 5, no. 5 (24 April 1996), p. 16.
32. For a more detailed synoptic discussion, see John English, "The Ottawa Process: Paths Followed, Paths Ahead", *Australian Journal of International Affairs* 52, no. 2 (July 1998), pp. 121–132.
33. For a report on the conference, see *Towards Ottawa and Beyond* (Sydney: International Campaign to Ban Landmines, 1997).
34. See *Australia to Sign Landmines Ban Treaty and Destroy Stockpiles* (Canberra: FA 139, Department of Foreign Affairs and Trade, 17 November 1997).
35. See Michael Flynn, "Political Minefield", *Bulletin of the Atomic Scientists* 55, no. 2 (March–April 1999), pp. 49–53.
36. Richard Price, "Reversing the Gun Sights: Transnational Civil Society Targets Land Mines", *International Organization* 52, no. 3 (Summer 1998), pp. 613–644.

7

Harnessing social power: State diplomacy and the land-mines issue

Iver B. Neumann[1]

As long as there are States, so there will be national pride, and nothing can be more warranted. But societies can have their pride, not in being the greatest or the wealthiest, but in being the most just, the best organized and in possessing the best moral constitution.[2]

There is nothing new about adding the epithet "new" to diplomacy. It was done in the 1600s, it was done again in the aftermath of the Napoleonic Wars, and once again at the beginning of the century, when Lenin and Wilson broke with the tenets of state-to-state diplomacy by targeting non-state actors like "the people" above the heads of their governments. When, in the aftermath of the Cold War, we have seen the epithet "new" crop up once again, it is in and of itself simply yet another indicator that the shape of the global system and of foreign policy-making are congealing into a new form.

The change in the international system brought about by the end of the Cold War is, however, only one of the ends which we have to take into consideration. The discussion about whether modernity is coming to an end so that we have reached a post-modern stage, or whether it is still an unfulfilled project so that we are living in a late modern age, has grown into one of those festering intellectual debates which easily becomes a goal in itself. Most of the debate has played itself out on the level of theory and meta-theory. Important as these debates may be, the time has now come for scholars of the social to do what sets them apart from philosophers, namely engage with specific social practices in order to ponder whether the changes one can observe are of such a character that the epochal metaphor is warranted.

Diplomacy is often defined as mediation between states. True, diplomacy is first and foremost about mediation. However, any system of suzereign or sovereign actors will be in need of diplomacy. There was dipomacy before the emergence of the European states system, and there will be diplomacy after the modern states system has disappeared. If the point is to discuss changes in diplomatic practice, it is therefore not unproblematical to start off by taking the state as a given, or even to start off by dividing agency into a state and a non-state kind. If the point is to trace changes at the level of the global system – which is constituted by a number of different kinds of actors – and not on the level of the international system of states, then it stands to reason that our starting point must be non-state-centric. And yet the hypothesis that states will not sit back and leave the initiating and agenda-setting sides of politics to others seems highly warranted. Thus, we are in need of at least two kinds of investigations: first, issue-specific and actor-specific studies, and secondly, state-specific studies which investigate changes in the foreign policy process of states. Analyses which are predicated on such a divide still lend themselves to a charge of state-centricity simply because it is the dichotomy state/non-state which is allowed to divide up the production of knowledge, and yet it seems to the writer that we simply do not have access to other perspectives from which to conduct empirical research.

The movement to ban land-mines is one of those cases which lend themselves handily to investigations of how states react when a particular activity involving both other state and non-state actors reaches a threshold where public interest is such that the activity cannot simply be treated according to standard operational procedures. We have here a case which emerges at the end of the Cold War, which involves a plethora of actors, and where the variations in agenda ranking (attention) and policy output are readily observable. John English has characterized it as

a new kind of diplomacy [...] a new texture in the international system where negotiating tables have new players and shapes, where linkages and networks transcend state limits, and even, perhaps, where moral sensibilities have a voice.[3]

There is a literature on the global movement to ban mines, and there are some studies of how states responded to the actions of this movement.[4] However, none of these studies reads state policy symptomatically – that is, not only as a question of the issue at hand, but for the insights state actions in this particular area have to offer into the question of how states as a class of actors are transformed in general terms. It seems apposite, then, to investigate what state responses to the land-mine issue tells us about state transformation today.

This chapter draws up the general outlines of the situation in one small European nation-state which also just happens to be the one the author knows best, namely Norway. It is based on in-depth interviews with central actors in the process, and on participant observation from the vantage point of the policy-planning cell of the Royal Norwegian Ministry of Foreign Affairs (MFA) in the period 1997–1998. Inasmuch as one of the points is to tease out how the actors themselves interpret what it is to perform politics and which place they are occupying in the greater scheme of things, extensive quotations will be used. Following a few introductory remarks about the chosen state, the rest of the chapter sketches the policy process on this issue as it has unfolded over the last decade with a view not to the substance as such, but in order to trace the agencies involved.

The case

Having been a part of Denmark for 400 years, as a result of great-power politics the territory known as Norway was transferred to Sweden in 1814 as a separate political domain with its own constitution. Norway became a sovereign state in 1905, and followed a foreign policy of neutrality until April 1940, when the country was occupied by the Nazis. It shares a border with the Soviet Union/Russia in the high north and was, not unrelatedly, a founding member of NATO.

Norway's social history offers four features which are immediately apposite. First, inasmuch as the local aristocracy was wiped out by the Black Death, which actually first reached Europe by way of the city of Bergen, the Norwegian social structure is somewhat truncated. Secondly, although industrialization was late, it was highly successful when it came, and with the added income from petroleum since the mid-1970s it has made Norway into an affluent society. Thirdly, and growing out of the two former factors, Norway is a highly institutionalized and consensus-based society. Fourthly, there is a humanitarian tradition tied up with Protestant missionary work and humanitarian relief work (for example, the first Commissioner of Refugees of the League of Nations, Fridtjof Nansen, was a Norwegian). One particularly relevant feature of all this to the case at hand is that Norway has a whole plethora of issue- and value-based non-governmental organizations.[5] As they are in varying degrees tied in with the political system, there exists a tightly knit and highly institutionalized network of organizations which is not sealed off from society at large.

The Norwegian Parliament – the Storting – was at one stage a central arena, and thus a word on the party system is merited. A large Labour Party has been in power for most of the post-war period. There is a small Socialist Left Party which harbours a certain intellectual power. Three small centre parties, the Christian People's Party (CPP), the Cenre Party (CP), and the Liberals, worked closely together during the period in question. There are also a Conservative Party and a populist rightist party, neither of which will concern us here. Traditionally, the entire Socialist Left Party and a whole swathe of Labour have taken a keen interest in the South, as has, with more missionary cadences, the Christian People's Party.

There are a number of NGOs with activities in the South, but the "five big ones" are the Norwegian Red Cross, Norwegian Church Aid, Norwegian Save the Children, Norwegian People's Aid, and an umbrella outfit for these four organizations and others known as the Norwegian Refugee Council. One point which must be made here is that the Norwegian People's Aid (NPA), which plays a key role in this story, is part of the workers' movement and has strong filial ties to the Labour Party. It was formed in 1939 as part of the interwar drive by the workers' movement to parallel what they saw as bourgeois civil society organizations (the Red Cross serving as an example at the time). As social democracy took root in the post-war era and state funding grew, it became a standard Norwegian developmental NGO with 125 local divisions and projects in 33 countries. Another much younger and smaller NGO which featured prominently in the initial stages of the process of concern here was the Norwegian Afghanistan Committee, founded in the aftermath of the 1979 Soviet military intervention to do political solidarity and humanitarian relief work.

One last introductory remark regards the state of play in Norwegian foreign policy during the 1980s. This was the decade when the NGOs, and particularly the big five, became integrated into the conduct of Norwegian foreign policy.[6] Having decided to try to adhere to the UN goal of setting aside 1 per cent of its GNP (later GNI – gross national income) for its Southern policy, the state found itself with a need to spend the money somehow. One way of doing this was to channel it through the state directory for aid, NORAD. Another was to donate money to NGOs, and particularly to the five big ones. From 1983 to 1999, annual sums allocated to the NGOs rose from NK350 million to over NK2 billion, which equals around 240 million Euros. Interestingly it was only in the wake of the Norwegian "no" to EU membership in a referendum in autumn 1994 that discussion of these things began to be framed as a question of foreign policy; before that, developmental discourse tended to lead a life of its own. When the issue emerged, it was intimately tied to the question of personnel. Specifically, the politician and then Junior Minister of Foreign Affairs Jan Egeland was attacked for what was considered his overblown interest in new diplomacy, especially in mediation of conflicts, aid work, and, as things have it, his intense interest in landmines. Already as a student of political science, Egeland wrote a MPhil thesis on human rights implementation at the Institute of Peace Research, Oslo.[7] He then went to Geneva to work for the International Committee of the Red Cross (ICRC). His political work centred on developmental issues, but his broadest exposure internationally has been as one of the key facilitators of the Middle East Olso Agreement. He now serves as a special UN envoy to Colombia. In a word, if there is such a thing as a politician of "new diplomacy", he would be it. Consequently, this chapter will begin by demonstrating how Jan Egeland's trajectory from the Red Cross to the Foreign Ministry may be seen as one of those personnel shifts which are indicative of wider structural change.

Playing the operational field: Mine clearance

Here is Egeland's version of how and why he was recruited as an adviser to the Norwegian Foreign Minister, Thorvald Stoltenberg:

Stoltenberg contacted me during his stint as High Commissioner for Refugees in 1989–1990. I think he had seen me on TV, I was the head of international relief and media face of the Red Cross at the time. I did not know him personally, and he did not know me. Later I found out that he had me in mind already when he became Foreign Minister before that; he had discussed it with [his junior minister] Helga Hernes, and she had been positive. I quit my job at the Red Cross and started to pack my bags, but before I had a chance to go, Thorvald was called back to Oslo to become Norwegian Foreign Minister once again. So he turned to me and said, there has been a change of plans, would you like to be my personal adviser at the Foreign Ministry instead? In the beginning, junior ministers were recruited from the ranks of the diplomats. Then it was a woman, and then it was an activist – me. From the very beginning he gave me wide reins, and I more or less continued to do what I had been doing before [*jeg fortsatte omtrent med å gjøre det jeg gjorde i Røde kors, jeg*], and that was to work with what I see as the greatest challenges of our time – conflicts, humanitarian aid, societal crises – and of course, at the Foreign Ministry there was money for this, around a billion [approximately 125 million Euro], much of it being non-earmarked cash.

One notes from this account that the media crops up here as an aid for new diplomacy in a rather unexpected way – as a showcase for politicians not only from which to learn about what are being presented as going concerns and who is authorized by the media to say what about what, but also as as a review of prospective aides. Aides are being picked not only for their telegenic potential, but also because they are active in areas which the incoming foreign minister deems to be politically salient. Looking back on this recruitment from his position as President of Red Cross Norway, Stoltenberg himself tells the story a bit differently:

I had met him a couple of times, and wanted him because he was capable, and because he came from the voluntary sector. The very day he came to Geneva, I had to tell him that I was to become Foreign Minister for the second time. So he came back with me, first as my personal adviser, because I wanted to retain Helga Hernes as my Secretary of State, then, when I had established the second post, he too became Secretary of State. Land-mines were a typical example of an issue which fell between the private and the public sector, and which it therefore fell to us in the voluntary sector to take care of. Land-mines were a Red Cross issue, and then it popped up on the government agenda. The voluntary sector takes on more and more importance as foreign policy becomes the direct concern of more and more Norwegians. When I set out in the 1940s, we were no more than 300 people throughout the country who were interested in this, the rest said that [then Foreign Minister] Halvard Lange and [then principal thinker on third world issues] Finn Moe would take care of it all.

Egeland had served at the Geneva headquarters of the Red Cross before he became its media face in Norway, and in Geneva he had been involved in land-mines issues. Once installed in the Foreign Ministry, he was confronted with the issue again when he received a visitor from the UN system:

The International Red Cross had worked with mines long before the International Campaign to Ban Land-mines, and I knew of their work from my Geneva days. The person at the Cambodia desk at the UNHCR came to the [Norwegian] Foreign Ministry and said "Cambodia is coming around", and that Norway was one of the best operators to enlist help from. OK, I said, what can we do? "Money." Anything else? "Repatriation and mines." So, I thought, time to call a meeting. This is how I work. I had heard there was a colonel who was the grand old man amongst the military engineers who had directed UN programmes for mine-clearing in Afghanistan. Then I invited about 10 people from the MFA, perhaps five from the MoD and the Joint Military Staff, and then all the NGOs, perhaps 50 people all in all, we filled the big meeting hall. This was in 1991 or 1992.

Being asked what was the more important trigger of his interest, his NGO work or the contacts with the United Nations, Egeland responded as follows:

It was both of those things. I felt that here there was work to be done and I coined a couple of soundbites, you know "from penny provider to partner, from observer to operator [*fra pengesekk*, lit. moneybag *til partner, fra observatør til operatør*]". So, we had to own up, but we did not have the people. There were only a group of persons at Hvalsmoen [the relevant military training camp]. We had to train people, and we had to do it professionally. The UN was not up to doing this, and instead of working along that slow path, I rather wanted us to do this ourselves. We could have donated the money to the UN and let them buy the services from the UK-based Halo Trust or from the Australian corps of military engineers, but I rather wanted us to develop our own capacity. This came up at the time when we were just founding NOREPS [an MFA set-up to make Norwegian firms put together instant packages of aid relief-related services ready on demand], and we had a dialogue going with all the five major NGOs. We challenged them to build up their capacity.

In 1992, using the NGOs to carry out MFA-initiated and MFA-financed projects was, as mentioned above, a growing trend in overall Norwegian policy, particularly towards the South. The framing here was that people had to be trained. It would be easier for the NGOs to be employers than for the MFA, and also for the MoD for that matter. Egeland, who served in a social democratic government, turned to the Norwegian People's Aid with the knowledge that they had the backing and the financial resources to follow through on the initiative:

I had a meeting with Jan Erik Lindstad, who was the foreign head at the NPA, and told them that here the NPA had a golden opportunity. This was after the meeting with the UNHCR, so I told him that things would be coming up fast. I think I was the first politician to sit down and trawl through the [MFA] budget, and to keep tabs on what was there and what was being spent. I also knew how to influence the biannual reallocation of development budget funds so that we would have more cash for our humanitarian operations from the Storting.

What Egeland is describing here is the emergence of what has locally come to be referred to as "the Norwegian model" – a set of flexible procedures for allocating resources from the MFA to societal actors and co-ordinating their activity with that of the MFA.[8] Egeland placed himself in an excellent position to mediate between the need reported by the UNHCR and the costly training needed to establish the NPA in the field of mine clearance:

The NPA was keen, I was actually a bit worried about how keen they were, they are willing to do everything for everybody. But we needed top quality, and I insisted that they use professional military personnel. The issue of mine clearance was proceeding all too slowly, and it was wholly necessary for the MFA [to supervise things]. Our civil servants had to make sure that the NGOs recruited professionals, but we also wanted the enthusiasm that the NGOs could provide. They also had the major comparative advantage of knowing what the mine situation was out there in the field.

This initiative looked rather similar from the perspective of the NPA. Interestingly, however, its leader, Halle Jørn Hansen, stressed Egeland's impatience with the way things were proceeding (or not proceeding) in the United Nations:

Jan [Egeland] had no faith in the UN's capacity in this area. He is extremely action oriented, and felt that the UN system was too full of roadblocks. He wanted to build new capacity and a new channel. I do not know who else he asked, but he asked the NPA. [NPA foreign head] Jan-Erik Linstad and Egeland were extremely action oriented and could talk. The researchers, particularly the people at the Christian Michelsen Institute [the major academic institution on the study of the South in Norway], they ridiculed us. The NPA, however, has maintained as a subterranean undercurrent the pacifist tradition of the workers' movement. We simply decided to try.

The distinction Hansen draws upon here is the one between a utopian-oriented NPA and a realism which is not placed at the MFA but in the camp of the knowledge producers who uphold the order of things. Having been granted a monopoly on recruiting military personnel the NPA went into the field in Cambodia in 1992, as the first Norwegian clearance force ever to operate outside of Norwegian territory.[9] This action was clearly taken on the instigation of, and at least indirectly even under the auspices of, the Norwegian state. Indeed, as it stands, this story looks like a case of a politician who has taken with him his INGO training and, with a push from a UN official, has used the state's resources to get things moving. This story can be embellished, however, by reference to another key aspect. There had actually been an initiative in favour of mine clearance taken already before this, in 1989. Kristian Berg Harpviken was the representative of the Norwegian Afghanistan Committee in Peshawar in 1990, and has a supplementary story to tell:

For the NAC, which had done work in Afghanistan throughout the 1980s, mines were a going concern, and things literally exploded in 1988, when two of the organization's people and nine others were killed as the car they were riding hit an anti-tank mine. In 1988 or 1989 the organization sent a letter to the MFA where they signalled that we were ready to start with mine clearance in Afghanistan and asked the MFA to finance the undertaking. This, I think, was the very first mine clearance initiative in Norway. The answering letter came right away and was signed by [junior minister] Helga Hernes. It stated that it was too much of a risk for an organization like the NAC to run their own mine-clearance campaign. With hindsight, of course she was right. In 1989, the UN started its work on mine clearing in Afghanistan. The UN approached the [Norwegian] MFA, which decided to finance this work. On this occasion, as on others, the NAC was an important decision-shaper [*premissleverandør*] where Norwegian Afghan policy was concerned. We were always asked when new initiatives were afoot. We had regular meetings, for example the annual meetings on disaster aid allocation [*nødhjelpsbevilgningen*] as well as informal ones; quite often they took place when our local representative in Peshawar was in Oslo. Actually, the MFA people around Peshawar also discussed things with them on location, and we had good contacts with the Norwegian military personnel – you know how expat circles work, you talk to compatriots you would never have approached at home even if you had been neighbours. They [the MFA] would show us stuff they had received from the UN with a view to hearing how this looked from out in the field. Actually, a meeting never went by without them putting out at least one of these feelers. The MFA rarely asked us just like that, however, they were a bit invisible in the way they asked their questions.

For the student of diplomacy, this account rings true. Diplomats are well known for their indirect approach, which often proves baffling to their interlocutors, particularly those who are not part of the established foreign policy circles. The NAC definitely falls into this category. It recruited amongst young people with little interest in the minutiae of how foreign policy is formulated. Diplomats and diplomatists alike are often blind to how well integrated their diplomatic culture is, and the degree to which this makes for a cultural barrier between them and others working in fields which are becoming part of foreign policy.[10] A lot of work remains to be done in this area on the clash of developmentalist culture and diplomatic culture. For our purposes, the point is that the NAC tended to treat the MFA as a monolithic organization. This approach seems to hold even when they were aware that there were tugs-of-war going on inside the organization, as was the case with their view of Jan Egeland and his people forming a "circle" inside the ministry. Despite this awareness, the NAC did not make contact with other parts of the MFA (which they must have deemed either irrelevant and/or out of reach); they were satisfised with maintaining their contact with Jan Egeland and his circle. Even more interestingly, their perception seems to have been that, through their contacts with the military people who were doing the actual work of clearing away bombs, they had established rapport with the armed forces as such. This lack of variegated military contacts beyond the field would prove crippling to the NAC when the emphasis moved away from mine clearance and on to a campaign in order to achieve a total ban.

Playing the political field: The campaign to ban anti-personnel mines

Due to its activist character, it is no surprise that the NAC was actually the first Norwegian group to be involved with what was to become the political campaign to ban anti-personnel mines. Kristian Berg Harpviken recalls:

In Peshawar, Norwegian Church Aid and the Norwegian Refugee Council had a joint representation, and then there was the NAC. In the late 1980s, Rae McGrath was an important operator around Peshawar. When he was establishing the Mines Advisory Group, we supported him with money from the Astrid Morken and Saifurrahmen Memorial Fund, which had been established to honour the memory of the two people we lost in the mine acccident in 1988. The Mines Advisory Group was a core group in the establishment of the ICBL, so that proved to be a wise decision.

However, apart from this incident and the continuing contacts between the NAC on the one hand and McGrath and also some other international activists on the other, there seems to have been little direct Norwegian involvement with the global movement to ban land-mines. The important crucible for what happened in Norway was definitely the heterologous milieu in Geneva. At least three lines emanate from this network node to Norwegian actors back in Oslo. The first is the MFA. According to the desk officer on land-mines Jørn Gjelstad, who had served at the Norwegian delegation in Geneva before taking up his present post, it was indeed this delegation which pushed the MFA into action.

In the Norwegian MFA the work on revising Protocol II proceeded apace, without much outside involvement. On a French initiative, there was a UN resolution calling for a conference. The first of these was held in the autumn of 1993. The MFA started to look at it, going over the substance and reviewing procedures for the upcoming conference in 1995. In Sweden, parliamentarians took an interest already in 1994. Swedish Save the Children (*Rädda barnen*) had been important. However, Sweden did not signal an interest in a unilateral total ban; the whole thing had that touch of rhetoric which Swedish foreign policy often has. Actually, it was not outside forces which put the question on the agenda. It was the system itself which picked up what was going on. The energy emanated from Geneva, which is teeming with diplomats and it is easy to talk things over and exchange ideas. Then they may put the capitals to work. Things started to happen within the Western group. Geneva reported home and insisted that Norway had to do something [*måtte dra noe*], because this case might go off [*gå av*].

One notes that the MFA's interest was first ignited by the standard disarmament timetable. This is in keeping with Andrew Latham's[11] point that, rather than being a result of direct transnational NGO pressure, the land-mine issue gained centrality in the first place simply through its happening to be the first major arms control development to appear after the event of Gorbachev's coming to power. One hypothesis does not rule out the other; at the very least, however, there is reason to doubt the claim that the transnationals simply moved the case up the political agenda on their own.[12]

The second thread from Geneva concerned the well-known and ongoing involvement of the Red Cross, which proceeded apace. As a junior minister at the MFA, Jan Egeland maintained his contacts with the Red Cross. The third thread concerned the Norwegian Afghanistan Committee, which had maintained its contacts with Rae McGrath and expanded them in parallel to the building up of the ICBL. In the summer of 1994, NAC activist Kristian Berg Harpviken intended to do something in Norway, and went to a seminar in Geneva in order to seek inspiration:

When the NPA started their work on mines, we [the NAC] tried to gain access to their work, but the NAC seemed to keep too high a profile for a social democratic organization with its high need of control to accept that. Even when we arranged a broad meeting in the autumn of 1994, after we had participated in a meeting in Geneva, they were sceptical.[13] This meeting I think was something of a turning point, because it established the mine question towards the centre of the political debate, and that is why we organized it. With hindsight, this looks like the beginning of the entire political campaign to ban mines [in Norway]. I invited Rae McGrath, and this was the first time that he came across as something more than an extremist. We also had [key mine specialist and military officer] Henriksen from the Norwegian People's Aid, we had a colonel from the Norwegian military engineer corps, and we had the Red Cross. This was an important event not least because it stirred [*vekket opp*] the NPA [on the total ban question]. Then the NPA took over the political work, and that was OK for the rest of us, for they had all the prerequisites for doing it.

The said Svein Henriksen, who first came into contact with the land-mine issue on an army mission in Afghanistan, concurs:

Before the 1994 seminar, some of us had been talking about doing something, but we had not talked about *what* to do. After the seminar, where Rae McGrath delivered a rousing speech, we just got together and decided to meet on the premises of the NPA a few days later in and set up a Norwegian chapter of the ICBL. We elected an interim board, which became the board [laughs]. It was never a democratic organization, in that respect as in so many others it was like the international organization at large. And there were lots of conflicts with us, too. It was a personal thing, the four core people were Lars Grønseth of Norwegian Save the Children, and then [Norwegian veteran peacenik] Mari Holmboe Ruge, who had a number of hats, myself, and then Thorleif Johnsen of the Working

Group Against Mines. That working group consisted of two people and some hangers on, really; they had gone to Cambodia as election observers, befriended one another, seen the rot, and then after their return they decided to do something about it. Some of us had received this fax invitation from the ICBL to attend a seminar in Rome. I went for the inspiration, a number of the people who were destined to become central were there. Even that late we still haggled over strategy, and it was only at that meeting that we decided to target anti-personnel mines and leave anti-tank mines out of it. We said that we did not intend to come back to the issue, but that was of course not entirely true.

What we have here is a transnationally instigated mustering of tailor-made knowledge. To be more concise, the build-up of political pressure reached Norway – NGOs and the MFA alike – through Geneva. For the MFA, the land-mines issue involved a need to keep up with the Swedes (a standard theme in Norway generally and for the Norwegian MFA specifically),[14] as well as a feeling of political urgency all around. This feeling was aggravated by the action taken by the NAC which, calculating that it did not have the potential to stir the MFA directly, chose to target the NPA and other NGOs and go for a knock-on effect which would eventually involve the MFA as well. Institutionally, this was the kick-off for the formation of the Norwegian chapter of the International Campaign to Ban Land-mines.

As seen from the MFA, which was at this time negotiating Protocol II, with an MoD representative taken from the technical side (a major from the engineering corps) participating from February 1994 onwards, it was during autumn 1994 and spring 1995 that NGO involvement started to grow. There was a feeling of events threatening to overtake the ministry. Jan Egeland's version of how this happened is as follows:

In the Norwegian MFA the work on revising Protocol II [for the 1995 Review Conference of the Convention on Conventional Weapons] proceeded apace, without much outside involvement. The NPA created an environment for mine clearing. And then this circle, which also consisted of the Norwegian Red Cross, their Geneva office, Norwegian Church Aid, and their international branches – the Lutheran World Federation and the World Council of Churches – began to argue in favour of a total ban. Suddenly, I was on the defensive. I had seen the need for this, I had put the NPA on the case, I had even provided the money, and then there they were! I remember sitting down to a TV programme on mines, you know, rest a little on my laurels, and there was this person from the NPA being interviewed out in the field in Cambodia saying now the Norwegian state must wake up and see the enormous need etc. etc. [...][15] I was called names – you know, reactionary, all that – by the people who thought of themselves as progressive activists. So I thought it was time to follow up on my previous good experiences and simply talk to them. This was when I initiated a series of meetings, but there I had to argue the case for why a total ban was unrealistic. This I had not done before. I had been neither in favour nor against, because the idea of a total ban had not existed as such. [. . .] So why, they said, why cannot we be the first ones to be in favour of a total ban? Well, I said, because Canada and Belgium are bordering other NATO allies only [and not Russia, as does Norway]. In Norway, the MoD and the Department for Security Affairs were in the driver's seat, and to put it mildly, I had no power of instruction over them.

The binary opposition which does the discursive work here is one of humanitarian versus disarmanent, an opposition which is to be refound in the framing of the international process as one where a global movement to ban land-mines involving a plethora of actors is working under a humanitarian banner, in opposition to a UN-based disarmament process where states, and particularly the great powers, are in charge. As seen by Jan Egeland, he had landed in a squeeze. The NGO people he had been instrumental in involving were lobbying for a total ban along three axes. First, they were mobilizing other people, such as the head of the Trade Union Conference and the primas of the Norwegian Church, by means of a signature campaign. Secondly, and decisively, in the spring of 1995 they managed to talk two politicians from the Centre Party into forwarding a motion in the Storting in favour of a total ban.[16] The motion made its way to the Foreign Committee of the Storting. This moved the issue on to the central public arena (but of course not the central arena measured by most other means), and made the entire issue much more transparent. Thirdly, they were using these victories to sway what is traditionally the powerhouse of Norwegian policy-making – the Labour Party, which was at this time also the ruling party.

As seen by NPA hitman Henriksen, Egeland was a problem, not a giver of mirth:

Egeland was very negative towards us; he told us to stick to clearing mines and that launching a political campaign would simply be destructive. We quickly understood that there was little point in trying to convince the key politicians directly, so we decided to build momentum and to target the media, too. We asked the MFA for money in order to set up a documentation centre, but the whole thing was simply a cover [skalkeskjul] to wage the campaign. We got the money, and used most of it on hiring a full-time activist by the name of Petter Quande. He sat down and drew up a list of 500 organizations and names – everybody, peace organizations, women's rights groups, Christian organizations, bishops, environmentalists, political parties, trade union chapters, you name it – and then we drew up a rather woolly resolution and passed it around: 120 organizations signed up, and that gave us the platform we needed. Of course, the ICBL was not a membership organization, but we pitched it so that the media reported that 120 organizations backed us up, and we got away with it. We spent a lot of energy on enrolling the big five [aid organizations], and even persuaded them to set up a coordinating council consisting of their secretaries-general. That was really important. Every week, we met at a local cafe [*Kaffistova*] to divide the tasks and talk it all over. Those who wanted to come along simply popped up. In addition to the signature campaign, we worked along three other tracks. We continued targeting the media. Then there was the Labour Party. During their annual meeting in the autumn of 1994, we tried to have a resolution passed from the bench, but [Defence Minister] Kosmo himself shot it down. We had not polished our arguments and overall strategy well enough, and with hindsight it was only fair that we lost out. Instead, we turned to the annual meetings of the county chapters. Starting with Buskerud [county], we pursued their annual meetings one by one, and had them pass resolutions. And then we also continued to target top politicians in the Storting. The break came when Thorleif Jensen of the Working Group Against Mines was able to sit down with their contacts in the Centre Party and draw up what was to become [resolution to the Storting] Doc 8–52.

The NGOs were attacking Egeland and his government under the banner that Egeland considered his own: humanitarianism. Egeland's response was twofold. First, he invited a clutch of NGOs to a talk in the autumn of 1994. In June 1995 there was a follow-up meeting, where the largest meeting room in the MFA was crammed with people from the NGO sector. As recalled by MFA desk officer Gjelstad, "some of these were way out on the activist side, with Norwegian People's Aid being the most vocal of these. They were the main argumentative challenge [*de innebar den største begrunnelsesutfordringen*]. Others were rather moderate." What made the NPA a formidable challenge, Gjelstad maintains, was their pool of knowledge:

Norwegian People's Aid were able to draw in people who were working in the field clearing away mines; they understood where the possibilities for improvement were to be found, how concretely to strenthen security; they had the best practical grounding in areas where we lacked it.

One general reading of this would be that diplomats take their identity from being "operative" – that is, not only conceptualizing academics, but real movers.[17] Diplomats tend to acknowledge expertise of the same type which diplomats pride themselves in having, namely operational skills. Egeland and other MFA sources repeatedly stress the complementarity of the operational knowledge NGO representatives possess when they want to explain why they maintain contacts with these people and why they even increasingly include them in official delegations.[18]

Jan Egeland's other countermove was to work his own party, particularly at the Storting:

The focus was the Labour faction for foreign policy, particularly [the chair] Håkon Blankenborg. In April–May 1995 Canada went in for a total ban, with Belgium and Austria following on. Then I said that we had two choices; either we could sit there and do nothing, which would mean that we would eventually be forced [*tvunget*] to adopt the total ban policy by public opinion and international actors, or we could bite the bullet and go in for a total ban ourselves. I argued in favour of the latter option, from an interest-based perspective.

As seen from the MFA, on the other hand, it was a question of filling in the diplomatic background to educate the parliamentarians:

The problem with Parliament was that they did not really bear in mind that what we were talking about at this stage was a UN resolution, which of course has to be brought about by consensus-building. There was no basis from which to call for a total ban at this stage; we could not proceed too quickly. During the period April–June 1995 there were a number of informal conversations about this and what was about to happen in Vienna, how to relate to China etc., with Egeland and the most active parliamentarians talking it over in the Storting canteen and so on.

The motion on a total ban was carried. With hindsight, the head of the Socialist Left Party Erik Solheim describes the process as follows:

After the committee work, the issues are taken to the party groups (*gruppemø-tene*), which is where the going often gets hot. The major showdown was inside the Labour Party. With Anne [Enger Lahnstein, head of the Centre Party] behind it and Kjell Magne [Bondevik, head of the Christian People's Party] as spokesman, that was where the remaining insecurity was to be found.

At this point, too, mine clearance and the ban issue became the topic of a heated debate between the MFA and the MoD. The MoD seems to have been caught on the hop. According to one official working in its security division:

It was the materiel division of the MoD which was in charge of of mine clearance. [One of the key MoD security analysts] was very sceptical regarding a total ban, because he saw land-mines as a central and legitimate part of the country's defence. The process was going on without us being sufficiently alert, however. We made the mistake of leaving the running to the lawyers in our juridical division. The division for coordination of resources was also in on it. The security division was only meant to keep an eye on things. If you want something political done in the MoD, however, we must be fully in charge. In this case, nobody really watched the thing closely.[19]

The showdown between the ministries became public when the two ministers spoke at cross-purposes to the Storting during debates, and the newspapers ran stories exposing the internal tugs-of-war. This further enhanced the status of land-mines as a media issue. According to the head of the Socialist Left Party, Erik Solheim, "Until the confrontation between the ministers, this was one of a thousand cases. When it went through at first, I think it was because nobody really thought it would materialize." Interestingly, the committee's work was also permeated by the NGO presence. Henriksen of the NPA recounts how the Norwegian ICBL

had a lot of contact with the MFA and with [MFA officer seconded to the Foreign Committee of the Storting as their secretary] Åge Grutle. I fed him a lot of info and even drew up some memos. We asked for a meeting with the committee, and I went there with the secretaries-general of the big five and the secretary of the Handicap Council. We tried to speak only on humanitarian issues, but they [the members of the committee] asked a lot of questions about technicalities and military strategy, and that was really for me to answer. The armed forces had briefed the Defence Committee, but it was their issue and they were all very interested. In the end, in June 1995, they all came around and Parliament did not even need a vote.

However, the fissions between the two ministries were not the only ones in evidence. The military were not necessarily all that interested in keeping extant land-mines, pointing out that many of the Norwegian mines were getting old, with some of them even having been bought with Marshall Aid money. On the other hand, the MoD argued that due to the planned strategy of deploying clusters of anti-personnel mines against attacking tanks, Norwegian defence capability would be seriously weakened if mines were abandoned.[20] If one started with the technical condition of the mines, then one might as well get rid of many of them, and in this case there was no pressing reason not to support a total ban. That was the engineers' angle. If one started from a strategic angle, on the other hand, the costs of reshaping strategy were substantial. As seen by MFA desk officer Gjelstad:

We had a problem dealing with the MoD and Headquarters Defence Command Norway [FO]. We would send things over, but they were not really followed up. When headquarters [FO] say that they were not involved, it is true enough where the top brass is concerned, but it does not hold true for the organization as such. During the initial stages, there was precious little interest.[21]

In the parliamentary arena, Labour eventually came around to supporting a total ban. Head of the NPA, Halle Jørn Hansen, recalls that:

on 15 May 1995 I was on my way to a meeting with [head of Labour Torbjørn] Jagland, and I met [Prime Minister] Gro [Harlem Brundtland] at the stairs of the Storting. She was a bit stiff, and when the meeting started, Jagland announced that they had just discussed the mine issue in the faction and decided to drop their resistance [to a ban].

This is interesting not least because it goes to show that the party organs were not really that involved, at least not at this stage, and probably not before either. The final decision was taken by the party faction in the Storting. This is in keeping with a general trend that the party organs are not really in the thick of things on questions of foreign policy-making. Interestingly, it was then the NGO representative, Hansen, and not Labour's own people at the Storting who went and informed the Norwegian Broadcasting Corporation, which duly staged an interview with head of the Labour Party Jagland the same evening.

On 2 June, only a few weeks after Labour decided to back the ban, the Storting moved to support a total ban on production, stockpiling, sale, purchase, and use of anti-personnel mines.[22] This was a major breakthrough for the campaigners, and, given Norwegian consensus traditions and the way the enlarged committee of the Storting acts as a consensus-building clearing-house for difficult decisions, a high road to victory in the long run. Yet with the devil being in the details and the government being involved in diplomatic negotiations, it was not at all an immediate victory, and it was not perceived as such by the NPA and the other key lobbyists.

This is also where reports from the diplomatic arena give glimpses of frivolous moments. One such came in the autumn of 1995. MFA desk officer Gjelstad:

Things got really interesting at Vienna on 25 September 1995. To the great surprise of the MFA, the armed forces had simply begun to destroy mines, the idea seemingly being to set a good example. We had held our main speech two days before, and had of course made no mention of anything like this whatsoever. During the conference [MoD representative] Laugerud, who was sitting with us on the conference floor, simply informed us that they had begun. [MFA's] Petter Wille was slated to speak as number 11 or something when this occurred, so we began to draft right away. When he announced the news from the rostrum, you should have heard how the gallery at the back with all the NGO people just went off! It was a victory for the MFA too, since at this stage the relationship with the Norwegian People's Aid was marred by us not supporting the total ban actively enough. We demonstrated that we were able to set our own house straight.

Then things really got rolling. Gjelstad:

In January 1996, there were technical talks between Sweden and those who had not yet warmed to the idea of a ban. A result emerged in Geneva in April–May 1996. The USA was no problem. The Swedes were a bit sore about not having been able to keep up the momentum. In the morning of 3 May, we understood that there would be a result, but a damn bad one – a total ban on mines which could not be detected and dumb bombs, that sort of thing. We thought this was absolutely ridiculous. We were worrying about how to sell it to the public. Some of us had been talking a lot, over breakfast and things; there was Canada, and New Zealand, and Belgium which was under parliamentary pressure just as we were, and the Netherlands, not Austria and Switzerland really. At this stage the international campaign [ICBL] was already the main umbrella of the INGOs. We had an open dialogue, you know we did not have to carry on as if these were nuclear weapons. We had also been talking to the Danes about maybe trying to tweeze the whole thing into a Protocol V situation [a total ban], maybe trying to draw up a new track for those who wanted to strike out on their own! What we wanted was a process based on some kind of majority vote, absolute or qualified majority, instead of a consensus-based process. Suddenly the Canadians just grasped this idea, without any preliminary moves, and invited everybody to Ottawa for the autumn of 1996, with the only criterion for participation being an allegiance to the *goal* of a total ban, nothing more. [Canadian Foreign Minister Lloyd] Axworthy said that within December of next year we want to have that protocol ready. This way of doing things came over as a rather arrogant way of straightlacing the process. The South Africans were livid, and there were others who reacted strongly as well.

The Ottawa meeting was duly held in October 1996. At that meeting, Norway made a bid for the follow-up meeting, what was to become the Oslo conference:

Johan Løvald delivered Norway's major speech during the general debate in Ottawa [October 1996], and announced that we had just destroyed the last of the country's mines. You could just hear the gallery take off. Then he said that we were ready to host a conference in Oslo the following autumn. We were thinking in terms of a three- or four-day meeting. This was the initiative of the system. It is nice to be a host, Austria hosted in February, the Germans arranged something, a core group was forming, and attempts were made to make it as geographically diverse as possible. We wanted to host the meetings where the formal negotiations were to take place.

Egeland presents a somewhat different narrative:

After a while, the civil servants understood how I and the others thought. There were two cases which stand out. We sent Johan Løvald to a meeting in Brussels, and there he was approached by Jill Sinclair – the Canadian number two on disarmament and a real mover. Unlike us, the Canadians have some damned good progressive diplomats; we don't have that, we have NGOs and some politicians. She aired this idea, that we needed a real negotiating session. She presented it simply as an idea that suddently happened to materialize then and there. Løvald came back and went straight to my office and said, "Listen, you are going to like this, the Ottawa process may culminate with a major dipomatic conference, and I think we have a good shot at getting it." So we went to Foreign Minister Godal, and of course he was on his way somewhere, it is just incredible how many decisions are actually made on the stairs. We walked down the stairs talking to him and into the waiting car, and then he said "OK" and was off. So we landed this conference, which is the largest diplomatic conference ever to have taken place in Norway, and the decision was taken in two minutes. And one of the reasons was that we were able to say yes straight away and go for it; there was no need to clear it with others than the Foreign Minister. That's the Norwegian model for you: ability to act fast due to the wide authorities [fullmakter] given by Parliament, and a dose of good NGOs with access to a lot of cash. The other case was at the Oslo conference, when Bjørn Skogmo suggested that [South Africa's] Selebi should chair the conference instead of himself, or Løvald, or me. That was a good move!

At the Oslo conference itself, that typical intermingling of state representatives and NGO representatives which had characterized the entire process continued. Egeland stresses how the NGO representatives were accommodated on a grand scale:

After some discussion I invited the ICBL to join me for the official press briefing before the conference started. During the Oslo conference, the ICBL delegation and the ICRC sat along with the government delegations in the hall itself. We gave them this large recreation area ajacent to that of the dipomats in return for a promise that they would not heckle the diplomats during coffee breaks.

The NGOs adhered to the stipulations, but kept up the pressure. Halle Jørn Hanssen of the NPA stresses how the NGOs lobbied in tandem, in order to blanket all the state representatives. This was particularly important when the USA launched a last-minute counterattack against the ban:

The NGOs divided the world between themselves for lobbying purposes. I got Europe and Africa. I was a member of the [Norwegian] delegaton, and had the information. There were certain diplomats who simply had to be stopped – a Chilean, and a Pole. We just shot them down. On 15 September we swayed Africa, well Abdul Minty swayed (vippet) Africa with our help. [...] We had the info we needed about the American counteroffensive during the conference from the American NGO representatives who knew the hill and what went on inside the Beltway. So, we went around and stiffened the backs of the delegates.

The conference duly concluded their work according to plan. In deference to the leading role played by Canada, the result was not named after its immediate place of origin: "The Oslo Conference produced a draft treaty, 'Convention on the Prohibition of the Use, Stockpiling, Production and Transfer of Anti-personnel Mines and on Their Destruction' (generally referred to as the Ottawa Convention)."[23] This example of like-minded solidarity where Norwegian-Canadian relations were concerned contrasted sharply with developments in Norwegian-US relations. Having been thwarted in their attempt to hold up the work of the conference, the USA intensified pressure on how the ban would affect the status of the American equipment which was stored in Norway as part of the preparations for US support of Norway in case of a military attack by a third party. At this stage, the MoD finally came to life. As seen by a medium-ranking officer:

when the working meeting in Oslo was coming up in the autumn of 1997, we suddenly realized that things were taking a dangerous turn. It was a combination of us being a bit out of it and the MFA not having informed us properly. They agreed to solutions internationally without having consulted fully with us about what the military side looked like. The MoD is supposed to gather information from the Chief of Defence Staff and then provide politico-military input to the MFA. It is very counterproductive when the MFA makes direct contact with the military authorities. In the autumn of 1997, the working definition of land-mines pointed in a direction which would involve us having to remove tripwires from anti-tank mines in order to keep them from being defined as anti-personnel land-mines. This set a huge apparatus in train. We tried to have the definition changed, but to no avail. The armed forces could not see why they should change something which had worked well, and was defensive as well as legitimate. The Norwegian Army Materiel Command [*Hærens forsyningskommando*] tried to specify costs. [...] That autumn, NATO also became involved. Inasmuch as it seemed clear from the very beginning that Turkey, Greece, and also Poland would not participate, there was a problem with interoperability. It was also taken up by the council, at ambassadorial level. The military committee was looking into it, and it was decided to await their report. At this stage, we also discovered that the smart mines that were included in the US advanced depots would fall within the proposed definition. This was when there was really a collective gasp going through the ministry. We tried to change the definition so as to have them exempted, because these particular mines were self-destructive after a 24-hour period. We also took bilateral action *vis-à-vis* the Americans. We went to the Pentagon twice, and had tough talks. They said that Norway was a good ally, but if you make us remove some of our equipment you may as well forget about us, then we will take it all away. It was bordering on a threat that we would not receive aid in crises and in war [*hjelp i krise og krig*]. That was when we really started thinking hard about alternative costs! The MFA also worried, and they went to see State, but the Pentagon were really the tough ones, as they always are. We were able to negotiate a transition period up until 2003, and we are still in dialogue with the Americans. Actually, the mine issue has moved into the running portfolio of our US desk officer. We really hope that technological developments may spawn a system which is as good as what they have now and which will make it possible for us to stay inside of the definition at the same time. The key is to find a replacement for the mixed munitions/smart bomb concept.

The MoD does not seem to have seen the relevance of playing the open field. In the words of the same official, "In the MoD, it is only Press and Information which has, or is supposed to have, contacts with the outside world." From this official's perspective, the problem was first and foremost one of the MFA not being able to curb the activists:

The humanitarian pharisees in the MFA should exercise some self-critique. On the other hand, we did not understand how important this was about to become before it was too late. The MFA had not really thought things through, they had not given as much as a thought to matters military.

By way of contrast, Henriksen of the NPA's assessment has a rather different focus. He maintains:

The armed forces were simply not very professional when it came to the politics of the thing: they did not use the media, they sent only young technical personnel to the committees, and even when the MoD had a person from the legal department in Ottawa and he wrote home what was about to happen, nobody paid any attention.

Conclusion

There can be no doubt that the transnational movement to ban antipersonnel mines was instrumental in swaying the Norwegian state's policy on land-mines. Neither can there be any doubt that Norwegian NGOs played a central role where both agenda-setting and decision-shaping were concerned. The analysis demonstrates how different NGOs played to their different strengths, with the NAC using its early contacts with the rest of what we may call the epistemic community of mine specialists to sensitize the rest of the NGOs and also the state to the issue, and the NPA using its intimate links with the rest of the labour movement and also a whole swathe of politicans and NGOs with an interest in humanitarian work to launch an effective lobbying campaign. Technical expertise stands out as a key policy asset as long as the decision-making process is operating within normal parameters. Those who have it are granted access to the key desk officers in the MFA on a regular basis. When their expertise is not challenged by rival data from other quarters, they have considerable influence on how the MFA assesses the situation. Similarly, know-how emanating from transnational NGO networks can be converted to an asset on which the Norwegian NGOs can draw in their attempts to get the attention and shape the decisions of the MFA and the politicians. These processes are constitutive of like-minded states, and are interesting in and of themselves.[24] It would be rash, however, to conclude that this transnational upgrade of traditional agenda-setting and lobbying skills is the only drama playing itself out here. The chapter will conclude by highlighting another aspect of the process. States have a need to be perceived as key political players. Due to limited numbers of people working in central administrations, they suffer under a constant dearth of operational capacity, which is only made worse as globalization presents them with ever-new challenges. There is, therefore, a constant pressure in the direction of cooptation and outsourcing.

One will recall that, upon becoming Foreign Minister, Thorvald Stoltenberg turned to Jan Egeland of the Red Cross in order to stock up on people with skills in humanitarian affairs. One way of reading this move on his part is as an attempt to nudge new diplomacy forward by harnessing key personnel from social movements to the wagon of the state's foreign policy. If so, one could expect a clash of perspectives between the diplomats who were already manning the system on the one hand, and Egeland on the other. Stoltenberg's answer when asked how he thought the apparatus reacted to having someone like Egeland act as their political superior is very telling:

You are asking the wrong man. If there were any negative reactions, I would rarely hear them, and then only after a long stretch of time. I understood that there were reactions to new ways of doing things, but that was one of the reasons I had asked him to come in the first place. [*Du vet jo at du er kommet til feil adresse. Eventuelt negative reaksjoner ville jeg sjelden høre, og da eventuelt først etter lang tid. Jeg skjønte at det var visse reaksjoner på aktiviteten og på den nye håndteringen av saker, men det var jo blant annet derfor jeg hadde bedt ham om å komme.*]

One will also recall that Egeland proved to be an ace politician, keeping tabs on funds, reallocating funds through the Storting, boosting the organizational capacity of the MFA to deal with these issues by creating and staffing a new department for global affairs, etc. etc.[25] One will also, and in the author's view crucially, recall that once the Norwegian NGOs caught up with the rest of the INGOs and launched the political campaign for a total ban on anti-personnel mines, Jan Egeland's reaction was, in the words of an NGO representative, "to double deal". As he himself tells it, it was to try to mediate between the NGO pressure and those – inside and outside the MFA – who insisted on framing the question of mines not as a humanitarian issue, but as one of state-to-state disarmament policy and Norwegian security policy. We have here a classic example of the statesman as a mediator between different forces, and of the state as that institution where the discursive work of making the world look as if it is of one piece is being done. On this view, it is not the functional role of the state which has changed as such, but the intermeshing of the networks which has become so much denser that it qualitatively changes how the state goes about minding that function – how it recruits its personnel and orders its work. The change in operating mode is potentially so far-reaching that we may have here an example of a new type of state formation – the disaggregated state.

The picture which arises out of this material is not one of national interest, hard-and-fast borders, and state sovereignty. On the contrary, the decision-making process involves mediating between the different views and actions emanating from identities such as engineers, activists, strategists, negotiators, humanitarians etc. The name of the game is setting up a node in a network, rather than securing sovereignty. The Norwegian MFA harnesses the social power of NGOs, and also the military sector, and in order to do so more effectively is itself taking on a more disaggregated shape, one more compatible with the network in which it wants to be the most powerful node. In similar fashion, on the international level, where the network also includes more state nodes and offers a number of other possible relations, the issue is to be as central a node as possible. Put differently, the issue is to place oneself in a position where one's capacity to manage the flow of events is maximized to the limit. Social anthropologist Marilyn Strathern has suggested that this way of acting is a characteristic of globalization: actors try to "cut the network", in the sense of shaping its flows such as to place themselves in a central position, and in the sense of taking a cut of the added value which is being produced by the ensuing transactions. Crucially, however, one does not have to read this as a result of the specific actions of transnational NGOs working transnationally. After the globalization of politics, the intermeshing of states and NGOs, and the resulting disaggregation of states, the states remain powerful actors in world politics. However, power is tied to the state's position in a multi-actor network, not to its ability to manage and defend its own territory and its own "national interests" relative to those of other states. States can have their pride in being as centrally placed in those networks as possible. For like-minded states, which have the advantage over other states of being able to harness the resources of well-ordered societies without being overly threatened by them, one way of doing this is to disaggregate agency nationally in order to aggregate centrality globally. The upsurge in transnational activity is often read as the coming of global society and as a challenge to the centrality of the system of states. Arjun Appadurai has generalized the present situation in the following terms: "the relationship between states and nations is everywhere an embattled one [...] state and nation are at each other's throats, and the hyphen that links them is now less an icon of conjuncture than an index of disjuncture".[26] Looking specifically at the case of the land-mine campaign, Richard Price[27] maintains that the success of the NGOs challenges the central role of states. As this case study demonstrates, however, these generalizations are in need of specification. At the very least, their area of validity seems to be somewhat narrower than suggested. Like-minded states have found a way to maintain their political centrality under these new conditions. Like-minded states by definition have strong non-state actors. Under conditions of globalization, these non-state actors strengthen themselves even more by widening their transnational networks and forming transnational alliances. Like-minded states do not seem to react to this by trying to curb the power of their civil societies. On the contrary, they try to harness it and use it as a source of strength in order to maintain its centrality vis-à-vis their own polity. Furthermore, like-minded states draw on these sources of power in their dealings with other states. One consequence of this strategy is that like-minded states become even more disaggregated and so even more different from other states than they were prior to the acceleration of globalization.

Notes

1. The interviews which form the lion's share of the research for this chapter were carried out after the author stepped down as a planner with the Norwegian MFA on 31 December 1998 and before taking up a similar job with the Norwegian MoD on 20 March 2000. The argument in no way draws on specific information that was obtained in those two posts, but is a result of interviews which were clearly advertised as research related. The author would like to thank all the interviewees for their cooperation, and the Landmines Discussion Forum at the International Peace Research Institute in Oslo for their response to a talk delivered in January 2000. Many thanks to Andrew Cooper and his team for helping to place the findings in the wider context.
2. Emile Durkheim, *Professional Ethics and Civic Morals* (London: Routledge, [1913] 1992).
3. Quoted in Geoffrey Wiseman "'Polylateralism' and the New Modes of Global Dialogue", Leicester: Diplomatic Studies Programme, Discussion Papers, no. 59, 1999, p. 19.
4. Richard Price, "Reversing the Gun Sights: Transnational Civil Society Targets Land Mines", *International Organization* 52, no. 3 (1998), pp. 613–644; Maxwell A. Cameron, Robert J. Lawson, and Brian W. Tomlin, eds, *To Walk Without Fear: The Global Movement to Ban Landmines* (Toronto: Oxford University Press, 1999); Raamesh

Thakur and William Maley, "The Ottawa Convention on Landmines: A Landmark Humanitarian Treaty in Arms Control?", *Global Governance* 5, no. 3 (1999), pp. 273–302.

5. Terje Tvedt, *Angels of Mercy, or Development Diplomats? NGOs and Foreign Aid* (London: James Curry, 1998).

6. Iver B. Neumann, "Norsk sørpolitikk: Den disaggregerte stats diplomati", *Internasjonal Politikk* 57, no. 2 (1999), pp. 181–198.

7. Jan Egeland, *Impotent Superpower – Potent Small Power: Potentials and Limitations of Human Rights Objectives in the Foreign Policies of the United States and Norway* (Oslo: Norwegian University Press, 1988).

8. *Ibid.*

9. The recruitment effort included people in the reserve, which makes for a rather large pool: Norway has trained conscripted personnel to be officers instead of having a separate professional corps of non-commissioned officers.

10. Neumann, note 6 above.

11. Andrew Latham, "Global Cultural Change and the Transnational Campaign to Ban Antipersonnel Landmines", ms, 1999.

12. This argument is made by Price, note 4 above.

13. A summing up of that meeting is an op-ed by Kristian Berg Harpviken in Norway's leading newspaper, "Miner – krigerne som aldri blir trette", *Aftenposten* (Oslo), 5 June 1994.

14. Iver B. Neumann, "The Foreign Ministry of Norway", in Brian Hocking, ed., *Foreign Ministries in a Time of Change* (London: Macmillan, 1998).

15. "Of course, Norway's positions on the additional protocol [to the 1980 treaty] at this time was not carefully planned as people seem to think. When the seven o'clock news [*Dagsrevyen*] heard about the campaign for a total ban, they absolutely wanted me to comment. So I called the desk officer, Gjelstad, in order to find out how the Norwegian positions had emerged. He provided the four or five points Norway had jockeyed with earlier, and given what had been at all doable within a NATO context, we had taken up the most radical positions possible. So I find myself in a position where in the course of two hours I have become an actor, having to defend this 'old and outdated position of ours'."

16. A so-called Document 8 suggestion, which may be used by single representatives of parties regarding all issues which are not already circulating in the system. It is, therefore, not correct as stated in *Landmines Monitor*, 1999, p. 634, that the motion was forwarded on a regular party basis. The Centre Party was also divided between those who, like the two persons behind the motion, saw this as a humanitarian issue, and those like its chairman, who saw it mainly as a question of Norwegian security policy. In a discursive reading, this fault line crops up all over the place in this phase – also inside the Conservative Party, where a former chair spoke publicly in favour of a ban on humanitarian grounds, while the party as such were not swayed until later. Arnstad and Lahnstein followed up on their motion with a letter to the Foreign Minister. There was also a letter from Erik Solheim (SLP). These came apropos of the preliminary work leading up to the preparatory conference in the spring of 1995. The reading of an MFA source is that "the receptive representatives had been fed all the info that the Norwegian People's Aid had been able to lay their hands on".

17. This is the light in which one must read Gjelstad's claim, and particularly his use of the word "but", when he maintains that Canadian DFAIT's "Bob Lawson was the driving force, a former academic, but he had done practical things as well. The Canadians had really burnt their fingers in Somalia, and wanted something which could re-establish their image. I think Axworthy saw that here was the cause he needed." Amongst Nor-

wegian activists, academics like Harpviken seem also to have been central in hammering out the consistent, overall arguments. See for example Kristian Berg Harpviken and Mona Fixdal, "Anti-Personnel Landmines: A Just Means of War?", *Security Dialogue* 28, no. 3 (1997), pp. 271–285, a Norwegian version of which appeared as an op-ed in *Aftenposten*.

18. Egeland reveals that the key issue here was the identity and solidarity of diplomats: "During the mine campaign, NPA people like Hanssen and Henriksen were often included as a members of the Norwegian delegation. I had to insist on it, but there was not that much resistence. The major problem was the fear that they would be present when diplomats described other diplomats during strategy talks; they feared that our NGO people would talk to representatives of other NGOs about that, and maybe use it." Henriksen's representation of how these meetings worked is telling:

I attended a lot of seminars. In Otttawa in October 1996 it was really party time. At that time, it was Halle [Jørn Hansen] who had a seat in the official delegation, and I was there for the ICBL, but that was basically a technicality. We were all in it together. When Canada announced that they were going to go for the endgame, some of the MFA people were a bit put out, you know this was something new, this is not the way we do things, but all that fell into place really quickly. Actually, in May 1998 the MFA brought me in as their technical background and field experience land-mine specialist. They both need me, the section for security which is in charge of the convention and the section for humanitarian affairs which pays for it all. I report directly to the special adviser on humanitarian affairs, and am the one who is on the case all of the time. I started work as a military man, and I am still a captain in the reserve. I have worked for the UN, for humanitarian organizations, and now for the MFA, so I do not see myself as an MFA man, but then again nobody expects me to. I have a paid contract, and can pose as an MFA representative when that is called for, and an NGO person when it is time for that kind of thing. It goes down well all around [*det passer alle godt*].

19. A senior servant from the juridical division concurs: "We were taken unawares." Interestingly this interviewee had the impression that the MFA officers involved "were very activist-oriented [Š] They were more NGO than bureaucrats, and we were simply moved aside."

20. Interestingly, the MoD ordered a classified report from the Norwegian Defence Establishment (FFI, a research outfit) on the matter. The 35-page report emerged in 1998 and concluded that a ban would not have a strong negative impact on Norwegian defence. The report was not widely distributed and was, as one FFI employee put it, "not particularly well received by the military".

21. The importance of levels appears even more clearly if one considers Egeland's answer when the author asked him why he and his Foreign Minister did not settle their differences with Defence Minister Kosmo in party organs. The answer was that "No, that would have had to be done by the PMO, and the PMO was not particularly efficient at that time. Living with political differences is sometimes not so bad. Here we had a seemingly unsolvable conflict between two important considerations, we simply represented the two sides, and so there was a good basis for discussion internally. I was a sector politician, and partly for this reason, my influence on others was limited." The MFA/MoD relationship during the process seems to parallel the Canadian case; compare with Brian W. Tomlin, "On a Fast Track to a Ban: The Canadian Policy Process", in Cameron, Lawson, and Tomlin, note 4 above, pp. 185–211.

22. St.prp. no. 73 (1996–1997).

23. David Mutimer, *The Weapons State: Proliferation and the Framing of Security* (Boulder,

CO: Lynne Rienner, 2000). When the ICBL was awarded the Nobel Peace Prize, there was a debate in Norway over whether Axworthy should have been a co-recipient. Where the prize is concerned, its administration also has some of the features one would expect in a like-minded state. While all the other prizes are awarded by Swedish committees, the administration of the Peace Prize was given to Norway when it was still in union with Sweden. After the disbandment of the union in 1905, the first Norwegian Foreign Minister also served as the first chair of the committee. When Hitler vehemently protested the award of 1936 going to Carl von Ossietzky, the Foreign Minister was also a member, but chose to respond to the criticism by leaving the committee. After the Second World War, the committee has been nominated by the Storting and has consisted mainly of senior if perhaps fading politicians (although the chair at the time was an academic), and has acted on its own accord. A paper should be written on whether it qualifies as a quango.

24. What is mentioned as the historical first in this connection is invariably the process leading up to the Geneva Convention, where "the role played by a few morally committed individuals and the organization they built, the International Committee of the Red Cross (ICRC), in promulgating and transmitting humanitarian norms" seems to have been crucial in getting states to the conference table, to sign, and to implement. See Martha Finnemore, *National Interests in International Society* (Ithaca, NJ: Cornell University Press, 1996), p. 70. The sequence, which basically lasted from 1859 to 1864, involved ignition of activism by war experience, book publication, a wide political reception, institutionalization, and lobbying. These are all elements which are present in the land-mine case as well, in Norway as well as globally. The newness of the land-mines case is to do with the scope of action and the kind of relationship which exists between state and non-state actors – not with the humanitarian impulse or the process of state lobbying as such.

25. Egeland: "The secretariat expanded from two to five, and the humanitarian field from one office [*annet politiske kontor*] with three people into a separate department with 15–20 people. When we discussed postings, I asked about creativity and innovatory skills, but this was always laughed off. They told me that the point was for these people to be good bureaucrats with a capacity to handle and follow up on all the initiatives which emanated from me. I got what I wanted when I asked for it [*Jeg fikk det jeg ville ha når jeg bestilte det*]. I was rarely dragged into ongoing processes; the rule was that I could adjust the strategy myself. We lagged behind on the mine issue. Then we came up with this mine clearance and caught up by initiating the work of the NPA. Then we lagged behind on the political front due to our defence considerations. We were not amongst the four or five front runners in spring 1995. Then we moved up front at the end and finish as a good number two right after Canada. South Africa moved with us, really."

26. Arjun Appadurai, *Modernity at Large: Cultural Dimensions of Globalization* (Minneapolis: University of Minnesota Press, 1996), pp. 37–39.

27. Price, note 4 above.

8

Peace, justice, and politics: The International Criminal Court, "new diplomacy", and the UN system

Alistair D. Edgar

Introduction

In supporting the growing movement to establish a permanent international criminal court, UN Secretary-General Kofi Annan observed that global justice would remain an impossible goal for as long as the "worst crimes" – such as genocide and crimes against humanity – remained beyond the reach of international law. After the terrible atrocities witnessed in Rwanda and Bosnia in the early 1990s the proposed new court, he argued, "will ensure that humanity's response will be swift and will be just" if ever again faced with such heinous actions.[1]

In May 1998, when Mr Annan was making these remarks, it was not at all clear just how swift the international community might be in agreeing upon the creation of the court. Five decades had passed since the UN General Assembly had asked the International Law Commission to study the possibility of establishing such a body, in the wake of the Nuremberg trials and the Assembly's own adoption of the Convention on the Prevention and Punishment of the Crime of Genocide. However, between 15 June and 17 July 1998 the so-called Rome summit witnessed intense negotiations, numerous compromises, and a final vote in favour of the Rome Statute of the International Criminal Court.[2] Despite the strong and vocal opposition of the US negotiator to several elements of the final statute, and the negative votes of the American, Chinese, and five other states' representatives, delegates attending the summit approved the statute in a non-recorded vote by 120 in favour, seven against, and 21 abstentions.[3]

That the Statute of Rome and the International Criminal Court (ICC) became the subject of a substantive conference at all was a considerable achievement; that they were adopted in the face of active opposition by two permanent members of the UN Security Council was even more remarkable. To some extent, the groundwork already had been laid by the earlier and equally dramatic accomplishment of the campaign to ban anti-personnel land-mines.[4] The so-called "Ottawa process" of middle- and small-power multilateralism and active agenda-setting participation of non-governmental organizations (NGOs), which had been developed during the land-mines campaign and boosted by the strong support of Canadian Foreign Minister Lloyd Axworthy, did much to set the political stage for the success at Rome. The horrors which occurred during the conflicts in Rwanda and Bosnia, and the subsequent establishment under UN Security Council directives of the International Criminal Tribunals for the Former Yugoslavia and Rwanda, raised the profile of public debate over the need for a permanent court instead of these inevitably post hoc and ad hoc measures. Within the UN system too, the International Law Commission in 1994 had submitted to the General Assembly a final draft statute for a permanent court, and six preparatory commission meetings had worked for two years between 1996 and 1998 on revising the text for the conference. Still, the accomplishment of the governmental and non-governmental delegates at Rome was remarkable, and probably not expected by many of them as they travelled to the Italian capital for the summit meeting.

The analysis presented in this chapter is not concerned directly with recounting the general story of the creation of the court, nor with the specifics of the process of negotiation in Rome and the tactics there of the various players involved. Considerable material of all sorts already exists, proffering critiques, rebuttals, and explanations of these questions and topics.[5] Some of these issues and debates certainly will filter through into the focus of this chapter, which considers instead a critical but still underassessed element of the ultimate fate of the court – namely the several questions surrounding the very practical and highly political matter of state cooperation with, and enforcement of, the court's powers of indictment and detention or arrest of alleged offenders. In particular, the chapter discusses practical aspects of the enforcement of the court's decisions against those states and individuals who refuse to provide "full and timely cooperation" with its activities and judgments. As will be seen, such support is by no means certain even after a successfully completed ratification process (which has made progress but at the time of writing still possesses under half of the state ratifications required to come into force); and there are potential problems related to the issue of enforcement which have not been addressed, nor often raised, whether by advocates or opponents of the court.

In addition to this more specific focus, the underlying theme of the broader study being presented in this book is the extent to which the Ottawa process and the expressions of that process – the land-mines ban and the ICC treaty – constitute the prototype of an emergent "new diplomacy", or else are no more than anomalies in a world of traditional international (power) politics. Can shifting coalitions of "like-minded states" and NGOs develop new political processes that avoid, or even confront and overcome, the opposition of the traditional leading states in the UN system and in international politics outside of the UN system? To what extent can such alternative international groupings be effective, if and when they proceed in the absence of the support of one or more of the major powers – especially if such political, financial, and/or material support is, in the end, critical to the practical implementation of the "new" initiative or process? And what does "new diplomacy" imply for the United Nations itself as an institution that gives a special place to the major powers (or which recognizes their unavoidable influence), and which has cherished and defended the sovereign state as the central actor in world politics?

In the words of one analyst of the land-mines convention, a key question thus is "the potential of state/civil society partnerships as vehicles for substantive change" in international politics. Putting this into the context of the present chapter, the question is the extent to which the International Criminal Court provides an example of *transformative* or less fundamental *reformative* practices.[6] To both the specific topic of this chapter and the broader theme of the text, the argument advanced here is neither entirely positive nor completely negative towards the court. It is suggested, however, that the most likely outcome for the court – upon completion of the ratification process – will be sufficiently modest and constrained by the "traditional realities" of political, economic, and military power that a reasonable conclusion can only be that the court represents no more than a moderate reformative practice. While certainly representing a political victory for its advocates, neither the UN system, nor the sovereign state as actor in international politics, nor the centrality of the most powerful states will be undermined by the court and the "new diplomacy" of the Ottawa process.

The United Nations faces a host of pressing challenges regarding its credibility and legitimacy, as well as its day-to-day functioning, as it seeks to deal with seemingly intractable problems of ethnic conflicts and failed states, and increasing demands for its assistance around the world. The Ottawa process may indeed highlight the emergence of a range of non-state actors into the arena of international political agenda-setting, but so far it appears to be safe to agree with Richard Falk that "we have yet to experience the definitive waning of the state system, which is the form of world order that has dominated political imagination and history books for several centuries".[7]

The statute and the court: Elements of continuity and development

In order to evaluate the degree to which the court is an expression of either reformative or transformative tendencies in world politics and international law (and in the UN system), and to provide some context to the discussion of such a court's actual conduct, it is worth considering political and legal history and precedent to see what is not new or revolutionary but rather a continuation of, or development from, the past. By doing this it also will be easier to highlight later what may be new issues raised by the court and the Statute of Rome, and to identify the core challenges that advocates of the court are likely to face in attempting to make their "new" creation an effective functioning body.

Part 9 and Part 10 of the Rome Statute of the International Criminal Court deal respectively with matters of "international cooperation and judicial assistance" and with "enforcement". Part 9 begins with the statement in Article 86 that "States Parties shall, in accordance with the provisions of this Statute, cooperate fully with the Court in its investigation and prosecution of crimes within the jurisdiction of the Court." Such cooperation extends to detaining, arresting, and when required surrendering indicted persons to the court (Articles 89 and 92); as well as permitting the examination of "places or sites" of suspected criminal activities, providing records and documents, protecting victims and witnesses, and arranging when needed for the tracing and freezing or seizure of "proceeds, property and assets and instrumentalities of crime" (Article 93). Part 10 of the statute sets out states parties' obligations with respect to enforcement of sentences of imprisonment (Articles 103–107), and of fines and forfeitures (Article 109). Should a state party fail to comply with a request for cooperation by the court and its reasoning for this failure not be accepted by the latter, then the court is authorized to refer the matter to the Assembly of States Parties or to the UN Security Council for consideration (Article 87).

These are not new or novel requirements to be placed upon states as they sign on to international treaties. Under emerging international criminal law and following on from the post-Second World War Nuremberg trials, the four Geneva Conventions of 1949[8] established the obligation of all signatory states ("states parties") to cooperate in identifying, arresting, and punishing individual persons who breached the terms of the conventions.[9] It also is worth noting, while on the subject of the Geneva Conventions, that these were developed in large measure outside of the formal intergovernmental structure of the relatively new United Nations, at international conferences organized and hosted in Geneva by a nongovernmental organization – the International Committee of the Red Cross. NGO participation was limited in scope, but the ICRC was pivotal in bringing states together in this forum and helping to set the context of the discussions. Subsequent to the Geneva Conventions, and this time within the UN structure, the General Assembly in 1953 passed Resolution 3074 on "Principles of International Cooperation in the Detection, Arrest, Extradition and Punishment of Persons Guilty of War Crimes and Crimes Against Humanity". Resolution 3074 again called on states parties to cooperate in identifying, arresting, and prosecuting alleged offenders, and declared that these grave crimes were subject to universal jurisdiction – thus allowing any signatory state (not just the state in which the alleged crime took place, or a state whose citizen committed the crime or had the crime committed against them) to arrest an alleged offender.[10]

These agreements on universal prohibitions against designated international crimes, and on states' obligations to enforce such prohibitions and to punish individual offenders – not just other states – offer clear precedents for some aspects of the 1998 Rome Statute. The important role of a NGO in the negotiation process for the Geneva Conventions is likewise worthy of note as a precursor to the land-mines and ICC negotiations. Other legal and political precedents may also be found in the general field of international human rights law as this began to emerge in the latter half of the twentieth century.

As Hurst Hannum observes, international human rights instruments of many types have been adopted by the United Nations after being introduced and formalized by a wide range of means and actors: by state initiation, by UN organs, NGOs, and UN-appointed individual experts.[11] The best-known form of instrument, if not the most common by sheer numbers, is the convention adopted by the UN General Assembly. Included in this category is the 1948 Universal Declaration of Human Rights, plus the two associated Covenants on Civil and Political Rights and on Economic, Social, and Cultural Rights. Together these measures are considered to constitute "the most comprehensive conventional human rights law yet adopted".[12] Amongst subsequent conventions which have been proposed and adopted are those on the rights of refugees

(1951); against racial discrimination (1965) and against apartheid (1973); against torture and inhuman treatment (1984); and on the rights of the child (1989).[13]

In addition to these General Assembly conventions, both the Assembly and other specialized UN agencies may adopt resolutions, statements of principles, and declarations. Some, such as the initial Declaration of Human Rights and the Declaration on the Rights of the Child, may be broadly supported and in turn become formally accepted as conventions. Others on narrower subjects such as the administration of criminal justice, or on controversial topics such as the Declaration on Social Progress and Development, may be less widely accepted. The International Labour Organization, the World Health Organization, the UN Educational, Social, and Cultural Organization, and other specialized agencies have adopted literally hundreds of declarations and statements of principles which have been ratified on topics such as forced labour, collective bargaining, and the rights of indigenous peoples.

A frequently cited criticism of these sorts of measures is that they do not create legally binding common law obligations upon states. Even the conventions formally adopted by General Assembly votes do not automatically create legally binding obligations – most, like the Universal Declaration of Human Rights and the two covenants, are aspirational or promotional documents rather than "restatements or reaffirmations of legal norms". They do, however, promote the development of widespread "common practice". Hannum rightly notes that "to suggest that they do not contribute to law-making is to underestimate the impact of 'merely' moral or political statements in the area of human rights".[14] The UN Office of Legal Affairs commented in 1962 that although formally non-binding statements and declarations obviously did not constitute legally binding documents in and of themselves, "in so far as the expectation is gradually justified by State practice, a declaration may by custom become recognized as laying down rules binding upon States".[15] Hence the Universal Declaration, while explicitly aspirational in its descriptions of human rights, is generally argued to have "ripened" over the past five decades into customary international law binding upon all states.[16]

Since the conventions, declarations, and other statements noted above were not approved initially as binding and hence enforceable sets of rules and principles, however, they were not accompanied by the establishment of permanent international bodies with jurisdiction and power to render authoritative judgments against states that failed to live up to their agreed commitments. The Covenant on Civil and Political Rights did create the Human Rights Committee to examine the reports periodically required from signatory states, but only 51 states parties also signed the optional protocol giving the commission the right to consider information from individual persons alleging violations of the covenant. Otherwise it was left to the states themselves to prepare and submit reports of their activities. The Covenant on Economic, Social, and Cultural Rights merely required the submission by signatory states of reports on their "progress" towards the goals of the covenant. It is reasonable to say, therefore, that the standards of actual state cooperation, compliance, and support for enforcement have been limited.

Despite this caveat, which might be argued to demonstrate the ultimately limited influence of international law over the concerns of international politics, it is the case that some less formal development towards functioning oversight bodies has taken place. This has occurred particularly under the auspices of the Commission on Human Rights. During the 1980s, working groups and official UN rapporteurs were appointed to examine compliance with UN conventions. The Working Group on Enforced or Involuntary Disappearances was established in 1980, and rapporteurs on arbitrary execution, torture, and religious intolerance and discrimination were appointed in 1982, 1985, and 1986 respectively. These offices were mandated to receive allegations of violations, to attempt to prevent potential imminent violations, and to prepare annual country reports for submission to the commission. In turn, the commission could adopt a public resolution either condemning or expressing its concern over a state's actions and policies. While such a resolution, again, holds no formal legal standing in international law and thus cannot bind states to amend their policies, "the efforts exerted by states to prevent such actions testify to the power of diplomatic embarrassment and isolation".[17]

Taken altogether, this admittedly cursory overview of existing international legal and political precedents provides reasonable grounds to argue that the 1998 Statute of Rome and the International Criminal Court ought not to be seen as entirely novel or revolutionary and "transformative" developments. The list of international crimes laid out in the statute as falling within the jurisdiction of the court certainly are by no means new – war crimes, crimes against humanity, and the crime of genocide each have a history that can be traced back at least to the Nuremberg Tribunal, and well before that in the case of war crimes.[18] The fourth criminal activity noted in the statute, the crime of aggression, has yet to be defined in a manner acceptable to the signatory states, and hence remains outside of the court's jurisdiction. It was, however, recognized at least *de facto* by the League of Nations and the United Nations, as well as by the Nuremberg Tribunal. The latter also made the important observation that "crimes against international law are committed by men, not abstract entities, and only by punishing individuals who commit such crimes can the provision of international law be enforced".[19]

The coalition of middle- and small-power states and non-governmental organizations, which together formed the core of the global political movement known as the Ottawa process, brought a firm commitment and provided a major impetus to the demand for a new, permanent international criminal court. As much as this is true, it is argued here that calling the process and the court a revolutionary expression of international law and politics would be a significant exaggeration. To the extent indicated in the preceding analysis, neither the provisions of the Statute of Rome, nor the mandate, jurisdiction, or powers of the court, nor the involvement of non-state actors and smaller states in the negotiation process represents a startling or transformative development in international politics. Thus the "new diplomacy" is not all that new. To say this, however, begs the question: if this was not as revolutionary a "victory" as was sometimes claimed, why has it been surrounded by the degree of political controversy and – from some sources – outspoken opposition that arose during and after the negotiations? What if anything is new and novel, potentially transformative, or otherwise notable about the agreement that finally was reached by 120 states in Rome?

The court as a transformative agent

An independent court?

At the core of the criticisms directed towards the new court, especially by conservative opponents in the USA, as well as at the core of the victory claimed by its supporters, is the relationship between the Office of the Prosecutor and the UN Security Council. Unlike the two International Criminal Tribunals for the Former Yugoslavia and Rwanda, which were established at the behest of the Security Council and received their mandates from that body, the International Criminal Court is to a considerable degree independent of the immediate authority, direction, and control of the Security Council. Investigations by the court and the Office of the Prosecutor may be initiated by the new body without prior Council authorization, and therefore conceivably could take place against the wishes and interests even of a permanent member of the Council.

The power of the Security Council over the court rests instead on a limited and post hoc right to request temporary deferral only of an investigation or prosecution, and must come in the form of a resolution adopted under the provisions of Chapter VII of the UN Charter.[20] The deferral is for one year only, so that the request has to be renewed – and thus debated in the Council and before "the public", a process that inevitably places a potentially uncomfortable political spotlight on the state

or states seeking the deferral. For supporters of the court, including notable international figures such as the former special prosecutors of the
international criminal tribunals, Chief Justice Richard Goldstone and
Madam Justice Louise Arbour, the distancing of the ICC from the veto
power of the Security Council's permanent members and from the politics of the Council generally was critical to the court's success. Only a
clearly independent court and a legal structure that stood above all
states, not just the lesser ones, could provide a credible system of justice
that would be accepted by the vast majority and could act as a deterrent
to potential future transgressors.[21]

The removal of the court from the direct control of the Security Council, in so far as this has now shifted from the realm of debate and into that
of a formal international agreement, is an innovative aspect of the Statute of Rome. Since the end of the Cold War in particular, the continuing
veto privilege of the five permanent members of the Security Council has
been raised on numerous occasions as a source of resentment for the
other UN members and as an obsolete relic of the power politics of the
1940s and 1950s. It has never appeared likely or realistic, however, to
expect the USA, Russia, China, Britain, and France voluntarily to surrender their veto power: serious discussion of the subject has not taken
place within the Council, despite such debates in the public sphere.
While recognizing the popularity of calls for ending the veto power there
also do remain reasonable arguments for its retention, which will not be
addressed in any detail here.[22] Still, the victory of the advocates of the
court – even with the limitations noted here regarding its transformational character – may now be used as a model for future agreements
between middle and small powers, and other more powerful states which
do not enjoy permanent status on the Security Council such as Japan,
Germany, or India.

The persistence of state sovereignty

A second issue upon which the court may be argued to represent some
elements of transformative change – and hence a truly "new" diplomacy
– is that of its relationship to the traditional, and in the UN Charter fundamental, legal and political concept of state sovereignty. A most basic
precept and value of the United Nations since its inception has been the
protection and promotion of the political independence and the territorial integrity of the state. Although unequal in levels of power, the
United Nations nonetheless recognizes all states as enjoying and being
entitled to an equal right to exercise sovereignty. In 1965, with decolonization well under way, the members of the General Assembly adopted
by a vote of 109–0 with one abstention a declaration reinforcing the pre-

cept that no state had the right for "any reason whatsoever" to intervene in, threaten, or interfere with "the personality of the State or against its political, economic and cultural elements".[23]

Court advocates initially sought to establish a new body which would be empowered to exercise universal jurisdiction – that is, a court able to claim jurisdiction over crimes (at least those falling within its scope) committed anywhere, regardless of state consent. In fact the statute is argued by these same advocates to be, in the end, somewhat more restrictive and limited than other existing international treaties and agreements.[24] They note that the court gives precedence to national legal systems in the first instance to investigate and where necessary to put on trial alleged offenders. Article 12 of the statute on "Preconditions to the Exercise of Jurisdiction" limits the court to jurisdiction over the state in which the conduct allegedly took place, or the state of which the person accused of committing the crime is a national. In either case the state must be a party to the statute or else have accepted the jurisdiction of the court by declaration.

The wording of the Statute of Rome does, however, allow of an interpretation that would provide the court with a far broader jurisdiction than this portrait suggests. Article 12 could also be read to allow the court to investigate and take action against an individual or group – including state political and military leadership – either serving in or directing a military or other mission, who might be a national of a non-state party but who is engaged in actions on the territory of a state party, or of a state that has accepted the court's jurisdiction by declaration. This concern for a broader interpretation of the statute, and the potential for those who might try to use the court for mischievous or frivolous (or merely deliberately anti-American) purposes, was one major reason for the opposition of the US government to the Rome agreement.[25]

Attempts to use – or abuse – the court in bad faith might not succeed, but at the least they would be distractions and possibly disruptive tactics, since both time and political attention would be absorbed in responding.[26] Of course, domestic court systems also are equally or more open to frivolous accusations laid by persons seeking to manipulate the system for personal gain or other motives – even the legal system in the USA! That such may be true is nevertheless not taken to provide a compelling reason to oppose or abandon these domestic legal systems. What could be a result in the international realm, however, is that the existence of the court and the potential for such accusations might cause states to choose not to participate in otherwise legitimate international actions, including UN peacekeeping and peace enforcement missions. This would be especially so if such frivolous accusations arose even once. The efforts of some critics to have an international criminal tribunal investigate

NATO's actions in Kosovo might be an indication that such actions are not beyond the realm of possibility.[27]

To the extent that these consequences of the ICC became reality, they would represent new and novel limitations on states' political independence and on aspects of state sovereignty. An international non-state body would be able to lay claim to jurisdiction and authority over the actions, and individual persons, of a state – possibly even in the absence of that state's consent. This does, indeed, appear to have been the ideal goal of several of the NGOs engaged in the negotiation process at Rome in June–July 1998. It also appears, judging from the votes cast at the Rome conference, that 120 states were prepared for reasons of their own to accept this possibility. If so, the ICC may represent an important but underemphasized shift in the values and priorities of many states in the international political system.

Putting purpose into practice

The third and last transformative potential of the Rome Statute and the court is related to the topics of compliance, cooperation, and enforcement. According to a transformative interpretation, the Ottawa process, the land-mines treaty, and now the ICC have opened up avenues for circumventing the obstructive, status quo policies and actions of the major powers within and outside of the United Nations. These new coalitions of state and non-state actors can coordinate and cooperate to raise matters of peace and security – not "just" of human rights but of other human security issues too – on to the agenda of international political debate. This new form of coalition politics might be argued to be an approximation of "international civil society",[28] or perhaps of what other international relations scholars have labelled the idealized (but unrealized) form of "complex interdependence" wherein state and non-state actors and large and small powers alike act on relatively equal footing, and there is no clear hierarchy between "high" and "low" politics.[29]

This vision of what might indeed be a real transformation in, and of, international politics does not seem likely to proceed either as far and as fast as its advocates might hope, nor as its opponents might fear. As of 31 December 2000, the Rome Statute had been signed by 139 states, including most recently and most notably the USA and Israel (and the Islamic Republic of Iran), and ratified by 27 states including France, Germany, Italy, Canada, and South Africa. In their ratification, however, France included significant "interpretive declarations" regarding its right of self-defence; the list of acceptable weapons including nuclear weapons; the description of acceptable targets of military attacks; and the extent of the court's jurisdiction.[30] The US signature, made at the direction of outgoing President Bill Clinton, was a limited success in that the statute will not in the foreseeable future go before a hostile Republican-dominated Senate for ratification. Indeed Senator Helms, the Republican senator for North Carolina and the influential chair of the Foreign Relations Committee, immediately responded by saying that "this decision will not stand". China and India thus far remain significant non-signatories to the statute. As much progress as has been made, there clearly remains a significant distance to cover and internal disagreements or divergences to address.

The idealism of the conception of the court may also prove hard to match in practice. This disjuncture comes from two sources, the first being the concern that the court might have legal jurisdiction but no real or practical enforcement capability; and that if it did have such capability this might be counterproductive and even dangerous to international order. The second concern is the sometimes awkward, complex, and perhaps even contradictory relationship between peace and justice in the resolution of international and intrastate conflicts.

On the first of these questions, Yale University law professor Ruth Wedgwood – a moderate supporter of the court – commented that "the international tribunal for the former Yugoslavia has found that its orders are paid little heed unless the United States and its allies lend their diplomatic, economic and military muscle".[31] Former US Attorney General and Assistant Secretary of State John Bolton, a stronger critic of the court, likewise argued that its advocates "make a fundamental error in trying to transform matters of power and force into matters of law" and that "the Court and the Prosecutor will not achieve their central goal because they do not, cannot, and should not have sufficient authority in the real world".[32] In this view the court would lack the capacity to enforce its judgments against individuals or states indicted or convicted of international crimes but who refuse to accept the judgment or to "surrender" to the court. If it cannot enforce its judgments then eventually the court would become a sham – again, perhaps, in the same manner that the League of Nations ultimately proved to lack the capacity to enforce its decisions, especially against its more powerful members.

Practical enforcement of the statute and the court means the willingness of states parties to act politically, economically, and militarily in support of the court's decisions against transgressors, and to do so at some potentially significant financial, material, or other cost to themselves.[33] While a coalition of smaller states and NGOs may be able to push an item on to the agenda or into the court's docket, they realistically simply do not possess the capability to enforce a judgment without the active support of larger, wealthier, and (when necessary) militarily more powerful states. Thus far the record of states parties – including the

USA, Britain, and France – in fulfilling their obligations to cooperate with the ICTY in apprehending indicted Serbian leaders has been quite poor. Yugoslav and Bosnian Serb leaders Slobodan Milosevic, Radovan Karadic, and Ratko Mladic each proved to be either too elusive or else potentially too difficult to target for seizure and arrest.[34] The difficulties of enforcement, the required military and economic capabilities, and the associated risks and costs all multiply as the individual or state against which the action is to be taken is more powerful. It is virtually inconceivable, for example, to imagine the court being able to issue a judgment against China, Russia, or the USA which could be enforced against the strongest opposition of that state.

The dilemma, of course, is that to accept the practical inevitability of this situation, and to exclude the major powers (such as by allowing the Security Council to have sole authority to initiate court investigations), would be tantamount to creating a new instrument of "great-power imperialism". Eliminating the possibility of such accusations or those of Western legal-cultural imperialism was an important dimension of the formulation of the Rome Statute. In his study of the development of human rights instruments in the UN system, Hurst Hannum cites the 1986 UN General Assembly Resolution 41/120 on "Setting international standards in the field of human rights". The resolution included amongst its guidelines the notion that any proposed new standards must provide realistic and effective implementation machinery and systems. Hannum rightly observes that "no one has yet drafted the perfect treaty".[35] In the case of the court, the problem may prove to be that what is realistic is also the opposite of what is required for effective implementation or enforcement. A satisfactory and workable answer to the awkward – and thus far too often simply ignored or set aside for later consideration – question of how to address this unavoidable problem of reliance on the major powers for enforcement capabilities has not been found. The existence of this limitation is recognized even within Canadian government circles otherwise strongly supportive of the Ottawa process, the Rome Statute, and the establishment of the International Criminal Court.[36]

A second consideration that has not been widely debated in the discussions surrounding the International Criminal Court is the ambiguous relationship that exists between the pursuit of peace and the demand for justice in states suffering through, or recently emerged from, profound and widespread violence. Kenneth Roth, of the non-governmental organization Human Rights Watch, argues that the expectation of ultimate immunity for their actions renders warring groups and their leaders more willing to commit atrocities against each other and against innocent civilians. A permanent court with broad jurisdiction over these sorts of internationally condemned crimes would, in Roth's view, "undermine this confidence by divorcing the quest for justice from efforts to secure peace, making clear justice is not a bargaining chip".[37] On the other side of this debate, John Bolton cautions that "it is by no means clear that 'justice' is everywhere and always consistent with the attainable political resolution of serious disputes, whether between or within states".[38]

The cases of Chile's General Pinochet, Pol Pot and the Khmer Rouge in Cambodia, the apartheid regime in South Africa, and even of the Franco regime in Spain all are instances in which peaceful transitions between political regimes might well have proven impossible without tacit or explicit guarantees that earlier crimes would be left largely unpunished. Two members of the Chilean government who had previously been jailed under the repressive Pinochet dictatorship found themselves in the position of criticizing the decision of a Spanish judge to indict the former Chilean leader, and asking what would happen if a Chilean judge chose to indict any living former members of the Franco government.[39] Initially rejecting the calls for an independent international tribunal to try former Khmer Rouge leaders, especially while Pol Pot remained alive, Cambodian Prime Minister Hun Sen argued that his government had to "carefully balance, on the one hand, the need for providing justice [with] the paramount need for national reconciliation and the safeguard of the hard-gained peace" that had been achieved in that country.[40] Most notable of all in this regard, no doubt, is the relatively successful and peaceful transition from apartheid regime to Nelson Mandela's "rainbow nation" in the Republic of South Africa. It is by no means clear that this transition could have occurred when or how it did if the remarkable Truth and Reconciliation Commission led by Desmond Tutu had not been established, instead of a formal judicial process with a criminal tribunal directed to punish the supporters and leadership of the apartheid government.[41]

The analysis of compliance, cooperation, and enforcement issues offered here is not intended to make a particular case either for or against the Rome Statute and the court. Rather, the goal is to show that the debate is not a clear and simple one between "right" and "wrong", power politics and law, or sovereignty and justice. As these recent examples suggest, there exist a range of competing goals and values. The central appeal of the International Criminal Court model is that it avoids the ad hoc and post hoc nature and the political bargaining of "temporary" tribunals; and that a permanent court would be a deterrent to possible future transgressors. On the other side of the argument, it is not certain how much deterrence would be provided by an unworkable court; the existence of the ICTY did nothing to deter Yugoslav President Slobodan Milosevic from his subsequent campaign of cynical repression and ethnic cleansing against Kosovar Albanians. Finally, a permanent court also might create a barrier to already sensitive political negotiations in situations where a choice between peace and justice, however painful, may nonetheless need to be made.

Reflections on the court: International politics, civil society, and the United Nations

From what has been seen in this review of the Ottawa process, and especially its recent expression in the form of the 1998 Statute of Rome and the International Criminal Court, any claims of either historical and conceptual uniqueness or a profound transformation of international politics must be said to be exaggerations. International law has been evolving slowly since at least the emergence of the "modern" state system marked by the Peace of Westphalia ending the Thirty Years' War in 1648.[42] To paraphrase the subtitle of the 1977 text by Robert O. Keohane and Joseph S. Nye Jr,[43] the nature, form, content, and actors in world politics – and in international law – have been "in transition" for some considerable time.

If the argument for a fundamental or transformative change is an overstatement, it still may be reasonable to wonder if the somewhat unexpected success of the Ottawa process in accomplishing a ratified treaty banning anti-personnel land-mines, and in taking some major steps towards the creation of the court, does not still represent a significant shift in power and initiative. The coalition of "like-minded" states and non-governmental organizations did take for themselves a considerable level of active leadership, not just participation. Their experiences and their example can be put forward as evidence to support P. J. Simmons's argument that even the most powerful states now must "learn to live with NGOs".[44] The new diplomacy might not be here in its entirety (whatever that is), and indeed it might never supplant completely the forces of traditional international politics and diplomacy; but civil society groups in the form of NGOs may have won themselves a greater ability to move politics and diplomacy in directions of their choosing.

It is an interesting and perhaps provocative question to ask whether the International Criminal Court in fact shows not the decline of the sovereign state but rather the obsolescence of the UN organization. It is true that those delegates who actually voted in favour of the statute did so as representatives of sovereign states, and that the ratification process depends on the acceptance of the terms of the statute by the domestic legislatures of those same sovereign states. As Ian Clark notes in a separate study, states have been actively, busily, and centrally engaged in shaping and supporting many of the activities and developments that are said to be indicators of their demise![45] The United Nations, it should also be noted, is an organization initially premised on protecting the inviolability and integrity of the sovereign territorial state; and the supporters of the court were adamant that the court must be independent of, and even placed above, the state-centric logic and structure – and the politics – of the United Nations. The court might be seen as representing a potential break away from, rather than an extension of, the current UN system. After all there is nothing inevitable about the continued existence of the United Nations, just as there was nothing historically inevitable about the emergence of the sovereign state in its present form. This is a large topic, however, and one better left for a separate treatment.

Notes

1. Quoted in "The Draft Statute", DPI/1960/D-May 1998-10M (United Nations Department of Public Information, May 1998), p. 2.
2. Officially titled the United Nations Diplomatic Conference of Plenipotentiaries on the Establishment of an International Criminal Court, the summit was named more simply after the city in which the final conference was held. The text of the statute is available from several sources and is reproduced at the UN website: http://www.un.org/icc.
3. States reported as voting against the statute were the USA, China, Israel, Libya, Iraq, Yemen, and Quatar. India, Japan, and Mexico were amongst those delegations choosing to abstain. In one of his last acts as President of the USA, Bill Clinton finally authorized the US ambassador-at-large for war crimes, David J. Scheffer (who was also the chief American representative at the Rome summit) to sign the statute on 31 December 2000; Israel signed on the same day.
4. A useful account and analysis of the land-mines campaign and associated issues is given in Maxwell A. Cameron, Robert J. Lawson, and Brian W. Tomlin, eds, *To Walk Without Fear: The Global Movement to Ban Landmines* (Toronto: Oxford University Press, 1998).
5. For critiques see David J. Scheffer, US State Department, "America's Stake in Peace, Security, and Justice", http://www.state/gov/www/polic_remarks/1998/980831, 31 August 1998; from the conservative Heritage Foundation, Lee A. Casey and David B. Rivkin Jr, "The International Criminal Court vs. The American People", available at http:www.heritage.org /library/backgrounder/bg1249es.html; Jeremy Rabkin, "International Law vs. the American Constitution – Something's Got to Give", *The National Interest* (Spring 1999), pp. 30–39; and John R. Bolton, "Courting Danger: What's Wrong with the International Criminal Court", *The National Interest* (Winter 1998–1999), pp. 60–71. Moderate or supportive evaluations of the court and the statute, and rebuttals of these criticisms, may be found in Ruth Wedgwood, "Fiddling in Rome: America and the International Criminal Court", *Foreign Affairs* (November/December 1998), pp. 20–24; Kenneth Roth, "Roman Compromise", *Foreign Affairs* (March/April 1999), pp. 163–164; and Human Rights Watch, "The ICC Jurisdictional Regime: Addressing U.S. Arguments", available at http://hrw.org/campaigns/icc/icc-regime.html.
6. See J. Marshall Beier and Ann Denholm Crosby, "Harnessing Change for Continuity: The Play of Political and Economic Forces Behind the Ottawa Process", in Cameron, Lawson, and Tomlin, note 4 above, p. 269. As these authors note, critical security theo-

rists (as opposed to "traditional" security theorists) are interested in counter-hegemonic alternative understandings of the meaning, means, and objects of security – alternatives which are "rooted in historical experience but shaped by existing material, political, social, and cultural relations" and which "will result in a remapping of international politics reflective of a global community with a global consciousness" (p. 271). This would be the basis of transformative change; reformative change refers to change within, rather than of, the existing system. One of several useful introductions to the growing critical security literature is Ronnie D. Lipschutz, ed., *On Security* (New York: Columbia University Press, 1995). Elsewhere in the literature of international relations theory, regime theorists might refer to these as norm-governing and norm-governed change: change of, and change within, an international regime.

7. Richard Falk, "World Prisms: The Future of Sovereign States and International Order", *Harvard International Review* (Summer 1999), p. 30. For two excellent historical surveys which examine the development of the modern state system and international society from different perspectives, see Adam Watson, *The Evolution of International Society* (London: Routledge, 1992), and Hendrik Spruyt, *The Sovereign State and Its Competitors: An Analysis of Systems Change* (Princeton: Princeton University Press, 1994). A study that offers a critique of the notion that the sovereign state retains its unchallenged primacy is Joseph A. Camilleri and Jim Falk, *The End of Sovereignty? The Politics of a Shrinking and Fragmenting World* (Aldershot: Edward Elgar, 1992). A recent historical and (constructivist) theoretical argument supporting the continued centrality of the state as actor in world politics comes in two texts by Ian Clark: *Globalization and Fragmentation: International Relations in the Twentieth Century* (Oxford: Oxford University Press, 1997), and *Globalization and International Relations Theory* (Oxford: Oxford University Press, 1999).

8. The Convention for the Amelioration of the Conditions of the Wounded and Sick in Armed Forces in the Field; the Convention for the Amelioration of the Condition of Wounded, Sick, and Shipwrecked Members of the Armed Forces at Sea; the Convention Relative to the Treatment of Prisoners of War; and the Convention Relative to the Protection of Civilian Persons in Time of War.

9. States parties to the Geneva Conventions were obliged to enact any necessary domestic legislation to allow the imposition of criminal sanctions against those who committed or ordered to be committed grave breaches; to search for alleged offenders and either to prosecute them or else allow their extradition to another state party; and to ensure the right of the accused to a fair trial. See John F. Murphy, "International Crimes", in Christopher C. Joyner, ed., *The United Nations and International Law* (Cambridge: Cambridge University Press, 1997), p. 375; and Gerhard von Glahn, *Law Among Nations: An Introduction to Public International Law*, seventh edition (Boston: Allyn and Bacon, 1996), pp. 715–716.

10. The resolution did note that as a general rule alleged offenders should be tried in the state(s) in which the crimes took place.

11. Except where otherwise noted, the following discussion draws on information from Hurst Hannum, "Human Rights", in Joyner, note 9 above, pp. 131–154.

12. *Ibid.*, p. 138. For the full texts of the declaration and the two covenants, along with associated optional protocols, see Ian Brownlie, ed., *Basic Documents in International Law*, fourth edition (Oxford: Clarendon Press, 1995), pp. 256–306.

13. Convention and Protocol on the Status of Refugees; Convention on the Elimination of All Forms of Racial Discrimination; Convention on the Suppression and Punishment of the Crime of Apartheid; Convention against Torture and Other Cruel, Inhuman, or Degrading Treatment or Punishment; Convention on the Rights of the Child. A more comprehensive list of conventions may be found in William R. Slomanson, *Fundamental*

Perspectives on International Law, second edition (Minneapolis/Saint Paul: West Publishing, 1995), pp. 497–498.

14. Hannum, note 11 above, p. 147.
15. Quoted in *ibid.*, p. 145.
16. See for example Rebecca M. M. Wallace, *International Law*, second edition (London: Sweet & Maxwell, 1992), pp. 197–198; Michael Akehurst, *A Modern Introduction to International Law*, fifth edition (London: George Allen and Unwin, 1984), p. 77; and Slomanson, note 13 above, p. 501. The same argument has been made for the concept of "war crimes" since the Nuremberg trials; see Murphy, note 9 above, p. 364.
17. Hannum, note 11 above, p. 137.
18. A valuable recent addition to the literature on this general topic is Brian Orend, *War and International Justice: A Kantian Perspective* (Waterloo: Wilfrid Laurier University Press, 2000).
19. The Nuremberg judgment, later adopted as the "Nuremberg principle" in UN General Assembly Resolution 95(1), stated that a state and its agents – that is the political and military leadership – who waged an aggressive war committed a crime punishable under international law and could be punished by any state able to bring the planners to account. Slomanson, note 13 above, pp. 384–386.
20. Rome Statute of the International Criminal Court, Article 16: "No investigation or prosecution may be commenced or proceeded with under this Statute for a period of 12 months after the Security Council, in a resolution adopted under Chapter VII of the Charter of the United Nations, has requested the Court to that effect; that request may be renewed by the Council under the same conditions."
21. Timothy Appleby, "UN Urged to Give War Court Freedom", *The Globe and Mail*, 5 March 1988, p. A8; and Barbara Crossette, "U.N. Prosecutor Urges New International Criminal Court", *New York Times*, 9 December 1997, p. A8. Also see "Sign On, Opt Out", *The Economist*, 6 January 2001, p. 28.
22. Principal amongst these arguments is that the Council and the United Nations could not act militarily or otherwise against a major military (especially nuclear) power – the USA, China, Russia, Britain, or France – without risking either precipitating a disastrous conflict or else arriving at deadlock and failure (as happened to the League of Nations). The veto is thus a practical political necessity which has thus far helped to ensure that the United Nations does not self-destruct: the founders of the Charter learned well the lesson of the League's dismal record in that respect.
23. Declaration on the Inadmissibility of Intervention in the Domestic Affairs of States and the Protection of their Independence and Sovereignty, GA Resolution 2131. Quoted in John F. Murphy, "Force and Arms", in Joyner, note 9 above, p. 98.
24. See Human Rights Watch, "The ICC Jurisdictional Regime: Addressing U.S. Concerns", at http://www.hrw.org/campaigns/icc/icc-regime.html.
25. Bolton, note 5 above, p. 63, argues that the ambiguousness of the statute, and especially the open-ended list of crimes it encompasses, is such that if it were domestic American law it would be prohibited by the Supreme Court as being "void for vagueness".
26. Supporters respond that frivolous investigations and potential expansion of the lists of crimes would be very hard to accomplish, and unlikely to be accepted by a court whose judges recognize the importance of upholding the court's international reputation: see Roth, note 5 above, pp. 163–164.
27. A short but nuanced and careful judgement of the Kosovo intervention is provided by Robert Jackson, *The Global Covenant: Human Conduct in a World of States* (Oxford, Oxford University Press, 2000), pp. 277–287. Reviewing Russian, Chinese, and American critics of the NATO intervention as well as the views of supporters, Jackson suggests that the intervention "skirted the edge of international law" and flouted the tra-

ditional interpretation of the UN Charter. He quotes a legal scholar's argument that the action was, however, "compatible with the emerging international humanitarian law that recognizes the rights of individuals to be protected from genocidal practices, torture and other gross human rights abuses". While Milosevic had existing "procedural international legality" on his side, Jackson concludes that the Yugoslav President "could still be condemned for political recklessness and callousness of the worst kind" and for "disregard[ing] his fundamental national responsibility", pp. 285–286.

28. See *ibid.*, chapter 5; and Hedley Bull, *The Anarchical Society: A Study of Order in World Politics*, second edition (London: Macmillan, 1995).

29. Robert O. Keohane and Joseph S. Nye Jr, *Power and Interdependence: World Politics in Transition* (Boston, MA: Little, Brown, 1977).

30. See the chart "Rome Statute: Ratification Status" available at http://www.un.org/icc/statute/status.htm.

31. Wedgwood, note 5 above, p. 21.

32. Bolton, note 5 above, p. 66.

33. A useful analysis of the types of measures of enforcement needed is provided in *Making Justice Work*, Report of the Century Foundation/Twentieth Century Fund Task Force on Apprehending Indicted War Criminals (New York: Century Foundation Press, 1998).

34. Two critical reviews of the work of the International Criminal Tribunal for the Former Yugoslavia are Charles Trueheart, "A New Kind of Justice", and Chuck Sudetic, "The Reluctant Gendarme", *The Atlantic Monthly* (April 2000), pp. 80–90 and pp. 91–98 respectively.

35. Hannum, note 11 above, p. 152.

36. Interviews, Ottawa, May 1999.

37. Kenneth Roth, "Sidelines on Human Rights: America Bows Out", *Foreign Affairs* (March/April 1998), p. 5.

38. Bolton, note 5 above, pp. 66–67.

39. Ricardo Lagos and Heraldo Munoz, active opponents of Pinochet during the latter's rule, compared their state's situation with those that had taken place in Brazil, Portugal, Spain, South Africa, and Uruguay, which had all been "long on forgiveness, short on justice". Lagos and Munoz argued that although "deals" should not be set by the dictators, and measures should be taken to repudiate past wrongdoings and compensate victims, there must be room left for "the notion that the state may forgive under some circumstances in order to safeguard values – such as democracy and stability – that are as important to society as justice." See Ricardo Lagos and Heraldo Munoz, "The Pinochet Dilemma", *Foreign Policy* (Spring 1999), pp. 26–39.

40. Quoted in Steven Edwards, "Hun Rejects UN Bid to Try Leaders of Khmer Rouge", *National Post*, 21 September 1999, p. A12. Since then an agreement has been reached whereby a joint international tribunal will be established to indict up to 30 former Khmer Rouge officials on the crime of genocide. No additional trials will be held. The tribunal will be composed of a majority of Cambodian and a minority of foreign judges; the agreement passed the Cambodian Senate and lower house, and must be approved by King Sihanouk, the Cambodian Constitutional Council, and the United Nations.

41. One thoughtful contribution amongst the many studies of this transition period and the role of the Commission is provided in Brian Frost, *Struggling to Forgive: Nelson Mandela and South Africa's Search for Reconciliation* (London: HarperCollins, 1998).

42. Akehurst, note 16 above, chapter 2, and von Glahn, note 9 above, chapter 2, offer brief historical reviews.

43. Keohane and Nye, note 29 above.

44. P. J. Simmons, "Learning to Live with NGOs", *Foreign Policy* (Autumn 1998), pp. 82–96.

45. Clark, *Globalization and International Relations Theory*, note 7 above.

9

Between counter-hegemony and post-hegemony: The Rome Statute and normative innovation in world politics

Philip Nel

The ICC process as normative innovation

Once ratified by a minimum of 60 countries, the Rome Statute of 17 July 1998 will give birth to the first permanent *international* enforcement mechanism in the evolution of the humanitarian law regime: the International Criminal Court (ICC).[1] This will change this regime from a declaratory-proscriptive regime into a declaratory-cum-enforcement regime. In terms of norms typology, the ICC has the potential to change the proscriptive norms against genocide, crimes against humanity, and war crimes into *instrumental* norms; that is, norms that not only reflect social expectations (intrinsic norms) but also encourage compliance through repeated and consistent application.[2]

Based on the principle of complementing rather than replacing municipal enforcement mechanisms, the ICC will be an international rather than a supranational institution. Complementarity means that state responsibility is not diminished, and while the Rome Statute strengthens the role of the UN Security Council, it would be a mistake to interpret the ICC as relieving states of their responsibilities in terms of treaty obligations. States are still the main agents of humanitarian law, and mechanisms should be developed to compel states to take up their duties.

The Rome Statute makes provision for some significant innovations in humanitarian law.

- A state which becomes party to the statute automatically accepts the jurisdiction of the ICC with respect to the crimes referred to in Article 5 of the statute (that is, crimes against humanity, and war crimes as defined by various existing international instruments).
- Apart from further codifying existing prohibitions, the statute also prohibits certain war crimes not yet prohibited, such as deportation, and specifically gender-related crimes such as rape and enforced sterilization.[3]
- Non-state actors such as rebel groups and warlords can also be brought to trial for crimes mentioned in Article 5.
- Due process is guaranteed, including a pre-trial chamber of three judges who will exercise judicial supervision, and mechanisms to handle sensitive information.
- Principles for making reparations to victims are established.
- Provision is made for a trust fund to receive fines and forfeited property for the benefit of victims and their families.

Important though these innovations in humanitarian law are, they are by far not the only important features of the Rome Statute and the process leading up to it. From the viewpoint of the study of world politics, the Rome Statute also entails normative innovation on a broader scale than that represented by humanitarian law. In fact, one could argue that the very basis of the prevailing global normative order has been modified by the content of the statute, and by some of the diplomatic practices that gave birth to it. "Modified" seems appropriate because it is much too early to speak about the emergence of a completely new set of global norms. But considered together with other recent major innovations, such as the Ottawa Treaty banning the use and stockpiling of and trade in anti-personnel land-mines,[4] it becomes clear that strong, if somewhat underappreciated, tendencies towards change in global affairs characterize the late 1990s. The question, of course, is how fundamental is the change promised by these normative innovations? This is an important question, specifically for the developing world, which is looking forward to a century whose reigning norms will be less discriminatory than those of the twentieth century.

This chapter highlights some of the more important and broader normative innovations brought about by the Rome Statute process, and also tries to fathom the depth of these changes. Theoretically, it links up with what can be broadly called "the constructivist turn" in international studies, which sees norms – that is, standards of acceptable and appropriate behaviour – as constitutive elements of global order.[5] One of the main challenges for this literature is to specify the conditions under which fundamental change becomes possible.

Hegemonic, counter-hegemonic, and post-hegemonic norms

In this chapter, a distinction between counter- and post-hegemonic norms will be introduced and developed. However, the important question from a critical perspective is whether the ICC and the process surrounding its introduction reveal some post-hegemonic tendencies as well. Despite being state-based, and in that sense being a reinforcement of current world order norms, the process leading up to the establishment of the ICC and the statute of the ICC itself contain a number of potential counter-hegemonic tendencies.

Hegemonic norms are those that legitimize and uphold the current division of power and privilege in world affairs. An exhaustive list will have to contain many more than those listed below, but these are important in terms of the points made in this chapter. The main hegemonic norms of our time are:

• the acceptability of sovereign impunity – that is, the practice whereby limits to sovereignty are defined by power and not in terms of justice;
• the primacy of state-based, conventional "secret" diplomacy;
• the acceptability of great-power unilateral or multilateral "vetoism", which implies that initiatives in world politics are accepted only if the great powers initiate or agree to them;
• élitism in decision-making and distributive structures;
• interest-based differentiation between humanitarian crises that "deserve" attention and those that do not.

None of these norms is necessarily "given" as part and parcel of the modern state system. Like all norms, they are constructed and learnt and can therefore also be deconstructed and unlearned.

Counter-hegemonic norms are not necessarily "good" norms in all respects simply because they contribute to delegitimizing hegemony. In fact, it is conceivable that a specific counter-hegemonic norm may be questionable because it can be shown to lead to an outcome that may be as problematic, if not more so, than is the case under current hegemony. For instance, if the hegemonic norm of sovereign impunity is countered by restricting sovereignty, but the practice associated with such restrictions leads to selective and arbitrary interventions – ostensibly for humanitarian reasons – a new form of hegemony will be established. Similarly, replacing great-power "top-down" vetoism by transnational activism of the sort exemplified in the successful scuttling of the Multilateral Agreement on Investment and in the land-mines ban will indeed undermine one kind of hegemony, but may replace it with another kind of hegemony: softer and subtler, perhaps, but nevertheless hegemonic.

It is therefore necessary to distinguish between counter-hegemonic and post-hegemonic norms and practices. In doing so, the crucial criterion to apply is whether a particular practice or norm itself legitimizes or delegitimizes forms of exclusion and privilege.[6]

In the rest of this chapter the norms and practices related to the ICC process will be examined in order to determine the extent to which they can be said to give birth to a post-hegemonic order.

What will replace sovereign impunity, and how selective will it be?

Sovereignty may never have been more than a fiction for many of the weaker states of the world, but it is nevertheless a necessary fiction, as they rightly believe. Although it provides the legal screen behind which dictators and murderers have been hiding for too long, it nevertheless remains one of the very few safeguards that developing countries have against arbitrary intervention in their domestic affairs. It may be difficult for people living in an essentially post-sovereignty security complex, such as the one provided by the NATO umbrella, to understand the fears of us poorer souls who find ourselves out there in the real world of anarchy and security dilemmas. When the Non-Aligned Movement or China insists on upholding the principle of sovereignty and non-interference, they do so not only because they want to hide from the normative eyes of the world – which is in any case impossible – but also because they have a real fear that any downplaying of sovereignty would remove the only effective guarantee against the power of the strong to dictate and intervene at their leisure. In terms of democratic theory (not that all leaders who stand on sovereignty are necessarily democratic), the will of the people can only be heard if we settle the question "who are the people?" beforehand. National sovereignty is one, up until now quite successful, way of answering this question.

The fact that some developing countries, despite their firm belief in sovereignty, nevertheless support the ICC, and in some cases even took a lead in promoting it (witness the leading roles played by Malawi, Lesotho, and South Africa, for instance), shows their commitment to undermining sovereign impunity. Nevertheless, some of these same countries have grave concerns that the ICC will provide justification for a new form of great-power interventionism, now legally sanctioned, similar to what has been perceived to be the case with NATO's intervention in Kosovo. While it is clear that the legal process prescribed by the ICC statute would hardly allow this body to be used for such practices, the fear is that this is only the thin edge of the wedge that would make selective intervention, under the pretext of "humanitarian concerns", all the more likely. For some, like China, the fact that the ICC will not fall under the control of the UN Security Council removes the only safeguard that the PRC had. For others, it was important to safeguard the independence of the ICC from great-power machinations in the Security Council, but they still have concerns about what the ICC would imply for the evolution of humanitarian intervention norms. While the norms of humanitarian intervention, legally circumscribed as they are in the Rome Statute to apply only to war crimes, crimes against humanity, and genocide, are clearly counter-hegemonic, they would not in themselves guarantee a post-hegemonic world in the absence of effective safeguards against arbitrary intervention. Activating an indictment against the crime of aggression, once an acceptable definition has been included in the foreseen amended ICC statute, may help, but not much.[7] More important would be that the UN framework for humanitarian intervention be strengthened and codified so as to prevent selective application and ensure unilateral application as far as possible.

Great-power vetoism under threat?

Great-power vetoism can be seen as the main hegemonic norm of our time. It is difficult to see how this norm, based as it is on the specific provisions of the UN Charter, is going to change, even if the composition of the UN Security Council is to change. Nevertheless, we may be witnessing a more subtle whittling away at this norm in various dimensions of multilateral diplomacy. One is the way in which majoritarianism is creeping back into multilateral fora. In the case of the Rome conference, the treaty was eventually accepted by an "unrecorded" majority of the 160 states that took part. Although "unrecorded', the fact that such an overwhelming majority voted in favour adds an element of legitimacy to the treaty and the process that cannot be undermined by attempts to the contrary by powerful states.

There are at least two further ways in which great-power vetoism was undermined. Firstly, during the final meeting of the Committee of the Whole (plenary) of the Rome conference, the US delegation proposed an amendment that the ICC's jurisdiction would only apply to those cases where the state of the accused has accepted the jurisdiction of the ICC. This was part of the so-called "core-issue package" around which a number of US proposals have been attended to and accepted by the conference. Knowing full well that the proposed amendment would scuttle aspects of the finely tuned compromise that was already reached, the USA still went ahead in proposing this amendment. To counter this implicit veto tactic, Norway proposed (as it did with two amendments proposed by India) that "no action" should be taken on the US proposal.

This shifted the focus in voting from the substance of the amendment to the question of whether delegates believed that no action should be taken. Norway's proposal carried the day, with 113 in favour to 17 against, and 25 abstentions. As such "no action" procedural tactics can also be used against any other attempt to undermine a majority consensus, they do provide a powerful action against the veto power of the strong.

A more particular undermining of the veto-power norm is contained in the eventual agreement reached on the role of the Security Council *vis-à-vis* the ICC. In terms of the statute, the UNSC can refer "situations" (not "cases") for investigation to the prosecutor of the ICC, and also has the right to stop impending or ongoing proceedings of the ICC. In terms of what became known as the "Singapore compromise", the original ILC (International Law Commission) proposal that recognized the right of the UNSC permanent members to veto a prosecution has been replaced with a formulation that allows a prosecution to proceed unless the UNSC decides by at least a majority of nine votes that it should not. Thus the negative veto is now replaced with the positive arrangement that the court could exercise its jurisdiction (before and during proceedings) unless otherwise directed by the UN Security Council. Such decisions must be reconsidered within 12 months (as proposed by Canada).

Formally, thus, the ICC process and statute have contributed to undermining the veto power of the great powers in at least some respects. However, it should be obvious that these restrictions have no bearing on the role of the great powers in determining which "situations" can be referred to the ICC and which cannot. Until the composition and operating procedures of the UN Security Council change, it is too soon to speak about a post-hegemonic norm replacing the current hegemonic norm of great-power vetoism.

Élitism undermined?

The sheer extent of participation in the Rome conference (15 June–17 July 1998), the public nature of the process, and the intensity of the process were important blows to the élitism and exclusivity of "established" multilateral diplomacy. The 160 states that participated were the largest group of states ever to participate in a UN codification conference. UN Secretary-General trust funds were used for the first time at a public law codification conference to make it possible for poorer states to attend and stay at the conference for the duration. The trust funds eventually assisted 35 delegates from 33 least developed countries and 19 delegates from 19 developing countries.

Furthermore, the membership of the crucial general committee was increased from the traditional 25 to 34, and of the drafting committee from 21 to 25. Although this meant that the representation of all the UN regional groupings was increased, except for Western European and Other, the move allowed for a strong participation team specifically from Africa, with member states of SADC, notably South Africa, Lesotho, and Malawi, eventually playing lead roles as coordinators of working groups.

Also notable was the large NGO participation at the Rome conference, and the role played by the NGO coalition (the CICC – Coalition for an International Criminal Court) before the conference and since then to provide a forum for public debate on and scrutiny of the process. Two hundred and thirty-six NGOs were accredited to participate (most of them members of the coalition), represented by 450 individuals. Some of the NGO delegations, such as those from Amnesty International and Human Rights Watch, were in fact larger than some government delegations. The coalition secretariat directly or indirectly assisted 50 experts from NGOs in developing and transitional countries to attend and participate in the conference.

The activities of the CICC consisted of the following.

- Facilitating NGO participation by keeping everyone informed of matters to be discussed, facilitating NGO accreditation, and acting as a link between NGOs and the UN Secretariat.
- Regional caucuses were organized to facilitate coordination. This activity led to a very effective tri-continental alliance formed by groups from Africa, Asia, and Latin America.
- Twelve monitoring teams were set up, each to cover a specific aspect of the negotiations. These teams prepared daily reports that were of great assistance in keeping everyone, including the media, informed about what was going on, and on which issues pressure could be applied on which participants.
- The coalition also provided legal experts and interns who could participate as members of government delegations.
- It organized regionally focused meetings that provided opportunity for informal intergovernmental negotiations and interactions between governments and NGOs.
- The CICC organized three news teams, *Terra Viva*, *On-the-Record*, and the *CICC Monitor*, which provided the only print and electronic coverage for the conference. News packages were prepared for the use of journalists, and to date it would be true to say that the CICC is the main supplier of information on the ICC to world civil society.
- The CICC continues to play a leading role in trying to secure the 60 ratifications needed to put the ICC into operation.

The ICC process thus stands out as one of a number of recent examples of how public diplomacy is changing the contours of world politics (the others are the scuttling of the MAI and the success of the Ottawa Treaty process). While less pronounced in bilateral diplomacy (although not absent), public diplomacy has become a major feature accompanying "complex multilateralism". It is on this level that the ICC process harbingers more than just counter-hegemonic norms.

However, effective NGO participation is still limited to only a few very specific issues, and can by no means be seen as a permanent feature of multilateralism. In addition, a critical perspective should be entertained on the role of NGOs themselves. While aspiring to represent civil society, there exist very few means to secure accountability on the part of NGOs, except by their main donors and via the public space they open for debate on issues. Greater prominence of NGOs does not in itself mean the greater democratization of world affairs. The role of grassroots social movements may become crucial in this respect, giving reason to appreciate the distinction regarding "new multilateralism" being based on a broader social base than "emerging" multilateralism ("complex multilateralism" in O'Brien's words[8]), where semi-élitist NGOs form a counterpart, but an exclusivist one, to governments.

Conclusions

The ICC process, and the statute setting up the ICC itself, represent a major example of normative innovation through multilateral negotiations. Their effect will in due course be comparable to the two Hague Conferences of 1899 and 1907. The ICC, however, not only advances international humanitarian public law to new heights, but the diplomacy accompanying it also introduces new practices and norms that can be said to be at least counter-hegemonic, and even post-hegemonic in some respects.

Justified though our enthusiasm for this and similar projects is, it would be a mistake to assume that all attempts at breaking out of the stranglehold of established great-power-dominated, top-down diplomacy are necessarily good simply by virtue of being counter-hegemonic. At the end of the twentieth century we probably need little reminding that new hegemonies lurk in the shadows of counter-hegemonic projects. We should therefore make sure that our criteria of assessment of the new diplomacy have built into them a healthy dose of self-criticism.

Of particular concern for the developing countries (if one may be so bold as to speak on their behalf) is the fear that the unchecked evolution of humanitarian intervention, justified though it may be in certain circumstances, has a sting in the tail that can be used by the strong against the weak if the legal fiction of sovereignty is not upheld.

In one of the funding proposals for a project on the "new diplomacy" as exemplified by the Ottawa Treaty and the Rome Statute, it was suggested that the processes leading to these two international agreements can be likened to an "end run" in grid iron, where immediate power obstacles are circumvented by a run behind the last lines of defence and a well-timed long-distance pass. The problem with this metaphor is that it may not evoke the intended associations among people from the global South, where soccer (and to some extent rugby) are *the* games. In both rugby and soccer, "end runs" are illegal moves, implying offsides or forward passes. What the developing countries rightly fear, therefore, is that end runs by middle powers and NGO coalitions of the North, counter-hegemonic though they may be, can constitute a new form of illegality. One should be careful not to assume that metaphors and norms necessarily travel well.

Notes

1. For comprehensive information on the Rome Statute and the process leading up to it, see the website of the international coalition of NGOs which helped to establish the International Criminal Court: http://www.iccnow.org. See also F. Benedetti and J. Washburn, "Drafting the ICC Treaty: Two Years to Rome and an Afterword on the Rome Diplomatic Conference", *Global Governance* 5, no. 1 (January–March 1999), pp. 1–39. In preparing this chapter, the author was much assisted by the publication of an edited volume detailing the process and content of the Rome Statute, namely R. Lee, ed., *The International Criminal Court: The Making of the Rome Statute – Issues, Negotiations, Results* (The Hague: Kluwer Law International, 1999).
2. M. Cheriff Basiounni, "Policy Perspectives Favoring the Establishment of the ICC", *Journal of International Affairs* 52, no. 2 (Spring 1999), pp. 795–810.
3. Common definitions of such crimes have to be presented by the preparatory committee of the ICC conference by June 2000. One of the reasons why by the end of November 1999 only four states had ratified the statute (89 have signed) is that legislators still await these specific definitions.
4. See specifically R. Price, "Reversing the Gun Sights: Transnational Civil Society Targets Land Mines", *International Organization* 52, no. 3 (1998), pp. 613–644; R. Thakur and W. Maley, "The Ottawa Convention on Landmines: A Landmark Humanitarian Treaty in Arms Control?", *Global Governance* 5, no. 3 (July–September 1999), pp. 273–302.
5. The literature representing "the constructivist turn" is extensive, but good summaries and expositions can be found in R. Price and C. Reus-Smit, "Dangerous Liaisons? Critical International Theory and Constructivism", *European Journal of International Relations* 4 (1998), pp. 259–294; J. Ruggie, "What Makes the World Hang Together? Neo-utilitarianism and the Social Constructivist Challenge", *International Organization* 52 (1998), pp. 855–885; M. Finnemore and K. Sikkink, "International Norm Dynamics and Political Change", *International Organization* 52 (1998), pp. 887–917.

6. Readers familiar with critical theory of international relations would recognize the gene-alogy of the terms "legitimize" and "delegitimize". See R. Cox, "Multilateralism and World Order", *Review of International Studies* 18, no. 2 (April 1992), pp. 161–180; F. Gareau, "International Institutions and the Gramscian Legacy: Its Modification, Expansion, and Reaffirmation", *Social Science Journal* 33, no. 2 (1996), pp. 235–247.

7. The international crime of aggression is included in the Rome Statute as a crime in terms of which prosecution can be initiated, but a commonly accepted definition of what aggression is still has to be developed by the preparatory committee.

8. R. O'Brien, "Complex Multilateralism: The Global Economic Institutions – Global Social Movements Nexus", unpublished paper (Warwick: Centre for the Study of Globalisation and Regionalisation, University of Warwick, 1997). See also R. O. Brien, Anne Marie Goetz, Jan Aart Scholte, and Marc Williams, *Contesting Global Governance: Multilateral Economic Institutions and Global Social Movements* (Cambridge: Cambridge University Press, 2000).

10

Industry regulation and self-regulation: The case of labour standards

Virginia Haufler

Globalization has made the regulation of multinational corporations one of the most contentious issues in relations between states and within societies. What is striking about current debates, however, is the degree to which they now centre on the issue of private sector self-regulation, an idea that would have been laughed off the table only a few decades ago. Many multinational corporations are adopting a variety of self-regulatory policies and are doing so at an increasing rate. Self-regulatory policies include corporate codes of conduct which lay out the social commitments the company makes; management and accounting systems that translate those commitments into specific roles and responsibilities within the organization; implementation programmes that involve the expenditure of resources to achieve specific goals; and monitoring, auditing, certification, and labelling programmes testifying to successful achievement. Industry self-regulation also shades into "co-regulation" at times, when the policies and programmes are developed in cooperation with governments or non-governmental actors. Much of this activity falls under the more popular headings of "corporate social responsibility", "corporate citizenship", and "business ethics".

The Organization for Economic Cooperation and Development (OECD) recently analysed a sample of 233 corporate codes of conduct. This analysis demonstrated that a growing number of companies either adopted or revised their codes of conduct in the past decade.[1] In a recent survey, KPMG reported that of 1,000 large Canadian companies 86.4 per cent had some sort of corporate code.[2] A recent International Labour Organization (ILO) report on voluntary initiatives found the same upward trend for codes addressing labour issues.[3] Indirectly, corporate interest can be gauged by, for instance, the huge audience for the annual meetings of Business for Social Responsibility, a US-based business membership organization. The Prince of Wales Business Leaders Forum in the UK, made up of British firms, has gained increasing visibility and influence in promoting corporate social responsibility. The Sullivan Principles, originally developed for companies in apartheid South Africa, have been revised to become general global guidelines, and many companies are signing up. The UN Global Compact, while still in its early stages, is beginning to attract major multinational corporations. Even the US Chamber of Commerce – not usually viewed as a progressive organization – recently established a Corporate Citizenship Center.

Corporate codes of conduct are generally the most visible measure of industry self-regulation. However, there are now a wide array of other elements of this emerging self-regulatory system. An increasing number of management programmes support the implementation of those codes within the corporate bureaucracy. These include auditing, accounting, monitoring, and reporting requirements. In fact, there has been such a proliferation in environmental reporting alone that the UNEP, in partnership with business organizations and NGOs, has convened a global reporting initiative in an effort to standardize and make sense of the competing formats. Hundreds of international firms have adopted environmental management systems, including the ISO14000 standards, which are designed to help link their environmental code to actual organizational implementation.[4] Monitoring and auditing of performance have become so common that the major auditing and accounting firms now have well-established practices in this new market, with Pricewaterhouse Coopers the market leader in social audits of factories. Businesses have created new associations to assist in developing standards and implementing them, often partnering with NGOs – for example, in the Fair Labor Association for apparel manufacturers in the USA. Many companies have moved from simple codes of conduct developed by top management to bottom-up policy processes within the entire company. Still others have moved from codes developed "in-house" to collective efforts within an industry or business group. Others have developed more elaborate systems that institutionalize new practices and certify their implementation.

Few people trust business to implement higher standards and stick by them. This is complicated by the fact that, fundamentally, much of current self-regulation is about the activities of corporations *in other countries*. Governments and publics in the industrialized countries, where regulatory systems are strong and well developed, want the private sector to raise standards in developing countries. Industry self-regulation may be one way to raise standards, but codes of conduct are voluntary, unenforceable, and lacking credibility. Even more troubling for many, however, is the issue of accountability. If these efforts are an indirect means for public goals to be met by private interests, then how does the public influence their content? How can the public make sure the private sector upholds its end of this one-sided bargain? Without the public having a voice, these new forms of regulation appear to be undemocratic and illegitimate.

Attempts at international regulation of multinational corporations

Comprehensive international regulation of the private sector has generally failed. Since multinational corporations first emerged as a significant force after the Second World War, regulation of them generally has been by individual countries and not by international law and organizations, although this issue has certainly been on the agenda for the entire postwar era. The effort to use international law to regulate corporations reached a high point in the 1970s, when the United Nations sponsored negotiations over a proposed voluntary Code of Conduct on Transnational Corporations, the OECD developed its Guidelines for Multinational Enterprises, and the ILO adopted its tripartite Declaration on Multinational Enterprises. Governments also developed sectoral agreements as a result of contentious debates over specific industry practices, such as the marketing of infant formula in developing countries. In Latin America, countries responded to the entry of foreign investors with the creation of a set of regional investment codes.[5] Both developing nations and trade unions in the 1970s agreed that the power of international business needed to be reined in as part of a new international economic order, but their efforts failed.[6]

The climate of the early 1970s played an important role in capturing the collective attention of the United Nations and others on the issue of corporate behaviour. Corporate influence on national politics had become a concern, particularly in newly independent states still uncertain of their sovereignty. Scandals had erupted – for instance, over the role of ITT in Chile. In response to developing country demands, the UN Economic and Social Council (ECOSOC) in 1972 adopted a resolution to monitor closely the behaviour of transnational corporations (TNCs). ECOSOC established the Commission on Transnational Corporations in 1974 with the mandate to negotiate a code of conduct for transnational corporations. Under the proposed UN code, states would pledge to ensure that foreign investors respected national sovereignty and human rights, disclosed relevant information to host governments about their operations, refrained from transfer pricing, and resolved other points of contention.[7] From the very start, the United Nations assumed the end result would be a comprehensive, single international instrument.

Developing countries, empowered by the success of the OPEC oil embargo in 1972, insisted that the industrialized world make the code mandatory and apply it only to transnational corporations and not to the governments that hosted them. The major industrialized nations, on the other hand, supported a voluntary code that addressed both host government and corporate behaviour. In the early negotiations, the issues of nationalization and compensation of foreign corporate assets and the national treatment of foreign companies tied up the discussions. The UN debate over a corporate code became a flashpoint for conflicts between the developing and industrialized countries, exacerbated by Cold War tensions and the ideological fight between capitalism and communism. The negotiations dragged on throughout the decade.

By 1985, efforts to develop an international corporate code had stagnated.[8] In both the USA and the UK, by the 1980s the political wind had turned and new governments ardently pursued free-market policies that went against further regulation of corporations. Many developing countries were suffering through a debt crisis, and, under IMF guidance, adopted deregulatory policies themselves. They were no longer very interested in the UN code negotiations. In 1991, the Bush administration argued that private corporations played a critical role in the world economy, and therefore they should not be regulated. In 1992, despite agreement on about 80 per cent of the content of the code, the international negotiations ended.

Simultaneously with the UN negotiations, the OECD managed to negotiate and adopt its Guidelines for Multinational Enterprises in 1976 as part of a broader Declaration on International Investment and Multinational Enterprises. The member states – the industrialized nations – negotiated principles that governments would apply voluntarily to the private sector. The guidelines broadly covered issues ranging from financing and taxation to employment and environmental protection. They had little influence, however, and little visibility, despite the fact that the OECD revised the guidelines twice in the following decades.

A year after the initial guidelines were adopted by the OECD, the ILO also formulated and adopted a Declaration of Principles Concerning Multinational Enterprises and Social Policy. The declaration established voluntary guidelines covering employment, training, working conditions, and industrial relations. As in all ILO conventions, the declaration applied to governments and relied upon them to ratify and implement its provisions. The ILO instrument places more restrictions on TNC activity than the OECD document, but is not as comprehensive as the UN code would have been. Both the OECD guidelines and the ILO declaration did not have much direct and measurable effect, but they laid the groundwork for later efforts.

The concern over multinational corporate behaviour did not pass with the formulation and adoption of the OECD guidelines or the ILO declaration. Although interest in developing a multilateral code of conduct waned in the 1980s, specific issues did grab the headlines. The most significant was the movement to use corporations as levers to change the apartheid regime in South Africa and facilitate peace in Northern Ireland. In 1977, the Reverend Leon Sullivan, a member of the board of General Motors and an activist against apartheid, developed a set of principles to guide companies operating in South Africa, hoping the private sector could change the system from within. By 1984, 128 of about 350 US companies operating in South Africa had agreed to abide by these principles. Despite this, Sullivan himself began to lose faith in their efficacy, as too many companies did not actually implement the principles and the apartheid regime appeared firmly entrenched. Yet, in hindsight, the Sullivan Principles were an important piece in the ultimately successful movement against apartheid and demonstrated the value of using companies to pursue political objectives.[9]

In the past decade, smaller groups of states have been able to negotiate and implement rules governing corporate behaviour. These regional regulations are fairly comprehensive, covering both corporate rights and responsibilities. The two major advances in this area are the Social Protocol of the European Union and the labour and environment side agreements of the North American Free Trade Agreement (NAFTA). These two, despite significant weaknesses, establish wider acceptance of the idea that corporations must be held to high standards.

In the 1990s, as the backlash against globalization and corporate power gained strength, the OECD launched two new efforts: one to revise the existing Guidelines for Multinational Enterprises, and the second to sponsor negotiations over a comprehensive and enforceable Multilateral Agreement on Investment (MAI). The latter would lay out such principles as national treatment for foreign investment, protection of property rights, and arbitration requirements. The MAI, a complicated document full of trade-offs to protect the interests of different industries and countries, garnered only weak support among the member governments. A loose coalition of environmental, human rights, and anti-corporate organizations put the final nail in the proposed MAI by mobilizing energetically against an agreement that they argued protected the rights of corporations without paying equivalent attention to their responsibilities.[10]

In contrast, the OECD successfully concluded another revision of the original Guidelines for Multinational Enterprises in June 2000, strengthening their provisions significantly. The new OECD guidelines have wider acceptance, with some non-OECD newly industrializing countries such as the Republic of Korea and Brazil indicating a desire to adopt them. These guidelines will be monitored through national contact points in each country. It is too early to tell whether they will eventually become a strong instrument of corporate regulation, but the history of earlier efforts leads one to doubt it.

Interest in international regulation of multinational corporations has waxed and waned over the past three decades. The United Nations, ILO, and OECD all attempted to develop comprehensive frameworks for corporate behaviour, but these early initiatives had little impact. In recent years, all three organizations have revitalized their attention to corporate activities. At the same time, however, the private sector has not remained immune to the pressures of their changing social environment. The public's expectations regarding corporate behaviour have changed, and many companies are responding to these changes with their own principles, guidelines, practices, and codes.

Why self-regulate?

Regulation broadly defined is the formal rules or standards that dictate what is acceptable and required behaviour, putting limits on what is permissible.[11] Self-regulation occurs when those regulated design and implement and perhaps even enforce the rules themselves. Corporate self-regulation is all about the private sector setting rules that govern its behaviour. They are adopted voluntarily, and either go beyond current regulatory requirements or establish new standards in areas where government rules or standards are lacking. While they are adopted voluntarily, the rules may be backed up with a variety of formal and informal enforcement mechanisms, including written agreements among companies or between companies and other groups. The basic document of such an initiative is typically a "corporate code of conduct".

The main participants in self-regulation are multinational corporations based in the industrialized countries. Changes in the international system provide them with increasing access to a large number of markets hitherto closed to them. The most dramatic opportunity is China's entry into the WTO, portending a great reorganization of the world economy. Both large and small firms have an international presence through trade, joint ventures, strategic alliances, outsourcing of production to local manufacturers abroad, and, in recent years, via the internet.[12] Intense competition for markets pushes all firms to produce at lower cost with higher quality, and respond to changing consumer demands almost instantaneously. In their operations in developing countries, they face myriad conflicting cultures, often weak national governments, and markets so thin of economic activity that foreign corporations easily dominate them. They also find themselves dealing with a tangle of law and regulation at multiple levels of government on a variety of policy issues. Many corporations that invest and transact business internationally are torn between a desire for harmonization and standardization of the rules of the game, and strategic calculations about the competitive edge that they could gain from taking advantage of such a mixed system.[13]

Self-regulatory strategies are chosen to reduce risk, enhance reputation, and respond to new ideas within the business community. Political risks include everything from war and riot to changes in regulatory systems. Government regulation can be a burden and a cost, to be avoided if at all possible, and therefore often constitutes the biggest risk. There are, of course, situations in which an industry or set of firms prefers to have the government step in, in order to restrain competition or promote consumer confidence. But this typically happens at the national level, where industry representatives may feel they have more control over the process. There exists a lot more uncertainty about the transnational aspects of corporate operations. In these situations, the company may face the possibility of at least three sources of regulation: regulation in one or more host countries where the company operates; regulation by the home country of activities both at home *and* abroad; and international regulation. One would expect most transnational companies to favour government negotiation to design global rules, so that they would not have to deal with such a welter of conflicting national regulatory systems.[14] But the process of negotiating intergovernmental agreements can be slow, clumsy, often wrong-headed, and highly political, which means the design of rules – even rules the private sector desires – can be fraught with risk. Some corporate decision-makers may prefer instead to calculate how to use the differences in national regulation to gain a competitive advantage. For instance, different companies may take advantage of differences in the way that national regulatory systems affect the skills and wages of the labour pool. Recent successful efforts to negotiate international rules that affect corporate interests do indicate that the political risk in this area is high.

Transnational activist pressure is a key feature of current calculation of

political risk. Until recently, most companies discounted the effect of social mobilization on their operations. They calculated that they could win
their position through lobbying national governments, litigating in the
courts, or stonewalling. Recent successes by activist groups in raising the
costs of doing business through boycotts, shareholder activism, media
campaigns, and litigation have changed this calculation.[15] Shell Oil lost a
lot of business when it tried to dispose of an old oil platform in the North
Sea and Greenpeace launched an extensive and successful European
campaign, using both media exposure and boycotts, against it. In the
USA, activists are using the Alien Tort Claims Act to bring companies to
court over human rights violations abroad, effectively using litigation as a
tool against the company.[16]

Shareholder activism is on the rise. Socially responsible investment
(SRI) funds, which screen out corporations deemed illegitimate in some
way, are growing ever larger, with some major institutional investors
such as the California Pension System (Calpers) now considering social
screens too.[17] Such funds are primarily found in the USA, UK, Canada,
and Australia.[18] In the USA, over $2 trillion are now handled by SRI
funds, and over 120 institutions and mutual fund families have used their
ownership of assets to bring shareholder resolutions on social issues.[19] A
recent survey of the top 500 British occupational pension funds showed
that 59 per cent of them, representing 78 per cent of assets, had some
form of socially responsible investment policy.[20] Another survey found
that 71 per cent of the financial community in London believe social and
ethical considerations are more important for them today than five years
ago, and 77 per cent expect them to become more so in the coming five
years.[21]

Joining these political risks, and interacting with them, are a number of
significant economic risks that can also drive a company to adopt new
higher standards. One of the most obvious is the competitive position of
the company or industry on a global basis. When markets are highly
competitive, every added cost is harder for management to justify in terms
of bottom-line profits and market share. Self-regulatory programmes
often entail significant financial costs, and may undermine a firm's competitive position – especially if no other major competitor adopts similar
standards. This is why it is difficult for a single corporation to adopt a
highly restrictive code of conduct. When corporations can agree on setting standards together, however, the competitive position of each is
maintained. This is why oligopolistic markets are the most likely candidates for collective self-regulatory action, since it is easier to get a
smaller number of firms to agree.[22] At the same time, these costs of self-
regulation can be offset by significant benefits in terms of new markets

for high-quality goods and services, or lower costs of production. For instance, if a company sets a higher standard for the elimination of industrial waste it may discover greater efficiencies in the production process.

Another economic risk that influences the decision to develop self-regulation is the degree to which the business of a company is tied to a specific locale, people, or production process (what economists call "asset specificity").[23] Assets tied in this way are difficult if not impossible to disentangle. For instance, extractive industries such as mining are literally tied to the places where the minerals exist. They are unlikely to leave a particular place voluntarily, even when the political situation around them deteriorates. This puts them in a unique political and economic position, subjecting them to more attention from activists and more government regulation.[24] A company that cannot pick up and move must learn to manage other risks, such as the risk of transnational activism or of government regulation. Other companies, for instance consumer goods manufacturers, have very low asset specificity. These firms often collaborate closely with a chain of suppliers around the world, and yet maintain their distance and ability to drop one supplier and pick up another fairly easily. They can reduce the risk of too much specialization or dependence through outsourcing and partnerships. More flexible firms would be less subject to political pressure of all kinds; in fact, long supply chains are themselves the object of criticism for this very reason.

Neither competitive pressures nor the threat of government regulation and public activism can entirely explain the convergence across sectors and issues on a self-regulatory strategy, however. Reputation has become increasingly important as a corporate and industry asset, and is one of the key explanatory factors behind the rise of self-regulatory behaviour. When a company develops a reputation for making a quality product, this gives the company a stronger brand name. Increasingly, we see competition in many markets based not just on how cheap a product is, but also on the quality of the product. Corporations that are close to consumers and can sell directly to them are likely to feel bottom-line effects when consumers shun them if they believe the firm has behaved reprehensibly. Reputation affects not just sales to customers, but also a range of other relationships on the production side as well. A company with a positive reputation is attractive to potential employees, and in tight labour markets those potential employees favour working for firms with a strong positive image. The same is true for potential business partners and even governments, both of which may be more willing to work closely with a reputable company and trust it to behave well. Once reputation becomes a significant asset of a company, then that company will be more vulnerable to activist campaigns. Many NGO critics use the leverage of corporate reputation to try to influence a company's behaviour.

In response, a company may try to enhance its reputation by setting high standards in a variety of areas. As a company values its reputation more, it will be more likely to try to preserve it and promote it through a variety of corporate codes and other voluntary initiatives.

The trend towards industry self-regulation would not be pushed forward very far without the spread of knowledge, information, and ideas within the business community regarding the relative costs and benefits of voluntary initiatives. Any self-regulatory system requires some consensus on what the rules ought to be, and expertise on how to implement them.[25] In the case of self-regulation, learning is a process in which consensual knowledge is applied by business leaders to change their policy projects and political strategies.[26] Industry self-regulation is still at a relatively early stage of development, so there are only scattered areas of consensus that vary across issue areas. In those areas where there is some business agreement over appropriate norms and standards, firms within an industry are more likely to self-regulate. Where consensus is deep, that self-regulation is likely to be collectively developed and implemented. The role of leadership in this process cannot be underestimated. Particular business leaders may adopt new strategies, lobby other business leaders to join them, and even put economic pressure on business partners through their business relationships, such as supply networks. In the past few decades, businesses have created organizations dedicated to spreading information and knowledge about these ideas while highlighting their leadership on these issues. Business leaders and industry associations establish business "best practices", and these influence what other managers view as the normal range of options available to them.

The case of industry self-regulation for labour standards

Existing data on the disparity in wages and working conditions cross-nationally are not very good, but even the rough information we have highlights the huge gulf between industrialized and developing countries. The ratio of average income in the richest country in the world to the poorest is about 60:1 today, and inequality around the world is on the rise.[27] Manufacturing costs in the newly industrializing economies of Asia are 36 per cent of US costs, while they are only 10 per cent in Mexico. In 1997 the average hourly compensation of German manufacturing workers was $28.28, Japanese $18.37, and American $18.24; at the same time, Mexican workers took home only $1.75 per hour in compensation.[28] Compensation costs in newly industrializing countries such as Taiwan, however, have increased relative to US costs.[29] Variations in working conditions – from hours of work and overtime, to health and

safety, to discrimination, to collective bargaining – are even more difficult to summarize. Child labour, for instance, makes up about one-third
of the workforce in many African countries, about 9 per cent in Indonesia, 14 per cent in India, but close to zero in South Korea.[30] Practices
viewed as unacceptable, even immoral (such as child and bonded labour), by many are all too common in some developing countries.

Many companies now produce goods by farming out portions of the
production process to subcontractors – and to their subcontractors and
sub-subcontractors, sometimes numbering in the thousands, mostly located in the developing world where labour costs are so low. Disney
alone has over 6,000 subcontractors for its various products. Long supply
chains are particularly common in the sectors where criticism of labour
standards is most common: textiles, apparel, footwear, toys, and sporting
goods. The result of this complex outsourcing is that brand-name companies now sell goods made by people who are not direct employees.
Nike, for instance, does not own factories itself but rather contracts with
factories around the world to supply the products it designs and puts its
logo on. This new organization of production makes it extremely difficult
for labour to maintain a balance of power with management, especially
since a national union does not have the ability to take effective action
against the overseas operations of a corporation. Foreign buyers have a
huge influence on working conditions in these countries, even without
directly owning any production facilities.

Three traditional means for redressing poor working conditions are,
in the eyes of many critics, inadequate to meet the needs of labour in a
period of rapid economic globalization. First, the idea that governments
will protect workers through appropriate legislation and enforcement is
unrealistic in many developing countries. Even with the best will in the
world, the political infrastructure may not be in place to ensure that
working conditions meet established standards. In many cases, the will
itself is missing. Some governments deliberately pursue policies that lead
to lower labour standards, for a variety of reasons – repression of labour
unrest, desire to attract foreign investment, policies that favour one
group over another, resistance by industrial élites, and other reasons.
However, we cannot say this is true everywhere, and in fact wages and
working conditions have improved in some of the newly industrialized
countries. In general, the most problematic countries for labour rights,
such as China or Viet Nam, are the ones that are fairly impervious to
political demands for change, especially when made by foreign governments or activists.

Historically the most potent tools in the hands of labour have been
unionization and collective bargaining. Many of the countries where the

conditions of work have become an international issue are countries where unions are either outlawed or suppressed, where collective bargaining is uncommon, and where the power of labour as a political force is weak. Major international labour organizations, such as the ICFTU (International Confederation of Free Trade Unions) and AFL-CIO (American Federation of Labor-Congress of Industrial Organizations) and others, have tried to promote and support labour organizers abroad, but the political barriers to success can be quite high. Finally, another means towards raising worldwide labour standards is through the ILO. It has great, but as yet unrealized, potential to be a bulwark against the exploitation of workers.[31] In recent years, the role of the ILO has been revitalized with the reaffirmation and acceptance of the fundamental or core principles of the ILO.

Major human rights groups put labour on the international agenda by the late 1980s and early 1990s. Human Rights Watch, Amnesty International, and the International Labor Rights Fund, plus unions, consumer groups, churches, and social justice campaigners forcefully began to pressure governments around the world to address – and redress – the exploitative conditions found in many developing countries. They focused on an array of related issues: unsafe and unhealthy working conditions, extremely long working hours, exploitation of child labour, discrimination against women or particular ethnic groups, the use of forced labour, the suppression of freedom of association and collective bargaining, and the lack of a "living wage". They pointed in particular to what they saw as the inevitable results of intense economic competition in labour-intensive industries such as apparel, footwear, toys, and sports equipment. The broader human rights activist networks took up the cause of labour.

The business community woke up to the increasing power of this labour activism though a number of high-profile cases. Activists accused the TV personality Kathie Lee Gifford of complicity in sweatshop labour because she endorsed a line of clothing for Wal-Mart. Much of this clothing was stitched in factories in Honduras that employed children in 20-hour working days. In recent years, activist campaigns have specially targeted Nike with accusations that it uses sweatshop labour in developing countries, and its profits and market share have been declining.[32] In 1996, CBS reported on sweatshop conditions in a factory in Viet Nam that supplied Nike products, and within a year Vietnam Labor Watch formed to monitor Nike's actions publicly. The "campaign of embarrassment" against retail giants and media personalities brought home to consumers the conditions of work in the places where imported clothing was made.[33] A new anti-sweatshop movement began to gain headway among activists, consumers, and especially students in the USA, Canada, and Australia. Campus activism emerged as a significant factor in the late 1990s, as students across the USA demanded that university logo goods be certified as sweatshop-free.

Many firms strongly resisted outside demands, refusing to provide information about working conditions and subcontractor operations, rejecting any community engagement, opposing unions and collective bargaining, and accepting existing poor living conditions in developing countries. But others have pursued a more accommodationist policy, responding to new political pressures by launching voluntary initiatives addressing labour conditions at home and abroad. Their efforts fall into three basic categories: individual corporate initiatives, such as a corporate code of conduct; group initiatives, either within an industry sector or in partnership with public interest groups; and acceptance of third-party oversight. Those three categories reflect the evolution of the self-regulatory movement on labour issues, as corporations have moved from weak individual codes to ever-stronger collective public commitments.

Initially, a number of corporations simply handed down a new corporate code of conduct developed by management or by an outside consultant. These codes would lay out high-minded principles for ethical behaviour and establish a commitment to treating workers fairly. They were often empty statements of sentiment suitable for public consumption and marketing purposes. The codes languished at headquarters and were never publicized widely within the corporation, or else they were trotted out for public consumption to burnish the image of the company when necessary. Workers often knew little or nothing about them – especially workers in foreign factories looking at statements written in English. The weaknesses of these codes gave them a bad reputation.

Nike unveiled a corporate code of conduct in the early 1990s, but suffered unrelenting criticism due to the weakness of its provisions and implementation. At first, Nike defended itself by arguing that it could not be responsible for the actions of its suppliers. Many other firms also began to develop codes of conduct in the 1990s. A number of them also tried to ensure they were properly implemented by establishing management procedures within the corporations, as part of a wider human relations/personnel function within the firm. They set up systems to encourage workers to report violations (often setting up a toll-free number for such reports), translated all documents into the native language of the workers, and monitored their own compliance. These codes applied primarily to direct employees.

Levi Strauss & Co. developed and implemented global sourcing and operating guidelines, which rest fundamentally on its business partner terms of engagement. These guidelines became a model for codes that regulate the behaviour of suppliers and subcontractors. The document is a set of guiding principles for choosing business partners and identifying potential problems ahead of time. The Levi's code states that contractors are expected to be ethical, law-abiding, and to meet employment standards including paying minimum wages or prevailing wages, setting reasonable working hours not exceeding 60 hours per week, not using child labour less than 14 years old or prison or forced labour, maintaining a safe and healthy work environment, and not discriminating among employees or using corporate punishment or coercion to discipline workers. Levi's also produces country risk assessments to understand how likely violations might be in different cultural settings. Most importantly, top management is committed to these principles. For instance, Levi's at one time withdrew its business from China when it could not be sure these standards could be met.

Reebok, seeing the writing on the wall after the media tarring of Nike, chose to adopt better practices itself. Reebok instituted a policy of refusing to buy soccer balls from factories using child labour. Instead of going it alone, however, it obtained support first from the World Federation of Sporting Goods Industries and the US Sporting Goods Manufacturers Association. These collective commitments can create stronger incentives, for the buyer and seller alike. In this case, Reebok felt reassured that other manufacturers would be reluctant to undercut it in this market. Sellers, faced with a collective refusal to buy soccer balls made by children, had to change their practices.

At the same time as the corporate code "movement" advanced, many other groups began to promote the adoption by companies of various codes. Labour advocates, unions, governments, and international organizations all began experimenting with "cooperative" approaches to regulation. In these cases, the standards and systems of implementation are designed in concert, but the final result is a voluntary initiative and not new regulation. By the mid-1990s, Amnesty International, the Interfaith Center on Corporate Responsibility, the Clean Clothes Campaign in Europe, and others all had labour codes they asked businesses to adopt.

Clinton administration officials turned to an ambitious programme in the mid-1990s, facilitating negotiations between business and its critics. It helped launch the Apparel Industry Partnership (AIP), consisting of 18 garment-makers and labour and human rights groups. The AIP began meeting in 1996 to develop basic labour standards to govern factories and suppliers in textile, apparel, and footwear industries.[34] The US government had no direct vote on the outcome of negotiations among these groups, but helped bring the participants together. The outcome of the negotiations under the AIP would be developed through a multi-party process with representatives from a range of interested groups, and not just business alone. The negotiations lasted for three years, and almost broke down completely at one point. The participants engaged in often contentious debate over the appropriate set of standards and how to implement them. The most divisive issues concerned the design of a monitoring system, unionization, and especially the issue of a living wage. Some original members of the AIP, including the Union of Needletrades, Industrial, and Textile Employees (UNITE), withdrew from the process. After UNITE withdrew, a handful of major corporate participants, including Nike, Liz Claiborne, Phillips Van Heusen, and Reebok, stayed in and finally agreed to some basic principles. They decided to establish an independent Fair Labor Association (FLA), a private entity split between corporate and human rights/labour representatives. The FLA would accredit auditors to certify company compliance with the agreed standards. The FLA officially began to operate in late 1999, and it is still too early to tell its ultimate impact.

Partly in response to the negotiations in the AIP, the American Apparel Manufacturers Association (AAMA) developed its own industry guidelines for its member companies. These responsible apparel production (RAP) principles are intended to help companies police their factories and suppliers. Members of the AAMA had been targets of high-profile attacks, and the AIP at times seemed either on the verge of collapse or about to include what members viewed as unreasonable standards. The AAMA ensured that the RAP principles include many fundamental labour rights, but exclude contentious elements such as freedom of association and collective bargaining. Each company that signs on to the RAP principles makes a commitment to have its factories independently inspected.

The UK government under Tony Blair also launched an initiative designed to harness corporate voluntary action to "ethical" foreign policy goals. The Blair government launched what it called the Ethical Trading Initiative in January 1998. The ETI is a programme that includes equal representation by business, workers' organizations, and NGOs. It aims to develop and encourage voluntary adoption of a set of standards, and monitoring and auditing methods, for the apparel industry. Unlike in the USA, a fairly large number of British corporations, non-profits, and unions have signed on to it.

Other voluntary initiatives focused on the carpet industry in India, soccer ball manufacturing in Pakistan, and others. For instance, the Confederation of British Industry, UNICEF, and the UK government launched a combined campaign against child labour. Carpet industry officials in India negotiated with child and labour activists and UNICEF to eliminate child labour in the carpet industry, largely due to pressure from German consumer groups. They developed the Rugmark programme, which monitors worksheets and certifies carpets have been made without child labour. The negotiations addressed one of the most difficult issues – the future of the children themselves, given the poverty of their families. The Rugmark programme includes funding to place former child workers in school and replace their wages with aid. The ILO developed a similar programme with soccer ball manufacturers and exporters in Pakistan, which was initiated in 1996. In both cases, the voluntary programme by industry involved an explicit commitment by governments and international organizations to treat the elimination of child labour in part as a development aid issue.

One of the most significant developments in the area of industry self-regulation was not an actual corporate or industry code or standards programme. In 1998 the Council on Economic Priorities (CEP), a non-profit association with a long history of promoting corporate social responsibility, launched an effort to develop social accounting standards. The system was modelled on the ISO standards-setting process, and is called SA8000. The CEP developed it with the input of retail associations, Amnesty International, SGS International Certification Services, Reebok, the International Textile Workers Union, and others. SA8000 is a set of verifiable standards that includes child labour, forced or slave labour, worker safety, and freedom of association. Unlike ISO14000, the SA8000 standards are both process and performance standards. Social Accountability International administers it, and trains and certifies individuals to conduct social audits. Companies hire SAI-certified auditors who can assess whether or not the firm can be certified as meeting SA8000 standards. The incentives for other businesses to join in are the reputation effects of certification, and inclusion in socially screened mutual funds. Neil Kearney, Secretary-General of the International Textile, Garment, and Leather Workers Federation, joined the board of SA8000. Kearney argues that it is impractical to construct codes and monitoring systems industry by industry, and that professional certification firms would be an improvement over the current alternatives.[35]

The AIP, RAP, Rugmark, and other programmes came at about the same time as international pressure mounted to link trade and labour in international negotiations. By the end of the 1990s, unions, labour activists, and human rights organizations pressed national governments from around the world to put labour standards on the agenda of the next round of global trade negotiations under the World Trade Organization (WTO). Representatives to the WTO steadfastly refused to admit any link between free-trade negotiations and labour standards up until the ministerial meeting in Singapore in 1997. There, WTO leaders acknowledged a link between trade and labour, but reaffirmed the role of the ILO as the competent body to handle labour issues. The new Secretary-

General of the ILO, Juan Samovia, saw an opportunity to reinvigorate the organization. After only one year of discussion, in 1998 the ILO declared that eight of the ILO conventions constituted fundamental principles for rights at work, and the membership voted to make them binding on all members, whether or not each nation formally adopted the relevant conventions.[36] The following year, the ILO adopted a new convention against the worst forms of abusive child labour, which came into force in November 2000, one of the fastest ratification processes in ILO history.[37] In contrast, that same year the members of the WTO met in Seattle to launch a new round of trade negotiations, but the launch was scuttled by deep divisions among governments about whether to continue, and massive protests from a wide variety of pressure groups opposed to globalization.

In concert with activism against globalization, many students mobilized against sweatshops by the end of the decade. The leadership of major US universities reacted swiftly by adopting guidelines for university logo-wear. Recently, five universities worked with Business for Social Responsibility, the Investor Responsibility Research Center, and a consultant to gather information about working conditions in countries where university logo apparel is manufactured.[38] They concluded that working conditions are poor, corporate codes and monitoring are too weak, and the proliferation of codes and monitoring efforts does not lead to greater compliance.[39] Clearly, many of those leaders did not want a repeat of the stonewalling that faced anti-apartheid activists a decade earlier. The students demanded that the universities use a monitoring system; most went for the Fair Labor Association, although the students preferred an alternative monitoring association. In 1999, the Reverend Leon Sullivan also launched the new Global Sullivan Principles, a code of corporate conduct promoting human rights, economic justice, racial and gender equality, and a healthy environment.

In early 1999, keeping up the pressure on corporations, activists filed a lawsuit against Wal-Mart, The Gap, The Limited, Sears, Dayton-Hudson, and others. It accuses them of a "racketeering conspiracy" to use indentured labour to produce clothing in Saipan. Two class-action lawsuits were filed on behalf of Saipan workers, and a third was brought by four labour and human rights groups – Sweatshop Watch, Global Exchange, Asian Law Caucus, and UNITE.[40] The goal was to convince US corporations to cut off their contracts with Saipan factories or enforce higher standards on them. Litigation as a tactic depends on a court system that allows lawsuits for actions taken abroad. In the USA the Alien Tort Claims Act allows such lawsuits, and they are increasingly being brought against companies accused of labour abuses.

Throughout the 1990s, new sources of pressure against corporations emerged in the rapidly growing financial markets. Activist groups, taking a page from the book of anti-apartheid activists, took advantage of the widening pool of investors and consumers who are willing to use their investment money to support a cause. A small but growing group of US, UK, and Japanese mutual funds began to screen for socially responsible companies and included labour standards as one of their screens. Large institutional investors serving thousands of individual investors, such as TIAA-CREF (Teachers Insurance and Annuity Association–College Retirement Equities Fund) in the USA, began to offer socially screened alternatives. A number of religious groups, unions, and NGOs submitted resolutions to shareholders at annual meetings, proposing for instance that company management should refuse to do business in countries with abusive labour practices. In the USA the Investor Responsibility Resource Center and the Interfaith Center for Corporate Responsibility have both promoted shareholder activism. In April 1999 Disney committed to auditing the labour practices of 15,000 of its overseas subcontractors after being pressured to do so by shareholders. Mattel developed its own set of supplier guidelines, asked an independent group to establish a global monitoring system, and made its final report public.

The Canadian government, under pressure for not doing enough on international labour issues, watched closely what was happening in the USA and Britain. Canadian officials watched the negotiations over the Apparel Industry Partnership in the USA for lessons about how this issue might play out, and what role voluntary self-regulation could play. As John English details in his chapter, promotion of corporate codes appeared to be a way to further the Liberal government's commitment to human security as the keynote of its foreign policy. In 1998 the Canadian government issued a handbook for business on codes of conduct, declaring codes a supplement and even an alternative to traditional regulatory approaches.[41] Government officials also facilitated meetings between business and NGOs throughout 1999 to develop a consensus code of conduct for Canadian business. Canadian manufacturers, under fire from human rights and labour activists, actually invited the government to help.[42] Labour and NGO representatives formed a coalition called the Ethical Trading Action Group (ETAG) to negotiate with business and government. The working group on these codes included a representative from UNITE, a union that had participated in and then withdrawn from the US AIP.[43] Industry associations which had already been considering corporate codes joined in these government-sponsored efforts, including the Canadian Chamber of Commerce, the Retail Council of Canada, and the Alliance of Manufacturers and Exporters. The Canadian Partnership for Ethical Trading (CPET), as it came to be called, spent a year negotiating a Canadian code of conduct. The CPET negotiations broke down in spring 2000, although industry representatives made a commitment to develop their own codes.

By summer 2000, efforts to link worker rights with trade sanctions in global and regional institutions had met with only limited success. The WTO now engages better with civil society organizations, and international labour organizations continue to be active.[44] There has been some softening of the position of pro-labour groups from a preference for punitive enforcement (which looked like protectionism and neo-imperialism) to a focus on promoting core labour standards that would give workers the means to claim an equitable share of the benefits of freer trade.[45] Union groups such as the International Confederation of Free Trade Unions support core labour standards within a regional strategy. Social clauses have been inserted into the EU and NAFTA, are being discussed in the Latin American Mercosur, and have been proposed in the Southern African Development Community and APEC.

Clearly, the pressures facing business on labour issues reached a peak in the mid-1990s. The threat of government regulation or strong international action to link trade and labour were real possibilities, and in NAFTA that link was made concretely for the first time. Activists had become increasingly adept at using diverse and innovative tools to press their cause against high-profile corporations, using shareholder activism and litigation in concert with media attention, boycotts, and protests. Human rights groups, unions, anti-globalization activists, religious groups, and others successfully mobilized over the sweatshop issue. They became increasingly successful at lobbying policy-makers in Europe and North America to take action on labour conditions abroad. Many business leaders had to figure that the political risks of inaction outweighed the perceived cost of action.

Businesses learned in different ways about the significance of labour issues and corporate social responsibility. High-profile activist campaigns directed against brand-name manufacturers such as Nike taught them the cost of being targeted. Once Nike had been chosen as a target by activists, Reebok executives realized their company would be next in line for attention and began to develop stricter corporate policies on sweatshop issues. Unfortunately, some businesses learned the "wrong" lesson from this: when Nike, Reebok, and Levi Strauss all suffered from critical attention *after* they adopted a code of conduct, some business leaders decided it was safer to take a low profile in order to stay out of the public eye. Watching what happened in the USA, businesses in Canada realized that attention would soon turn to them, and they took the proactive step of asking the Canadian government to facilitate negotiations with NGOs.

In general, business leaders have been unresponsive to the argument that even the lowest-level, unskilled, or semi-skilled workers will be more productive if they are treated well. And even when they respond and implement self-regulatory programmes, each firm defines good treatment differently, and there is relatively little consensus over the standards to promote abroad.

Conclusions

Industry self-regulatory initiatives, from single-firm corporate codes to industry association standards to broader partnerships with other actors, all suffer from three perceived significant weaknesses: disagreement over the standards; lack of strict enforcement mechanisms; and no well-defined way to hold companies accountable. Corporate codes can be a tool to facilitate some kinds of improvements, but there are limits on what they can do. In general, evidence demonstrates that foreign investment improves the lot of working people, and that workers in foreign subsidiaries or in factories that supply world markets have better wages and working conditions than local firms. Corporate codes can improve their operations further, especially when they are extended beyond the firm to cover suppliers. This can set up a positive dynamic that has the potential to create real change.

One of the big changes in industry self-regulation over time has been the evolution of increasingly sophisticated systems of monitoring and compliance. Initially, most of these systems were internal to the corporation, and the companies essentially self-certified or audited their own behaviour. Many corporations now outsource this function to accounting and auditing firms, which see a growing market in global social accounting and auditing. A handful of firms now also accept external monitoring. External monitors can include traditional auditors and accountants who make their reports public or certify the company to a particular set of standards. The AIP established its own independent monitoring organization, the Fair Labor Association (FLA), which will evaluate how well particular factories meet the AIP standards. Mattel funded an independent auditing group, MIMCO (Mattel's Independent Monitoring Council), to conduct thorough reviews of working conditions at its supplier factories. MIMCO published its first report in 2000. And of course, the SA8000 social auditing and certification process has great potential for creating uniform measures of comparability and benchmarking of factories and firms.

One of the primary concerns of those suspicious of industry self-regulation is that of accountability. Critics see self-regulatory processes as inherently illegitimate, since the companies are essentially making up their own rules. Once the rules are developed, the degree of compliance is often determined by the company itself. There are, however, certain mechanisms of accountability in place in some voluntary initiatives. Multinational corporations that adopt a corporate code often establish a system of accountability within the corporate organization, establishing particular positions and people who are responsible for implementing corporate policy. Increasingly, as described above, companies conduct internal and external auditing of their performance. Public reporting of the results is a form of accountability. In addition, companies that do not work alone but in cooperation with NGOs and governments can be held accountable by those partners. More companies today adopt these practices than did 10 years ago. At the same time, however, the majority of companies with business overseas do not self-regulate either their own or their suppliers' labour standards, and relatively few subject themselves to external monitoring or certification programmes.

Industry self-regulation in the area of worker rights has great potential to improve the lives of many people living in developing countries. To date, however, these codes have not lived up to their claims. The companies that are most prominently pushing their corporate codes of conduct have been accused of laxness in implementing their own policies. Individual companies have struggled to develop a means of applying their standards not just to their own organizations, but to suppliers and the suppliers to suppliers. In some political and economic contexts, there simply is no way for a company to be absolutely sure that its code is being upheld 100 per cent. After a series of reports on poor working conditions in Asian subcontractor factories, a number of groups combined to launch a Boycott Nike Campaign in 1999. Levi Strauss, which was a leader in developing its global sourcing guidelines, has also been a target of critical reports and claims that it has not fully implemented the excellent guidelines it established.[46]

Nevertheless, private sector initiatives could be one avenue for exporting labour standards from high-standard to low-standard countries without resorting to government mandate. These standards could establish a floor on global working conditions. Although it is hard to see at times, these initiatives are a breakthrough in relations between the private sector and society. Major companies are admitting publicly that they are responsible for the welfare of workers, at home and abroad. Even some unions and labour advocates take the position that voluntary self-regulation is a way to set minimum standards, raise consciousness about the need for standards, and provide guidance for national laws in the absence of a good governmental framework.

Governments in industrialized countries may view private sector voluntary initiatives as a means to deal with public pressure to apply sanctions and other punitive measures against low-standard countries. For governments in emerging markets, however, these initiatives pose a real challenge. From their point of view, foreign corporations, in league with activist organizations and unions and even their home-country governments, are interfering in local affairs. In fact, some of what the companies propose is positively subversive. Developing country governments accuse the companies of creating inequities between workers in export industries and all others. The codes that companies attempt to implement in one country are developed elsewhere, rarely with any local input. The price of entry into world markets may be getting higher, which may reduce the comparative advantage of low-wage countries. Both the WTO and the OECD are exploring whether cooperative agreements among businesses on labour standards will distort trade flows, act as a non-tariff barrier, and perhaps even violate anti-trust law.

Ultimately, something so intimately tied to the historical development of social relations as labour standards cannot be addressed completely by corporations alone. Two other elements are even more critical to improving the working conditions of labour around the world. The first is a growing economy that provides enough opportunity for citizens to move beyond subsistence. The second is an effective national regulatory system that establishes a floor beneath labour standards, and that creates a framework for labour-management relations. Once these are in place, private voluntary initiatives can be an important tool in the fight for better living conditions around the world.

Notes

1. OECD, *Codes of Corporate Conduct* (Paris: Organization for Economic Cooperation and Development, Trade Directorate Trade Committee, 1998).
2. KPMG, *KPMG Ethics Survey 2000*, http://www.kpmg.ca/english/services/fas/publications/ethicssurvey2000.html.
3. International Labour Organization, *Further Examination of Questions Concerning Private Initiatives, Including Codes of Conduct*, ILO Working Party on the Social Dimensions of the Liberalization of International Trade (Geneva: ILO, 1999), pp. 1–18.
4. The International Organization for Standardization (ISO) is an international body whose members are national standards associations. The ISO14000 establishes standards for designing a management system to implement the environmental policy of an organization.
5. Charles Lipson, *Standing Guard: Protecting Foreign Capital in the Nineteenth and Twentieth Centuries* (Berkeley and Los Angeles: University of California Press, 1985). The International Chamber of Commerce developed the first international corporate codes, which addressed ethical issues involved in advertising and marketing. The ICC also developed an International Code of Fair Treatment for Foreign Investment after

the Second World War, but it was not influential in affecting how governments treated multinational corporations.

6. John Kline, *International Codes and Multinational Business: Setting Guidelines for International Business Operations* (Connecticut: Quorum Publishers, 1985).

7. "Transfer pricing" refers to the practice by multinational corporations of minimizing or evading taxes by the way they manipulate the sales prices of goods sold by one subsidiary or branch to another across national borders.

8. Kline, note 5 above.

9. Audie Klotz, *Norms in International Relations: The Struggle Against Apartheid* (Ithaca: Cornell University Press, 1995). In 1984, the Irish National Caucus in the USA developed the MacBride Principles for US companies operating in Northern Ireland. These principles ban discrimination in employment practices. Sixteen states and over 40 cities in the USA have passed legislation upholding the principles, and some city pension funds, including New York, only invest in companies that adhere to them. Companies adopting them include AT&T, Dupont, Federal Express, GM, 3M, Phillip Morris, and Viacom.

10. The MAI collapsed under the weight of many competing interests among governments, and not just because of the sudden mobilization of NGO opponents. Despite this, the anti-MAI story has become one more example of the strength of transnational activism today.

11. A regulation is "a principle, rule, or law designed for controlling or governing behavior", *Webster's II New Riverside University Dictionary* (Boston: Houghton Mifflin, 1984), p. 990.

12. Benjamin Gomes-Casseres, "Group Versus Group: How Alliance Networks Compete", *Harvard Business Review* (July/August 1994), pp. 62–73. A recent report by the OECD points out that foreign operations are no longer limited to the largest companies. Even small and medium-sized enterprises from non-OECD countries today participate in international markets. Stephen Thomson, *Investment Patterns in a Longer-Term Perspective* (Paris: OECD, 2000), pp. 1–27.

13. An excellent examination of these issues in the context of US-EU relations is Michelle Egan, *Mutual Recognition and Standard-Setting: Public and Private Strategies for Regulating Transatlantic Markets* (Washington, DC: American Institute for Contemporary German Studies Seminar Papers/Policy Papers No. 10, 1998), pp. 1–36.

14. According to UNCTAD, only a handful of companies can be called truly "transnational", though this number is growing steadily. UNCTAD, *World Investment Report* (Geneva: UNCTAD, 2000).

15. Robin Broad and John Cavanagh, *The Corporate Accountability Movement: Lessons and Opportunities* (Washington, DC: World Resources Institute, 1998).

16. Elizabeth Amon, "Coming to America: Alien Tort Claims Act Provides a Legal Forum for the World", *National Law Journal*, 23 October 2000, p. A1.

17. There are three main types of investment activism: investment funds that screen out companies which do not meet certain standards; the use of resolutions by owner-activists at shareholder general meetings; and community-based investment. Numerous research reports in the past few years have shown that socially responsible investment does not necessarily conflict with profits when you compare the return on investment of screened and non-screened funds. Social Investment Forum, *1999 Report on Socially Responsible Investing Trends in the US*, SIF Industry Research Program, 4 November 1999, http://socialinvest.org/areas/research/trends/1999-Trends.htm.

18. Differences in the legal framework in the USA and other countries mean that socially responsible investing takes different forms. The US system allows and facilitates shareholder activism by requiring only 2 per cent of shareholders to file a proxy resolution. In much of Europe, proxy resolutions are impossible. In the UK, Canada, and Australia

SRI consists primarily of screening, advocacy, and dialogue with company management. Oxford Analytica and the Prince of Wales Business Leaders Forum, *Changing Corporate Roles and Responsibilities: Business and Socially Responsible Investment* (London: Oxford Analytica and Prince of Wales Business Leaders Forum, 2000).
19. Social Investment Forum, note 16 above.
20. Peter Moon and Ray Thamotheram, "Corporations Become 'Socially Responsible'", *The Independent*, 12 December 2000, p. 8.
21. Opinion Leader Research, *Does the City Have a Social Conscience?* (London: Control Risks Group, 2000), pp. 1–12.
22. Mancur Olson, *The Logic of Collective Action: Public Goods and the Theory of Groups* (Cambridge, MA: Harvard University Press, 1965).
23. For more on asset specificity and the organization of markets, see Oliver Williamson, *The Economic Institutions of Capitalism* (New York: Free Press, 1985).
24. Evidence indicates that, over time, the initial bargain between a foreign investor and the host-country government "obsolesces", as the government gains more leverage the longer the company is invested in the country. This can lead to incremental increases in taxation and regulation.
25. Kathryn Gordon, *Rules for the Global Economy: Synergies between Voluntary and Binding Approaches, Conference on Corporate Citizenship Linking CSR Business Strategies and the Emerging International Agenda* (London: Royal Institute of International Affairs, 1999).
26. The discussion within the business community on these issues is framed in terms of "corporate citizenship", "corporate social responsibility", and "business ethics". It is not referred to as self-regulation.
27. Nancy Birdsall, "Life is Unfair: Inequality in the World", *Foreign Policy* 111 (1998), pp. 76–94.
28. US Bureau of Labor Statistics, *International Comparisons of Hourly Compensation Costs for Production Workers in Manufacturing, 1975–1997* (Washington, DC: US Department of Labor, 1998). Total compensation includes direct hourly wages, benefits, and all other direct and indirect payments.
29. US Bureau of Labor Statistics, *International Comparisons of Hourly Compensation Costs For Production Workers in Manufacturing, 1999* (Washington, DC: US Department of Labor, 2000).
30. The World Bank, *1998 World Development Indicators* (Washington, DC: World Bank, 1998).
31. The founders of the ILO believed the organization would prevent a repeat of the Russian Revolution by raising living standards in an international process negotiated among business, labour, and government. The ILO has adopted numerous voluntary conventions, but few governments have ratified all its conventions. It has no enforcement powers, but relies on monitoring, persuasion, and technical assistance to enhance the conditions of work around the globe.
32. There are a number of causes for Nike's current financial weakness, and not all can be laid at the doorstep of anti-sweatshop attacks upon it.
33. Pamela Varley, ed., *The Sweatshop Quandary: Corporate Responsibility on the Global Frontier* (Washington, DC: Investor Responsibility Research Center, 1998).
34. The US government persuaded the participants to negotiate, but did not itself have a direct vote or seat at the table. Officials believed that any direct participation would drive away American business participants, who tended to shy away from any hint of government participation that might lead to regulation.
35. The launch of SA8000 created a lot of controversy. An industry group, Industry Cooperation on Standards and Conformity Assessment, complained of the proliferation of standards and certifications, and the high costs of complying with them all, particu-

larly pointing to SA8000. At a meeting in Munich in 1998, about 58 members put forth a "manifesto" in protest, arguing in favour of harmonization of standards and self-certification to lower costs. Amy Zuckerman, "Global Standards Can Be a Drag on the Bottom Line", *Journal of Commerce*, 7 July 1998, p. 1. One report on the launch of SA8000 commented that it "stunned" the international standards community and directly challenged the pre-eminence of the ISO on international standards. Amy Zuckerman, "Many Stunned by Social Accountability Standard from Little-Known Organization", *Journal of Commerce*, 8 April 1998, p. 14.

36. The passage of the Declaration of Fundamental Principles spurred many countries to re-examine why they had not adopted the relevant conventions. This led in turn to a rash of ratifications in the past two years. Still, as of December 2000, only 22 countries have ratified all eight of the conventions that make up the fundamental principles.

37. Prior to the 1998 annual ILO conference, the Global March Against Child Labour traversed the world, ending in Geneva, to draw global attention to the worst forms of child labour. One year later, the ILO adopted a new ILO Convention Concerning the Prohibition and Immediate Elimination of the Worst Forms of Child Labour.

38. The five universities were Harvard, the University of Michigan, Notre Dame, Ohio State, and the University of California.

39. Business for Social Responsibility, Investor Responsibility Research Center, and Dara O'Rourke, *Independent University Initiative Final Report, 2000*, http://www.ucop.edu/ucophone/coordrev/policy/initiative-report.pdf.

40. Wal-Mart claims that it does not conduct business with Saipan factories, and there is some evidence to support that claim. The companies say they follow US law in hiring subcontractors, and Nordstrom promised to hire an investigator itself.

41. Government of Canada, *Voluntary Codes: A Guide for their Development and Use* (Ottawa: Government of Canada, 1998).

42. The contrast between Canadian and US business preferences in similar negotiations is striking. US business clearly did not want official government participation or voting on the AIP. The Canadian business representatives, on the other hand, insisted that the government should play a prominent role in the process. See John English's contribution to this volume.

43. Jay Mazur, President of UNITE and Chair of the AFL-CIO International Affairs Committee, pointed to the danger that too eager support for voluntary codes could lead policy-makers to view them as a substitute for enforcement of existing laws, prevent adoption of new legislation, and further block the linkage of trade with labour standards. Jay Mazur, "Labor's New Internationalism", *Foreign Affairs* 79, no. 1 (January/February 2000), pp. 79–93.

44. Rorden Wilkinson and Steve Hughes, "Labour Standards and Global Governance: Examining the Dimensions of Institutional Engagement", *Global Governance* 6, no. 2 (2000), pp. 259–277.

45. *Ibid.*, p. 262.

46. Levi Strauss found itself the target of criticism, too. When its growth rate slowed and sales declined, it had to shut down plants and let workers go in Belgium and France. Up until recently, Levi Strauss was one of the few major US apparel manufacturers to produce much of its product without extensive subcontracting to overseas factories. *Financial Times*, 23 February 1999, p. 21.

11

Negotiating a code of conduct: A Canadian experience

John English

In 1996 a 13-year-old Canadian boy followed Prime Minister Jean Chrétien on a trade mission to Asia. Rather than presidential palaces, Craig Kielburger visited slums, factories, brothels, and child labourers; and television cameras were always close at hand. CNN paid little attention to the Prime Minister until he met with Kielburger at, in Kielburger's words, "the predictably ritzy hotel" in Islamabad. The teenager lectured the Prime Minister on human rights and the need to link trade with human rights; and, after the encounter, told the press that the Prime Minister would now "bring up" the issue of child labour with Asian governments.[1]

In 1995 Kielburger and some teenage friends had created a non-governmental organization called Free the Children. Through the internet, Free the Children had linked itself with Asian-based NGOs, such as Child Workers in Asia, and had developed a common platform. As its 12-year-old President, Kielburger had spoken to 2,000 members of the Ontario Federation of Labour, attracted the favourable attention of Canada's largest newspaper, and raised C$150,000 to support its work, including the celebrated Asian journey.[2] His success was remarkable, but his techniques are familiar: a focus on the media and emotional images; a linkage with organizations traditionally associated with such issues, notably organized labour and liberal churches; and international organization through the internet. Major political events, such as a Prime Minister's trip or an international trade gathering, become magnets that quickly gather together dispersed fragments and create politically irresistible forces. Immovable objects then begin to move.

In a recent article, Craig Warkentin and Karen Mingst discuss the success of the international campaign to ban anti-personnel land-mines and the failure of the Multilateral Agreement on Investment. They conclude:

In both cases, the nature and possibilities of the World Wide Web combined with those of an emergent global civil society to create a new international political environment, one in which state sovereignty was constrained and NGOs – as key actors in civil society – were able to work in novel and notably effective ways.

Criticizing state-centric approaches, they stress the significance of NGOs as "effectual political actors in their own right capable of acting independently of international institutions and states".[3]

The political effectiveness of NGOs also seemed apparent on an early summer night in Winnipeg, Canada in 1998, where thousands had gathered for a tribute to Foreign Minister Lloyd Axworthy's twenty-fifth year in politics. Blocking the entrances to the Winnipeg Convention Centre, protesters called upon Axworthy to commit to the creation of a task force on sweatshops. One of the minister's assistants satisfied the crowd that their pleas were heard; and then the party began.

The NGO coalition demanding the task force on sweatshops urged that the Canadian government "should follow the lead of governments in the United States, the United Kingdom, and Australia in convoking a federal task force on sweatshop abuses in the garment and footwear sectors, and providing financial and other forms of support" for it. The linkage between "the spread of sweatshop practices in other countries and the emergence of similar practices in Canada" was strongly asserted, as was the need to address the problem in Canada and elsewhere at the same table simultaneously. As in the USA and elsewhere, the apparel sector was the major target, not least because campaigns against well-known brands such as Nike, Reebok, and Levi Strauss had been so successful in the USA. The issue had gained great force in the mid-1990s when American television celebrity Kathie Lee Gifford tearfully confessed that she never knew that clothing she had endorsed had been stitched together by 13-year-old children working 20-hour days in Honduran sweatshops. Organized labour, government, and the textile industry, however, had another concern: the promise made to developing countries in trade negotiations that the World Trade Organization's Agreement on Textiles and Clothing meant the phasing out of the import quotas established under the Multifibre Arrangement in 1972.[4] Already Canadian employment in the textile and clothing sector was falling rapidly, from approximately 168,000 in 1988 to 130,000 in 1996. It was not all bad news. While imports had increased from approximately C$5 billion to C$8 billion, exports had more than doubled from less than C$2 billion to well over C$4 billion because of notable success in so-called high-end products, the type that offered a future for the Canadian industry.[5]

The Canadian Liberal government, which came to office in 1993 at the end of the worst recession since the 1930s, had a strong trade agenda, one which took the Prime Minister throughout the world on so-called Team Canada missions. After Kielburger's trip and the 1996 appointment of new Trade and Foreign Ministers, Sergio Marchi and Lloyd Axworthy, the government became more attentive to human rights concerns. In July 1997, Marchi said that "increasing economic activity and allowing free flow of goods is absolutely central. But it needs to take into account both the labour aspect as well as the environment." His comments, which did not reflect departmental policy papers that warned against linking "core labour rights of the International Labour Organization with World Trade Organization rules", drew a quick rebuke from the influential President of the Business Council on National Issues, Thomas d'Aquino. He warned against labour rights becoming "integral parts of trade deals" and expressed confidence that "bureaucrats and the federal cabinet as a whole have more influence on Canada's trade policy than a single minister". According to d'Aquino, "the portfolio and issues drive the minister, not the other way around".[6]

Two years later, the Business Council on National Issues retained its scepticism,[7] but other business groups and leaders were attentive to the issue of corporate social responsibility. George Soros's worries about globalization, Ted Turner's gift to the United Nations, the collapse of the MAI, and Shell's troubles in Nigeria deeply influenced public debate in Canada. When Peter Sutherland, the Chairman of BP Amoco, declared that "Good business is sustainable, is part of global society, not at odds with it, and reflects values which are shared across the world", Canadian environmentalists and business leaders involved in the oil and extractive industry took notice. With the assistance of an academic, Canadian Occidental Petroleum developed a voluntary code of conduct that attracted attention but also some criticism because of the absence of NGO participation in its creation. By 1998, placards were common, conferences on corporate social responsibility abounded, and shareholder activists bothered company presidents at annual meetings. On 25 February 1999, the Montreal-based and government-funded International Centre for Human Rights and Democratic Development held a conference entitled "Commerce with Conscience: Options for Business in the Global Economy". Government and some business representatives heard Simon Zadek, a brilliant speaker and founder of the UK's Ethical Trading Initiative, and Kevin Sweeney, a business leader who co-founded the American Apparel Industry Partnership, and representatives from the South argue passionately for the place of conscience in international trade.[8]

Shortly after this event, the government of Canada approached the author about the possibility of being the "facilitator" of discussions between, on the one hand, the apparel and related sectors and, on the other hand, labour and NGOs, with the view to the development of a voluntary code of conduct.[9] The Apparel Manufacturers of Canada had written to the Ministers of Foreign Affairs and International Trade expressing a willingness to develop such a code. By this time, the NGO community, leading churches, and organized labour had developed a focused campaign for the proposed task force. Churches had parishioners sign tens of thousands of postcards, which were then forwarded, postage free, to Axworthy's office. The linkage of the issue to the minister's broader human security agenda, with its emphasis on individuals, was emphasized in sermons and statements. The minister's own comments about the need for business to be socially responsible and about the importance of NGO partnerships were invariably part of the text.

The initial task was to identify the parties at the table. On the side of business, industry associations facilitated the process. On the side of labour and NGOs, a coalition took form in the Ethical Trading Action Group (ETAG), which embraced Roman Catholic, Anglican, and Protestant churches, organized labour, and several NGOs. The leading Canadian NGO umbrella group, the Canadian Council on International Cooperation, was a member, as were prominent research institutes. Notable among the research institutes was the North-South Institute, which had extensively studied Canadian business activities in the South and which had stressed the importance of the involvement of Southern NGOs in the development and operation of codes of conduct. The Canadian Chamber of Commerce, the Retail Council of Canada, and the Alliance of Manufacturers and Exporters were significant business organizations that were discussing among themselves codes of conduct and were attending public meetings on corporate responsibility. The government encouraged such discussions; indeed, it issued in 1998 a primer for Canadian businesses on codes of conduct. "More and more firms and organizations," the Minister of Industry and President of the Treasury Board declared, "are exploring the possibilities of voluntary codes. A supplement and, in some circumstances, an alternative to traditional regulatory approaches, voluntary codes can be inexpensive, effective, and flexible market instruments."[10]

Early meetings with industry, NGO-labour, and government representatives indicated less possibility for consensus than numerous public declarations had suggested. In the case of business, there was concern about costs (especially in the case of monitoring), legal liability, publicity, and government involvement. Some pointed out that those who had tried to work with NGOs, such as Nike and Levi Strauss, became larger targets; those who did not seemed to attract less attention. In the case of labour and NGOs, there was worry about how the new partnerships with business would "be perceived by their own constituencies and by their union and NGO allies in the countries where manufacturing is taking place".[11] For government, the demand that a task force look at the linkage between domestic and international sweatshops was unacceptable because labour fell within the constitutional purview of the Canadian provinces, not the federal government. There was also concern that the codes should be voluntary, that government financing would be minimal, and that trading partners in the North and South did not perceive such codes as protectionist in character. In this last respect, there was evidence supporting such arguments. A leading Canadian company committed to ethical trading practice had as one item in its code that purchases should be made from Canadian companies wherever possible.[12]

Although the author's discussions with the principal actors raised serious concern about different perceptions and goals, the process continued with a meeting at a Toronto garment manufacturing and import plant on 11 May 1999. In a unionized factory where many familiar logos adorned hundreds of thousands of neatly hung trousers, shirts, and topcoats, 22 participants agreed to create a working group of six people, three from business and three from labour/civil society, with the facilitator as the chair. The larger 22-person group would become a steering committee to which the working group would report. A confidential government report on the meeting concluded that "This was the first time business, labour and civil society representatives in Canada had been able to agree on a concrete initiative on the issue of business ethics, and as such the meeting can be considered a success." Some regretted that an official government task force had given way to a more limited process. Others, however, were concerned about how much the stripped-down process would eventually cost. The government would fund the facilitation work, but the facilitator would not represent government. On 12 May, Foreign Affairs Minister Axworthy, International Trade Minister Marchi, and Labour Minister Claudette Bradshaw announced the appointment of a "facilitator to encourage private sector discussion of voluntary business codes of conduct". The appointment, the press release continued, reflected "the Canadian government's commitment to encouraging domestic and international partnerships that promote fair and equitable global business practices".[13]

The announcement also reflected some differences within government, between trade officials who were concerned about protectionist tendencies and business distrust of government and foreign affairs officials who believed that Canada was falling behind its counterparts in promoting ethical practices for its international businesses. One was continually struck by the impact of international experiences, contacts, organizations, and trends upon the Canadians. Civil society was closely linked with counterparts in Europe, the USA, and the UK. Zadek of the UK Ethical Trade Initiative (ETI) was a frequent visitor to Canadian NGO gatherings and government offices. The compatibility between Robin Cook's ethical foreign policy and Foreign Minister Axworthy's human security agenda was accepted and emphasized by British and Canadian government and civil society representatives. Although there were no Southern voices at the steering committee table, civil society representatives emphasized their continuing contact with Southern NGOs. In the case of labour, the experience at the International Labour Organization (ILO) was extremely important. The attempts in the later 1990s to strengthen and broaden the ILO conventions were reflected in labour's approach to code negotiations. During the code negotiations, the Canadian Labour Congress elected a new leader, Ken Georgetti, whose campaign for the presidency reflected labour's greater concern with international issues and social policies. Business, of course, was much influenced by events in the USA, where the apparel sector was considering several different approaches to codes of conduct, notably the Apparel Industry Partnership (later the Fair Labor Association) and the Worldwide Responsible Apparel Production Certification Program (WRAP).

The working group included a representative of the Union of Needletrades, Industrial, and Textile Employees (UNITE), the Steelworkers' Humanity Fund, and the Maquila Solidarity Network, whose representative, Bob Jeffcott, acted as the secretary. The business representatives were the executive directors of the Apparel Manufacturers and the Retail Council of Canada and the president of the Shoe Manufacturers of Canada. Each member was to report to and consult with the wider constituency he or she represented. The labour/civil society side had a formal structure for such reporting. The need for confidentiality created difficulties because the broader constituencies were not directly responsible to the process. Otherwise, the approach was generally successful.

Meetings began in May 1999 with general discussions of codes, of basic principles, and of international precedents. By that time, the Apparel Industry Partnership (AIP) had broken apart as labour and religious groups and some NGOs objected to the failure to include a "living wage" provision in the AIP code.[14] Leading the exodus was UNITE, a participant in the Canadian process, which in the American context objected strongly to the failure to deal with China and the limits on freedom of association and collective bargaining in that country. In the USA, Jay Mazur, UNITE's President and Chair of the AFL-CIO International

Affairs Committee, angrily attacked "the forces behind global economic change – which exalt deregulation, cater to corporations, undermine social structures, and ignore popular concern". He demanded that core labour standards be included in trade agreements, and that national and local government take appropriate action if the WTO and similar institutions failed to act.[15]

The Retail Council of Canada incorporated virtually all of the major Canadian retailers and most of the small operations. During the period of negotiations, the Canadian retail sector was profoundly changed by the collapse of Eaton's, for most of Canadian history its leading retailer, and by the weakness and eventual disintegration of Dylex, a major Canadian retailer whose president was chair of the Retail Council during the code discussions. These events were almost certainly the result of Wal-Mart's entry into Canada in 1994 and its rapid expansion, which made it Canada's largest retailer by 1999. A labour/civil society newsletter of September 1999 warned that "the downfall of the Eaton's empire raises questions about how global trends will affect our ability to win greater respect for worker's rights". The Gap, it pointed out, made all purchasing decisions for Canada in San Francisco, although Sears Canada retained control of purchasing and sourcing. Wal-Mart, it feared, emulated the former rather than the latter.[16] Moreover, Sears and The Bay, the largest retailers after Wal-Mart, were part of the steering committee of the code negotiations and had developed their own codes of conduct. In the case of Sears, a senior vice-president was specifically assigned to the social responsibility file. Nevertheless, the fragility and volatility of the Canadian retail sector troubled working group members, especially since codes covering the entire retail sector did not exist elsewhere and such a Canadian code would create a clear precedent.[17]

The two sides brought forward separate ideas for discussion. The Retail Council expressed the opinion that the working group, which became the Canadian Partnership for Ethical Trading (CPET), should be "a forum for discussion, review, exploration and education with respect to ethical sourcing issues". It hoped for a sectoral set of guidelines that would "establish the minimum standard of behaviour and allow individual companies to exceed the requirements". These guidelines should be "accompanied by standards for monitoring", and there should be "an affordable and effective means" for monitoring. The Council did stress that the guidelines must "operate within the legal framework of the jurisdictions to which they will be applied" and must not "expose signatories to unwarranted private legal liability". The federal government, it urged, should "have a prominent role in the process". The apparel and shoe manufacturers shared concerns about monitoring costs, but were initially less concerned about legal liability matters. All agreed with the principle of independent monitoring, although there was considerable vagueness about the form that monitoring should take.

When the Apparel Manufacturers' representative brought forward guidelines touching upon only a few items at an early meeting, the labour/civil society side responded at the following meeting with an extensive code that clearly bore the influence of international precedents and events. The influence of labour was most apparent in the emphasis on ILO recommendations and conventions, which were the basis of specific items in the code and its preamble. The base code drew its language from non-Canadian codes, including Social Accountability 8000 (SA8000), the ETI, and the Apparel Industry Partnership. Exploitative child labour was not only barred but remedial action was prescribed.[18] Such provision was explained by the tragic outcome of some interventions to end child labour in South Asia, where children freed from exploitation in rug factories were soon imprisoned in the sex trade. Implementation principles were detailed and required Canadian companies to cooperate with contractors, subcontractors, and licensees to assure compliance and ensure that workers were aware of the code. There were provisions for corrective action and for a transparency in commercial transactions that would allow that "prices negotiated for work performed and services provided are sufficient to allow for supplier compliance with the Code". Although based on American and British codes, the proposed code went beyond the other models, especially in its attempt to integrate ILO conventions within the text and the preamble.

When presented with this detailed code in July, the business side reacted to its length, its scope, its uncertain costs, and the adoption of ILO standards for the individual provisions of the code. There was acceptance, however, of the base code subjects: forced labour; child labour; harassment or abuse; discrimination; hours of work; freedom of association; and the right to bargain collectively concerning health and safety, wages and other compensation, and the employment relationship. On the content of those subjects, there was fundamental disagreement on all except forced labour and harassment. One business representative objected more to the complexity than to the content of the code. He urged that businesses and suppliers needed a clear, direct, and brief document, one that was as easily understood in Montreal as in Mexico. His point was generally accepted, and both sides agreed to strive for greater simplicity. Nevertheless, the meeting ended with business either rejecting or reserving comment on most of the code.

Several other areas of concern emerged. Both business and labour worried about the source of financial support for trial projects on monitoring, which both considered essential to future collaboration. In the UK, ETI trial projects had the support of business, labour, and government. In Canada, the industry itself was weak and unable to share the burdens. Government was a possible source, but existing programmes required partner contributions. Both business and labour worried about their constituencies and recognized the need to "educate" them on the subject. The apparel and shoe manufacturers met regularly with government officials who briefed them on international trends, and the Retail Council had participants in a series of workshops on corporate social responsibility sponsored by the Alliance of Manufacturers and Exporters. These workshops, however, did not endorse the concept of a code negotiated between business and labour with provision for independent monitoring. Indeed, some speakers pointed to the difficulties of the AIP and other programmes.

The development of the Worldwide Responsible Apparel Production Certification Program by the American Apparel Manufacturers Association without NGO or labour input into its development or monitoring system troubled labour representatives, particularly when they learned that Canadian manufacturers had met with WRAP representatives. WRAP would place the onus on the suppliers and on compliance with local labour legislation rather than on the importing company or retailer. Moreover, the freedom of association clause was unsatisfactory because, again, it stressed local legislative requirements rather than ILO standards.[19] Although UNITE was a full and active participant in the Canadian negotiations, Neil Kearney, Secretary-General of the International Textile, Garment, and Leather Workers Federation, joined the board of SA8000 where certification was done by independent auditing agencies linked to the major accounting firms. He argued that industry-by-industry codes covering thousands of factories were impossible to develop. Professional certification firms were the best answer, and the role of NGOs and labour was to brief these firms and monitor them.

The issue of monitoring challenged both business and labour. Jeff Otis of Grand National and President of the Canadian Apparel Manufacturers pointed out that the average Canadian firm bought only a part of a supplier's production, unlike Levi Strauss, which would contract the production of an entire factory. George Hanna, President of the Shoe Manufacturers and a manufacturer/importer himself, asked how one could monitor the suppliers to the suppliers in a country like China. Quite apart from the question of monitors getting into China, one faced the possibility that the Chinese factory would subcontract the work to another factory in the hinterland where monitors would not or could not tread. There was some discussion of a study that would evaluate how the Canadian retail and importing sectors were unique. No study was undertaken, although a NAFTA study that revealed the relative limitations of the Canadian market offered important insights. Government officials also offered advice and information on such questions as ILO conventions, UN Secretary-General Annan's Davos speech and his presentation of the Global Compact, and the development of OECD guidelines. The compact and the OECD guidelines were particularly important because the former was developed in cooperation with the International Chamber of Commerce and the latter process brought cooperation among government, business, and labour in developed countries.

The internet may melt distance and time across continents and oceans, but it did not speed the process of negotiation in Canada. Major decisions required working group members to meet with their broader constituency, and such meetings took place throughout the summer of 1999. Not surprisingly, the business side, led by the Retail Council, rejected the draft code presented by civil society/labour. Objections concentrated on the detailed reference to ILO standards, to the freedom of association clause, to potential legal liability issues, and to the implementation provisions. Challenged by civil society/labour to produce their own code, the business representatives, led by the Retail Council, promised in November to bring forward their code. The result profoundly disappointed civil society/labour representatives. Some representatives of ETAG wrote directly to Sears and The Bay, noting their own codes and expressing concern that the Retail Council code would be a "lowest common denominator" approach to the issues and would not be as comprehensive as those of the two companies. Sears replied that the Retail Council was "the most effective venue for resolution of complex issues such as this", and a withdrawal of the Retail Council in favour of direct participation by the companies "would deal a fatal blow to the process".[20]

The document presented by the business side was not a code but only guidelines for retailers. The apparel and shoe manufacturers accepted the document but pointed out that it would have to be adapted for their use. It was aspirational, in that companies could opt out of particular provisions of the guidelines. Moreover, the Retail Council would recommend rather than require that its members accept the guidelines. Although there were disagreements about individual items, the major objections were to the lack of reference to ILO standards, the absence of a monitoring regime, and the weakness of the freedom of association clause. Business argued that ILO commitments were for governments, not corporations, and pointed to the absence of significant reference to ILO conventions in most other codes (SA8000 being an exception). However, the absence of verification and compliance language did not trouble the civil society/labour side as much as one might expect. The business side remained committed to working towards a monitoring regime and expressed willingness to work on trial projects with NGOs. The freedom of association clause, however, brought the strongest objections from the civil society/labour side.

The business side eventually proposed a clause stating that "The employer shall respect lawful rights of free association." ETAG responded with an alternative: "Workers, without distinction, have the right to join or form trade unions of their own choosing and to bargain collectively." The business side said many of their members simply would not accept this direct statement, which many interpreted as a method of imposing trade unions on states that limited union activity. This, it argued, would require businesses to ask their suppliers to go beyond local law. What does one do about free-trade zones or about China, the major source of textile and clothing imports to Canada? ETAG argued that the Retail Council proposal "does not address how freedom of association would be interpreted in countries like China, where it is not legal to organize independent unions; or in Bangladesh, where employers in export processing zones are exempted from legal requirements to respect the right of workers to join and form unions; or in Mexico, where the government's interpretation of the legal right to join and form unions of workers' own choosing effectively prohibits independent unions in maquiladora assembly-for-export factories". They feared that the business proposal might even encourage Canadian signatories to the guidelines to source from countries where freedom of association was restricted by law.[21] ETAG offered to add a general provision in the code stating that nothing in the code should be interpreted as requiring employers to be in violation of local laws or other legal obligations. In dealing with China, the so-called Sullivan Principles, which had been used with apartheid South Africa, were suggested as an alternative.[22]

A final meeting of the working group took place during the first week of March 2000 after the Retail Council polled its members on whether it could remove the term "lawful" from the free association clause. The response was negative. The manufacturers spoke to their groups, but there was an unwillingness to act independently. The Retail Council and the manufacturers indicated that they intended to present their own codes later, and that the codes were, in part, a product of the process that had taken place in CPET. There would be no further collaboration in the development of the codes, and no provision for monitoring involving NGOs and labour from either North or South. Later collaboration, however, was not ruled out. Sharon Maloney, the Retail Council representative on CPET, told Naomi Klein, the Canadian author of a best-selling book on globalization and workers, that the Retail Council's goal was to have members and their contractors abide by the laws of countries in which they do business. She added, pointedly, that countries such as

China restrict independent unions and "we should not recommend what our members cannot achieve". Klein argued that the breakdown of the CPET talks pointed to "a fundamental impasse in the debate about how to end international sweatshop labour". Economic growth "with the help of a few weak codes of conduct" would not end sweatshops in developing countries, just as it was not "capitalism's natural evolution that eliminated sweatshops in the 1920s and '30s. It was labour unions." Klein ended her comment:

Many of the same companies who made sacrificing workers the entry pass into the global economy are now claiming that they can't mention unions in their code of conduct. Why? Because they don't want to interfere with the sovereign decisions of foreign countries. It's a little late for that.[23]

In their discussion of the new capabilities of non-state actors, Warkentin and Mingst point to how the campaign against the MAI trade liberalization progressed from the abstract realm of economics to the more practical and publicly accessible areas of human security and democracy. They continue:

The effect of these shifts, particularly combined with NGOs' extensive use of the Web, was to open to public scrutiny and participation private discussions and political processes conventionally considered the (foreign policy) domain of states. Although arguably few governments recognize that this process is occurring, some (e.g. Canada) have moved to capitalize on it.[24]

These comments contrast strongly with the NGO assessment of what went wrong with CPET. In their view the state remains central, whether it is the state sovereignty of China, Canada, or the USA. Although civil society/labour could have engaged directly with business, they did not but rather waited until the appointment of a facilitator paid for by government, a government that, in the NGO view, was not willing to "capitalize" on the opportunity it had. ETAG complained: "The government did not come through with needed funding for the process. More importantly, it was not willing to put pressure on the associations and companies in support of ILO core labour rights."[25] Moreover, it was the limits imposed by Chinese sovereignty, ETAG pointed out, that made Canadian companies, which import one-third of all clothing by value from China, "extremely reluctant to deal seriously with the issue of freedom of association". Finally, there was the American factor. There was the growing domination of the Canadian market by US retailers, especially Wal-Mart, which in only six years had increased its share of the Canadian department store market from zero to 40 per cent. There was also the failure of the Clinton-inspired Apparel Industry Partnership and the development of an alternative (WRAP) by the American Apparel Manufacturers Association. When the Clinton administration, in response to domestic political pressures, proposed the inclusion of environmental and labour issues in the Seattle meeting of the WTO, the unilateral action by Canada's largest trading partner profoundly affected the way in which business, labour, and government viewed the future of voluntary codes. Canadian academic Robert O'Brien told a December 1999 World Civil Society conference that the key explanation for the proliferation of codes in the 1990s was "increased competition between firms, increased awareness of labor abuses, and the failure of governments to legislate in this area". For labour, legislation was always the preferred route, and American legislation would determine the international agenda.[26]

The NGO assessment of the failure of the attempt to create a Canadian voluntary code of conduct is, as we have seen, much more state-centric than one might expect. Indeed, one comes away from the facilitation process deeply aware that barriers of sovereignty remain very high at the beginning of the new millennium. Conversely, international organizations, notably the ILO, that bear responsibility for labour issues within the UN system remain very weak. The intense focus by the civil society/labour side on ILO standards was a response to the inability of organized labour to achieve stronger commitments from government and business in Geneva in the late 1990s (similar to the response to the weak action taken in Geneva in 1995 in the case of land-mines). Business and labour representatives both pointed at the failure of the Canadian government itself to ratify some ILO conventions when ministers urged them to carry through on their commitments. Both also agreed that monitors paid for and supervised by an international organization were preferable to ad hoc arrangements between Northern and Southern NGOs and businesses, but such internationally sanctioned monitors were the dream of visionaries.

One heard much talk of globalization at the working group table and, as mentioned above, international example was a constant concern. There was, however, a curious remoteness in the discussions about what codes would actually mean in Bangladesh, Honduras, or Mexico's maquiladora zones. There were many shades, particularly those created by sovereignty, that fell upon the operations of the system that brought clothing and textiles to Canadian department-store shelves. How would we know whether a Chinese factory producing T-shirts allowed its workers to observe tenets relating to sexual orientation or religion? If China seemed very much another country, the worlds of the Canadian working group members were also surprisingly far apart. They did not know each other's concerns well. There are no national tripartite institutions that bring labour and business together in Canada. Unlike Europe, which has strong corporatist traditions and social democratic parties, and the USA, where both major parties have had union and business support, Canadian labour stands apart from the major federal parties. As a result, the discourse of business and civil society/labour is markedly different, and those differences created difficulties in the discussions. Two generations ago, a Canadian academic, Marshall McLuhan, coined the term "global village" that has such contemporary currency. In that village the chatter is loud today, but do we really hear the same sounds?

Notes

1. See the account of the meeting in Craig Kielburger with Kevin Major, *Free the Children* (Toronto: McClelland and Stewart, 1998), ch. 10.
2. *Ibid.*, pp. 34–36.
3. Craig Warkentin and Karen Mingst, "International Institutions, the State, and Global Civil Society in the Age of the World Wide Web", *Global Governance* (April–June 2000), pp. 237–238. See also Peter Willetts, "From 'Consultative Arrangements' to 'Partnership': The Changing Status of NGOs in Diplomacy at the UN", *Global Governance* (April–June 2000), pp. 191–212. Warkentin and Mingst argue that Willetts has taken a narrow approach in treating NGOs as "pressure groups".
4. North American Agreement on Labour Cooperation, *The Clothing Industry in Canada, Mexico and the United States* (Ottawa: NAFTA, 1999). This study revealed that garment sector employment had fallen steadily since 1973 in the USA, had remained stable in Canada through the 1980s but had fallen in the 1990s, and had risen steadily in Mexico.
5. *Ibid.* and figures from Apparel Manufacturers. Success had come in exports of men's suits to the USA after the Free Trade Agreement of 1999.
6. *The Globe and Mail*, Toronto, 8 July 1997. Robert Stranks, a policy adviser in Marchi's Department of International Trade, had written a cautionary paper, "Look Before You Leap: 'Core' Labour Rights", Policy Staff Commentary No. 14, Department of Foreign Affairs and International Trade, April 1996.
7. One often heard reference to the comments of American economist Milton Friedman that the only responsibility corporations had was to their shareholders and that social responsibilities were not within the purview of company boards or managers.
8. See www.bpamoco.com/about/policies/policy.htm and www.ichrdd.ca for the Montreal centre's interest in the area. The Canadian Occidental Petroleum code is not on their website. On Shell, see www.shell.com/values/0,1169,99.html.
9. The author had no experience as a facilitator or negotiator. He had come to know some of the groups and officials because he chaired the House of Commons Subcommittee on Sustainable Human Development which, in 1997, had produced the report *Ending Child Labour Exploitation – A Canadian Agenda for Action on Global Challenges* (Ottawa: Standing Committee on Foreign Affairs and International Trade, April 1997). The report urged a test of a label marketing scheme for rugs, consideration of development pacts with specific countries with a view to eradicating child exploitation, and the possibility of incorporating into multilateral trade and economic liberalization agreements the ILO convention prohibiting child labour exploitation. It did not make a clear declaration about a child labour social clause in the WTO, as was later recommended by American officials. For the author's assessment of the process, see " 'Imitating the Cries

of Little Children': Exploitative Child Labour and the Growth of Children's Rights", *International Journal* (Summer 1997), pp. 432–444.

10. Kernaghan Webb, a lawyer in Industry Canada who has taken a prominent role in assembling information on the subject, prepared this booklet. *Voluntary Codes: A Guide for their Development and Use* (Ottawa: Government of Canada, 1998).

11. This comment was made by Bob Jeffcott and Lynda Yanz, leading personalities in ETAG, in "What Can Be Gained from the New Codes of Conduct", in *Visions of Ethical Business* (London: *Financial Times*, April 2000). See the website: www.web.net/ ~msn.

12. The World Trade Organization Agreement on Technical Barriers to Trade incorporates a code of good practice which stated that "the standardizing body shall accord treatment to products originating in the territory of any other Member of the WTO no less favourable than that accorded to like products of national origin and to like products originating in any other country". The labour/civil society side drew this to the attention of the working group, and the government was aware of its implications.

13. The representativeness of the group was never questioned. There were four labour representatives including the president of the major apparel union and the senior international vice-president of the Canadian Labour Congress. The Canadian Council of International Cooperation represented broader NGO interests, and a representative of the Canadian Conference of Catholic Bishops represented religious interests. On the industry side, two of the three largest retailers were represented, as was the umbrella organization, the Retail Council of Canada. The President of the Apparel Manufacturers hosted the event, and the President of the Shoe Manufacturers attended. The Canadian Chamber of Commerce and the Alliance of Manufacturers and Exporters also sent representatives.

14. Some NGOs remained supportive of the AIP, which became the Fair Labor Association, an organization that had support from major brands.

15. Jay Mazur, "Labour's New Internationalism", *Foreign Affairs* (January/February 2000), pp. 79–93. In abandoning the Apparel Industry Partnership, UNITE expressed concern that the AIP "will reinforce the tendency to view voluntary corporate codes of conduct as a substitute for the enforcement of existing laws and the adoption of legislation and trade agreements designed to protect the rights of workers in the global economy". UNITE Statement on the Apparel Industry Partnership, 5 November 1998.

16. *Maquila Network Update*, September 1999, pp. 4–5.

17. There were many codes that covered more than one retailer, especially in Europe. The Dutch, for example, had a code covering most middle-range retailers.

18. "Company shall develop or participate in and contribute to policies and programs which provide for the transition of any child found to be performing child labour to enable her or him to attend and remain in schooling until no longer a child."

19. See the comments of Jeffcott and Yanz, note 11 above. They also complained that there were weaknesses in the area of transparency and public disclosure. Only the names of certified factories would be revealed; other information would be considered proprietary.

20. Robert Kitson, Sears Canada, to Moira Hutchinson, Ethical Trading Action Group, 28 January 2000.

21. These quotations and others are taken from the negotiating documents in the author's possession.

22. These were principles developed in the USA in the 1980s that permitted trade while requiring adherence to principles such as free collective bargaining. Although strongly criticized by anti-apartheid activists at the time, some later credited the principles with the development of some African trade unions.

23. Naomi Klein, "No Sweat", *The Globe and Mail*, Toronto, 3 May 2000. Her book is *No Logo: Taking Aim at the Brand Bullies* (Toronto: Knopf, 1999). She had received an anonymous copy of the Retail Council guidelines on her fax machine on 2 May.
24. Warkentin and Mingst, note 3 above, p. 253.
25. A full text of this assessment is found at www.web.net/~msn/3codeassess.htm.
26. "Commentary", in Tatsuro Kunugi and Martha Schwartz, *Codes of Conduct for Partnership in Governance* (Tokyo: United Nations University Press, 1999), p. 159.

12

Doing the business? The International Chamber of Commerce, the United Nations, and the Global Compact

Brian Hocking and Dominic Kelly

The central theme of this book is that the demands of global governance require the development of what is termed in the introduction "innovative diplomacy". As the various perspectives to be found in other chapters clearly illustrate, this reflects the growing complexity of the myriad issues confronting the global community and the diffusion of authority amongst its constituent actors, both governmental and non-governmental. As a consequence, diplomacy as a concept is confronting, if not a crisis, then at least a set of questions as to its character and the processes through which it is capable of achieving its goals. Inseparable from the development of the Westphalian system (although as Cohen and others have demonstrated, it predates this[1]), diplomacy is now often regarded as a mode of communication that transcends the activities of governments, embracing a range of actors located in civil society as well as those spawned by regional and global institutional structures. Often the consequent debate that this shifting scenario engenders is designed to demonstrate either that diplomacy remains a matter for governments or that it has become an irrelevance in an era preoccupied with processes that deny the significance of the territoriality which it appears to encapsulate. With this in mind, the ensuing discussion has a broad and a more specific aim.

The broader aim is to contribute to the debate on the changing nature of diplomacy and the diffusion of diplomatic activity as it embraces a more extensive cast of players than is to be found in the traditional structures and processes of state-centred diplomacy. The related and more focused aim is to examine the role of business in this changing diplomatic milieu by examining the nature of the International Chamber of Commerce (ICC) as a diplomatic actor and its relationship to the United Nations. During the period of Kofi Annan's Secretary-Generalship of the United Nations, the ICC appears to have become one of the former's major interlocutors in a bid to align the business community with its global governance objectives, particularly in the broad realm of human security. Although this was hailed by the press as a radical change for both organizations, in one sense it is not a "new" phenomenon.

As is demonstrated below, the ICC has been involved in world affairs since its creation in 1919. Emerging from a network of nationally and locally based chambers of commerce in the nineteenth century, it assumed the form, after the First World War, of a federation of national chambers with a Paris-based secretariat and an extensive web of specialist committees covering most of the key areas of concern to the business community. However, its activities have not been limited to the area of "low politics", as its key role in the reparations issue during the interwar years demonstrates.[2] A key feature of its strategy over the decades has been to seek access to and, where possible, develop a presence in key policy fora, including multilateral agencies. Thus its various specialist committees developed close relationships with the relevant sections of the League of Nations and the International Labour Organization as these bodies developed during the 1920s.

But what have changed are the context within which this access and presence is sought and utilized, and the broad objectives and strategies that underpin it. Partly, of course, this reflects environmental changes broadly subsumed under the conditions associated with globalization which simultaneously establish the need for and facilitate the creation of coalitions of interests with interrelated goals. These are underpinned by significant changes in norms and values to which all actors, whether governmental or non-governmental, are required to be sensitive in the fashioning of their policy strategies. The result of these developments, it is argued, is that business organizations, such as the ICC, find themselves engaged in a quadrilateral relationship with national governments, civil society organizations, and multilateral institutions. The consequent patterns of interaction can be uneven and often unpredictable, varying from issue to issue and displaying differing modes of engagement. The dynamics of these relationships are informed by adaptive behaviour underpinned by organizational learning as each set of actors seeks to utilize the resources of the others in the attainment of their respective goals.

Against this background, the authors suggest that the involvement of the ICC in multilateral diplomacy can be understood in terms of a change in strategies and norms on the part of multilateral organizations and business which are changing business attitudes towards a range of social issues, such as those in the environmental sphere.[3] Alongside this, the norms underpinning NGO actions and strategies are also changing, reflecting a redefinition of their objectives and how these might be achieved.[4]

Pursuing this theme, the chapter begins by considering the changing context of diplomacy and the impetus towards less state-centred patterns produced by changes in the character of world politics. It then considers the nature of the ICC as an international actor and the development of its relationships with multilateral institutions since its creation in 1919. Finally, it analyses the nature of the relationship between the United Nations and the ICC in the context of the Global Compact launched in July 2000, evaluating the motivations of both organizations in developing their linkages.

Towards a changed diplomatic milieu: "Polylateral" structures and "catalytic" processes

The demands of governance in a globalizing world pose challenges for all categories of actor that carry us well beyond the familiar, if more easily conceptualized, arguments resting on assumed patterns of dominance and decline in their relationships. The realities of the emerging patterns of world politics, however fuzzy, are much more complex: underpinned as they are by a growing recognition of the mutuality of interests and concerns that require actors to bargain, learn from one another, exchange resources, and adapt their roles according to the shifting demands of more intricately configured policy milieux. Thus national governments are increasingly required to develop strategic and tactical relationships with non-governmental organizations, whilst the latter, traditionally portrayed as hostile to government, often seek to work with it rather than against it.[5] In short, the legacy of the dominant inter-paradigm debate in international relations, which encouraged an image of patterns of inter-state relations differentiated from transnational patterns embracing a growing diversity of non-state actors, fails to provide us with helpful explanatory images.[6] This is equally true of attempts to fit business into world politics. Here, the traditional state-centred image of international relations is challenged by a growing literature that explores the complexities of the government-business relationship.[7] Not only are firms and their agents in the form of business associations able to affect the outcomes of issues on the international agenda by inserting themselves at critical points in policy processes, but they are also increasingly agents of global governance through the creation of self-regulatory regimes and standards-setting.[8]

Against this background, traditional conceptualizations of structures and processes in international relations have to be re-evaluated. In the present context, this can be seen to be true of our images of diplomacy where this term conjures up state-centred notions of government-to-government patterns of communication. It is increasingly clear that the practice of diplomacy is having to adapt to an environment in which pressures from both outside and within the state are eroding the capacity of governments in important respects. No longer is it the case that national policy-makers possess either the sole authority, the expertise, or the material resources to achieve their policy goals in complex negotiating environments. In terms of bilateral diplomacy, the traditional agents of interstate communication – to the extent that they historically exercised a monopoly over the state's interaction with its international environment – are reconstituting themselves by means of redefining their roles and patterns of behaviour. This can be conceived in terms of layers of transformational adaptation that occur within the machinery of the state as the management of international policy becomes more diffuse but, increasingly, demands engagement with the representatives of civil society.

At the multilateral level, too, it is clear that significant change is afoot. The identification of what O'Brien *et al.* term "complex multilateralism" is a mirror image of the kinds of pressures to which national diplomatic systems are seeking to respond.[9] In brief, this might be identified in terms of challenges stemming from diminishing material resources, the diffusion of policy expertise amongst a growing range of non-state actors, and the erosion of governmental legitimacy. A "crisis of multilateralism" began to set in during the 1970s and 1980s, compounded by US budgetary withdrawals from the United Nations and a growing disillusionment on the part of third world states in terms of the influence to be gained through their participation in international organizations.[10] Whereas the post-Cold War world initially foreshadowed something of a renaissance for the United Nations, it has become increasingly clear that a new "crisis" has emerged which challenges both its relevance and its reputation. This is by no means unique to the United Nations, but is shared by other multilateral institutions such as the World Bank and the IMF. One manifestation of this trend has been enhanced pressure from civil society, in the shape of global social movements as well as business interests.

One way of conceptualizing these developments is to differentiate – as do O'Brien *et al.* – between "old" and "new" forms of multilateralism. The former focuses on multilateralism in its traditional, state-centred form as the coordination of relations amongst states.[11] The latter is conceived as attempts to reconfigure multilateralism by building it from the "bottom up" rather than the "top down", basing it on the active participation of a global civil society.[12] Although this particular definition of "new" multilateralism focuses on global social movements, it is equally clear that there is a growing role for business in these arenas. This not infrequently results in an increasingly complex set of interactions between multilateral institutions, business, and global social movements. Whether this is, indeed, a new phenomenon or a reworking of characteristics identifiable in earlier phases in the evolution of the states system is not the key issue.[13] What are significant are the interests that each set of actors brings to bear on its relationships with the others, and the extent to which the behaviour of each is modified through processes of organizational learning. Thus it is obvious that the "reformist" objectives of NGOs and their desire to gain access to and presence in multilateral organizations are varied, but also likely to be markedly different from those of the business community.

It is equally true, however, that there is a strong impetus for actors to engage with one another, as one recent study of the interactions between business and NGOs notes:

... something is happening in the relationships between governments, NGOs and companies which draws them to engage more closely together to deal with certain issues. There is a desire to understand better the terms of engagement, and an interest in making the engagement constructive – to create social value rather than to destroy it by confrontations which would be costly and risky for all concerned.[14]

This affects both governmental and non-governmental actors in ways which, whilst related, are differentiated by their distinctive organizational characteristics (their "actorness"). In the case of business, this is reflected in the growing concern with corporate citizenship which, by its nature, focuses on redefining a firm's relations with an expanded range of "stakeholders".[15] In the case of governments, it is reflected in the reform of diplomatic services to enhance their interaction with civil society and reinforce and redefine the "public diplomacy" function. In the case of NGOs, it is reflected in debates about purpose, strategies, and engagement with both business and government, and, for multilateral organizations, in reaching out beyond the realm of states in a search for funds, expertise, and legitimacy.

Increasingly, as noted above, the changing policy milieu reinforces mutual needs rooted in autonomy dilemmas and growing capacity constraints along three planes: tangible resources, access to knowledge and expertise, and legitimacy. Put another way, actors seek to preserve their autonomy to pursue core policy objectives whilst recognizing that resources possessed by others are critical to their ability to do so. This requires the utilization of "catalytic" strategies in which actors bring to a policy milieu a differing mix of resources without which neither can their objectives be sustained nor a diplomatic conflict resolved.[16] In turn, this demands the development of appropriate strategies and structures – formal, informal, or a hybrid mix – through which communication can be maintained and successful outcomes pursued.

Such a theme is reflected in the growing role of the private sector within multilateral organizations and negotiations, as bodies such as the World Intellectual Property Organization, the International Telecommunications Union, the International Maritime Organization, and the International Tropical Timber Organization have responded to the changing trade agenda and developed closer relationships with business.[17] The trend is also evident in studies on climate change negotiations. As both Rowlands and Benedick argue, industry had a vital input into the negotiations on ozone depletion which produced the Montreal Protocol, through both the activities of individual chemical companies such as Du Pont and industry groupings as represented by the Business Council for Sustainable Development (BCSD) and the ICC itself. Not only did the major chemical companies possess financial and technical expertise but, of course, they were able to develop the alternative chemicals that made progress in phasing out chlorofluouro carbons (CFCs) possible.[18]

In short, success or the lack of it in some policy environments depends on the capacity of public and private actors to engage in processes of organizational learning through which knowledge and legitimacy-generating resources are developed and exchanged to manage unpredictable policy environments. Failure in this respect can have serious consequences, in terms of both the interests of the sets of actors involved and the successful outcome of certain types of international negotiation. Of course, the authors are not suggesting that all policy environments exhibit these characteristics – their nature will depend on the terrain of a given diplomatic "site" – nor that, even when they do so, they will be marked by patterns of uniformity.

Inevitably, this has led some observers to question the conventional distinctions that seek to contrast bilateralism and multilateralism as modes of communication and negotiation. The synergy between the two forms has been noted in a variety of arenas, not least the European Union and, indeed, the UN system itself. The attempt to integrate the two forms is reflected in other usages, such as "associative diplomacy" and "minilateralism". Yet others, recognizing the need to enhance the incorporation of transnational actors into negotiating environments, have suggested alternative designations such as, for example, "polylateralism".[19]

Underpinning these various conceptions is the proposition that networks are indispensable in managing increasingly complex policy environments by the promotion of communication and trust. In this sense, a policy network can be defined as "a set of relatively stable relationships which are of a non-hierarchical and interdependent nature linking a variety of actors, who share common interests with regard to a policy and who exchange resources to pursue these shared interests acknowledging that co-operation is the best way to achieve common goals".[20] This is the fundamental principle on which Reinicke's concept of global public policy networks rests.[21] Starting from the premise that globalization has highlighted the deficiencies of governments, acting both alone and in concert, in terms of their scope of activity, speed of response to global issues, and range of contacts, he identifies the significance of the emergence of networks incorporating both public and private sector actors. It is not, he suggests, that multigovernmental institutions are irrelevant, but that the more diverse membership and non-hierarchical qualities of public policy networks promote collaboration and learning and speed up the acquisition and processing of knowledge. What he terms "vertical" subsidiarity, in which policy-making is delegated within public sector agencies, has to be supplemented by "horizontal" subsidiarity through outsourcing to non-state actors.[22]

This theme is clearly reflected in a number of Kofi Annan's public pronouncements since assuming the role of UN Secretary-General, notably his speech to the World Economic Forum at Davos in 1997 in the course of which he observed: "The United Nations once dealt only with governments. By now we know that peace and prosperity cannot be achieved without partnerships involving the governments, international organizations, the business community and civil society."[23] This was further underscored by a joint press release issued by the United Nations and the ICC at the end of a meeting between the two bodies convened in February 1998:

There is great potential for the goals of the United Nations – promoting peace and development – and the goals of business – creating wealth and prosperity – to be mutually supportive. Development and peace are essential for trade and investment to occur and for business to grow. At the same time, thriving markets are a precondition for creating jobs, improving standards of living, spreading more widely the benefits of globalization and integrating developing countries into the world economy.[24]

Similar sentiments can be found in a statement from the ICC announcing the establishment of the ICC Geneva Business Dialogue, which met in September 1998. This stressed the importance of establishing a dialogue between business and international organizations "so that business action, knowledge experience and expertise become a part of the decision-making process for the global economy".[25]

Since then, of course, the momentum of the UN-business dialogue has gathered pace, manifesting itself in the Global Compact launched in July 2000. Under its aegis, 50 major multinationals committed themselves to observing a voluntary set of principles on the environment, child labour, and freedom of trade unions.[26] As we have seen, this partnership reflects the needs of both multilateral institutions and the business community. For the United Nations, it has provided an enhanced sense of relevance in an environment where, after the first glow of post-Cold War euphoria had faded, the growing impact of globalization threatened to downgrade its significance. Not least was this manifested in the growing transborder flows of private capital that overshadowed the aid programmes of the United Nations and its agencies. At the same time, the Janus-faced characteristics of globalization were to become equally clear to the business community as GSMs (global social movements) and NGOs successfully projected the growing concern at its impact. From the business perspective, on the one hand, the United Nations is significant as a promoter of regulatory frameworks for globalization, specifically on matters such as standards-setting, telecommunications, and aviation. But additionally, Annan's initiatives have provided a valuable supportive voice advocating the benefits of free trade and arguing that issues such as human rights and the environment should not be loaded on to the WTO system. Not surprisingly, many NGOs have been highly critical of this development, arguing that the United Nations is simply providing legitimacy to companies such as Shell and Nike – which stand accused of major transgressions on the human rights and environmental fronts – and for little more than adherence to loosely monitored principles. As suggested earlier, it is in this changing context that the present role of the ICC has to be viewed. Just as in earlier phases of its evolution it had adapted to the shifting sands of world politics and the evolving patterns of institutional structures and norms, so it can be seen to be doing now.

The ICC as an international actor: Adapting roles and the changing nature of its "actorness"

The decision to create a permanent organization serving the interests of world business was taken in Atlantic City, New Jersey in late October 1919 at a meeting of "influential industrialists and traders from Belgium, France, Italy, the UK, and the United States, all of whom were called together by the US Chamber of Commerce".[27] The ICC was officially inaugurated on 24 June one year later. This means, of course, that it outlasted the League of Nations and pre-dates the United Nations and all its associated organs. It pre-dates the major institutions created at Bretton Woods, including the World Bank, the International Monetary Fund, and the ITO/GATT/WTO triumvirate. It is older, finally, than many of the states in which its constituent national committees reside. Although there have been periods of relative inactivity (during the war years, for example), this longevity is in itself a key resource, facilitating as it does efforts to foster a sense of tradition and associated "standing" upon which to focus and build a sense of legitimacy in the modern era. In addition to simply "being there", however, the ICC claims to have been involved not only in the formulation of policy within these institutions of global governance and others over the long term, but also to have been influential in bringing them into being in the first place. What follows outlines some of these claims and, in so doing, suggests that states and intergovernmental organizations have been communicating and bargaining with non-state actors such as the ICC from the moment of their creation: sharing information with them and drawing on their resources whenever and wherever it seemed appropriate.[28] As a corollary of this, the "actorness" of the ICC has slowly changed, so that at one moment it can be seen as "an international movement",[29] at another as a "world parliament of business",[30] at another as a "defender of the multilateral trading system"[31] and a "private sector policeman for world trade",[32] at yet another as a sort of epistemic community pursuing a "diplomacy of technics",[33] and so on as long as each of these images is seen as cross-cutting and contradictory as well as forward-moving and complementary.

The organization was brought into being against the sombre backdrop provided by the efforts at national and international reconstruction and rehabilitation in the aftermath of the First World War and, as might be expected in such times, spent the early part of its life attempting to contribute to those efforts and ensuring that the interests of business were well served in the process. It began with a prolonged campaign to break the deadlock over the settlement of post-war reparations, actively sponsoring and heavily contributing towards the Dawes Plan, which was brought into effect by the 1924 Treaty of London. As the following quotation suggests, the work of the ICC proved fundamental to the successful resolution of this problem:

The Dawes Plan was really the work of the International Chamber of Commerce. Without official standing, without any means of coercion, by the sole force of its competency and the weight of the interests it represents, the International Chamber of Commerce was able to play a decisive part in the settlement of a great international question ... In brief, what thirty-two diplomatic conferences with the help of countless meetings of ambassadors and interviews between heads of governments were unable to achieve, has been done by a private business organization.[34]

There is little doubt that in confronting the issue of war reparations, albeit from the perspective of satisfying the needs of business, the ICC won an important victory at this early stage of its existence in the battle for recognition and standing in the world of sovereign states. This achievement was followed in 1931 by a successful campaign, conducted through the media and behind closed doors, to reverse President Hoover's decision not to make any concessions with regard to the payment of war debts.[35] There is thus evidence already in the 1920s and 1930s that the informal attribute of "competency" matters more at certain times than the attribute of formal sovereignty, even when issues of "high" politics are at stake.

From the very start, then, the ICC concerned itself with and involved itself in the business of politics and diplomacy at the highest levels, and did so with a degree of success that might surprise those analysts who reserve the practice of "diplomacy" solely to states and the official representatives of states. It is clear, however, that these efforts represent only the tip of a very large iceberg: most of the ICC's labours were (and, it is worth noting here, still are) directed toward less dramatic aims, the achievement of many of which also required the ICC to engage in diplomacy as defined here. Indeed, the first decade or so of its existence was dominated not by the sort of top-table discussions outlined above, but by efforts (ambitious in themselves) to effect the reintegration of the European heartland in the world economy, and to deepen and soothe connections with the emerging hegemon, the USA.[36] As to the mechanics of this operation, these focused on four major areas: transport, communication, finance, and trade.[37]

Innumerable conferences and commissions produced, over the next few years, initiatives, proposals, and agreements in each of these areas supportive of the growth of efficient, peaceful, and, above all, profitable world trade.[38] Perhaps most noteworthy was the ICC's involvement with the World Economic Conference (WEC) in 1927, called by the League of Nations in order to effect a lowering of tariff barriers. In the words of an anonymous chronicler:

The ICC submitted a celebrated 150-page report described by the legal secretariat as "in some respects the most important document before the Conference". Certain sections of the report could be regarded as the conceptual origin of the General Agreement on Tariffs and Trade: others gave virtual draft texts for conventions on specific issues. The Conference ... very largely accepted the report's recommendations. One significant result was the 1928 convention on import and export prohibitions – the world's first multilateral agreement on trade policy.[39]

Notwithstanding the self-congratulatory tone of this statement, the influence of the ICC at the WEC is difficult to ignore, particularly in light of the fact that it was directly represented at the conference by five delegates and six experts, and indirectly by 64 other members of the organization (serving the ICC as either members of the council, the working committees, or national committees) who had been selected to attend by their respective governments.[40] One might also suggest that if success could be measured by the virulence of the criticism generated by its actions, then the ICC was at this time successful indeed. Witness the following statement, relating to the direct representation of the ICC on the Economic Consultative Committee of the League of Nations, on behalf of another venerable NGO, the International Cooperative Alliance:

Our attention has been drawn to the extraordinary claims which have been publicly made that the organized private traders of the world had not only succeeded in entrenching themselves at Geneva in the authorities of the League on a basis of equality of voice and voting with the National Governments, but wielded such influence on behalf of their clients – the capitalist private traders – that they practically dominated the situation and were even able to repudiate their own National Governments ...[41]

In the area of transport the ICC once more led the way, agitating for and securing an international conference at the Hague in 1926 on the extension of the airmail system worldwide.[42] Sustained pressure again succeeded in bringing about a preliminary agreement that was to be widened and deepened in the years that followed, and did so against a backdrop suffused with difficulty. In the first place, the ICC was forced to act by what it saw as the refusal of the responsible body (the International Commission for Air Navigation) to deal with the problem in a timely fashion. In the second place, it did so via a rather surprising mechanism: transmitting its proposal through the official channel provided by the postal administration of the Soviet Union.[43] Similar initiatives followed in the areas of communications (restraining increases in telegraph rates scheduled for 1938) and finance (assisting the League in its deliberations on the problem of double taxation in 1928).[44]

None of this prevented the outbreak of the Second World War, of course, nor the economic and political events (the Wall Street crash, the Great Depression, and the collapse of the League) that preceded it. Due largely to the financial constraints imposed upon the organization by the severing of funds from national committees, the ICC effectively halted its operations during the war years, although it did switch its country of domicile from France to Sweden for the duration, where several meetings took place attended by nationals of states already at war with one another. These financial constraints did not necessarily apply at the national level, however, and the US and British national committees remained particularly active throughout.

If anything, the second global conflagration hardened the resolve of the ICC to become involved in the great political and economic decisions of the day. Even before the war, at the Berlin Congress held in 1937, the organization adopted as its motto the slogan "World Peace through World Trade": convinced that business had much to offer politicians and diplomats in their search for international accommodation.[45] These convictions stemmed not only from the view, widely held in the ICC and throughout international business circles, that the nature of the market is such that political boundaries and national differences are transcended, obscured, and effectively dissolved by it, but also from the success that the ICC had already enjoyed at the international level in resolving seemingly intractable problems between states. Moreover, these convictions were boosted through collaboration between the ICC and the Carnegie Endowment for International Peace (CEIP), and confirmed by the meeting of minds which took place between members of the two organizations at a conference sponsored by the CEIP and held at the Royal Institute of International Affairs (Chatham House) on 5–7 March 1935.[46] One of the concrete outcomes of this conference was the formation in that same year of a joint CEIP/ICC Committee, attended by business leaders and academics from various countries – including amongst their number Dag Hammarskjöld (who later became Secretary-General of the United Nations) and Per Jacobsson (later head of the Bank for International Settlements and the International Monetary Fund) – with the aim of laying the groundwork for the improvement of commercial and, thus, political relations between nations. In addition to the publication of a two-volume compendium of technical reports focusing on the improvement of commercial relations between nations and on monetary stabilization, this collaboration was to be followed in 1938 by the publication under CEIP auspices of a history of the ICC entitled *Merchants of Peace*.[47]

In the early post-war years attention once more turned to reconstruction and rehabilitation, with the ICC pressing for expansive monetary and trade regimes. Its support for the formal inauguration of the International Trade Organization was made strongly dependent upon acceptance of the provisional agreement on commercial policy and trade restrictions (the GATT) reached during preparatory studies on the ITO charter.[48] However, when the draft charter was put before the UN Conference on Trade and Employment (Havana, November 1947–February 1948), it became clear to many in the ICC – the only NGO granted the opportunity to address plenary sessions and discussion meetings – that as far as the interests of business were concerned it contained so many loopholes and extraneous provisions that it was virtually useless.[49] This recognition led the organization, after a short period of internal debate, to withdraw its support for the ITO charter and concentrate instead on building the GATT into a permanent organization.

In 1946 the ICC began its long association with the United Nations when it was granted Category A consultative status with the UN Economic and Social Council (ECOSOC), a position it still holds.[50] Although an active participant at the United Nations from that day to this, the emergence and deepening of the Cold War combined with the emergence of the G77 as a voting bloc to freeze effectively the policy options of the United Nations into a series of stances dictated by the dominant contending ideologies, with the result that from the perspective of the ICC "relations between the UN and business were frequently marred by mutual suspicion, and sometimes antagonism".[51]

Notwithstanding this dissatisfaction, the ICC actually had very little to complain about over the following three decades as the world (capitalist) economy first recovered and then entered its boom years. The dominant theme remained integration and expansion under the rubric of free trade, whilst key objectives were the development of close relations with the European Economic Community (EEC) following signature of the Treaty of Rome on 15 March 1957, and expansion of ICC membership beyond the Atlantic heartland – and especially into the hinterland of Asia. In 1955 the first ICC congress to be held in Asia took place in Tokyo, and by 1959 seven new national committees had been set up, along with a regional Commission on Asian and Pacific Affairs whose brief it was to coordinate their activities and represent the ICC to the regional office of the United Nations in Bangkok.

Trouble was brewing, however, and it can be argued that it was in these same years, the 1950s and 1960s, that the "success" of the ICC, and of international business as a whole, came home to roost. Instead of the goose that laid the golden egg, international business was, in these years of dramatic growth in the industrialized world juxtaposed against stagnation and decline in the economic well-being of the decolonizing and developing world, in danger of being seen not only as a lame duck as far as the satisfaction of the economic needs of developing countries was concerned but, more seriously, as the proverbial cuckoo in the nest: squeezing out indigenous firms and stifling domestic economic growth. Moreover, by the 1970s the impact of business activities appeared, especially in the industrial states, increasingly to be endangering the health of the biosphere. Lumped together, these issues raised questions in the mind of concerned publics (at this stage in no way a "global civil society") the world over concerning the ethical implications and repercussions of the unfettered pursuit of capitalism throughout the "free" world, as these impacted upon the public and private spaces of the industrialized states and the economic and social welfare of their less developed and newly independent brethren. In these circumstances, public anger found an easy target: the multinational corporation – bastion and boiler-room of the physical and intellectual resources of the ICC.

There can be little doubt that the organization reacted swiftly to this new challenge, as evidenced by the major themes considered at the six congresses held by the ICC between 1959 and 1969. Whilst in 1957 (Naples) attention had, quite understandably, focused on the formation of the EEC under the heading "New Factors of Economic Progress", by 1959 (Washington) attention had turned in a different direction to consider "Today's Challenge to Businessmen – Their Responsibility in Domestic and World Affairs". In 1961 (Copenhagen) the theme was "Private Enterprise in Economic Development". The 1963 congress (Mexico City) considered the theme of "Economic Growth through World Interdependence", while the 1965 congress (New Delhi) dealt with "World Progress through Partnership". At the 1967 congress in Montreal the theme was "Private Enterprise in a Changing World", while at the final congress in that decade, Istanbul in 1969, attention zeroed in on the apparent villain of the piece under the theme "International Economic Growth – The Role, Rights and Responsibilities of the International Corporation".

All of this might have been so much hot air, of course, but for the fact that the ICC took genuine steps both to protect itself from the wrath of a number of hostile publics and to turn the situation to its advantage by seizing the opportunity to "educate" those self-same publics in the many ways that business aids and abets economic development whilst at the same time preserving the environment for future generations of consumers and businessmen alike. One of the first steps was for the ICC to establish a presence at the inaugural UN Conference on Trade and Development (UNCTAD) held in Geneva in 1964, and again at UNCTAD II in New Delhi four years later. The message delivered by the ICC at these and other intergovernmental conferences was that free trade and unimpeded private foreign investment were wholly beneficial for economic development no matter what the context. This message was reinforced by the arrangement on behalf of the ICC of periods of "training" in industrialized countries for staff of chambers of commerce and associated bodies from less developed states, all facilitated by the International Bureau of Chambers of Commerce (IBCC).[52] It was further complemented by the development and public announcement (at the 1967 Montreal congress) of a set of principles, under the heading of a "Charter for Private Enterprise", outlining the ethical responsibilities of business operating in a free-enterprise system.[53] Considered crucial to the success of these initiatives was the development of still closer relations with the key intergovernmental organizations and agencies dealing with economic and legal matters. Efforts in this direction bore fruit in 1969 with the creation of the ICC-UN-GATT Economic Consultative Committee, which "brings together the heads of all principal UN agencies in the economic field, plus those of GATT and the OECD, for two days of high-level [but low-profile] discussions each year with leading ICC members".[54]

At one and the same time, however, the ICC was manifestly seeking to use these enhanced connections to improve and standardize regulatory conditions for its members across the globe. In 1969 the organization initiated a series of discussions on the roles, rights, and responsibilities of the multinational corporation. These led, in December 1972, to the launch of its *Guidelines for International Investment*, urging governments to investigate and adopt standard investment and insurance practices covering all aspects of private foreign investment. Four years later the OECD published its own views on this subject, warmly welcomed by the ICC, in the form of the OECD *Guidelines for Multinational Enterprises*.[55] Meanwhile, the ICC became involved in the major projects initiated by the newly created UN Commission and Centre on Transnational Corporations – including a code of conduct for transnational corporations (TNCs), international standards of reporting and accounting, and the creation of a database on TNCs for government use.

The ICC and the United Nations: Shared interests and mutual needs

As the intensity of the Cold War waxed and, finally, waned, so the pressure on the ICC to lead the way in justifying the activities and rights of international business has steadily increased. The organization has had, as a consequence, to tread an increasingly fine line between the assertion of the private interests of its members and the satisfaction of the interests of an increasingly knowledgeable and wary public. As such, the courting of government favour and public opinion more widely has slowly been pushed to the forefront of ICC activities. In the 1970s, the organization reacted to the oil crisis and the subsequent slowdown in economic growth with a vigorous campaign focused on heading off protectionist pressures in the world economy before they could do too much damage to business interests and relations. Meanwhile, it continued to defend the environmental record of international business and – in the context of a growing rejection in some parts of the world of consumerism and the attendant commercialization and indeed commodification of all aspects of life, and in other parts of the world a rejection of Western prescriptions regarding the possibilities for securing economic development – to argue the case for the benefits of continued and sustained economic growth driven by the engine of private enterprise.[56]

Be that as it may, as memories of the decade of the 1970s began to fade, the influence of the ICC seemed to fade along with them. So much so in fact that by the time Helmut Maucher (Chairman of Nestlé since 1990) assumed the presidency of the organization in 1997 the ICC was regarded as rather old-fashioned and "fusty" by contemporary standards.[57] Maucher, who under ICC rules would have been Vice-President between 1994 and 1996, began to bring the organization back into the public eye: initiating a series of internal reforms designed to streamline and focus the structure and activities of the organization, and bringing in new staff at top level, such as Maria Livanos Cattaui (who had spent 19 years at the World Economic Forum in Geneva with responsibility for the annual meeting at Davos) as ICC Secretary-General.[58]

The consequence of this has been to lend the organization a more visible profile centring around activities designed to achieve three aims: each of which, as we have seen, has been at the core of ICC policy from the very beginning. Set within the context of a broad aspiration "to make the voice of business heard in global decision-making",[59] these are to facilitate global trading flows, promote the self-regulation of business, and extend the capitalist economy into every corner of the globe. In the contemporary age, the ICC seeks to achieve these aims in a number of (interrelated) ways: by extending its network of member chambers throughout East and Central Europe, Asia, Latin America, and Africa, by pre-empting national and international legislation and regulation through the adoption of self-regulation and standards-setting laid down by a large network of issue- and sector-specific committees drawn from member multinational corporations, and by deepening already close relationships with national governments and regional and global institutions such as the EU and the UN system.

At one and the same time, the United Nations, as noted above, has been struggling to maintain its status and legitimacy in the face of a number of challenges emerging from a global political economy that has undergone deep change in the recent past. Some, but by no means all, of these are as follows.[60] First, each of its major sponsors has vacillated in its approach to the organization. The USA first bypassed it in favour of unilateral and bilateral management initiatives so as to avoid the entanglements threatened by calls (issued by the G77 with the tacit support of the Soviet Union and People's Republic of China) for a "new international economic order". It then took up the helm again as a way of lending a degree of legitimacy to its prosecution of the war against Iraq in 1991, before, most recently, demonstrating a degree of ambivalence exemplified on the one hand by its reluctance to place troops on the ground in the Balkans (following the debacle in Somalia), and on the other by its continued support for budgetary and structural reform begun by Boutros Boutros-Ghali and continued under his successor Kofi Annan.[61] For the former Soviet Union, meanwhile, as for the PRC, the

United Nations and its specialized agencies increasingly came to be seen as part of the answer to their economic and (geo)political problems, and accordingly both began to take a more conciliatory line in the Security Council just at the moment that they were seeking entry to the economic organs they once so virulently condemned.

Second, the increasing pressure being exerted on the UN system by the USA – designed to lessen the "burden" of its financial commitment, and to force the organization to support US foreign policy goals – has resulted in a growing "legitimacy deficit" for the United Nations which some argue is now too big to close.[62] Sceptical that the incremental reforms under way at the United Nations are meant simply to deflect criticism and entrench further the power of the major states, an array of the less powerful have begun to argue for a combination of either or all of the following: further and deeper structural reform (of the Security Council, for example), transformation of the underlying philosophy (that is, one based on "Western" interests) that drives the UN system, and outright abolition and its replacement with an institution or institutions reflective of the changed circumstances and varied social, political, and cultural viewpoints given expression around the world.[63] Third, and countering (though not foreclosing) arguments that suggest possibilities for a reform of multilateral institutions "from the bottom up",[64] the demise of the dream of a socialist alternative and the globalization of production, finance, and ideas has shattered the coherence of the G77, resulting in the emergence of hierarchies and rivalry in the developing world as states compete with each other for preferential access to markets and credit (public and private), for the attentions of (and influence within) multilateral organizations such as the IMF and World Bank, and for admission to regional organizations such as NAFTA, the EU, APEC, Mercosur, and so on.[65] Fourth, globalization has engendered an ever more vocal opposition, manifest in what are now being called "global social movements" that target their activities either against capitalism in general or against perceived injustices and "transborder damages"[66] inflicted by capitalism in specific areas, such as the environment.[67] More often than not, these activities are directed against multilateral institutions, of which the United Nations is the supreme embodiment, with a view to contesting global governance.[68]

In light of these shared difficulties it is (perhaps) fortunate that Maucher took the helm at the ICC at roughly the same time that Kofi Annan was beginning to put his own plans for the revitalization of the United Nations into operation.[69] Throughout 1998, Annan went to great lengths to push forward with a new agenda for the United Nations, based upon a perceived relationship between the promotion of peace and development and the creation of wealth and prosperity, that saw a major partnership role for business.[70] The ICC responded in kind, making this its key theme for 1998 and launching a barrage of press releases, speeches, and seminars on the motif of public-private partnership, culminating in the Geneva Business Dialogue. This series of meetings, held over two days between representatives of business and UN officials, covered the full range of issues currently exercising the minds of the ICC as well as those issues of economic development in least developed countries that lie at the heart of Annan's agenda for the United Nations. The ICC, through Maucher, used the meeting as a launch-pad for its globalization "manifesto", the Geneva Business Declaration, calling effectively for more globalization, faster.

The Global Compact

It is against this background that we must consider the demand for, and implications of, the Global Compact between business and the United Nations. Both the United Nations and the ICC (as representative of business) face challenges to their legitimacy variously expressed at local, national, and international levels: the United Nations for continued relevance in the emerging post-Westphalian world order, the ICC for justification of the place and role of business in a global economy that appears ever more inequitable. For both sides, the Global Compact is one answer to these shared challenges.

In short, the Global Compact is designed to work at a number of levels, taking in a variety of issue areas and along several trajectories. In material terms, it centres around the cash nexus, with the United Nations gaining much-needed funds in the form of both corporate philanthropy (Ted Turner has pledged $1 billion to support UN projects) and corporate investment in UN-sponsored development projects. From the perspective of the ICC this is money well spent, since not only can business "piggyback" into new (potential) markets, but it also benefits from the "soft infrastructure" (orderly, stable societies, operating within "a framework of essential rules administered by strong, efficient, transparent and impartial government"[71]) ostensibly promoted by UN development assistance. Thus, the ICC has made a major push into what have been called, often euphemistically, "economies in transition" and "developing economies".[72] Russia, Poland, and Cuba joined the ICC in May 2000, and there has also been a great deal of interest shown in Africa,[73] with Ghana and Nigeria joining in 1999 and Kenya, Uganda, Tanzania, and Zimbabwe scheduled to join in the year 2000.[74] Projects highlighted at the ICC website appear largely technical, and are focused in the areas of agriculture, energy, the environment, health, intellectual property, investment, telecommunications, trade, and transport. Typical of this approach has been the ICC's association with a joint project between the IBCC and the International Trade Centre designed to provide technical cooperation and assistance to chambers of commerce in developing and transition economies in order to facilitate the creation of "vibrant" private sectors in these countries.[75]

In terms of institutional relationships, the Global Compact affirms and reasserts the long-standing role of interlocutor that the ICC has sought and succeeded in playing between business and structures of governance. Influential relationships have been formed at the highest levels of national, regional, and global governance, including the EU, G8, and the OECD,[76] and the UN and its constituent agencies and organs. The major thrust of ICC activity at this level has been in the arena of self-regulation and standards-setting, in line with its frequently reiterated calls for the development of a "balanced" relationship between freedom and rules in the global economy, which appears to encapsulate all of the following: the encouragement of a deepening and widening of the "benefits" of the global knowledge economy (secured in this instance by the "flexible" regulation of the internet where this relates specifically to e-commerce), the encouragement of public acceptance of developments in innovation and technology (such as genetically modified organisms), the deepening and widening of opportunities for trade and investment (calls for a new trade round), and the apportionment of regulatory responsibilities according to a strictly defined set of criteria (excluding "non-trade" issues such as the environment and human rights from the remit of the WTO).[77]

In the realm of ideas, the Global Compact – which two leading academic practitioners suggest "is meant to be a 'social norming proposition'"[78] and "a platform for institutional learning"[79] – explicitly calls for the reaffirmation by the United Nations of a set of values and principles contained within the Universal Declaration of Human Rights, the ILO's Declaration on Fundamental Principles and Rights at Work, and the Rio Declaration of the UNCED (1992). The nine principles are:

- business should support and respect the protection of internationally proclaimed human rights within their sphere of influence;
- business should make sure that it is not complicit in human rights abuses;
- business should uphold the freedom of association and the effective recognition of the right to collective bargaining;
- business should uphold the elimination of all forms of forced and compulsory labour;
- business should uphold the effective abolition of child labour;
- business should eliminate discrimination in respect of employment and occupation;
- business should support a precautionary approach to environmental challenges;

- business should undertake initiatives to promote greater environmental responsibility;
- business should encourage the development and diffusion of environmentally friendly technologies.[80]

The ICC has not been afraid to commit wholeheartedly to these ideals, on the grounds that ordinary business people – the "human face" of capitalism – hold to them as closely as anyone else, since "a good place to live is a good place to do business".[81]

There is, however, a catch, and therein lies the first explicit indication that the Global Compact may not be the panacea for the woes of the United Nations and the ICC that both so obviously hope it will be. For the ICC has, quite quickly, sought to "clarify" its understanding of it as follows:

Business accepts the challenge and is eager to cooperate with the UN and other public sector bodies to enhance all three [human rights, labour standards, and environmental practices]. Alongside them however, we must place a fourth value – the economic responsibility incumbent upon any company to its customers, to its employees and to its shareholders.[82]

In its widest sense, this fourth "value" might be said to pre-figure a projected transfer between business and public sector bodies of the understanding of the necessity of sticking to the "bottom line" when it comes to ethical judgements and material outlays on human rights, labour standards, and environmental practices. More narrowly, it reflects a view of the Global Compact as "a management tool to create added value in our relationship with employees, customers and society at large".[83] Either way it is bound to cause problems with other constituents, as well as with officials at the United Nations.

Conclusion

This chapter has attempted to put forward a set of arguments suggestive of the increasingly complex nature of both the concept and the practice of diplomacy in the contemporary setting, and one, moreover, that moves beyond the debate on the "decline" of diplomacy as it has been traditionally understood in the academic literature. "New" forms of diplomacy have not supplanted the "old": they have supplemented and indeed complemented them. Against a background constituted by uncertainties and frailties generated by the end of the Cold War and the globalization of economic activity, the process by which this change has unfolded can best be apprehended in a series of separate steps which,

cumulatively, delineate the emerging shape and scope of patterns of diplomatic interactions. Thus, one can point to functional changes within the
machinery of state, international and multilateral organizations, and non-
governmental organizations reflective of a growing awareness of an array
of material and non-material autonomy dilemmas and deficits, to widening and deepening patterns of interaction (characterized, often simultaneously, by both conflict and cooperation) within and between this
quadrilateral matrix of actors, and to an evolving set of "norms" or "intersubjective meanings" attached to these patterns.

Driven by its own priorities, frailties, and dilemmas, the International
Chamber of Commerce is seeking to play a major role in this process:
a role informed by its long history of involvement in policy-making at
every level and in many issue areas, "high" and "low". It is seeking to
profit from the apparent "triumph" of capitalism by widening the scope
of business activity into previously untapped markets, deepening the extent of its influence in these and established markets through securing
lower barriers to trade (visible and invisible), and tightening its grip on
these same markets by pushing forward with an agenda of self-regulation
and standards-setting by business underpinned and guaranteed by legal
agreements hammered out between governments and their interlocutors
on a bilateral and multilateral basis. The place of the UN system, and of
the Global Compact, in this strategy is clear: it is to provide the "moral
authority" which business needs but lacks if it is to drive home the gains
it has already secured, act as the thin end of the wedge in securing greater
access to new and established markets, and clean up any messy loose ends
in whatever form – social protest, environmental degradation, armed
resistance – these take.

That there will be resistance is evident in the hostility generated on
all sides by the contested nature of the "intersubjective meaning" ascribed to the Global Compact. Leaving aside, for the moment, the not-
unexpected suspicion of NGOs and GSMs, a consideration of the length
of time taken and the number of meetings required between Kofi Annan
and his team and the ICC before the compact was officially launched hints
at the difficulties that arose before agreement on a common position was
secured. Six months later, the specific issues on which disagreement (or,
more charitably, lack of accord) may have arisen are becoming apparent
in ICC publications. Even the triumphal tone of the ICC-sponsored section on the success of the Global Compact cannot obscure the unease
and doubt being felt in corporate boardrooms the world over, and in the
USA most of all.[84] On almost every page of this special section fears are
raised that the compact will be "hijacked", either by NGOs pressing for
surveillance rights, or by UN suits micro-managing specific projects.[85]
The response is a familiar one: to assert the authority of the ICC – "not

as a narrow pressure group but rather by providing a business voice which is global, multisectoral, and represents a broad and diverse community"[86] – over and above that of other non-governmental actors, and, on that basis, effectively to neutralize them through processes both of inclusion in and exclusion from the corridors and hallways of power.[87]

Notes

1. R. Cohen, "Reflections on the New Global Diplomacy: Statecraft 2500 BC–2000 AD", in J. Melissen, ed., *Innovations in Diplomatic Practice* (London: Macmillan, 1999).
2. G. L. Ridgeway, *Merchants of Peace: Twenty Years of Business Diplomacy through the International Chamber of Commerce 1919–1938* (New York: Columbia University Press, 1938); C. N. Murphy, *International Organization and Industrial Change: Global Governance since 1850* (Cambridge: Polity, 1994), pp. 160–163.
3. V. Haufler, "Self-regulation and Business Norms: Political Risk, Political Activism", in A. C. Cutler, V. Haufler, and T. Porter, eds, *Private Authority and International Affairs* (Albany: SUNY Press, 1999).
4. D. Hulme and M. Edwards, eds, *NGOs, States and Donors: Too Close for Comfort?* (London: Macmillan in association with Save the Children, 1997).
5. This point is developed in A. F. Cooper and B. Hocking, "Governments, Non-governmental Organizations and the Re-calibration of Diplomacy", *Global Society* 14, no. 3 (2000), pp. 361–378.
6. T. Risse-Kappen, *Bringing Transnational Relations Back In* (Cambridge: Cambridge University Press, 1995).
7. J. Greenwood, J. R. Grote, and K. Ronit, eds, *Organized Interests and the European Community* (London: Sage, 1992).
8. J. Greenwood and H. Jucek, eds, *Organized Business and the New Global Order* (London: Macmillan, 2000).
9. R. O'Brien, A. Marie Gotz, J. A. Scholte, and M. Williams, *Contesting Global Governance: Multilateral Economic Institutions and Global Social Movements* (Cambridge: Cambridge University Press, 2000).
10. J. P. Muldoon Jr, J. Aviel, R. Reitano, and E. Sullivan, eds, *Multilateral Diplomacy and the United Nations Today* (Boulder, CO: Westview, 1999).
11. J. G. Ruggie, *Multilateralism Matters: The Theory and Praxis of an Institutional Forum* (New York: Columbia University Press, 1993), p. 11.
12. R. W. Cox, "Multilateralism and World Order", *Review of International Studies* 18 (1992), pp. 161–180; S. Gill, ed., *Globalization, Democratization and Multilateralism* (London: Macmillan for the United Nations University Press, 1997); K. Krause and W. A. Knight, eds, *State, Society, and the UN System: Changing Perspectives on Multilateralism* (Tokyo: United Nations University Press, 1995); M. G. Schechter, ed., *Innovation in Multilateralism* (London: Macmillan for the United Nations University Press, 1999), and *Future Multilateralism: The Political and Social Framework* (London: Macmillan for the United Nations University Press, 1999).
13. See, for example, the essays in J. Smith, C. Chatfield, and R. Pagnucco, eds, *Transnational Social Movements and Global Politics: Solidarity Beyond the State* (Syracuse, NY: Syracuse University Press, 1997).
14. J. V. Mitchell, "Editor's Overview", in J. V. Mitchell, ed., *Companies in a World of Conflict: NGOs, Sanctions and Corporate Responsibility* (London: RIIA/Earthscan, 1998).

15. G. Kelly, D. Kelly, and A. Gamble, eds, *Stakeholder Capitalism* (London: Macmillan, 1997).
16. For a discussion of catalytic diplomacy see B. Hocking, *Beyond "Newness" and "Decline"*, DSP Discussion Papers, No. 10 (Leicester: Centre for the Study of Diplomacy, 1995).
17. M. P. Ryan, *Knowledge Diplomacy: Global Competition and the Politics of Intellectual Property* (Washington, DC: Brookings, 1998); S. Sell, "Multinational Corporations as Agents of Change: The Globalization of Intellectual Property Rights", in Cutler, Haufler, and Porter, note 3 above, pp. 169–197; and Kelley Lee, David Humphreys, and Michael Pugh, "'Privatisation' in the United Nations System: Patterns of Influence in Three Intergovernmental Organizations", *Global Society* 11 (1997), pp. 339–357.
18. See I. Rowlands, *The Politics of Global Atmospheric Change* (Manchester: Manchester University Press, 1995), pp. 159–160; R. E. Benedick, *Ozone Diplomacy: New Directions in Safeguarding the Planet* (Cambridge, MA: Harvard University Press, 1991).
19. G. Wiseman, *"Polylateralism" and New Modes of Global Dialogue*, Discussion Papers, No. 59 (Leicester: Centre for the Study of Diplomacy, 1999).
20. T. Börzel, "A Way Out? Policy Networks as a Mode of Conflict-management in the Implementation of EU Environmental Policies", paper presented to the ECPR Workshop on "The Role of Subsidiarity in Managing Local Conflicts Related to the Spatialisation of National Policies", Bern, 1997, quoted in D. Stone, "Networks, Second Track Diplomacy and Regional Cooperation: The Role of South-East Asian Think-tanks", paper presented to 38th International Studies Convention, Toronto, March 1997.
21. W. H. Reinicke, *Global Public Policy: Governing without Government?* (Washington, DC: Brookings, 1998), and "The Other World Wide Web: Global Public Policy Networks", *Foreign Policy* 117 (1999–2000), pp. 44–57.
22. Reinicke, *ibid.*, *Global Public Policy*, pp. 89 and 229; "The Other World Wide Web", p. 46.
23. Quoted in L. Silber, "UN Reformer Looks for New Friends in World of Business", *Financial Times*, 17 March 1997.
24. UN Press Release SG/2043, 9 February 1998, p. 1.
25. ICC, "What is the ICC Business Dialogue?", *Business World*, 20 September 1998.
26. E. Alden, "Multinationals in Pledge on Standards", *Financial Times*, 28 July 2000.
27. ICC, *World Peace through World Trade: ICC 1919–1979*, Publication No. 342 (Paris: ICC, 1979), p. 1; Ridgeway, note 2 above, pp. 21–38.
28. An excellent general survey is Murphy, note 2 above. On the ICC in particular there are two studies of interest: Ridgeway, note 2 above, and L. C. White, *International Nongovernmental Organizations: Their Purposes, Methods and Accomplishments* (New York: Greenwood Press, 1968), both of which are heavily reliant on ICC publications and statements. The few references to the ICC in a recent collection of essays on the topic of NGO activity in the UN system – P. Willetts, ed., *"The Conscience of the World": The Influence of Non-governmental Organizations in the UN System* (London: Hurst & Company, 1996) – are almost wholly reliant on White's text.
29. Ridgeway, note 2 above, p. 3.
30. White, note 28 above, p. 20.
31. "History of the International Chamber of Commerce", available at the ICC website: http://www.iccwbo.org.
32. J. Marks, "Trade's Global Police Force", *FT Exporter*, 16 May 1996.
33. Ridgeway, note 2 above, part IV.
34. F. Delaisi, "The Contradictions of the Modern World", *Journal of the International Chamber of Commerce*, February 1926, p. 16. Cited in White, note 28 above, p. 27. See also Ridgeway, note 2 above, pp. 144–155.

35. See White, note 28 above, pp. 27–28; and Ridgeway, note 2 above, pp. 350–354.

36. As a symbol of this commitment to relations across the Atlantic, the Washington congress of May 1931 was the first such to be held by the ICC outside Europe.

37. For an overview see Ridgeway, note 2 above, pp. 263–331.

38. Between its constituent conference held in Paris in 1920 and its Madrid conference in 1975 the ICC held 25 major congresses on a biannual basis (with a break in the war years, 1939–1947). Thereafter, the conferences have been held on a triennial basis.

39. ICC, note 27 above, p. 3. See also White, note 28 above, pp. 21–22, who is similarly complimentary; and Ridgeway, note 2 above, pp. 217–259.

40. White, note 28 above, p. 21.

41. Cited in *ibid.*, p. 31.

42. Ridgeway, note 2 above, p. 301.

43. White, note 28 above, p. 25.

44. Limited space prevents the authors from discussing these here. See White, note 28 above, pp. 21–29; and Ridgeway, note 2 above, pp. 297–301 (on telegraph issues) and pp. 279–283 (on double taxation).

45. Ridgeway, note 2 above, p. 384. Adolf Hitler and Herman Goering were both in attendance.

46. For details see *ibid.*, pp. 379–385.

47. *Ibid.* A revised edition was published in 1958.

48. In the realm of financial and monetary affairs the ICC was less directly involved, although the central theme for its 1947 congress in Montreux, Switzerland, was financial and monetary reconstruction. The keynote speech by Per Jacobsson was timed to coincide with and wholeheartedly support the announcement of the Marshall Plan. ICC, note 27 above, p. 11.

49. References to the role played by the ICC in the proposed creation of the ITO are sprinkled throughout Steve Charnovitz and John Wickham, "Non-Governmental Organizations and the Original International Trade Regime", *Journal of World Trade* 29, no. 5 (1995), pp. 111–122.

50. In 1968 the labels for these categories were changed, but the ICC retained its place in the most influential of these (Category I), allowing it to circulate written statements to Council members, address Council committees, and even address the full Council on the recommendation of the NGO Committee. For details see Peter Willetts, "Consultative Status for NGOs at the United Nations", in Willetts, note 28 above, pp. 31–62.

51. "ICC and the UN – origins of a partnership", available at the ICC website: http://www.iccwbo.org.

52. This organization (which is responsible for the provision of the ATA Carnet scheme for temporary duty-free imports) was "spun-off" from the ICC in 1951.

53. ICC, note 27 above, p. 20.

54. *Ibid.* It is not clear whether these meetings continue to date, although top ICC representatives do meet with government officials in advance of the G8 summits.

55. ICC, note 27 above, p. 27.

56. See *ibid.*, pp. 19–26.

57. F. Williams, "The Voice of Business Heard Around the World", *Financial Times*, 29 December 1998.

58. Maucher was also Chairman of the European Round Table of Industrialists between 1995 and 1999. See B. van Apeldoorn, "Transnational Class Agency and European Governance: The Case of the European Round Table of Industrialists", *New Political Economy* 5, no. 2 (2000), pp. 157–181.

59. Williams, note 57 above.

60. See, amongst others, K. Krause and W. A. Knight, "Introduction: Evolution and Change in the United Nations System", in Krause and Knight, note 12 above, pp. 1–33;

and S. Gill, "Structural Changes in Multilateralism: The G-7 Nexus and the Global Crisis", in Schechter, note 12 above, pp. 113–165.

61. See H. K. Jacobson, "The United States and the UN System: The Hegemon's Ambivalence About its Appurtenances", in R. W. Cox, ed., *The New Realism: Perspectives on Multilateralism and World Order* (London: Macmillan for the United Nations University Press, 1997).

62. M.-C. Smouts, "United Nations Reform: A Strategy of Avoidance" and A. Morales, "The United Nations and the Crossroads of Reform", in Schechter, note 12 above, pp. 29–41 and pp. 42–60 respectively.

63. See, for example, the various contributions to Krause and Knight, note 12 above.

64. R. W. Cox, "Introduction", in Cox, note 61 above, p. xxvii.

65. See A. Gamble and A. Payne, eds, *Regionalism and World Order* (London: Macmillan, 1996); J. Grugel and W. Hout, eds, *Regionalism across the North-South Divide* (London: Routledge, 1999).

66. M. W. Zacher, "Uniting Nations: Global Regimes and the United Nations System", in R. Väyrynen, ed., *Globalization and Global Governance* (London: Rowman & Littlefield, 1999), p. 58.

67. See R. Cohen and S. M. Rai, eds, *Global Social Movements* (London: Athlone, 2000).

68. O'Brien *et al.*, note 9 above.

69. See United Nations, *Secretary-General Sets Course for Long-awaited UN Revitalization* (New York: UN Department of Public Information, January 1998). See also H. Maucher, "Ruling by Consent", *FT Exporter*, 2 November 1997.

70. See UN Press Release SG/2043, entitled "Co-operation between the United Nations and Business", 9 February 1998, and the corresponding release by the ICC.

71. ICC, "World Business Message for the UN Millennium Assembly on the Role of the UN in the 21st Century", press release, 26 January 2000.

72. The theme for the thirty-third World Congress of the ICC held in Budapest in May 2000 was "The New Europe in the World Economy".

73. This emphasis can, at least in part, be traced to the interest the ICC has in reintegrating the core economy, South Africa, into the global economy.

74. Adnan Kassar, "Private Sector Growth is Good News out of Africa", ICC news release, 23 March 2000. Tanzania was the only African country actually to secure membership in 2000.

75. For this and other projects see ICC news release "Working with the United Nations", available at the ICC website: http://www.iccwbo.org. See also *International Herald Tribune*, 25 January 2001, pp. 11–14, which is an ICC-sponsored section highlighting certain projects being undertaken under the rubric of the Global Compact.

76. See, for example, "Business States its Views on OECD Investment Agreement", and "Business tells G8 it Wants Clear Rules for Global Economy", ICC news releases, 16 January 1998 and 29 April 1998 respectively.

77. In this instance these aims are encapsulated in the "Budapest Business Declaration" made by former ICC President, Adnan Kassar, at the conclusion of thirty-third World Congress of the ICC held in Budapest in May 2000. On the specific issue of internet regulation see, for example, "ICC Revised Guidelines on Advertising and Marketing on the Internet" (issued 2 April 1998).

78. J. Bhagwati, cited in K. Mackenzie, "Part of a Tapestry of Actions", *International Herald Tribune*, 25 January 2001, p. 13.

79. J. G. Ruggie, "Globalization: Shared Risk, Shared Promise", *International Herald Tribune*, 25 January 2001, p. 12.

80. Paraphrased from UN Press Release SG/SM/6881 entitled "A Compact for the New Century", issued 1 February 1999.

81. Current ICC President R. D. McCormick, "Good Business Practices Make Sound Commercial Sense", *International Herald Tribune*, 25 January 2001, p. 11.
82. M. L. Cattaui, "Business Takes Up Kofi Annan's Challenge", ICC press release, 15 March 1999.
83. M. Hoelz (Global Director of Public Affairs at Deutsche Bank), cited by J. Stratte-McClure "The Business of Building a Better World", *International Herald Tribune*, 25 January 2001, p. 12.
84. J. Clerk, "US Business Back Annan's Concept but Want More Clarity", *International Herald Tribune*, 25 January 2001, p. 13.
85. See, for example, the text of an interview with Maria Livanos Cattaui conducted by K. Mackenzie entitled "Compact Must Avoid 'Command and Control'", *International Herald Tribune*, 25 January 2001.
86. Kassar, note 77 above.
87. The strategy of excluding some groups is clearly illustrated in the following passage taken from a statement issued by the President of the ICC in 1998:

[The] emergence of activist pressure groups risks weakening the effectiveness of public rules, legitimate institutions and democratic processes. These organizations should place emphasis on legitimizing themselves, improving their internal democracy, transparency and accountability. They should assume full responsibility for the consequences of their activities. Where this does not take place, rules establishing their rights and responsibilities should be considered.

"The Geneva Business Declaration", statement by Helmut Maucher at the conclusion of the Geneva Business Dialogue, Geneva, 24 September 1998.

13

Codes of conduct and children in armed conflicts

Deirdre van der Merwe and Mark Malan

Introduction

There are three broad interrelated areas where codes of conduct that are
under development can have a possible positive impact upon the plight
of children in armed conflict: humanitarian action; small arms; and the
military.

On humanitarian action, the most prominent codes are that of the International Committee of the Red Cross (ICRC) and the SPHERE Project. The ICRC is the "custodian" of the oldest of the modern codes established in 1949, when the ICRC updated its charter and established four
separate treaties known as the Geneva Conventions. The conventions
accept the inevitability of armed conflict, but seek to ensure that soldiers
conform to certain basic principles of humanity – the chief principle being to spare civilians and medical personnel. Thus two different traditions
and moralities – humanitarian laws and the laws of war – are blended
somewhat uncomfortably in the teachings and work of the ICRC.

The SPHERE Project represents a far more recent attempt at codification. It was established on 1 July 1997 by the Steering Committee for
Humanitarian Response (SCHR) and InterAction, with the aim of examining and setting the minimum standards of behaviour for those involved in humanitarian responses. The project has involved front-line
NGOs and the Red Cross and Red Crescent Movement, interested donor
governments, and UN agencies cooperating to develop a set of standards

in core areas of humanitarian relief. It is felt that these standards will help to improve the quality of assistance given in emergencies, and the accountability of agencies to their beneficiaries, their membership, and their donors. The standards will derive from a charter of humanitarian rights, drawn from existing international law and relevant to all with a legitimate claim to provide assistance in disaster situations.

The development of codes of conduct or conventions for the management of small arms is also a very recent innovation, focusing mainly around regional efforts to regulate arms transfers and illicit trafficking in small arms. Examples of such initiatives include the following.

- The International Code of Conduct on Arms Transfers, which obligates arms-recipient governments to uphold internationally recognized standards of democracy, human rights, and peaceful international relations. The drafting of this code was initiated in 1995, when Dr Oscar Arias, former President of Costa Rica, invited his fellow Nobel Peace laureates to join him in developing the code and providing moral leadership for the code campaign.
- The Wassenaar Arrangement of 1996, under which 33 states have agreed to promote transparency and greater responsibility in transfers of conventional arms and dual-use goods and technologies.
- The European Union's 1998 comprehensive code of conduct governing illicit transfers of conventional arms, which was adopted as a legally binding joint action committing member states to help developing countries stem illegal arms flows across their borders.
- The Inter-American Convention against the Illicit Manufacturing of and Trafficking in Firearms, Ammunition, Explosives, and other Related Materials of 1997, which commits parties to regulate import and export and cooperate in training and intelligence.
- The ECOWAS moratorium on the production and import of small arms to the West African region for three years as of October 1998. (Members of the EU and the Wassenaar Arrangement pledged to respect this moratorium.)
- The Southern Africa Regional Action Plan, adopted in 1998, which unites members of SADC and the EU in the effort to regulate arms transfers and combat illicit trafficking.

It is obviously too early to evaluate the long-term efficacy of such initiatives, but they are widely regarded as moves in the right direction which, if successful, can contribute to reducing the proliferation of armed conflicts and hence the plight of children in volatile areas of the world.

Military codes of conduct have been around for centuries, but what is new is the idea of codes of conduct for the military when involved in peace support operations, which is closely tied the realm of codes for humantarian actions. But what of codes that may contribute to the respect of soldiers for the rights of children in armed conflict – and for that matter, human rights in general?

The UNHCHR has initiated an ambitious programme that parallels the work of the ICRC in teaching the law of armed conflict (LOAC) to national militaries, but which focuses specifically on human rights training for soldiers and police officers – including the rights of "vulnerable" groups such as refugees, women, and children. Rädda Barnen has pioneered a programme aimed at sensitizing military personnel to the rights of the child, and in collaboration with ECOWAS began the first regional training course in Côte d'Ivoire on 12 June 2000.

The cumulative effect of all these efforts – aimed at restricting the circulation of light weapons and instilling respect for the LOAC, human rights, and child rights – must eventually have a beneficial effect on the plight of children affected by armed conflict. However, it is impossible to establish direct causal links between the development of international conventions and ethical codes at the higher level, as well as lower-level behavioural codes and training programmes, and an improvement on the ground, in respect of those most intimately involved in prosecuting armed conflicts, regarding the rights of people in general and children in particular.

The aim of this chapter, therefore, is to provide a brief overview of the status of international legal instruments, and to deliberate on the perceived utility of ethical codes in general, as a prelude to examining the notion of developing a code that specifically guides/governs the conduct of military forces and individual soldiers towards children in situations of armed conflict.

Existing international legal instruments

The body of international law governing the rights and treatment of children in armed conflict has a variety of sources. It is to be found in specific and general treaties dealing with the broad field of human rights at universal and regional levels, as well as in the rules of international humanitarian law, customary international law, and the law practices of specific states. The latter are possibly the most important, as these will be the laws that will be established and adhered to in practice in a specific country.

Existing international law governing the rights and treatment of children has only an indirect effect on non-governmental entities. Although international humanitarian law can be applied to both government and non-statutory armed forces, this cannot always be enforced with clarity and in practice. On the other hand, even if state actors have not ratified a particular treaty, they may still be held accountable if the treaty has become customary international law (in other words, it has become standard practice among world governments).

The most widely ratified human rights treaty in history is the Convention on the Rights of the Child. Drafted in 1979, it was unanimously adopted by the UN General Assembly on 20 November 1989, and was opened to ratification the following year. To date, all member states but two (the USA and Somalia) have ratified it. It is the first legally binding international instrument to incorporate the full range of human rights. It includes children's civil and political rights as well as their economic, social, and cultural rights, and gives all rights equal emphasis. The convention defines a child as every human being under 18 years, yet sets the minimum age for recruitment into armed forces and use in hostilities at the lower age of 15 years.

Another major breakthrough at international level was UN Security Council Resolution 1261 of 1999. In its first resolution dedicated to children in war zones, the Security Council unanimously condemned the "killing and maiming, sexual violence, abduction and forced displacement, recruitment and use of children in armed conflict". Resolution 1261 also instructs nations to "prosecute those responsible for turning children into killers and soldiers, and for murdering, maiming and raping them during the course of war". The Security Council also said that peacekeepers should receive special training on the treatment and protection of children and civilians. This is a landmark development, and a great leap forward to place at least some pressure on guilty parties to stop the use of child soldiers.

The African continent followed soon after the convention with its own regional instrument for protecting the rights of the child. The African Charter on the Rights and Welfare of the Child was adopted in 1991, but has not yet entered into force, as very few African states have ratified this particular treaty. Moreover, the charter addresses states parties only, and the question arises as to how the states parties will ensure that rebel or opposition groups abide by the rules. Because Africa is the focal point of a large proportion of the conflicts that affect the rights of the child, it will be interesting to observe the course and implementation of this instrument.

Another noteworthy development on the international level was the International Labour Organization's Worst Forms of Child Labour Convention, dated 17 June 1999, in which the use of child soldiers is recognized as a labour issue. Importantly, the convention sets the first international standard for 18 years to be the minimum age of child recruitment. The latest milestone in this regard is the optional protocol to the Convention on the Rights of the Child, on the use of children in armed conflict, adopted by a UNHCHR working group on 22 January 2000.

The protocol sets 18 years as minimum age for compulsory recruitment and prohibits rebel and other non-government armed groups from recruiting children under the age of 18 years or using them in hostilities. The noticeable failure is that it did not establish 18 as the minimum age for voluntary recruitment, allowing for states to recruit volunteers as young as 16. Nonetheless, the optional protocol was unanimously adopted by the General Assembly on 25 May 2000.

Although it is important to set international standards, all treaties need political will and public pressure for their implementation. There is thus clear need for an international standard and norms that would provide guidelines for states and other parties on what the view of the international community is on certain issues. For example, UNICEF has argued that:

It is worth re-emphasising that the power of humanitarian law does not lie only in the fact that its principles are in the form of legal instruments. This only adds additional weight. The power of humanitarian principles arises from the fact that they form a moral code rooted in a concept of the common good in the public conscience of men, women and children around the world and that those who violate them do so at the expense of their own legitimacy in the minds of humankind.[1]

This provides an essential linkage between international legal instruments and voluntary codes of conduct based on moral principles, and a possible way of addressing the problem of regulating the behaviour of non-state actors in situations of armed conflict. On the issue of non-government forces or rebel forces, the Machel report argues that:

Many non-state entities aspire to form governments and to invoke an existing Government's lack of respect for human rights as a justification for their opposition. In order to establish their commitment to the protection of children, non-state entities should be urged to make a formal statement accepting and agreeing to implement the standards contained in the Convention on the Rights of the Child.[2]

The development of relevant codes of conduct may play a fruitful role in the search for new ways to relate to rebel groups, to get them involved in the international humanitarian law, and to give them incentives to comply.

On the utility of ethical codes and codes of conduct[3]

Codes of ethics are controversial documents. There is no definitive statistical study that shows once and for all whether codes work or not. Some writers have suggested that codes of professional ethics are pointless and unnecessary. Many others believe that codes are useful and important, but disagree about why.

At one end of the spectrum, there are those who argue that codes of ethics serve no good purpose whatsoever; that ethics should be open-ended and reflective, and that relying on a code of ethics is to confuse ethics with law. There is also the notion that it is mistaken to assume that there is a special ethics for professionals or specific occupational groupings which is separate from the ethics of ordinary human beings within a moral society. Professionals, according to this viewpoint, have no special rights or duties separate from their rights and duties as moral persons, and therefore codes of ethics are pointless and possibly pernicious.

Others acknowledge that codes of ethics do have some sociological value; particularly in that the adoption of a code is significant for the professionalization of an occupational group, because it is one of the external hallmarks testifying to the claim that the group recognizes an obligation to society that transcends mere economic self-interest. The latter has been the cornerstone of the modern concept of military professionalism as pioneered by Samuel Huntington.[4]

However, codes of ethics can ultimately create moral problems rather than helping to resolve them – for example, where practising professionals rarely turn to their codes of ethics for guidance, or where the guidelines within the codes sometimes seem internally inconsistent. The implementation of a code of ethics may also be in conflict with the moral autonomy we expect of individuals.

On the other hand, even though most practising professionals do not routinely consult their codes of ethics, it does not follow that they do not know or care about the contents of these codes. Further, the fact that codes of ethics sometimes seem internally inconsistent can be addressed by understanding codes of ethics not as recipes for decision-making, but as expressions of ethical considerations to bear in mind. They may be viewed as an ethical framework rather than as specific solutions to problems. Moreover, it may be argued that moral autonomy is not necessarily compromised by codes of ethics. If an ethical code can be supported with good reasons, this does not preclude individual members from autonomously accepting those provisions and jointly committing themselves to their support.

Ethical codes and codes of conduct not only serve to protect the layperson from abuse of professional competence, but can also be understood as conventions between professionals. A code protects each professional from certain pressures created by the possible unethical conduct of other members of the same profession. It is, in a sense, a partial solution to problems of coordination and unsavoury competition that may favour "fly-by-nights" and the less scrupulous.

There are at least three sound reasons why professionals should be intested in supporting and adhering to a code.

- It helps to protect them from being associated with the poor performance or behaviour of others in the same occupation.
- It helps to create a working environment in which it is easier to resist pressures to do that which members of the profession would rather not do.
- Supporting a publicized code helps protect a profession against negative public images of members of that profession.

Possible functions of a code of ethics or code of conduct include the following.

- The collective recognition by members of a profession/occupation of their responsibilities.
- Helping to create an environment in which ethical behaviour is the norm.
- Guiding towards or reminding of the correct course of action in specific situations.
- The process of developing and modifying a code of ethics can be valuable for enhancing the overall quality and image of a profession. In this respect, a code can serve as an educational tool, providing a focal point for discussion in classes and professional meetings.
- Providing a clear indication to outsiders that the profession or occupation is seriously concerned with responsible, professional conduct.

Ultimately, a code of conduct increases ethical sensitivity and judgement, strengthens support for individuals' moral courage, and helps to hone an organization's sense of identity. Codes of ethics are reflections of the morally permissible standards of conduct which members of a group make binding upon themselves.[5]

Importantly, codes of conduct can be developed by small or large organizations – governmental or non-governmental – at the local, national, regional, or international level, and the adoption of such codes is generally based on voluntarism. The high contracting parties to international legal instruments, on the other hand, are sovereign states – thus excluding substate actors and non-governmental entities. The importance of this disctinction should not be lost on those familiar with the record of rebel armies' treatment of children in armed conflict.

Military codes

In modern times it is generally deemed essential for the upholding of the rule of law that the armed forces be bound by their national constitution and other laws of the land, that they answer to the elected government, and that they are trained in and committed to the principles of human rights and humanitarian law in the execution of their constitutionally defined roles and tasks.

While traditional military training, in many cases, includes attention to the laws of war, including the four Geneva Conventions of 12 August 1949 and their 1977 protocols, specific training in the area of human rights has been conspicuously absent. Indeed, the notion that human rights training and sensitization are inconsistent with effective military training is not uncommon in some military circles. According to this line of thought, soldiers are warriors, and the waging of war is, by its very nature, contrary to human rights.

Such arguments are based on fallacious logic and ignorance of the history of armed conflict. Although not based on a human rights culture as we know it, soldiers have since ancient times had codes of conduct based on a warrior's honour – from the Christian code of chivalry to the Japanese *bushido* which was developed in feudal Japan and codified in the sixteenth century. These codes were primarily concerned with establishing the rules of combat and defining the system of moral ettiquette by which warriors judged themselves to be worthy of mutual respect.

However, the codes also required warriors to distinguish between combatants and non-combatants, legitimate and illegitimate targets, moral and immoral weaponry, and between civilized and barbarous practices in the treatment of prisoners and the wounded. Although such codes were honoured as much in the breach as in the observance, Ignatieff observes that "without them war is not war – it is no more than slaughter".[6] But such codes were very particularist, applying to certain peoples and not to others. For example, the chivalric code applied only to Christians, while warriors could behave towards infidels without restraint. The Muslims, of course, responded with the concept of *jihad*.

It was the Geneva Conventions that both codified the European warriors' honour and sought to make it universal, to open its protections to everyone. However, adherence to law in times of war has always been uncertain, and there are no judges or policemen at the place where the killing is done in combat. Moreover, in post-modern warfare belligerents are often unconcerned with the Western universalist ethic based on notions of human rights, adhering rather to particularist ethics that define the tribe, nation, or ethnicity as the limit of legitimate moral concern.

Under such circumstances, Ignatieff believes that "the decisive restraint on inhuman practice on the battlefield lies within the warrior himself, in his conception of what is honourable and dishonourable for a man to do with weapons".[7]

Of course, where there is a functioning military hierarchy and disciplinary code, soldiers have been held accountable and brought to book for atrocities and excesses committed in the heat of battle. There is also some hope that the International Criminal Court will come to play the role of an effective judge, and that combatants will keep this in mind. However, notwithstanding the role of the international media and NGOs such as Human Rights Watch, it is warriors themselves (albeit of superior rank) who, in the main, "police" the profession of arms.

In addition to military disciplinary codes which form the basis of military law, it is common for national military organizations, and even units or branches of such forces, to adopt one or more codes of conduct, codes of honour, and/or credos. For example, a Code of Conduct for US Armed Forces was first published by President Dwight D. Eisenhower in Executive Order 10631 in 1955. It was later amended by President Carter in 1977.[8] However, like many other national military codes, this is rather "gung-ho", and based more on notions of sacrifice, bravery, and patriotism than on universal human rights principles.

Such codes are in urgent need of revision where the duties of many contemporary armies are not limited to the waging of war, but increasingly include civil policing duties, the maintenance of order and public safety under states of emergency, and assignment to international peacekeeping operations. The effective, professional, and humane performance of these duties requires a knowledge of and sensitization to international human rights standards, as well as the skills to apply them in the daily work of the military.

Within the broader ambit of promoting military adherence to international human rights standards, we need to find ways of ensuring that the basic human rights of the child are adhered to within the military. Beyond the issue of an internationally acceptable minimum recruitment age (which should place the issue of children *outside* the military organization *per se*) are a whole range of contingencies where soldiers will have to deal with children in armed conflict. These range from the treatment of juvenile members of civilian populations in war zones to confrontations with child-soldier adversaries in hostile forces and the treatment of boy and girl soldiers when supervising a disarmament and demobilization process as part of a third-party intervention force.

There is an evolving consensus that the military in general and peacekeepers in particular should be influenced to be sensitive to the needs of the child. The idea is that soldiers should be trained to protect the children and ensure that if minors are inevitably caught up in war, their experiences will be less traumatic because of the sensitivity of soldiers towards the position of these children. This type of reasoning supports the West African training initiative of Rädda Barnen, which took place in Abijan in 2000.

The United Nations is also taking the issues of human rights and child rights within peace missions very seriously. Thanks to the efforts of Olara Otunnu, the special representative of the Secretary-General for children in armed conflict, it has been agreed that there will be child rights advocates in every new peacekeeping force, trained to understand not just the legal aspects involved, but also to have a knowledge of the emotional or psychological make-up and the physical needs of the child. A memorandum of understanding has also been signed by the UNHCHR and UNDPKO. This aims at integrating and "mainstreaming" human rights activities into the training and deployment of all UN peace missions, through enhanced cooperation between the Office of the High Commissioner for Human Rights and the DPKO. However, the annex to this MOU focuses more on the human rights "components" of peacekeeping operations than it does on affecting the attitudes and behaviour of peacekeepers themselves (though it does mention human rights training for civilian and military staff of peacekeeping operations, to be conducted under instructions of the head of mission).

The development of a military code of conduct that empasizes human rights and child rights would be a useful adjunct to the above intitiatives, and could contribute to the internalization, rather than the compartmentalization, of responsibility for upholding such rights. There needs to be an understanding in the military of critical issues involving young people, such as:

- the importance of youth to the nation's future;
- the various maturity levels of children;
- the physical development of children;
- the principle that children's interests should be held in higher regard than military interests;
- the need to prioritize the welfare of the child during disarmament and demobilization processes.

How understanding of such issues can or should be incorporated into a miliatary code of conduct depends on the answers to a host of questions relating to the elements of such a code and to the process of development and implementation. As it would be presumptious to propose a draft code of conduct at this stage, the discussion that follows deals with generic issues, rather than the content of a code related to human rights and children in armed conflict.

Elements and process

There is no blueprint for determining what elements to incorpoate in a code of conduct, for the variety of such codes is almost as great as the variety of groups that have seen fit to write codes (including such sectors as the "learned professions", the information technology industry, a variety of government and business sectors, and of course the military itself). The abundance and variety of codes of conduct can be ascribed to the fact that such codes are written by specific groups of people for specific groups of people, each group having its own purpose for existence and its own means of accomplishing its purpose. Consequently, each group encounters a unique set of ethical challenges. If codes of ethics were very similar, then the usefulness of codes of ethics specific to a group would be in jeopardy.

Often, codes of ethics prioritize commonly conflicting principles which underlie the standards of conduct within an organization, either by explicitly weighting the principles or by implicitly ordering the principles in order to give guidance on how one is to act as a morally responsible agent of the group when situations require an element of compromise between principles.[9] Borrowing from the "Toronto Resolution" on codes of ethics in science and scholarship, it can be suggested that a code should contain some or all of the following elements:

- a code should articulate as far as possible the underlying assumptions and guiding principles of a working ethic;
- a code should indicate specific measures designed to ensure that signatories adhere to its principles;
- a code should oppose prejudice with respect to sex, religion, national or ethnic origin, age, sexual preference, colour, or physical or mental disability;
- a code should forbid developing or using methods of torture, or other devices and techniques that threaten or violate individual or collective human rights;
- a code should urge its adherents to identify and report violations of its terms, and should correspondingly ensure their protection from retribution;
- a code should be widely disseminated through curricula at learning and training institions, to educate the rising generations, as well as practising soldiers, about their emerging responsibilities;[10]
- a code must be specific enough so that compliance is measurable.[11]

Codes of conduct should both state the underlying ethical principles and offer guidance in how the principles should be followed. Giving guidance encourages participants in the code to develop and practise moral reasoning based on the collectively agreed-upon principles of the group enumerated in the code.

The basic challenge is to write a code with enough information to be of use in the specifics of a situation, while remaining general enough to be used for a wide variety of situations. This challenge has prompted many authors to extend their codes of conduct with sections dealing with, for example: "suggested guidelines for use with the fundamental code of conduct"; "standards of practice"; or "rules and procedures".

Within these sections, the authors typically describe how one should interpret the principles of the code pertaining to one's specific situation. In many instances these guidelines will attempt to provide guidance on how to resolve conflicting principles. Such additional sections would obviously add time and effort to the drafting process, but much of what will be included in an additional "guidelines" section should surface in the initial consultative process.[12]

The process of developing a code must necessarily be inclusive and consensus-driven. To assure that a code of ethics functions properly, the group or a representative body of the group must formulate it. According to Davis:

Ethics consists of those morally permissible standards of conduct each member of a group wants every other (member) to follow even if their following them would mean he or she had to follow them too.[13]

If we accept this definition, then it is reasonable to assert that writing a properly functioning code of conduct is a collective task. Without a reasonable amount of group consensus concerning morally permissible standards of conduct relevant to the group, codes tend to become framed documents decorating office walls, rather than a guiding force for the actions and decisions of members of the group.

The issue of procedure is therefore no less important than content, and requires careful examination before any code-developing project is launched. For example:

- who should take the lead in setting up a code?
- who should participate in the drafting process, and how can broader consensus be achieved?
- what kind of monitoring and sanctions are to be incorporated to ensure adherence?
- do other bodies which currently have no codes consider them an appropriate way of dealing with "inappropriate" professional practices?

The question of enforcement is rather important and delicate, since it will evoke a host of questions related to sovereignty and independence. In the military realm, it is interesting to note that the South African National Defence Force recently promulgated a human-rights-oriented code of conduct that is to be incorporated into its military disciplinary code. Although it will become part of military law, the code enjoys elevated status in that it is carried in pocket-card format (like peacekeepers' ROE cards) by every soldier (and hopefully also in their heads).

The enforcement issue also reinforces the notion that one of the main concerns of the drivers of a code-creating process must be to create spaces for discussions. This could be done, for example, through:

- submission, through a newsletter for instance, of specific cases where a code could provide useful guides for behaviour, encouraging participants in the process to submit their own responses;
- making available existing codes of a wide selection of military and related organizations, with related pointers to existing documentation for further research;
- providing some forum (UNDPKO?) where discussion could be followed in terms of harmonizing the self-regulation, in order to prevent restrictions in one country being prejudicial to another;
- publishing those codes that have been the subject of a favourable opinion;
- assisting in the resolution of conflicts which could arise between different national codes.[14]

If we accept that a code of conduct is a means of uniquely expressing a group's collective commitment to a specific set of standards of conduct, while offering guidance in how to best follow those codes, then it should be organized and written in a way and a language that will be well received by its intended adherents.

Codes of ethics change with time due to changes in society, changes in organizations, and a desire to improve the effectiveness of a code. Like peacekeeping doctrine, a code of ethics should therefore be thought of as a dynamic or "living" document. It must be adapted to the changing atmosphere of an organization and the environment in which the organization operates. Through a process of revision, embryonic, rudimentary, or draft codes become what can be described as well-developed codes.[15] And a process of fluent discussion obviously reinforces the internalization of the principles and guidelines contained therein.

Using the peacekeeping framework to develop a code for African soldiers and peacekeepers

The development of military codes of conduct is least contentious and most effective in terms of process, if not content, at the national level. However, we are dealing with international human and children's rights standards that may not enjoy a high priority among the nations of the world. The same can be said for the virtues of international peacekeeping, and the need for effective training for nations to fulfil their obligations to the international community through this medium.

Ideally, the issues of enhanced peacekeeping training and respect for human and children's rights should be treated as global concerns, and be driven by the UN organization. In practice, however, there are limits to what can be accompished by the DPKO and UNHCHR in the realm of widespread skills training and value inculcation.

Since the mid-1990s, there has been a proliferation of intiatives aimed at enhancing the quality of troop contributions to UN and regional peacekeeping operations – primarily through donor assistance to peacekeeping training in Africa. Britain, France, and the USA have been prominent sponsors of a variety of projects ranging from large-scale, regionally based multinational field exercises to national battalion-level training and the establishment of regional peacekeeping training centres and specialized courses for senior officers. In Southern Africa, the Danish government sponsored the establishement of a regional peacekeeping training centre to serve the 14 countries of the SADC.

These intitiatives have paralled the development of regional/subregional frameworks for conflict management and the promotion and protection of human rights (such as ECOWAS and the SADC). Moreover, the peacekeeping training projects have recognized the need to involve governmental agencies, parliaments, civil society, and key components of the UN system in their activities. The evolving cooperative frameworks for peacekeeping training in Africa should enhance intergovernmental cooperation, intensify exchanges of experience, and promote best practices between countries in comparable situations. Eventually it is hoped that such cooperation may lead to the design of common policies and programmes for conflict management and the promotion of human rights.

The traditionally non-offensive nature of international peacekeeping means that individual countries do not feel threatened by combined exercises, and that participants in such exercises are willing to share doctrine and experience with one another. UN peace operations doctrine de-emphasizes the utility of naked force and stresses the importance of negotiation, mediation, and conciliation as means to resolve disputes and conflicts. It also emphasizes the international legal framework for the conduct of multinational operations, including the various human rights instruments.

Peace operations training, with its emphasis on communication and mediation skills, appreciation for cultural diversity, and respect for international humanitarian law and human rights, assists in breaking down attitudinal barriers between members of the various forces of the region.

It is therefore suggested that the notion of developing a code of conduct to address the needs and rights of children in armed conflict may be taken further via the mechanisms already in place in Africa to enhance peacekeeping training. The process could be "bottom up", concentrating on the subregions and eventually widening to a continental position that might be embraced by other regions of the world. The Pretoria-based Institute for Security Studies (ISS) has embarked upon a similar process to forge African consensus around an appropriate peace support operations (PSO) doctrine for African soldiers, which may provide some insights for the development of a code of conduct.

From 24 to 26 August 1999, the SADC RPTC (Regional Peacekeeping Training Centre) agreed to host an unofficial regional workshop of "military experts" (of the rank of lieutenant-colonel/colonel) on integrated principles for peace support operations.[16] The stated aim of this workshop was to:

Enhance mutual understanding of the principles and guidelines for the conduct of PSO at the operational and tactical levels, through the proposal of workable solutions to existing problems and the recommendation of research projects to address those key problems/issues that could not be adequately addressed by the participants.

A draft working paper was provided to orient participants and guide discussions. The idea was to initiate a deliberate process which examines the best evidence of past conflicts and draws on African opinions and African experiences to bring together a considered, robust set of statements that will inform the evolution of the doctrine for peace support. It was agreed that the workshop should focus on doctrine (the operational and tactical levels) rather than political, legal, or strategic matters. These higher levels normally result in nebulous discussions without form or conclusion. The working document contained some forthright questions.

- Is there such a thing as "UN doctrine for PSO"? If so, what are its strengths and limitations?
- If Western doctrinal publications are not suitable for Africa, where are they deficient?
- How can we express the doctrine deficit as regards Africa's requirements?
- How can we best approach the deficit – by a series of statements relating to Africa or a whole new doctrine?

Participants found that the much-vaunted UN doctrine on PSO consists of some training notes, manuals, and videos covering tactical matters. There is also a 17-page document on the conduct of peacekeeping operations, but it is thin on detail. Similarly, peacekeeping manuals from the Nordic countries emphasize "peacekeeping" techniques at the tactical level, largely to the exclusion of operational concepts. These publications all emphasize techniques, drills, and procedures and do not really address key issues of doctrine at the operational level.

Without the political baggage associated with "official status", participants readily agreed that the doctrinal deficit in Africa centres around the need to define circumstances which should trigger peace enforcement methods. They agreed that extant traditional peacekeeping doctrine is not sufficiently robust to confront the new challenges of conflict resolution in Africa, and that war-fighting doctrine is overly destructive. Furthermore, war-fighting doctrine is predicated upon the defeat of a designated enemy and does not address the peace-building and reconciliation challenges necessary to create a secure and self-sustaining society and environment. In terms of immediate steps towards addressing the "doctrinal deficit", the preference was expressed for a comprehensive draft publication which could be circulated for comment as widely as possible in the form of a discussion document.

The author of the extant NATO PSO manual[17] was therefore asked to produce a draft PSO manual which takes account of the special needs of PSO in the African context and incorporates the doctrinal ideas developed during the workshop. The product of this endeavour was published by the ISS in March 2000, under the title *Peace Support Operations: A Draft Working Manual for African Military Practitioners*. This document is presently being circulated to select African command and staff colleges (and other relevant institutions) with requests for comments.

This is seen as a first step in a process designed to develop a common approach among African national military contingents for the conduct of "grey-area operations". The draft manual is not meant to be a perfect product, nor is it complete. The endorsement of African multilateral organizations, such as the OAU and SADC, has therefore not been sought. The idea was not to claim universal applicability, but to invite African senior command and staff colleges to use that which they find useful for instructional purposes, and to discard/replace that which they do not find useful. The aspiration is to begin an interactive process of peer review and refinement that will lead to greater consensus on PSO doctrine in Africa and will eventually influence decision-making and training across the continent.

Conclusion

It is apparent that there is fairly wide consensus on the utility of codes of conduct as a means of achieving more ethical practices in the realm of trade and management of light weapons and in the field of humanitarian assistance. It is also evident that, while a significant number of international legal instruments exist to protect human rights and the rights of the child, there has been no noticable improvement in the record of soldiers and the plight of children caught up in contemporary armed conflicts. There is thus plausible reason to suggest that existing instruments may be reinforced by working to develop a code of conduct for soldiers that focuses on the rights of the child and on their behaviour towards children in armed conflict. Africa presents a plausible "laboratory" for the development of such a code. It is a continent with an estimated 100,000 child soldiers, and women and children remain vulnerable in at least 14 ongoing armed conflicts. Moreover, the preoccupation of the international community with promoting "African peacekeeping capacity" provides a ready vehicle for advancing the discourse on codes of conduct for both peacekeepers and the object of miltary peacekeeping operations: African armed forces in general, in the service of government and non-statutory political leadership.

It would probably be easier to focus initially on African peacekeepers, or potential peacekeepers, before widening the initiative to include military forces in general. Similarly, the content of such a code should probably be circumscribed around a few basic and non-controversial human rights principles and ethical statements around which minumum consensus can be forged, before engaging in a process of widening and fine-tuning further drafts of a more comprehensive code.

As with the development of all ethical codes, the process is every bit as important as the content, and this would require a funding commitment and political support for such a project from the outset if momentum is to be maintained. The "prime mover" for such a process would also have to be carefully selected and key partners identified, such as the UNDPKO, UNHCHR, coalition members such as Rädda Barnen, regional peacekeeping training centres, and national armed forces with a proud record of contributing to peace support operations (for example, Ghana, Kenya, and Nigeria).

The ultimate short-term prize would be the inclusion of a code of conduct in a standard training manual for peace support operations that is widely used in African military training institutions. This would link the issue firmly to that of the evolution of a common African doctrine for PSO, where doctrine is simply defined as "that which is taught". Once the miltary begins in earnest to teach respect for the rights of the child, we shall have a first step in place towards positive behavioural modification that will start to bridge the gap between international instruments and national compliance, and the gap between rhetoric and reality.

Notes

1. Everett M. Ressler, Joanne Marie Tortorici, and Alex Marcelino, *Children in War: A Guide to Provisional Services* (New York: UNICEF, 1993), p. 54.
2. Report of Graça Machel, Expert of the UN Secretary-General, "Impact of Armed Conflict for Children", A/51/306, United Nations, 26 August 1996, p. 54.
3. An analysis of existing codes shows that there is a distinction to be made between "codes of ethics" and "codes of conduct". The first expression could be favoured when the main idea is to envisage what would be called a "mission statement", giving visions and objectives. Some commentators consider that this title is related to codes which are more oriented toward the public, or society as a whole. The second expression seems to be related more to specific professions or occupations. For the purposes of simplicity, and to avoid a semantic quagmire, the terms "codes of conduct" and "codes of ethics" will be treated synonomously in this chapter.
4. See S. P. Huntington, *The Soldier and the State: The Theory and Politics of Civil-Military Relations* (New York: Sage, 1957).
5. Andrew T. Olson, *Authoring a Code: Observations on Process and Organization* (Chicago: Illinois Institute of Technology, 1998), http://csep.iit.edu/codes/coe/Writing_A_Code.html.
6. Michael Ignatieff, *The Warrior's Honour: Ethnic War and the Modern Conscience* (London: Vintage, 1998), p. 117.
7. *Ibid.*, p. 118.
8. The Code of Conduct for US Armed Forces was first published by President Dwight D. Eisenhower in Executive Order 10631 in 1955. It was later amended by President Carter in 1977. It outlines the basic responsibilities and obligations of all US service members to the USA, as follows.
   - I am an American, fighting in the forces which guard my country and our way of life. I am prepared to give my life in their defence.
   - I will never surrender of my own free will. If in command, I will never surrender the members of my command while they still have the means to resist.
   - If I am captured I will continue to resist by all means available. I will make every effort to escape and to aid others to escape. I will accept neither parole nor special favours from the enemy.
   - If I become a prisoner of war, I will keep faith with my fellow prisoners. I will give no information or take part in any action which might be harmful to my comrades. If I am senior, I will take command. If not, I will obey the lawful orders of those appointed over me and will back them up in every way.
   - When questioned, should I become a prisoner of war, I am required to give name, rank, service number, and date of birth. I will evade answering further questions to the utmost of my ability. I will make no oral or written statements disloyal to my country and its allies or harmful to their cause.
   - I will never forget that I am an American, fighting for freedom, responsible for my actions, and dedicated to the principles which made my country free. I will trust in my God and in the United States of America.
9. Olson, note 5 above.
10. Endorsed by participants to a workshop held in Toronto on 2 April 1992, with the aim of presenting a methodology for assessing particular ethical codes which comprises the key elements that all codes of ethics in science and scholarship should include. See the Toronto Resolution (TTR), http://courses.cs.vt.edu/~cs3604/lib/WorldCodes/IFIP.Recommendation.html, last updated 11 August 1995.
11. Cornelius von Baeyer, "Codes of Conduct: Panacea or Bunk?", *CDPA Report*, news-

letter of the Canadian Defence Preparedness Association XI, no. 3 (September/October 1997).

12. Olson, note 5 above.

13. Quoted in Olson, *ibid.*

14. Adapted from IFIP Ethics Task Group, "Recommendations to the Federation for Information Processing regarding Codes of Conduct for Computer Societies", http://courses.cs.vt.edu/~cs3604/lib/WorldCodes/Toronto.Recommendation.html, last updated 9 October 1994.

15. Olson, note 5 above.

16. The workshop was organized and facilitated by the Pretoria-based Institute for Security Studies in partnership with the Prague-based Institute for International Relations. It was funded by the government of Norway as part of the Training for Peace in Southern Africa project, and is seen as part of a process of building consensus around real regional capacity-building for peace support operations. However, participation was not based upon any regional grouping or mandate. Rather, the group was constituted through personal networks that enabled the identification of a number of experienced military officers and civilian experts who were willing and able to contribute to a candid debate in pursuit of the aim and objectives of the workshop. The group that finally assembled in Harare included military officers from Botswana, Britain, Kenya, South Africa, and Zimbabwe – as well as a few civilian scholars and experts.

17. Colonel Philip Wilkinson, British Army, who was a participant at the Harare workshop.

14

Smarter, sharper, stronger? UN sanctions and conflict diamonds in Angola

Kim Richard Nossal

Introduction

Among the most popular diplomatic tools of global governance in the 1990s were multilateral sanctions.[1] Yet international sanctions, particularly as they have been imposed by the UN Security Council, have tended to be both blunt and ineffective, imposing huge humanitarian suffering on both civilian populations and third countries without achieving political change. Moreover, most analyses of UN sanctions are pessimistic about the possibilities for reform, arguing that there are simply too many structural impediments and too little political will to fashion sanctions that would be "smarter" (in other words, not so indiscriminate in their effects), "sharper" (in other words, more carefully targeted and not so blunt), or stronger – more effective.

However, as Andrew Cooper noted in his introduction, and as many of the case studies presented in this book clearly demonstrate, innovative leadership on issues of global governance *is* possible. The UN sanctions against "conflict diamonds" in Angola provide a useful illustration of this dynamic at work. In this case, a few key actors sought to address what they saw as an intractable impediment to the achievement of peace in the civil war in Angola: the role of the diamond trade in fuelling and perpetuating the conflict. The purpose of this chapter is to explore the conflict diamonds initiative taken by the Canadian government when it began a two-year term on the Security Council in January 1999. It will examine the way in which UN sanctions against a rebel group in Angola – the União Nacional para a Independência Total de Angola (UNITA), under the leadership of Jonas Savimbi – were tightened, sharpened, and strengthened in 1999 and 2000. It will demonstrate that while the efforts of Robert Fowler, Canada's permanent representative to the United Nations, to press this case were an important catalyst for change, the cooperation of a range of other actors, including the global diamond industry, non-governmental organizations, and other "like-minded" governments, was crucial to the outcome.

In particular, this chapter will demonstrate the importance of the ability to transform norms as a feature of innovation and leadership in global governance.[2] The case of anti-personnel land-mines, explored by Iver Neumann, Max Cameron, and William Maley, shows clearly that one of the keys to the success of that initiative was the ability to strip land-mines of their legitimacy as a weapon of war; in this case, one of the keys to the success of the Angolan sanctions was the ability of Fowler and his allies in other governments and the NGO community to transform the legitimacy of the global diamond trade. This was done by engaging in what the editors of this book, following Fen Osler Hampson and Dean Oliver,[3] have called a diplomatic "end run" – an attempt to steer around the normal procedures and practices of global politics. In this case, the "end run" took a number of different forms.

First, it involved an attempt to taint diamonds from conflict areas sold on the international market to obtain funds to purchase weapons and perpetuate war as "conflict diamonds" or "blood diamonds".[4] This reconstruction of diamonds as a product with a possible negative taint had a powerful impact on the global diamond market, creating fears that diamonds could go the way of fur and tobacco as products increasingly reviled in the market-place. This prompted the key players in the global diamond industry to alter their attitudes towards diamonds from conflict areas, and change much of their market behaviour. Second, the "end run" involved using techniques of statecraft that were both unorthodox and undiplomatic, including the highly unusual practice of criticizing states and leaders by name in a UN report. While the "naming-and-shaming" approach was widely criticized, it did shake some of the entrenched norms that had shaped the UN's approach to sanctions in the 1990s.

The result was a sanctions regime that was somewhat smarter, sharper, and stronger; more importantly, because the Angolan conflict diamonds initiative has been replicated in other cases since, it can be argued that the efforts to improve the UN measures against UNITA moved the UN sanctions reform agenda forward, albeit in limited and only tentative ways.

The UN's "sanctions decade" and sanctions reform

The end of the Cold War brought what David Cortright and George A. Lopez have called the "sanctions decade": in the 10 years after 1991, the UN Security Council used the enforcement measures available to it under Article VII of the UN Charter six times as often as during the previous 45 years.[5] While UN sanctions had been used twice in the Cold War era – against the white-minority regimes of Rhodesia in 1966 and South Africa in 1977 – the Security Council proved itself willing to impose sanctions against an array of states in the 1990s: Iraq and occupied Kuwait in 1990, the former Yugoslavia in 1991, Cambodia, Liberia, Libya, and Somalia in 1992, Haiti in 1993, Rwanda in 1994, Sudan in 1996, Sierra Leone in 1997, and Afghanistan in 1999.[6]

In addition, the United Nations also began imposing sanctions against particular actors *within* sovereign states, rather than against states (and populations) as a whole. For example, in 1992, the UN General Assembly imposed sanctions against those parts of Cambodia controlled by the Khmer Rouge, which was refusing to cooperate with the UN Transitional Authority in Cambodia (UNTAC). Indeed, the Khmer Rouge was financing its continuing war against other factions in Cambodia by the sale of logs and gems exported from Khmer Rouge areas via Thailand. In an attempt to deny the Khmer Rouge funds, sanctions were imposed on the Khmer Rouge and its political wing, the Party of Democratic Kampuchea, putting in place an oil embargo and supporting a moratorium on the export of logs and gems from all of Cambodia.[7] And in September 1993, the Security Council imposed Chapter VII measures against UNITA in Angola for its refusal to accept the results of the September 1992 UN-supervised elections designed to bring an end to the civil war in that country.[8]

Paradoxically, the increased use of this tool of statecraft by the UN Security Council brought with it increasing dissatisfaction and a great deal of criticism. Some of the criticism focused on the blunt nature of sanctions and their undifferentiated impact on all those who happened to live within a state targeted by sanctions, regardless of their capacity to influence the behaviour of their governors that was attracting the sanctions in the first place. The key exemplar of this phenomenon was the comprehensive sanctions regime imposed against Iraq after its invasion of Kuwait in August 1990, for these sanctions had huge humanitarian and often gendered effects.[9] Some of the criticism focused on the unanticipated or unintended consequences of sanctions, in particular the criminalization of sanctioned societies,[10] or the impact on third parties.

But if some critics were arguing that UN sanctions were *too* effective, another line of criticism suggested that the sanctions being imposed by the United Nations were not effective enough, in the sense that these measures were clearly not producing the anticipated political results in the state targeted by sanctions. One result of what was widely seen as a string of UN sanctions "failures" in the 1990s was the growth of what might be thought of as a sanctions reform debate, supported by a host of studies detailing the problems evident in the UN Security Council's new-found enthusiasm for sanctions. Those contributing to this debate included a range of UN actors – two Secretaries-General, the chairs of the various sanctions committees established by the Security Council, the UN's Department of Humanitarian Affairs – and a variety of national governments. Added to these were studies commissioned by private groups, such as the International Peace Academy, the Carnegie Corporation, and the Fourth Freedom Forum; and studies by a number of students of sanctions.[11]

A number of common concerns were identified. Margaret P. Doxey, for example, argued that the UN sanctions in the 1990s revealed "significant shortcomings" in three areas: in the actual wording of the Security Council resolutions, which often left goals unclear and means ambiguous; in the national enforcement of UN measures, which often left large holes in the sanctions "net"; and in role of the United Nations itself in managing and supervising sanctions.[12] Some, like Paul Conlon, a former UN official, focused on the management of sanctions, arguing that the way in which the various sanctions committees established by the Security Council operated explained why sanctions were so porous.[13] John Stremlau's report for the Carnegie Corporation identified a range of comparable problems with the nature of the various sanctions regimes embraced by the United Nations.[14] For their part, the case studies collected by Cortright and Lopez demonstrate clearly the degree to which UN sanctions in the 1990s were ineffective in achieving their nominal goals while at the same time exacting a huge cost in pain and suffering by ordinary people caught in the crossfire between warring parties and sanctioning states.[15] In short, by the end of the 1990s there was widespread criticism of sanctions as an instrument for dealing with international conflict.

At the same time, however, there was no shortage of suggestions for reforming the UN sanctions regime, and making these measures more effective and less blunt. Most students who identified the shortcomings of UN sanctions were inclined to offer concrete suggestions for reform. One common suggestion was to make sanctions "smarter" in the way that bombs were made smarter in the 1990s – in other words, measures that would not be levied in blunt fashion against an entire population but only against those responsible for wrongdoing, or would target particular areas of the economy designed to maximize effectiveness.[16] And many of the suggestions focused on institutional reforms, such as Stremlau's suggestion for a resurrection of the Collective Measures Committee that the United Nations had established in 1951–1952 to suggest ways to improve UN sanctions.[17]

The Angola sanctions

The UN's Angola sanctions reflected many of these problems. International sanctions were first imposed by the Security Council following the collapse of attempts at a political settlement in Angola after Savimbi and UNITA refused to accept the results of the September 1992 elections, and instead continued to wage war against the government in Luanda. The rebel movement was able to continue the war largely because it controlled much of Angola's diamond production. In 1992 it occupied the diamond-rich Cuango Valley, and indeed for most of the 1990s its forces controlled the key diamond-producing areas in north-eastern Angola. UNITA was able to use revenues from the sale of the very high-quality diamonds from those areas on the international market to purchase weapons. As one newspaper report put it succinctly in 2000: "Diamonds have allowed [Savimbi] to convert a motley group of ill-trained fighters into one of the best armed irregular forces in the world, capable of fighting a war that has cost 500,000 lives."[18]

Moreover, it was becoming increasingly clear that the efforts of the United Nations to bring an end to the conflict were hampered by the ineffectiveness of the tools embraced by the Security Council. The Security Council had imposed sanctions against UNITA shortly after the collapse of the peace process. Resolution 864 of 15 September 1993 imposed an embargo on all arms to UNITA, and a ban on the sale of Angolan petroleum except through those ports designated by the government of Angola. Resolution 864 also established a sanctions committee to supervise and administer the measures, and the United Nations threatened further trade and travel sanctions against UNITA if it did not comply with the Bicesses peace accords by 1 November 1993. However, when UNITA responded to these demands by calling for further negotiations, the Security Council did not follow through on its earlier threat of harsher measures, but merely renewed its promise of further sanctions (Resolution 890, 15 December 1993). Moreover, the UN peacekeeping operation then deployed in the country – the UN Verification Mission in Angola (UNAVEM II) – was understaffed and incapable of effectively monitoring a country the size of Angola.

In the meantime, fighting in Angola intensified as UNITA's access to arms remained undiminished. In what is referred to as Angola's "Third War" or "War of the Cities", an estimated 180,000 people were killed between May and October 1993, with widespread destruction of the cities of the central highlands and the country's infrastructure. The military balance tipped towards the government side in 1994, leading UNITA to negotiate a peace agreement, the Lusaka Protocol initialled on 31 October 1994 and finally signed on 20 November 1994.[19] Under the protocol, a joint commission was established, consisting of the United Nations, the Angolan government, and UNITA, with a "troika" consisting of Portugal, Russia, and the USA as observers. In addition, in February 1995 the Security Council created yet another UN verification mission (UNAVEM III) But it is noteworthy that UN sanctions had little to do with the brief peace that followed; as Cortright and Lopez conclude laconically, "Sanctions were but a minor footnote in a bloody conflict determined primarily by the force of arms."[20]

The peace that was established by the Lusaka Protocol did not last long. While UNITA continued to negotiate with the government in Luanda, it also continued to accumulate military capacity, using the cease-fire as a cover for a major rearming exercise. Moreover, large numbers of UNITA troops were kept in hiding during this period. UNITA routinely violated the cease-fire. Attacks against civilians continued, and thousands were displaced as conflict spread throughout the provinces.

The UN Security Council responded to the resumption of fighting by continuing to threaten new sanctions. In October 1996, Resolution 1075 threatened UNITA with additional measures if it did not abide by the Lusaka accords. When UNITA did not respond to these pressures, the Security Council, instead of imposing the sanctions that had been promised two months before, began to wind down the UNAVEM III mission (Resolution 1087, 11 December 1996). By August 1997, however, it was clear that UNITA was continuing to engage in fighting, and so the Security Council decided once again to threaten sanctions. Resolution 1127 (28 August 1997) added travel and diplomatic sanctions to the existing measures. Under these sanctions, UNITA officials were banned from travelling and flights to and from UNITA-controlled territories were prohibited. In addition, UNITA offices in other countries were ordered to close. However, these measures came in the form of a suspended sentence: actual implementation was delayed so that UNITA could provide the Security Council with evidence of its compliance. Only after one further suspension of the sanctions did the Security Council's patience wear out: in October 1997, Resolution 1127 was finally implemented, and a small UN Observer Mission in Angola (MONUA) was established.

The fighting between UNITA and the Angolan government escalated over the course of 1998. In May 1998, UNITA began a series of coordinated attacks on diamond-mining operations in government-controlled areas, targeting expatriate workers in particular. As the war escalated, the Security Council adopted Resolution 1173 (12 June 1998), which imposed a number of additional sanctions, including a complete ban on travel to and from UNITA territory, a freeze on UNITA assets, a ban on all financial transactions with UNITA, and, most importantly, a ban on the importation of any Angolan diamond that had not been certified by the Angolan government.

However, these additional measures, by themselves, had little impact, for there was little enforcement on the ground. MONUA, far smaller than any of the UNAVEM operations, was even less able to provide monitoring. Arms continued to flow into UNITA and diamonds continued to flow out. UNITA had stockpiled large numbers of diamonds in 1996 and 1997, and when the UN imposed diamond sanctions in 1998 UNITA released all these gems on to the market. According to Global Witness, a British NGO which conducted an investigation into diamonds and sanctions-busting in the Angolan case, De Beers Consolidated Mines, the dominant firm in the global diamond market, moved quickly to prevent the market from being flooded and stabilize the price of diamonds by buying UNITA gems after the UN bans had been put in place.[21] Likewise, the travel ban was violated in numerous ways: some UNITA officials had other citizenships; other UNITA officials were given passports by Côte d'Ivoire and Togo. In short, Cortright and Lopez suggest that the failure of the Security Council to take harsher measures merely "encouraged Savimbi's tendency to be intransigent and made it easier for UNITA to violate previous peace commitments". More importantly, they argue, "the almost complete lack of enforcement efforts undermined the credibility of the entire sanctions exercise".[22] By 1999, according to Andrew Mack and Asif Khan, the UNITA sanctions regime was "largely moribund".[23]

Strengthening the Angola sanctions

Even before Canada began its two-year term on the Security Council on 1 January 1999, there had been some movement to address some of the deep problems with the Angola sanctions. Njuguna Mahugu, the Kenyan permanent representative and chair of the Angola sanctions committee in 1998, increased the frequency of committee meetings, and met with leaders in the Southern African region to try to secure greater compliance with the sanctions. However, it was not until the Canadian permanent representative, Robert Fowler, assumed the chair of the Angola sanctions committee in January 1999 that a concerted effort to strengthen the measures against UNITA began.

Trying to tighten the Angolan sanctions fitted well with the general

approach of the government of Canada to its two-year term on the Security Council. Ottawa had campaigned in 1998 for election to the Western European and Other non-permanent seat on the Security Council on
an explicit "election platform". Among the many promises made to the
voters was that if Canada were elected, one of its priorities would be to
address the leaky and ineffective UN sanctions regime. Indeed, the Canadian approach on sanctions followed a plan suggested by a study on
sanctions that had been commissioned by the Department of Foreign
Affairs and International Trade in preparation for a possible two-year
term on the Security Council. That study had proposed that "As a member of the Security Council, Canada should give priority to three tasks:
discouraging the use of sanctions wherever more constructive and humane alternatives exist; developing the capacity of the international community to design and administer strong, targeted sanctions; and ensuring
that the needs of innocent civilians in target states are given due consideration in the design and implementation of sanctions."[24]

Moreover, such activism on the issue of sanctions also fitted well with
the emphasis that Canada's Foreign Affairs Minister, Lloyd Axworthy,
was placing on what was called the "human security agenda" – an effort,
in the words of the Canadian Department of Foreign Affairs and International Trade, to define security more expansively. The essence of "human" security was what Ottawa called "a shift in the angle of vision"
that meant "taking people as its point of reference, rather than focusing
exclusively on the security of territory or governments".[25] Axworthy's
enunciation of a "human security agenda" for Canadian foreign policy
coincided with the beginning of Canada's term on the Security Council,
and it is not at all coincidental that the government's policy paper concluded with a clarion call to strengthen the capacity of international organizations like the United Nations to advance human security in conflict
areas. Likewise, given that anti-personnel land-mines were widely used
by UNITA, Angola was a natural focus for a government committed to
following through its anti-mine efforts. Thus when Axworthy appeared
before the Security Council in February 1999, he urged the Council to
place security and protection for civilians at the core of its efforts, and
stressed, *inter alia*, the importance of "fine-tuning" sanctions to maximize
the pain inflicted on wrongdoers and minimize the damage done to innocent civilians.[26]

Canada's attempts to try to "fine-tune" the Angola sanctions were
made easier by the fact that in January and February, the business of the
Security Council was dominated by sanctions issues. The bombing of
Iraq by Britain and the USA in December 1998 over the issue of weapons inspection prompted a debate on the Security Council over the sanctions regime against Iraq. Some members sought to ease the sanctions,

particularly in view of the humanitarian effects of these measures; other members, such as the USA and Britain, argued for a continuation of these measures as a means of pressuring the government in Baghdad into accepting a renewed UN weapons inspection regime. Canada's contribution to the debate over the Iraq sanctions was to call for the creation of panels of experts to examine three issues: the weapons inspection regime, humanitarian effects of sanctions, and missing persons and property.[27]

The Security Council was also forced to focus on Angola, for the conflict in that country had again intensified and there was renewed media attention given to the failure of UN sanctions. In large part this was a result of the wide publicity given to a report by Global Witness which detailed the links between the illicit trade in Angolan diamonds from UNITA-held areas and the continuing war. The report, entitled *A Rough Trade* and released on 14 December 1998,[28] detailed how the UN sanctions imposed in June were being routinely violated, with many "rough" diamonds (as uncut diamonds are called) being smuggled into other African countries, or sold on the grey market in Antwerp. Global Witness identified De Beers Consolidated Mines as the principal conduit for the smuggled gems, since at that time De Beers occupied a dominant place in the global diamond market. Using its Central Selling Organization (CSO), based in London, De Beers sought to maintain a stable price for diamonds by purchasing as many rough diamonds as possible, and then releasing them on to the global market. Global Witness claimed that De Beers, as the principal global buyer of rough gems, was primarily responsible for the flow of diamond revenues to UNITA. The report also criticized the government of Belgium for not regulating the principal centre of the diamond trade in Antwerp more closely, permitting through inaction and lax enforcement packets of illicit diamonds without appropriate certification to enter Belgium and be traded on the Antwerp bourse.

And merely days after the release of the Global Witness report, UNITA shot down two UN planes, killing 23 people. On 26 December 1998, UNITA forces shot down a UN-chartered C-130 Hercules, killing 14 people on board; on 2 January, the day after Canada took its seat on the Security Council, UNITA downed another UN Hercules, killing all nine aboard.[29] While the loss of 23 lives prompted the Security Council to withdraw MONUA from Angola, it also galvanized opinion on the Council about the need to take stronger action.

Thus, when Robert Fowler, Canada's permanent representative, sought the chairmanship of the sanctions committee that had been established by Resolution 864 in 1993, he had considerable support from other members of the Security Council for changing the UNITA sanctions. Once in position, Fowler was able to pursue a multifaceted diplomatic strategy designed to address the leakage in the measures against UNITA and thus to pursue Canada's broader UN agenda. Elements of this strategy included convincing the Security Council to conduct two full investigations of the diamonds-for-arms linkages; working with non-governmental organizations to raise public awareness of conflict diamonds; working on (and with) the global diamond industry to change the ways in which diamonds were traded; cooperating with other governments, including like-minded governments like Britain–governments with both an interest in the diamond trade and an interest in sustaining diamonds as a desired (rather than a reviled) product; and speaking out openly against those governments and actors deemed to be the primary obstacles to sanctions reform. To each of these interrelated elements this chapter now turns.

Investigating sanctions-busting

The first tactic embraced by Fowler was to convince the Security Council to allow a detailed investigation of the widely circulating allegations that Resolution 1173 was being disregarded by a number of other governments and actors. In his capacity as chair of the Angola sanctions committee, he worked to implement the suggestion made by the Secretary-General, Kofi Annan, in his report to the Security Council on 17 January 1999 that a panel of experts be appointed to investigate the UNITA sanctions. Because the appointment of a panel of experts had been well received by members of the Council in the case of Iraq (even if in the final analysis the Security Council was unable to reach agreement on any of the recommendations eventually put forward by the panel), the Canadian delegation decided to try to replicate it in the case of Angola. In May 1999 the sanctions committee proposed that a panel of experts be established and mandated to establish exactly how the UNITA sanctions were being violated, who was violating them, and how these measures could be strengthened; the Security Council established the panel by Resolution 1237 (7 May 1999).

Ten independent experts were gathered, with Anders Möllander, a former Swedish ambassador to Angola, in the chair. The other members were from Botswana, China, France, Namibia, the Russian Federation, South Africa, Switzerland, the USA, and Zimbabwe. After meeting in New York late in August 1999, panel members travelled to nearly 30 countries, holding meetings with government officials, NGOs, and other interested actors, including police and intelligence sources, firms, and industry associations. In January 2000, Fowler and two members of the panel visited Angola and videotaped interviews with several defectors from UNITA.

On the basis of the information gathered on their travels, members of the panel concluded in their report that UNITA was able to fight because of four factors: the availability of purchasing power from conflict diamonds; the willingness of certain countries not under sanction to give their end-user certificates to UNITA and allow their territory to be used to trans-ship arms to UNITA; the willingness of certain countries to sell arms without monitoring where those arms would end up; and the unregulated activities of global arms dealers. The panel report also recommended a number of ways in which the sanctions regime against UNITA could be strengthened.[30]

While the panel of experts was disbanded after delivering its report in March 2000, the Security Council decided to maintain a watching brief on the Angola sanctions that could also follow up on a number of leads uncovered by the panel. This new body was known as the monitoring mechanism. It was established under Resolution 1295 (18 April 2000), and was mandated to collect information on violations of sanctions; follow up leads of the panel of experts; and propose a mechanism for increasing the effectiveness and efficiency of the implementation of sanctions. Five members were appointed: Juan Larrain, the permanent representative of Chile, was appointed as the chair, plus representatives from Britain, Senegal, Sweden, and Zimbabwe. Like the panel of experts, the members of the mechanism traveled widely and interviewed numerous actors. They delivered their final report in December 2000, which not only broadly confirmed the conclusions reached by the panel of experts, but also managed to clarify some of the details that the members of the panel had raised earlier but which could not be confirmed.[31]

Working with CSOs

One of the hallmarks of Canada's approach to foreign policy-making during the period when Lloyd Axworthy was Foreign Minister was the privileged position accorded to global civil society and civil society organizations (CSOs). During this period, a conscious effort was made to bring non-governmental organizations deeply into the policy process: as Alison Van Rooy noted in 1999, "Canadian diplomats now work with non-diplomats to get diplomatic jobs done".[32] Indeed, the chapters by Neumann, Cameron, and Maley make clear the degree to which Axworthy's part in the campaign for a global ban on land-mines depended heavily on the active participation of NGOs in the Ottawa process.[33]

A similar approach was taken by Fowler at the United Nations: close relations were established with the NGO community, particularly with Global Witness and Human Rights Watch. Fowler had a number of meetings with Charmian Gooch of Global Witness and Alex Vines of Human

Rights Watch, and indeed encouraged the development of a synergy between Ottawa's efforts to strengthen the UN sanctions on UNITA and the efforts of NGOs to galvanize public awareness about the conflict diamonds issue by such means as the "Fatal Transactions" campaign, launched in October 1999 as a collaborative effort by four NGOs to draw attention to the link between diamonds and conflict – Global Witness, Medico International, a German NGO, the Netherlands Institute for Southern Africa, and Novib, a pan-European development NGO.[34] And in North America, Human Rights Watch spearheaded a public awareness campaign.

Recognizing the importance of the publicity generated by such campaigns, the Canadian government lent the efforts of the NGO community considerable support and legitimacy. For example, Fowler went out of his way to praise Global Witness and Human Rights Watch for having taken a "responsible" and collaborative approach to the issue, for having avoided the temptations to "grandstand", and for having "shown the way, the right way, to the rest of us".[35]

Working with the global diamond industry

Even before the panel of experts started gathering information in 1999, Fowler began to pursue a second line of pressure – seeking to convince the global diamond industry to cooperate with the UN sanctions and stop the trade in rough diamonds from UNITA-controlled areas. If diamond purchasers could be convinced not to buy diamonds from Angola that did not have appropriate certification from the Angolan government, then, it was hoped, funds to UNITA would dry up.

In July Fowler went to Antwerp, one of the key centres of the global diamond market and the location of the Hoge Raad voor Diamant (HRD, or Diamond High Council), the formal trade organization for the Belgian diamond industry. As Fowler reminded the World Diamond Congress a year later, "My challenge to diamond industry representatives ... was nothing less than a demand to know whether your industry was content to see the sanctions flouted and, thus, to run the real and present risk of seeking your industry branded as a principal culprit."[36]

The diamond industry responded to these pressures in a variety of ways. In October 1999, merely days after the launch of the Fatal Transactions campaign, De Beers announced that it was closing its Angola offices and would no longer purchase any Angolan diamonds. While Nicky Oppenheimer, chair of De Beers's board, claimed that Global Witness had an "exaggerated" view of his company's ability to solve African conflicts, he did acknowledge that De Beers may have bought UNITA-mined diamonds in the past.[37] In late 1999, the HRD moved to work with the Belgian government to curtail the trade in rough diamonds, and worked with the government in Luanda to create a certificate of origin that was forgery-proof. For its part, the Belgian government decided in February 2000 to require that all diamond imports from all those African countries that did not have certificate-of-origin systems be licensed by individual diamond dealers. Other diamond industry initiatives included a joint resolution of the World Federation of Diamond Bourses and the International Diamond Manufacturers Association at the World Diamond Congress in July 2000 calling for a global certification system of seals and registration for packets of diamonds and a code of conduct for diamond traders. This resolution led to the creation of a World Diamond Council (WDC) in September 2000. At its inaugural meeting, the WDC adopted a series of measures, such as supervised rough diamond import-export offices and a uniform international certification system for sealing packets. These "rough controls" would result in what the WDC called "a chain of assurance" for polished diamond traders.[38]

Working with other governments

Crucial for the success of the Canadian initiative to tighten the UNITA sanctions was the support of other governments, particularly those on the Security Council. Key allies for Canada included both the USA and Britain. While the US administration of Bill Clinton had been slow to take up concerns expressed by the US Department of State about the trade in illicit diamonds prior to 1999,[39] its attention was increasingly focused on the issue, in part because of the consumer awareness campaign in the USA and the active involvement of a number of members of Congress. Thus, while many of these members of Congress continued to find fault with the Clinton administration's policy[40] throughout 1999 and 2000, the US government was generally supportive of initiatives to strengthen UN measures against UNITA, and Madeleine Albright, the US Secretary of State, contributed to the global debate over conflict diamonds at the G8 Foreign Ministers' meeting on the prevention of conflict, held in Berlin in December 1999.

Likewise, the British Labour government of Tony Blair, which in 1999 had embraced the idea of pursuing an "ethical" foreign policy, also supported the Canadian initiative. Peter Hain, a Minister of State at the Foreign and Commonwealth Office, embraced the conflict diamond dossier, not only offering support for Fowler's initiatives, but indeed eventually pushing further measures of his own, such as convening an international conference in London in October 2000 in order to generate, in his words, "unstoppable momentum" for a UN-sponsored regime for the certification and regulation of trade in rough diamonds.[41]

The trade in illicit diamonds was also made the focus of the Miyazaki Initiatives for Conflict Prevention, embraced by the Group of Eight (G8) countries meeting in Miyazaki prefecture in July 2000. The major policy statement on illicit trade in diamonds committed all G8 countries to ending the trade in conflict diamonds, to establishing a system of certificates of origin for diamonds, and to supporting all UN measures aimed at these goals.

"Naming and shaming" sanctions-busters

The most controversial tactic of the Canadian delegation involved departing from the usual UN practice of diplomatically refusing to criticize countries and political leaders by name. Instead, when the report of the panel of experts was released in New York on 15 March 2000,[42] it openly named the governments of Belgium, Bulgaria, Burkina Faso, Congo (Brazzaville), Côte d'Ivoire, Togo, Zaire, and Zambia as responsible in some fashion for the numerous violations of the UN's mandatory sanctions. The report also explicitly named the current or former heads of state or heads of government of five African countries as sanctions-busters: Blaise Compaoré, the President of Burkina Faso; Pascal Lissouba, former President of Congo (Brazzaville) and his Prime Minister, Jacques-Joachim Yhombi-Opango; Henri Konan-Bedié of Côte d'Ivoire; President Gnassingbé Eyadema of Togo; and the former President of Zaire, Mobuto Sese Seko. It also named the Director-General of the Zambian security and intelligence service, Xavier Chungu.

The report was explicit about the involvement or complicity of these governments and officials in sanctions-busting. Belgium was criticized for not regulating the diamond market in Antwerp more carefully. Bulgaria was identified as selling arms to individuals with end-user certificates that the government should have known were bogus, and providing training to UNITA personnel on some weapons systems. Burkina Faso was named as a source of petroleum shipments to UNITA territories, as a transit point for illegal arms destined for UNITA forces, and as a supplier of Burkinabé end-user certificates to enable UNITA to purchase arms elsewhere. President Compaoré was personally implicated in sanctions-busting. Congo (Brazzaville) was identified as a transit point for arms. Côte d'Ivoire and its President were named not only for assisting UNITA in evading bans on financial transactions, but also for providing diplomatic passports to UNITA officials to enable them to travel in violation of the UN sanctions. Rwanda was named for allowing its territory to be used by UNITA for meetings with arms dealers and diamond traders. Togo was named for providing end-user certificates for arms to UNITA in return for diamonds given to President Eyadema, and for providing passports to UNITA officials. Zambia was criticized for turning a blind eye to dealings with UNITA; it was also claimed that the head of Zambian security and intelligence provided supplies to UNITA. In addition, the report named a number of individuals and firms operating in South Africa, Namibia, and Ukraine, but explicitly cleared the governments of those countries of any complicity in sanctions-busting.

Not surprisingly, this departure from the normal diplomatic niceties prompted much criticism and numerous denials of wrongdoing from the states named by what in the corridors of the United Nations was quickly dubbed the "Foul Report". Unrepentant, Fowler dismissed the critics as "squeaking wheels", saying bluntly that "Sanctions had been grievously flouted for nearly seven years. Every member of this organization knows these sanctions have been violated." He called the report a "blueprint for change".[43]

Conclusions

The case of the UN sanctions against UNITA in Angola provides a useful example of the possibilities of diplomatic innovation. In this case, a moribund UN sanctions regime was transformed by taking the initiative and doing diplomacy differently. Robert Fowler's general activism, his willingness to bring non-state actors such as NGOs and the global diamond industry into the processes of multilateral statecraft, and above all his refusal to play by the normal rules of UN diplomacy all contributed to the improvement in the effectiveness of the UN's Angola sanctions. Moreover, Fowler's claim in March 2000 that the process embraced by the Angola sanctions committee constituted a blueprint for change proved to be no idle boast: as diamond-fuelled conflicts in Sierra Leone and Congo intensified over the course of 2000, the UN Security Council did indeed use the lessons learned from the Angola sanctions to limit the ability of combatants to use their access to high-value commodities, particularly diamonds, to fuel continued conflict.

However, in assessing the longer-term impact of the Canadian conflict diamond initiatives of 1999–2000, it is important to trace causality in this case. For it can be argued that while embracing innovative initiatives and making diplomatic end runs may be a *necessary* condition for the transformation of entrenched UN practices, it surely is not a *sufficient* explanation for changes in this case. As the account above suggests, two factors were essential for the success of the Fowler initiative.

First, success in this case was heavily dependent on the nature of the global diamond market. Paradoxically, for all their high value, diamonds are basically unimportant to human beings and this essential *inconsequence* makes them exceedingly vulnerable to tainting. By contrast, as

Greg Mills and Raisaka Masebelanga point out, other products that have greater consequence for human existence generally do not get hung with pejorative modifiers; rarely is there a move to target "conflict oil", for example.[44]

Thus the diamond industry was in an exceedingly weak position. It had to go along – or perhaps more properly be *seen* to be going along – with the Canadian initiative if it did not want to face the hugely negative consequences of not taking action. For if the industry did *not* respond, people would be inclined to continue to use the terms "conflict diamonds" or "blood diamonds" that were anathema to the diamond industry. Politicians like Peter Hain, the British Minister of State, would continue to wonder openly whether young men would want proof that the diamonds they were placing on their fiancées' fingers were not the cause of the amputation of a finger or an arm of a person in Sierra Leone. CSO coalitions like Fatal Transactions would continue to investigate the industry and publicize illicit dealings. Diplomats like Robert Fowler would continue to "name and shame" and expose dirty deals involving packets of diamonds passed surreptitiously to corrupt presidents. And if that were the case, *all* diamonds ran the risk of being tainted, and turned into the kind of reviled luxury product that fur became in the 1970s and 1980s.

Second, the importance of the support or acquiescence of the permanent members of the Security Council cannot be underestimated. As Mack and Khan point out, there is nothing accidental in whether a UN sanctions regime is atrophic or robust: the interests of the major powers will always have a determining influence.[45] In the Angolan case, the cooperation of the P5 – the active support of the USA and Britain and the acquiescence of China, France, and the Russian Federation – was crucial for Fowler's initiative to work. Had any one of these governments cast a veto at any point in the process, the impact of the initiative would have been seriously compromised. However, as it happened, each of the P5 either had particular interests in tightening the sanctions noose around UNITA, or a more general desire not to get in the way of that occurring.

The corollary of this observation is that the end run in this case worked because of the political inconsequence of the targets of this initiative. The countries and officials named could be subjected to global shaming precisely because none was consequential enough to attract the support of one of the P5. Indeed, it is indicative that when states of greater power and consequence did become more deeply involved in the processes of global governance over the diamond trade, there was much less like-mindedness – and much less collaboration. Thus disagreement quickly emerged on the most appropriate way to reform the global trade in diamonds. The South African government, which has a deep interest in maintaining the legitimacy of the diamond trade, invited a number of governments, NGOs, and representatives of the diamond industry to

Kimberley in May 2000 to discuss ways of organizing the global diamond trade. The working group established by what came to be known as the Kimberley process recommended a more conservative approach to the issue of diamond certification. The British conference of October 2000 was seen by some diamond producers as an effort to undermine the Kimberley process by pushing the issue too aggressively, with the result that the Russian Federation withdrew its commitment to co-chair the conference and the government of South Africa refused even to attend.[46]

If we look at causality in this way, we might be somewhat more cautious about the prospect that this kind of diplomatic end run will yield longer-term changes in behaviour. In the specific case of diamonds, there is some evidence that the changes introduced by the diamond industry have made it more difficult for UNITA to sell its diamonds, and less profitable to do so because of the higher transaction costs that have come with illegality. On the other hand, of all high-value products, diamonds are among the easiest to smuggle. And although identification is possible,[47] certification schemes are made more difficult because the high value of diamonds encourages grey-market activity. As one Canadian official put it, "The best we can hope for is to affect this on the margins ... Diamonds will always find a way to market."[48]

More generally, it can be argued that the kind of undiplomatic end run conducted by Fowler in 1999 and 2000 has only limited reproducibility. The "naming-and-shaming" approach was dependent on the willingness of the P5 to tolerate such departure from the norms in this particular case. And that willingness, in turn, was dependent on the relative inconsequence of the targets of the Fowler initiative. In sum, it seems unlikely that had countries of greater consequence been the targets of this end run, we would have seen such unusual unanimity in the efforts to create smarter, sharper, and stronger UN sanctions.

Acknowledgement

The author would like to thank the Social Sciences and Humanities Research Council of Canada (grant 410-99-1498) for making the research for this chapter possible.

Notes

1. For a critical exploration of this theme, see Kim Richard Nossal, "International Sanctions as Instruments of Global Governance", *Global Society* 13, no. 2 (April 1999), pp. 125–137.
2. For an excellent exploration of this phenomenon, see Audie Klotz, *Norms in Interna-*

tional Relations: The Struggle Against Apartheid (Ithaca: Cornell University Press, 1995), especially chap. 2.

3. Fen Osler Hampson and Dean F. Oliver, "Pulpit Diplomacy: A Critical Assessment of the Axworthy Doctrine", *International Journal* 53, no. 3 (Summer 1998), p. 397.

4. See, for example, the efforts of Representative Tony Hall (Democrat of Ohio), one of the members of the US Congress who has been active in the area of conflict diamonds, to paint the purchase of diamonds as "blood trade": http://www.house.gov/tonyhall/pr185.html.

5. David Cortright and George A. Lopez, eds, *The Sanctions Decade: Assessing UN Strategies in the 1990s* (Boulder, CO: Lynne Rienner, 2000).

6. Margaret P. Doxey, *United Nations Sanctions: Current Policy Issues* (Halifax: Centre for Foreign Policy Studies, Dalhousie University, 1997).

7. See Cortright and Lopez, note 5 above, chap. 7.

8. For one account, see David Cortright, George A. Lopez, and Richard W. Conroy, "Angola's Agony", in Cortright and Lopez, note 5 above, pp. 147–165.

9. For example, David Cortright and George A. Lopez, "Are Sanctions Just? The Problematic Case of Iraq", *Journal of International Affairs* 52 (Spring 1999), pp. 735–755; Eric Hoskins, "The Humanitarian Impact of Economic Sanctions and War in Iraq", in Thomas G. Weiss, David Cortright, George A. Lopez, and Larry Minear, eds, *Political Gain and Civilian Pain: The Humanitarian Impacts of Economic Sanctions* (Lanham, MD: Rowman and Littlefield, 1997), pp. 91–147; on the gendered effects of the Iraq sanctions, see Lori Buck, Nicole Gallant, and Kim Richard Nossal, "Sanctions as a Gendered Instrument of Statecraft: The Case of Iraq", *Review of International Studies* 24 (January 1998), pp. 69–84.

10. See, for example, R. T. Naylor, *Patriots and Profiteers: On Economic Warfare, Embargo Busting and State-Sponsored Crime* (Toronto: McClelland and Stewart, 1999).

11. For a comprehensive survey of this literature, see Cortright and Lopez, note 5 above, chap. 12.

12. Doxey, note 6 above, pp. 27–39.

13. "Sanctions committee" is the informal name for the subsidiary organ frequently established by the Security Council under Article 29 to supervise and administer sanctions imposed by that body. Membership mirrors that of the Council itself, with the result that turnover on the committee is high. Paul Conlon, "The UN's Questionable Sanctions Practices", *Aussenpolitik*, English edition, 45 (1995), p. 327.

14. John Stremlau, *Sharpening International Sanctions: Toward a Stronger Role for the United Nations*, Report to the Carnegie Commission on Preventing Deadly Conflict (New York: Carnegie Corporation, November 1996).

15. Cortright and Lopez, note 5 above.

16. For example, Gary Clyde Hufbauer and Barbara Oegg, "From Blunt Weapons to Smart Bombs: The Evolution of US Sanctions", *Global Dialogue* 2 (Summer 2000), pp. 85–94.

17. See Stremlau, note 14 above, p. 57ff.

18. *Mail and Guardian*, Johannesburg, 15 May 2000. This was hardly a novel observation, however: seven years earlier, *The Guardian* (Manchester) had reported that "The UNITA rebel movement in Angola is helping to fund guerrilla war by selling hundreds of thousands of pounds worth of illegally mined diamonds to international buyers", 4 May 1993.

19. *Angola Peace Monitor*, 1, 3 April 1995: http://www.anc.org.za/angola/apm0101.html.

20. Cortright and Lopez, note 5 above, p. 153.

21. See Global Witness, *A Rough Trade: The Role of Companies and Governments in the Angolan Conflict* (London: Global Witness, December 1998), http://www.oneworld.org/globalwitness/reports/Angola/cover.htm; *Financial Times*, 14 December 1998.

22. Cortright and Lopez, note 5 above, pp. 162–163.
23. Andrew Mack and Asif Khan, "The Efficacy of UN Sanctions", *Security Dialogue* 31 (September 2000), p. 231, note 5.
24. For a published version, see Barry A. Burciul, "UN Sanctions: Policy Options for Canada", *Canadian Foreign Policy* 6 (Autumn 1998), pp. 5–50.
25. Canada Department of Foreign Affairs and International Trade, *Human Security: Safety for People in a Changing World* (Ottawa: DFAIT, April 1999), p. 5; see also Heather Owens and Barbara Arneil, "The Human Security Paradigm Shift: A New Lens on Canadian Foreign Policy?", *Canadian Foreign Policy* 7 (Autumn 1999), pp. 1–12.
26. Paul Knox, "Canada at the UN: A Human Security Council?", in Maureen Appel Molot and Fen Osler Hampson, eds, *Canada Among Nations, 2000: Vanishing Borders* (Toronto: Oxford University Press, 2000), pp. 309–310.
27. For an examination of the Iraq sanctions, see Cortright and Lopez, note 5 above, chap. 3, pp. 37–61.
28. Global Witness, note 21 above.
29. A year later, a defector from UNITA claimed that Savimbi himself had issued orders that any UN plane in range of UNITA anti-aircraft weapons was to be shot down on the grounds that the United Nations was in the service of the Angola government. *Globe and Mail*, 19 January 2000.
30. UN Security Council, *Report of the Panel of Experts on Violations of Security Council Sanctions against UNITA*, S/2000/203, 10 March 2000, http://www.un.int/canada/html/angolareport.htm.
31. UN Security Council, *Final Report of the Monitoring Mechanism on Angola Sanctions*, S/2000/1225, 21 December 2000, http://www.un.int/canada/html/s20001225.htm.
32. Alison Van Rooy, "How Ambassadors (Should) Deal with Civil Society Organizations: A New Diplomacy?", *Canadian Foreign Policy* 7 (Autumn 1999), p. 147; also Alison Van Rooy, *The Rise of Nongovernmental Voices in Multilateral Organizations* (Ottawa: North-South Institute, 2001).
33. See also Maxwell A. Cameron, "Global Civil Society and the Ottawa Process: Lessons from the Movement to Ban Anti-Personnel Mines", *Canadian Foreign Policy* 7 (Autumn 1999), pp. 85–102.
34. The Fatal Transactions website is http://www.niza.nl/uk/campaigns/diamonds/index.html.
35. Canada Department of Foreign Affairs and International Trade, "World Diamond Congress: Intervention by Ambassador Robert R. Fowler" (Antwerp: DFAIT, July 2000), p. 4, http://www.un.int/canada/html/s-18july2000fowler.htm.
36. *Ibid.*, pp. 1–2.
37. *Financial Times*, 7 October 1999.
38. Quoted in Nicholas Cook, *Diamonds and Conflict: Policy Proposals and Background* (Washington: Library of Congress, Congressional Research Service, November 2000), pp. 5–6.
39. *New York Times*, 8 August 1999.
40. See, for example, the criticism of the Clinton administration's policies of Representatives Cynthia McKinney and Tony Hall, http://waysandmeans.house.gov/trade/106cong/9-13-00/9-13mcki.htm   and   http://waysandmeans.house.gov/trade/106cong/9-13-00/9-13hall.htm, cited in Cook, note 38 above, pp. 9–10.
41. *Financial Times*, 25 October 2000.
42. For press reports, see "UN Names Violators of Sanctions on UNITA", *Financial Times*, 12 March 2000; "Report on Angola Sanctions is Challenged in the U.N.", *New York Times*, 16 March 2000; "African Nations Blast Charges of Sanction-busting", *Globe and Mail*, 16 March 2000.

43. *New York Times*, 16 March 2000; *Globe and Mail*, 16 March 2000.
44. Greg Mills and Raisaka Masebelanga, "Diamonds are Not the Enemy", *Financial Times*, 31 October 2000.
45. Mack and Khan, note 23 above, pp. 223 and 230.
46. "Russia and South Africa Snub Diamond Conference", *Financial Times*, 25 October 2000.
47. See, for example, the proposals made by Global Witness, *Conflict Diamonds: Possibilities for the Identification, Certification and Control of Diamonds* (London: Global Witness, June 2000), http://www.oneworld.org/globalwitness/reports/conflict/cover.htm.
48. "UN Losing Battle to Halt 'Blood Diamond' Trade", *National Post*, 2 November 2000.

15

Security in the new millennium[1]

Ramesh Thakur

Global governance

The threshold of the new millennium is also the cusp of a new era in world affairs. The business of the world has changed almost beyond recognition over the course of the last 100 years. There are many more actors today, and their patterns of interaction are far more complex. The locus of power and influence is shifting. The demands and expectations made on governments and international organizations by the people of the world can no longer be satisfied through isolated and self-contained efforts. The international policy-making stage is increasingly congested as private and public non-state actors jostle alongside national governments in setting and implementing the agenda of the new century. The multitude of new actors adds depth and texture to the increasingly rich tapestry of international civil society.

In today's seamless world, political frontiers have become less salient both for national governments whose responsibilities within borders can be held up to international scrutiny, and for international organizations whose rights and duties can extend beyond borders. The gradual erosion of the once sacrosanct principle of national sovereignty is rooted today in the reality of global interdependence: no *country* is an island unto itself any more. Ours is a world of major cities and agglomerations, with nodes of financial and economic power and their globally wired transport and communications networks. Cumulatively, they span an increasingly interconnected and interactive world characterized more by technology-driven exchange and communication than by territorial borders and political separation.

The meaning and scope of security have become much broader. The number and types of security providers have grown enormously, and the relationship between them has become more dense and complex. As well as armed terrorism, for example, states have to contend with eco-terrorism and cyber-terrorism (for example, the "I love you" bug). All three are cross-border phenomena of global scope and ramifications requiring active collaboration among the defence and constabulary forces, law enforcement authorities and non-government groups and organizations.

In this period of transition, the United Nations is the focus of the hopes and aspirations for a future where men and women live at peace with themselves and in harmony with nature. Over a billion people living in abject poverty have had neither the spirit nor the means to cheer the arrival of the new millennium. The reality of human insecurity cannot simply be wished away. Yet the idea of a universal organization dedicated to protecting peace and promoting welfare – of achieving a better life in a safer world, for all – survived the death, destruction, and disillusionment of armed conflicts, genocide, persistent poverty, environmental degradation, and the many assaults on human dignity of the twentieth century.

The United Nations has the responsibility to protect international peace and promote human development. The UN Charter codifies best practice in state behaviour. Universities are the market-place of ideas. Scientists have a duty to make their knowledge available for the betterment of humanity. The United Nations University has the mandate to link the two normally isolated worlds of scholarship and policy-making. It lies at the interface of ideas, international organizations, and international public policy. In an information society and world, the comparative advantage of the UNU lies in its identity as the custodian and manager of knowledge-based networks and coalitions that give it a global mandate and reach.

One recurring refrain in the UNU's projects in recent times has been the tension between the twin processes of globalization and localization; a second is the need for partnerships between different actors, including individuals, at all levels of social organization; and a third is the comprehensive and interconnected nature of many of today's major problems that require urgent policy measures. Solutions must be individual-centred, within a framework of human security which puts people first;

they must be integrated and coordinated; and they must be holistic, tackling the roots of the problems even while ameliorating the symptoms of stress and distress.

Globalization refers both to process and outcome. National frontiers are becoming less relevant in determining the flow of ideas, information, goods, services, capital, labour, and technology. The speed of modern communications makes borders increasingly permeable, while the volume of cross-border flows threatens to overwhelm the capacity of states to manage them. Globalization releases many productive forces that, if properly harnessed, can help to uplift millions from poverty, deprivation, and degradation. But it can also unleash destructive forces – "uncivil society" – such as flows of arms, terrorism, disease, prostitution, drug and people smuggling, etc., that are neither controllable nor solvable by individual governments. At the same time, and indeed partly in reaction to globalization, communities are beginning to re-identify with local levels of group identity.

Recommended solutions to the dilemma include decentralization and subsidiarity, on the principle that the locus of action and solution should be where the problems are. There must be active participation of the local government, non-government organizations, and private actors in all phases of planning and implementation. Thus international democracy promotion should be directed at building local capacity – supporting, financially and technically, the various pillars of democratization processes, the rule of law and the judicial system, and the legislatures, in addition to assisting in the conducting of elections.

The combined effect of globalization – both the process and the outcome – and localization is to erode the legitimacy and effectiveness of national governments and intergovernmental organizations. There has been a corresponding decline in levels of resources and support for international organizations, including the United Nations. In the meantime, a host of new actors from civil society – NGOs, labour unions, churches – have become progressively more assertive in demanding a voice at all top decision-making tables. Sometimes developing countries attach their concerns to NGOs, while at other times NGOs attack the state of affairs in developing countries (slave labour, child labour, environmental laxness).

The solution to many of these challenges lies in global governance. The goal of global governance is not the creation of world government, but of an additional layer of international decision-making between governments and international organizations which is comprehensive and not merely piecemeal social engineering, multisectoral, democratically accountable, and inclusive of civil society actors in the shared management of the troubled and fragile world order.

Partnerships are called for between governments, international organizations, NGOs, other civil society organizations, and individuals. Some countries are beginning to involve citizens more substantially in the political decision-making process through well-designed public choice mechanisms like referenda. We are likely to witness increasing issue-specific networks and coalitions. The United Nations has the moral legitimacy, political credibility, and administrative impartiality to mediate, moderate, and reconcile the competing pulls and tensions associated with both the process and outcomes of globalization. Human security can provide the conceptual umbrella that brings together the main themes of the Millennium Summit – security, development, environment, and governance – within one coherent framework. This would help to give practical content to the opening words of the UN Charter, "We the peoples".

Traditional security paradigm: Towards a world free of wars

War lies at the heart of traditional security paradigms, and military force is the sharp edge of the realist school of international relations. The incidence of war is as pervasive as the wish for peace is universal. At any given time, most countries are at peace and long to remain so. Yet most are also ready to go to war if necessary. Some of the most charismatic and influential personalities in human history – from Gautam Buddha and Jesus Christ to Mahatma Gandhi – have dwelt on the renunciation of force and the possibility of eliminating it from human relationships.

The twentieth century captured the paradox only too well. On the one hand, we tried to emplace increasing normative, legislative, and operational fetters on the right of states to go to war. Yet the century turned out to be the most murderous in human history, with over 250 wars, including two world wars and the Cold War, and more dead than in all previous wars of the past 2,000 years. Another 6 million more have died since the Cold War ended.

Confronted with a world that cannot be changed, reasonable people adapt and accommodate. The turning points of history and progress in human civilization have come from those who set out to change the world. This section is a story about a group of unreasonable people who met recently for the first steering committee of "GlobalAction to Prevent War: An International Coalition to Abolish Armed Conflict and Genocide".

The causes of war are many and complex. Our call to end it is single-minded and simple. Cynics insist that war is an inherent part of human society. To end war would indeed be to end history. Maybe. But so too have crime and poverty always been part of human history. Any political leader who admitted to giving up on the fight to end crime or poverty would quickly be returned to private life by voters. Paradoxically, in the case of war it is those who seek to abolish it who are considered to be soft in the head.

The deadly situation does not have to continue into the new century. We already have resources and knowledge that can drastically cut the level of armed violence in the world and make war increasingly rare. What has been missing is a programme for the worldwide, systematic, and continuing application of these resources and knowledge. Global-Action offers such a programme, and it is building a worldwide coalition of interested individuals, civil society organizations, and governments to carry it out.[2]

For internal conflicts, GlobalAction proposes a broad array of conflict prevention measures to be applied by the United Nations, regional security organizations, and international courts. For conflicts between neighbouring states, it recommends force reductions, defensively oriented changes in force structure, confidence-building measures, and constraints on force activities tailored to each situation. The possibility of conflict among the major powers can be reduced by fostering their cooperation in preventing smaller wars and through step-by-step cuts in their conventional and nuclear forces, eliminating their capacity to attack each other with any chance of success.

GlobalAction's conflict prevention and conventional disarmament measures will promote nuclear disarmament. Nuclear cuts in turn will facilitate conflict prevention and conventional disarmament. Achievement of nuclear disarmament will very probably require both reduced levels of conflict worldwide and some effective and acceptable way to cut back the conventional forces of the major powers, especially their force projection capability with naval and air forces. Countries like China, Russia, and India are not likely to relinquish their nuclear weapons if the main effect of doing so is to enhance the already large conventional superiority of the USA. Other governments are unlikely to be prepared to reduce their conventional armed forces drastically unless there is evidence that nuclear weapons are on the one-way road to elimination.

GlobalAction's deliberate focus is on violent armed conflict. The world also faces fundamental crises of poverty, human rights violations, environmental degradation, and discrimination based on race, gender, ethnicity, and religion. All of these challenges must be met before human security and a just peace can be fully achieved. To meet these challenges, many efforts must be pursued; no single campaign can deal with all of them. But efforts to address these global problems can and should complement and support one another. The abolition of war will make it possible to focus all remaining energy and efforts on resolving the fundamental structural problems.

One analogy is with domestic violence. Faced with incidents of violence within the family, the first and most urgent order of business is to stop the violence. Only then can we look at probable causes and possible solutions, including if necessary separation and divorce.

From national security to human security

The shift from the "national security" to the "human security" paradigm is of historic importance. The object of security changes from the state to the individual; the focus changes from security through armaments to security through human development; from territorial security to food, employment, and environmental security. The fundamental components of human security – the security of *people* against threats to life, health, livelihood, personal safety, and human dignity – can be put at risk by external aggression, but also by factors within a country, including "security" forces. Over the course of the twentieth century, 30 million people were killed in international wars, 7 million in civil wars, and an additional 170 million by their own governments.[3]

In his Millennium Report,[4] Secretary-General Kofi Annan writes of the quest for freedom from fear, freedom from want, and securing a sustainable future. A recurring theme in his report is the importance of making the transition from the culture of reaction to the culture of prevention. This is even more fundamental for the attainment of human security than for national security, as even a cursory glance at threats to human security will show.

Mankind – including the rich countries – will not be able to live free of fear, will not be able to secure a sustainable future, so long as over a billion people live in servitude to want. That is, freedom from want is precondition of the other two elements in the trinity. The safest and most peaceful communities are composed of individuals who have their basic needs and aspirations met.

The multidimensional approach to security sacrifices precision for inclusiveness. In order to rescue it from being diluted into nothingness, we need to focus on security policy in relation to crisis. Short of that it is more accurate to assess welfare gains and losses rather than increased security and insecurity. Security policy can then be posited as crisis prevention and crisis management, with regard to both institutional capacity and material capability.

Even if we limit "security" to anything which threatens the core integrity of our units of analysis (namely human lives), many non-traditional concerns merit the gravity of the security label and require exceptional policy measures in response: environmental threats of total inundation or desertification; political threats of the complete collapse of state structures; population flows so large as to destroy the basic identity of host societies and cultures; structural coercion so severe as to turn human beings into *de facto* chattels; and suchlike. The annual mortality correlates of Afro-Asiatic poverty – low levels of life expectancy, high levels of maternal and infant mortality – run into several million. Annual deaths – preventable killings – even on this scale cannot be accommodated within the analytical framework of "national security"; they can in "human security".

The traditional, narrow concept of security leaves out the most elementary and legitimate concerns of ordinary people regarding security in their daily lives. It also diverts enormous amounts of national wealth and human resources into armaments and armed forces, while countries fail to protect their citizens from chronic insecurities of hunger, disease, inadequate shelter, crime, unemployment, social conflict, and environmental hazards: "*Na roti, na kapara, na makan – par Bharat mera mahan.*"[5]

When rape is used as an instrument of war and ethnic "impurification", when thousands are killed by floods resulting from a ravaged countryside, and when citizens are killed by their own security forces, then the concept of national security is immaterial and of zero utility. By contrast, human security can embrace such diverse phenomena. To insist on national security at the expense of human security would be to trivialize the concept of security in many real-world circumstances to the point of sterility, bereft of any practical meaning.[6]

A recent report on health as a global security challenge concluded that health and security converge at three intersections.[7] First, faced with domestic economic crises and shrinking foreign assistance, many developing countries have had to make difficult budgetary choices to reduce the level of public services. But the failure of governments to provide the basic public health services, including garbage removal, water treatment, and sewage disposal, has two further consequences. It erodes governmental legitimacy, and encourages the spirit of "self-help" and "beggar thy neighbour" among citizens at the expense of the public interest. Often the competition degenerates into violence. Thus the withdrawal of the state from the public health domain can be both a symptom and a cause of failing states. Second, there has been an increasing trend in recent internal armed conflicts to manipulate the supplies of food and medicine. Indeed, the struggle to control food and medicine can define the war strategies of some of the conflict parties. And third, the use of biological weapons represents the deliberate spread of disease against an adversary.

The narrow definition of security also presents a falsified image of the policy process. The military is only one of several competing interest groups vying for a larger share of the collective goods being allocated authoritatively by the government. Environmental and social groups also compete for the allocation of scarce resources. There is, therefore, competition, tension, and conflict among major value clusters. The concept of military security as a subset of the national interest serves to disguise the reality of inter-value competition. By contrast, the multidimensional concept of security highlights the need for integrative strategies that resolve or transcend value conflicts. If they are rational, policy-makers will allocate resources to security only so long as the marginal return is greater for security than for other uses of the resources.

Once security is defined as human security, security policy embraces the totality of state responsibilities for the welfare of citizens from the cradle to the grave. The mark of a civilization is not the deference and respect paid to the glamorous and the powerful, but the care and attention devoted to the least privileged and the most vulnerable. Children in particular need and should have the most protection in any society. Regrettably, the many hazards to children's survival, healthy growth, and normal development, in rich as well as poor countries, constitute a pervasive threat to human security at present and in the foreseeable future.

UN calculations[8] show that in the last decade alone, 2 million children have been killed, 1 million orphaned, 6 million disabled or otherwise seriously injured, 12 million made homeless, and 10 million left with serious psychological scars. Large numbers of them, especially young women, are the targets of rape and other forms of sexual violence as deliberate instruments of war. The steps taken in defence of the rights of children remain small, hesitant, and limited. The biggest danger is compassion fatigue: we will get so used to the statistics that they will cease to shock us, and we will learn to live with the unacceptable.

Being wedded still to "national security" may be one reason why half the world's governments spend more to protect their citizens against undefined external military attack than to guard them against the omnipresent enemies of good health. Human dignity is at stake here. How can one experience the joys and the meaning attached to human life, how can one experience a life of human dignity, when survival from day to day is under threat?

From arms control to international humanitarian law

Human security gives us a template for international action. Canada and Japan are two countries that have taken the lead in attempting to incorporate human security in their foreign policies. A practical expression of this was the Ottawa Treaty proscribing the production, stockpiling, use, and export of anti-personnel land-mines. The first to impose a ban on an entire class of weapons already in widespread use, the convention was a triumph for an unusual coalition of governments, international organizations, and NGOs. Such "new diplomacy" has been impelled by a growing intensity of public impatience with the slow pace of traditional diplomacy. Many people have grown tired of years of negotiations leading to a final product that may be accepted or rejected by countries.[9] They look instead for a sense of urgency and timely action that will prevent human insecurity, not always react to outbreaks of conflict.

It would be as big a mistake to interpret the Ottawa Treaty from the analytic lens of national security instead of human security as to judge it by criteria devised for the evaluation of arms control regimes. Instead, it falls into the stream of measures that make up international humanitarian law.[10] Such measures derive from motives different from those which prompt the negotiation of arms control regimes, are concerned with different subject matters, involve radically different compliance mechanisms, and ultimately have different political functions. The basic purpose of international humanitarian law is not the exacting one of securing the absolute disappearance of particular forms of conduct, but rather the more realistic one of producing some amelioration of the circumstances which combatants and non-combatants will confront should war break out. While its rules are cast in the language of prohibition, it operates through the process of *anathematization.*

Sceptical observers of the Ottawa process have focused on such important non-signatories as the USA, Russia, China, and India; the allegedly perilous simplicity of the treaty, which creates scope for disagreement as to its exact meaning; and the relative ease with which a perfidious state party could move to violate its provisions. These criticisms are for the most part misconceived, and arise from a misunderstanding of the functions that the Ottawa Treaty can appropriately be expected to perform. In principle, every country whose participation is vital to the credibility and integrity of an arms control regime must be party to the treaty. A humanitarian treaty seeks to make progress through stigmatization and the construction of normative barriers to use and deployment. While major power endorsements of the convention would have added significantly to its political weight, amending the treaty provisions to accommodate their preferences would have greatly diluted the humanitarian content of the regime. The integrity of the convention as a humanitarian treaty was held to be more important than the inclusion even of the USA. The humanitarian impulse proved stronger than the arms control caution. Even those key states that have not signed the treaty have voiced sympathy for its objectives. To that extent, it has changed the parameters of discussion of anti-personnel mines from a strictly military framework to one that is strongly shaped by humanitarian concerns.

Non-governmental organizations

In recent major diplomatic landmarks like the Ottawa Treaty banning anti-personnel land-mines, the Rome Statute establishing the International Criminal Court, and humanitarian interventions in Kosovo and East Timor, the impact of NGOs on international public policy has been very evident. The consequence of the rise of NGOs as significant policy-influencing actors is to tilt the balance away from hard to soft security.

There are four broad reasons for the rise of NGO influence. Political space for them opened up with the end of the Cold War. New issues like human rights, environmental degradation, and gender equality came to the forefront of public consciousness. These are issues on which NGOs enjoy many comparative advantages over governments in terms of experience, expertise, and often, let it be noted, public credibility. These are also issues on which it is more difficult to marginalize and exclude NGOs than was the case with the hard security issues during the Cold War.

Second, the global scope and multilayered complexity of the new issues increased the need for partnerships between the established state actors and proliferating NGOs. They are partners in policy formation, information dissemination, standard-setting advocacy, monitoring, and implementation.

Third, the opportunities provided to NGOs have expanded enormously as a result of modern communications technology that enables people to forge real-time cyberspace communities on shared interests, values, and goals. The internet and the fax machine have expanded the range, volume, and quality of networking activity. Globally networked NGOs can serve as focal points for mobilizing interests shared by people living in different countries.

Fourth and finally, people with special skills and expertise have increasingly been drawn to work for and with NGOs, thereby muting some of their earlier amateurishness. The more effective and credible NGOs are increasingly professionalized in personnel and operations, including research, lobbying, fundraising, advocacy, and networking.

The expanding worldwide networks of NGOs embrace virtually every level of organization, from the village community to global summits; and almost every sector of public life, from the provision of microcredit and the delivery of paramedical assistance to environmental and human rights

activism. Much of the UN's work in the field involves intimate partnerships with dedicated NGOs. They can complement UN efforts in several
ways.

- The presence of NGOs in the field can be a vital link in providing early
  warning for dealing with humanitarian crises.
- Their specialized knowledge and contacts can be important components of the post-crisis peace-building process.
- They can mediate between the peace and security functions of intergovernmental organizations and the needs and wants of local civilian
  populations.
- They can exert a positive influence on the restoration of a climate of
  confidence for rehabilitation and reconstruction to take place.

This is not to imply that states are being replaced by NGOs and international organizations – far from it. Nor does it mean that all NGOs are
"good" ones, always on the side of angels. Instead we must confront,
address, and redress the problem of unelected, unaccountable, unrepresentative, and self-aggrandizing NGOs. They can be just as undemocratic
as the governments and organizations they criticize, and represent single-
issue vested interests such as the gun lobby. By contrast, most industrialized country governments are multipurpose organizations trying to
represent the public interest by the choice of the voters. In many developing countries, societies are busy building sound national governments
as the prerequisite to effective governance: good governance is not possible without effective government.

But it does imply that national governments and international organizations will have to learn to live with the rise of NGOs. Indeed, those
who learn to exploit the new opportunities for partnership between the
different actors will be among the more effective new-age diplomats.

Human rights

NGOs have been especially active, often intrusive, and sometimes even
obtrusive on human rights. Fifty years ago, conscious of the atrocities
committed by the Nazis while the world looked silently away, the United
Nations adopted the Universal Declaration of Human Rights. It is the
embodiment and the proclamation of the human rights norm. Covenants
in 1966 added force and specificity, affirming both civil-political and
social-economic-cultural rights, without privileging either set. Together
with the declaration, they mapped out the international human rights
agenda, established the benchmark for state conduct, inspired provisions
in many national laws and international conventions, and provided a

beacon of hope to many whose rights had been snuffed out by brutal regimes.

A right is a claim, an entitlement that may be neither conferred nor denied. A human right, owed to every person simply as a human being, is inherently universal. Held only by human beings, but equally by all, it does not flow from any office, rank, or relationship.

The idea of universal rights is denied by some who insist that moral standards are always culture-specific. If value relativism were to be accepted literally, then no tyrant – Hitler, Stalin, Idi Amin, Pol Pot – could be criticized by outsiders for any action. Relativism is often the first refuge of repressive governments. The false dichotomy between development and human rights is often a smoke-screen for corruption and cronyism. Relativism requires an acknowledgement that each culture has its own moral system. Government behaviour is still open to evaluation by the moral code of its own society. Internal moral standards can comply with international conventions; the two do not always have to diverge. The fact that moral precepts vary from culture to culture does not mean that different peoples do not hold some values in common.

Few, if any, moral systems proscribe the act of killing absolutely under all circumstances. At different times, in different societies, war, capital punishment, or abortion may or may not be morally permissible. Yet for every society, murder is always wrong. All societies require retribution to be proportionate to the wrong done. All prize children, the link between succeeding generations of human civilization; every culture abhors their abuse.

The doctrine of national security has been especially corrosive of human rights. It is used frequently by governments, charged with the responsibility to protect citizens, to assault them instead. Under military rule, the instrument of protection from without becomes the means of attack from within.

The United Nations – an organization of, by, and for member states – has been impartial and successful in a standard-setting role, selectively successful in monitoring abuses, and almost feeble in enforcement. Governments usually subordinate considerations of UN effectiveness to the principle of non-interference.

The modesty of UN achievement should not blind us to its reality. The Universal Declaration embodies the moral code, political consensus, and legal synthesis of human rights. The world has grown vastly more complex in the 50 years since. But the simplicity of the declaration's language belies the passion of conviction underpinning it. Its elegance has been the font of inspiration down the decades, its provisions comprise the vocabulary of complaint.

Activists and NGOs use the declaration as the concrete point of reference against which to judge state conduct. The covenants require the submission of periodic reports by signatory countries, and so entail the creation of long-term national infrastructures for the protection and promotion of human rights. UN efforts are greatly helped by non-governmental organizations and other elements of civil society. NGOs work to protect victims, and contribute to the development and promotion of social commitment and the enactment of laws reflecting the more enlightened human rights culture.

Between them, the United Nations and NGOs have achieved many successes. National laws and international instruments have been improved, many political prisoners have been freed, and some victims of abuse have been compensated. The most recent advances on international human rights are the progressive incorporation of wartime behaviour and policy within the prohibitionary provisions of humanitarian law, for example in the Ottawa Treaty, which subordinated military calculations to humanitarian concerns about a weapon that cannot distinguish a soldier from a child. In 1998 the world community established the first International Criminal Court. The US absence from both shows the extent to which human rights have moved ahead of their strongest advocate in the past.

Humanitarian intervention

The refusal to accept the discipline of universal norms of international humanitarian law is especially difficult to fathom in the case of a country that insists on the right to humanitarian intervention. We cannot accept the doctrine that any one state or coalition can decide when to intervene with force in the internal affairs of other countries, for down that path lies total chaos. Nevertheless, the doctrine of national sovereignty in its absolute and unqualified form, which gave the most brutal tyrant protection against attack from without while engaged in oppression within, has gone with the wind. On the other hand, war is itself a major humanitarian tragedy that can be justified under only the most compelling circumstances regarding the provocation, the likelihood of success – bearing in mind that goals are metamorphosed in the crucible of war once started – and the consequences that may reasonably be predicted. And the burden of proof rests on the proponents of force, not on dissenters.

If the Gulf War marked the birth of the new world order after the Cold War, Somalia was the slide into the new world disorder and Rwanda marked the loss of innocence after the end of the Cold War. Worse was to follow in the "safe area" of Srebrenica in July 1995 in a tragedy that, in the words of the official UN report, "will haunt our history forever".[11]

While Rwanda stands as the symbol of inaction in the face of genocide, Kosovo raised many questions about the consequences of action when the international community is divided in the face of a humanitarian tragedy.[12] It confronted us with an abiding series of challenges regarding humanitarian intervention: is it morally just, legally permissible, militarily feasible, and politically doable? What happens when the different lessons of the twentieth century, encapsulated in such slogans as "no more wars" and "no more Auschwitzes", come into collision? Who decides, following what rules of procedure and evidence, that mass atrocities have been committed, by which party, and what the appropriate response should be?

To supporters, NATO cured Europe of the Milosevic-borne disease of ethnic cleansing. The spectre of racial genocide had come back to haunt Europe from the dark days of the Second World War. Military action outside the UN framework was not NATO's preferred option of choice. Rather, its resort to force was a critical comment on the institutional hurdles to effective and timely action by the United Nations. To critics, however, "the NATO cure greatly worsened the Milosevic disease". The trickle of refugees before the war turned into a flood during it, and afterwards the Serbs were ethnically cleansed by vengeful Albanians.

The sense of moral outrage provoked by humanitarian atrocities must be tempered by an appreciation of the limits of power, a concern for international institution-building, and a sensitivity to the law of unintended consequences. In today's unstable world full of complex conflicts, we face the painful dilemma of being damned if we do and damned if we don't.

- To respect sovereignty all the time is to be complicit in human rights violations sometimes.
- To argue that the UN Security Council must give its consent to humanitarian war is to risk policy paralysis by handing over the agenda to the most egregious and obstreperous.
- To use force unilaterally is to violate international law and undermine world order.

The bottom-line question is this: faced with another Holocaust or Rwanda-type genocide on the one hand and a Security Council veto on the other, what would we do? Because there is no clear answer to this poignant question within the existing consensus as embodied in the UN Charter, a new consensus on humanitarian intervention is urgently needed.

The UN Charter contains an inherent tension between the principles of state sovereignty, with the corollary of non-intervention, and the principles of human rights. In the first four decades of the Charter's existence, state sovereignty was privileged almost absolutely over human rights, with the one significant exception of apartheid in South Africa. The balance tilted a little in the 1990s, and is more delicately poised between the two competing principles at the start of the new millennium. The indictment of President Slobodan Milosevic as a war criminal, as well as the arresting saga of former Chilean President Augusto Pinochet, show the inexorable shift from the culture of impunity of yesteryears to a culture of accountability at the dawn of the twenty-first century.

The UN Security Council lies at the heart of the international law enforcement system. The justification for bypassing it to launch an offensive war remains problematic, and the precedent that was set remains deeply troubling. By fighting and defeating Serbia, NATO became the tool for the KLA policy of inciting Serb reprisals through terrorist attacks in order to provoke NATO intervention. Communities bitterly divided for centuries cannot be forced by outsiders to live together peacefully. Another lesson that has been reinforced is that it is easier to bomb than to build. The willingness of the strong to fund a campaign of destruction stands in marked contrast to the reluctance of the rich – who happen to be almost the same group of countries – to find far less money for reconstruction. In turn this seriously, if retrospectively, undermines the humanitarian claims for having gone to war.

Many of today's wars are nasty, brutish, anything but short, and mainly internal. The world community cannot help all victims, but must step in where it can make a difference. However, unless the member states of the United Nations agree on some broad principles to guide interventions in similar circumstances, the Kosovo precedent will have dangerously undermined world order. Not being able to act everywhere can never be a reason for not acting where effective intervention is both possible and urgently needed. Selective indignation is inevitable, for we simply cannot intervene everywhere, every time. But community support for selective intervention will quickly dissipate if the only criterion of selection is friends (where the norm of non-intervention has primacy) versus adversaries (when the right to intervene is privileged).

In addition, we must still pursue policies of effective indignation. Humanitarian intervention must be collective, not unilateral. And it must be legitimate, not in violation of the agreed rules that comprise the foundations of world order. Being the indispensable power can tempt one into being indisposed to accept the constraints of multilateral diplomacy. But being indispensable does not confer the authority to dispense with the legitimacy of the United Nations as the only entity that can speak in the name of the international community. The reason for much disquiet around the world with the precedent of NATO action in Kosovo was not because their abhorrence of ethnic cleansing was any less. Rather, it was because of their dissent from a world order which permits or tolerates unilateral behaviour by the strong and their preference for an order in which principles and values are embedded in universally applicable norms and the rough edges of power are softened by institutionalized multi-lateralism.

The United Nations

It used to be said during the Cold War that the purpose of NATO was to keep the Americans in, the Germans down, and the Russians out. Does Kosovo mark a turning point, changing NATO into a tool for keeping the Americans in, the Russians down, and the United Nations out?

International organizations are an essential means of conducting world affairs more satisfactorily than would be possible under conditions of international anarchy or total self-help. The United Nations lies at their legislative and normative centre. If it did not exist, we would surely have to invent it. Yet its founding vision of a world community equal in rights and united in action is still to be realized.

For the cynics, the United Nations can do nothing right and is the source of many ills. For the romantics, the United Nations can do no wrong and is the solution to all the world's problems. Its failures reflect the weakness of member states, prevented only by a lack of political will from fulfilling its destiny as the global commons, the custodian of the international interest, and the conscience of all humanity.

The UN Charter was a triumph of hope and idealism over the experience of two world wars. The flame flickered in the chill winds of the Cold War, but has not yet died out. In the midst of the swirling tides of change, the United Nations must strive for a balance between the desirable and the possible. The global public goods of peace, prosperity, sustainable development, and good governance cannot be achieved by any country acting on its own. The United Nations is still the symbol of our dreams for a better world, where weakness can be compensated by justice and fairness, and the law of the jungle replaced by the rule of law.

The innovation of peacekeeping notwithstanding, the United Nations has not fully lived up to expectations in securing a disarmed and peaceful world. As with sustainable development, which seeks to strike a balance between growth and conservation, the United Nations must be at the centre of efforts to achieve sustainable disarmament: the reduction of armaments to the lowest level where the security needs of any one country

at a given time, or any one generation over time, are met without compromising the security and welfare needs of other countries or future
generations.

The UN system can take justified pride in mapping the demographic
details of the human family, and also in the stupendous improvements
to human welfare that have been achieved. The advances in health, life
expectancy, and satisfaction of basic needs and other desires were truly
phenomenal over the course of the twentieth century. The symbolic 6
billionth child was born just recently.

At the same time, as the sun rises on the new century and illumines
some of the darker legacies of the last one, we should engage in sober
reflection and sombre introspection. It is simply not acceptable that:
- at a time of unprecedented economic prosperity and stock market
  booms in some parts of the world, millions of people should continue
  to be condemned to a life of poverty, illiteracy, and ill health;
- the combined GDP of the 48 least developed countries should be less
  than the assets of the world's three richest people;
- the annual income of 2.5 billion – 47 per cent – of the world's poorest
  people should be less than that of the richest 225.

The need for international assistance in many continents is an unhappy
reminder of man's inhumanity against fellowman and his rapaciousness
against nature. Secretary-General Kofi Annan has noted that there were
three times as many major natural disasters in the 1990s as in the 1960s.[13]
Moreover, most disaster victims live in developing countries. Poverty and
the pressures of population force growing numbers of people to live in
harm's way at the same time as unsound development and environmental
practices place more of nature at risk. The rich reap the benefits, the
poor pay the price.

Success that is sustained requires us all to make a greater commitment
to the vision and values of the United Nations, and to make systematic
use of the UN forum and modalities for managing and ending conflicts.
People continue to look to the United Nations to guide them and protect
them when the tasks are too big and complex for nations and regions to
handle by themselves. The comparative advantages of the United Nations are its universal membership, political legitimacy, administrative
impartiality, technical expertise, convening and mobilizing power, and
the dedication of its staff. Its comparative disadvantages are excessive
politicization, ponderous pace of decision-making, impossible mandate,
high cost structure, insufficient resources, bureaucratic rigidity, and institutional timidity. Many of the disadvantages are the products of demands and intrusions by the 188 member states that own and control the
organization, but some key members disown responsibility for giving it
the requisite support and resources. For the United Nations to succeed,

the world community must match the demands made on the organization by the means given to it.

The United Nations represents the idea that unbridled nationalism and the raw interplay of power must be mediated and moderated in an international framework. It is the centre for harmonizing national interests and forging the international interest. Only the United Nations can legitimately authorize military action on behalf of the entire international community, instead of a select few. But the United Nations does not have its own military and police forces, and a multinational coalition of allies can offer a more credible and efficient military force when robust action is needed and warranted. What will be increasingly needed in the future is partnerships of the able, the willing, and the high-minded with the duly authorized. What we should most fear is partnerships of the able, the willing, and the low-minded in violation of due process. What if the UN Security Council itself acts in violation of the Charter of the United Nations? Unlike domestic systems, there is no independent judicial check on the constitutionality of Security Council decisions. No liberal democracy would tolerate such a situation domestically; why should liberal democrats, who generally lead the charge for humanitarian intervention, find it acceptable internationally?

The United Nations has to strike a balance between realism and idealism. Its decisions must reflect current realities of military and economic power. It will be incapacitated if it alienates its most important members. But it will also lose credibility if it compromises core values. The United Nations is the repository of international idealism, and utopia is fundamental to its identity. Even the sense of disenchantment and disillusionment on the part of some cannot be understood other than against this background.

The learning curve of human history shows that the UN ideal can be neither fully attained nor abandoned. Like most organizations, the United Nations too is condemned to an eternal credibility gap between aspiration and performance. The real challenge is to ensure that the gap does not widen, but stays within a narrow band. Sustained, coordinated efforts *can* turn killing fields into playing fields and rice fields. Success comes from having the courage to fail. If you have never failed, then you have not tried enough: you have not pushed yourself hard enough, not tested the limits of your potential.

Notes

1. This chapter was originally prepared as a paper for the workshop on Defence, Technology, and Cooperative Security in South Asia, Kathmandu, 10–12 September 2000.

The chapter expresses the personal opinions of the author, and does not necessarily reflect the views of the United Nations University.

2. GlobalAction's website address is www.globalactionpw.org.
3. "Freedom's Journey", survey in *The Economist*, 11 September 1999.
4. Kofi A. Annan, *We the Peoples: The Role of the United Nations in the 21st Century* (New York: United Nations, Department of Public Information, 2000).
5. The first part is a popular saying in India, the second is a patriotic boast. The two have been combined for ironic effect: "Neither food, nor clothing, nor shelter – but my India is great."
6. For an attempt to apply the human security concept to the Asia Pacific region, see William T. Tow, Ramesh Thakur, and In-taek Hyun, eds, *Asia's Emerging Regional Order: Reconciling Traditional and Human Security* (Tokyo: United Nations University Press, 2000).
7. *Contagion and Conflict: Health as a Global Security Challenge*, a report of the Chemical and Biological Arms Control Institute and the CSIS International Security Programme (Washington, DC: Centre for Strategic and International Studies, January 2000).
8. For details, see Kofi A. Annan, *We the Children: End-decade Review of the Follow-up to the World Summit for Children*, Report of the Secretary-General, A/S-27/3 (New York: United Nations, 4 May 2001). For the latest annual publication of the most authoritative compilation on the state of the world's children, see *The State of the World's Children 2002* (New York: UNICEF, 2002).
9. Jessica Tuchman Mathews, "Redefining Security", *Foreign Affairs* 68 (Spring 1989), p. 176. Mathews was writing in the context of environmental negotiations.
10. This section summarizes Ramesh Thakur and William Maley, "The Ottawa Convention on Landmines: A Landmark Humanitarian Treaty in Arms Control?", *Global Governance* 5, no. 3 (July–September 1999), pp. 273–302.
11. *Report of the Secretary-General Pursuant to General Assembly Resolution 53/35 (1998)* (New York: UN Secretariat, November 1999), para. 503.
12. See Albrecht Schnabel and Ramesh Thakur, eds, *Kosovo and the Challenge of Humanitarian Intervention: Selective Indignation, Collective Action, and International Citizenship* (Tokyo: United Nations University Press, 2000).
13. See Figure 11 in Annan, *We the Peoples*, note 4 above, p. 58.

Acronyms

AAMA	American Apparel Manufacturers Association
ACFOA	Australian Council for Overseas Aid
AFL-CIO	American Federation of Labor-Congress of Industrial Organizations
AIP	Apparel Industry Partnership (USA)
AP	anti-personnel
APEC	Asia Pacific Economic Cooperation
AUSAID	Australian Agency for International Development
BCSD	Business Council for Sustainable Development
CCW	Convention on Certain Conventional Weapons
CEIP	Carnegie Endowment for International Peace
CEP	Council on Economic Priorities
CFC	chlorofluorocarbon
CFPD	Center for Foreign Policy Development (Canada)
CHOGM	Commonwealth Heads of Government Meeting
CICC	Coalition for an International Criminal Court
CP	Centre Party (Norway)
CPET	Canadian Partnership for Ethical Trading
CPP	Christian People's Party (Norway)
CSO	Central Selling Organization
CSO	civil society organization
DPKO	UN Department of Peacekeeping Operations
ECOSOC	UN Economic and Social Council
ECOWAS	Economic Community of West African States
EEC	European Economic Community

EQ	entitlement quotient
ETAG	Ethical Trading Action Group (Canada)
ETI	Ethical Trading Initiative (UK)
EU	European Union
FLA	Fair Labor Association (USA)
GATT	General Agreement on Tariffs and Trade
GNI	gross national income
GNP	gross national product
GSM	global social movement
HRD	Hoge Raad voor Diamant (Diamond High Council)
IANSA	International Action Network on Small Arms
IBCC	International Bureau of Chambers of Commerce
ICBL	International Campaign to Ban Land-mines
ICC	International Chamber of Commerce
ICC	International Criminal Court
ICFTU	International Confederation of Free Trade Unions
ICRC	International Committee of the Red Cross
ICTY	International Criminal Tribunal on the Former Yugoslavia
IDEA	International Institute for Democracy and Electoral Assistance
IIR	Institute for International Relations (Prague)
ILC	International Law Commission
ILO	International Labour Organization
IMF	International Monetary Fund
INGO	international non-governmental organization
IPA	International Peace Academy
ISO	International Organization for Standardization
ISS	Institute for Security Studies (South Africa)
ITO	International Trade Organization
KLA	Kosovo Liberation Army
LOAC	law of armed conflict
MAI	Multilateral Agreement on Investment
MFA	Ministry of Foreign Affairs (Norway)
MIMCO	Mattel's Independent Monitoring Council
MoD	Ministry of Defence (Norway)
MONUA	UN Observer Mission in Angola
MOU	memorandum of understanding
NAC	Norwegian Afghan Committee
NAFTA	North American Free Trade Agreement
NAM	Non-Aligned Movement
NATO	North Atlantic Treaty Organization
NGO	non-governmental organization
NORAD	Norwegian Agency for Development Cooperation
NOREPS	Norwegian Emergency Preparedness System
NPA	Norwegian People's Aid
OAU	Organization of African Unity
OECD	Organization for Economic Cooperation and Development

OPEC	Organization of Petroleum Exporting Countries
PSO	peace support operations
RAP	responsible apparel production
RedR	Registered Engineers for Disaster Relief (Australia)
ROE	rules of engagement
RPTC	Regional Peacekeeping Training Centre (Southern Africa)
RSL	Returned and Services League (Australia)
RUF	Revolutionary United Front (Sierra Leone)
SADC	Southern African Development Community
SAI	Social Accountability International
SCHR	Steering Committee for Humanitarian Response
SRI	socially responsible investment
TIAA-CREF	Teachers Insurance and Annuity Association-College Retirement Equities Fund
TNC	transnational corporation
UNAVEM	UN Verification Mission in Angola
UNCED	United Nations Conference on the Environment and Development
UNCTAD	United Nations Conference on Trade and Development
UNDPKO	UN Department of Peacekeeping Operations
UNEP	United Nations Environment Programme
UNGA	UN General Assembly
UNHCHR	Office of the UN High Commissioner for Human Rights
UNHCR	Office of the UN High Commissioner for Refugees
UNICEF	United Nations Children's Fund
UNITA	União Nacional para a Independéncia Total de Angola (National Union for the Total Independence of Angola)
UNITAF	Unified Task Force in Somalia
UNITE	Union of Needletrades, Industrial, and Textile Employees (USA)
UNMCTT	UN Mine Clearance Training Team
UNPREDEP	UN Preventive Deployment Force
UNSC	UN Security Council
UNSG	UN Secretary-General
UNTAC	UN Transitional Authority in Cambodia
VVAF	Vietnam Veterans of America Foundation
WDC	World Diamond Council
WEC	World Economic Conference
WEO	Western European and Other
WRAP	Worldwide Responsible Apparel Production Certification Program (USA)
WTO	World Trade Organization

Contributors

Maxwell A. Cameron is an associate professor in the Department of Political Science at the University of British Columbia in Vancouver, Canada. He co-edited *To Walk Without Fear: The Global Movement to Ban Landmines* (1998) and co-authored *The Making of NAFTA: How the Deal Was Done* (2000). His current research focuses on problems of democratization in Latin America.

Andrew F. Cooper is co-director of the Centre on Foreign Policy and Federalism and a professor of political science at the University of Waterloo, Ontario, Canada. He is a former Fulbright Scholar and current assistant editor of the *Canadian Journal of Political Science*. His books include *In Between Countries: Australia, Canada and the Search for Order in Agricultural Trade* (1998), *Canadian*

Foreign Policy: Old Habits and New Directions (1997), and, as editor, *Niche Diplomacy: Middle Powers After the Cold War* (1997).

Alistair D. Edgar is an associate professor of political science at Wilfrid Laurier University, Waterloo, Ontario, Canada. His research and teaching interests centre on international security, international organization and law, Canadian defence and foreign policy, and post-conflict reconstruction. His publications include *The Canadian Defence Industry in the New Global Environment* (1995).

John English is co-director of the Centre on Foreign Policy and Federalism and professor of history at the University of Waterloo, Ontario, Canada. He served as a Canadian Member of Parliament (1993–1997), during which time he was Parliamentary Secretary to the President of the Privy Council and vice-chair of the Foreign Affairs and International Trade Committee. He was a special adviser on land-mines to the Minister of Foreign Affairs and International Affairs (1997–1998). He is currently working on a biography of Pierre Trudeau. Earlier work includes a biography of Lester Pearson.

Virginia Haufler is an associate professor of government and politics at the University of Maryland. She has been a senior associate at the Carnegie Endowment for International Peace, where she directed a project on the role of the private sector in international affairs. Publications include *A Public Role for the Private Sector: Industry Self-Regulation in a Global Economy* (2001), *Dangerous Commerce: Insurance and the Management of International Risk* (1997), and, as co-editor, *Private Authority and International Affairs* (1999).

Brian Hocking is professor of international relations at Coventry University, UK. Amongst his publications relating to the general role and character of diplomacy in contemporary world politics are "Catalytic Diplomacy: Beyond 'Newness' and 'Decline'", in J. Melissen, ed., *Innovation in Diplomatic Practice* (1999), and *Foreign Ministries: Change and Adaptation* (1999).

Dominic Kelly is a lecturer in international relations in the Department of Politics and International Studies at the University of Warwick, UK. He is the author and editor of several books on

international political economy and international relations, the latest of which is *Japan and the Reconstruction of East Asia* (2001).

W. Andy Knight is a professor in the Department of Political Science at the University of Alberta. He is former vice-chair of the Academic Council on the UN System and currently editor of *Global Governance Journal: A Review of Multilateralism and International Organizations*. His latest works are *A Changing United Nations: Multilateral Evolution and the Quest for Global Governance* (2000) and *Adapting the United Nations to a Post Modern Era: Lessons Learned* (2001).

Mark Malan is a senior researcher and head of the Peace Missions Program at the Institute for Security Studies in South Africa. He has published extensively on issues relating to civil-military relations, regional security, and peacekeeping in Africa. He most recent work is *Peacekeeping in the DRC* (2001).

William Maley is an associate professor of politics at University College, University of New South Wales, Australia. He is also chair of the Refugee Council of Australia. He edited, for the Australian Defence Studies Centre, *Dealing with Mines: Strategies for Peacekeepers, Aid Agencies and the International Community* (1994) and *Shelters from the Storm: Developments in International Humanitarian Law* (1995).

David Malone is President of the International Peace Academy (IPA) in New York while on leave from the Canadian foreign service. He chaired the negotiations of the UN's Special Committee on Peacekeeping Operations, 1992–1994, while serving as a Canadian Ambassador to the UN. He is the author of *Decision-Making in the UN Security Council: The Case of Haiti, 1990–1997* (1998), and *Greed and Grievance: Economic Agendas in Civil Wars* (2000).

Philip Nel is chair of the Department of Political Science at Stellenbosch, South Africa. His research and teaching interests include multilateralism, foreign policy analysis, and the political economy of science and technology. He is joint author/editor of *South Africa's Multilateral Diplomacy and Global Change: The Limits of Reformism* (2000).

Iver B. Neumann is a senior research fellow at the Norwegian Institute of International Affairs, and has worked as a policy planner in the Norwegian Ministry of Foreign Affairs and the Ministry of Defence. His latest book in English is *Uses of the Other: "The East" in European Identity Formation* (1999).

Kim Richard Nossal is professor and head of political studies at Queen's University, Kingston, Ontario, Canada. He is the author of *The Politics of Canadian Foreign Policy* (1997) and *Rain Dancing: Sanctions in Canadian and Australian Foreign*

Policy (1994). His latest co-edited book is *Diplomatic Departures: The Conservative Era in Canadian Foreign Policy, 1984–1993* (2001).

James Reed is a public policy consultant in Boston and a visiting scholar at Harvard University. A specialist on the USA and its role in world affairs, he is particularly interested in the domestic sources of foreign policy. He is the author of *The Missionary Mind and American East Asia Policy* (1983).

Ramesh Thakur is Vice-Rector of the United Nations University. He is a member of the UNU's senior academic staff and directs the university's Peace and Governance Programme. He is the author of numerous peace-related publications. His books include as co-editor *Asia's Emerging Regional Order: Reconciling Traditional and Human Security* (2000), *Kosovo and the Challenge of Humanitarian Intervention: Selective Imagination, Collective Action and International Citizenship* (2000), and *New Millennium, New Perspectives: The United Nations, Security, and Governance* (2000).

Deidre van der Merwe is a former researcher at the Institute for Security Studies in South Africa. She is the co-author of *ACT Against Child Soldiers in Africa: A Reader* (2000).

Index

293

IANSA (International Action Network on Small Arms), 47
IBCC (International Bureau of Chambers of Commerce), 216
ICBL (International Campaign to Ban Land-mines)
American individuals/organizations involved in, 4, 66
coalition of like-minded leadership in, 79–80
debate during Nobel Peace Prize awarded to, 131n.23
as "globalist organization," 75–76
"The Good, the Bad, and the Ugly" list kept by, 76
government-NGO partnerships and, 85–87
mobilization of shame and, 75–77
role of NGOs in, 10, 42, 69, 73–75, 77–79
role of Norwegian NGOs in, 110–126
See also AP (Anti-Personnel) mines
ICC Geneva Business Dialogue, 209
ICC (International Chamber of Commerce)
Global Compact and, 220–222
influence at WEC by, 212–213
as international actor, 210–217
involvement in multilateral diplomacy by, 204–205
joint statement with UN (1998), 209
shared interests/mutual needs of UN and, 215, 217–220
See also Business sector
ICC (International Criminal Court)
elements of Rome Statute on, 136–140
impact of international politics, civil society, and UN on the, 147–148
influence of NGOs on, 50
as normative innovation, 152–153
process leading to creation of, 22
push for permanent, 11, 46–47
as replacing sovereign impunity, 155–156
Rome Treaty establishing, 56, 66, 133–134
as threat to great power vetoism, 156–157
as transformative agent
as example of, 135
independence of court and, 140–141
political enforcement issues and, 144–147
putting purpose into practice, 143–147
state sovereignty and, 141–143

See also Genocide; War crimes
ICC-UN-GATT Economic Consultative Committee, 216–217
ICFTU (International Confederation of Free Trade Unions), 173, 180
ICRC (International Committee of the Red Cross)
Geneva Conventions organized by, 137
international principles leading to establishment of, 39
origins of, 10, 12
role in Australian Ottawa process by, 97, 98
role in Norwegian Ottawa process, 111
IDEA (International Institute for Democracy and Electoral Assistance), 45
Ignatieff, Michael, 236, 237
ILO Declaration on Fundamental Principles and Rights at Work, 221
ILO (International Labour Organization)
attempts to raise labour standards by, 173
corporate code report by, 162–163
Declaration on Multinational Enterprises, 164
Declaration of Principles Concerning Multinational Enterprises and Social Policy by, 165–166
elimination of child labour program by, 177, 178
influence on Canadian apparel sector reform by, 192, 194, 195, 196, 198
Marchi's warning regarding core labour rights of, 189
relative weakness of, 199
ILO Worst Forms of Child Labour Convention (1999), 232–233
Inhumane Weapons Convention, 99
Institute of Peace Research (Oslo), 110
InterAction, 229
Inter-American Convention against the Illicit Manufacturing of and Trafficking in Firearms, Ammunition, Explosives, and other Related Materials (1997), 230
Interfaith Center for Corporate Responsibility, 179
Interfaith Center on Corporate Responsibility, 175
International Centre for Human Rights and Democratic Development, 189